From Boycott to Economic Cooperation

The Political Economy of the Arab Boycott of Israel

GIL FEILER

Routledge
Taylor & Francis Group

NEW YORK AND LONDON

This edition published 2011 by Routledge

Routledge
Taylor & Francis Group
711 Third Avenue
New York, NY 10017

Routledge
Taylor & Francis Group
2 Park Square, Milton Park
Abingdon, Oxon OX14 4RN

British Library Cataloguing in Publication Data:

Feiler, Gil
From boycott to economic cooperation: the political
economy of the Arab boycott of Israel
1. Arab–Israeli conflict   2. Arab countries – Foreign economic
relations – Israel   3. Israel – Foreign economic relations –
Arab countries
I. Title
337.5'694'0174927

ISBN 0-7146-4866-3 (cloth)
ISBN 0-7146-4423-4 (paper)

Library of Congress Cataloging-in-Publication Data

Feiler, Gil, 1959–
From boycott to economic cooperation: the political economy of
the Arab boycott of Israel / Gil Feiler.
     p.   cm.
Includes bibliographical references and index.
ISBN 0-7146-4866-3 (cloth). – ISBN 0-7146-4423-4 (pbk.)
1. Economic sanctions, Arab countries–Israel.   2. Boycotts–Arab
countries.   3. Boycotts–Israel.   4. Arab countries–Foreign
economic relations–Israel.   5. Israel–Foreign economic relations–
Arab countries.   I. Title.
HF1610.Z41825   1998
327.1'17–dc21   98-24519
                                                             CIP

Typeset by Regent Typesetting, London

FROM BOYCOTT TO
ECONOMIC COOPERATION

Contents

Acknowledgements

I WAS first encouraged to start researching the subject of the Arab boycott of Israel by Mr Muzi Wertheim, President of Coca-Cola (Israel) and chairman of the United Mizrahi Bank. I have had the honour of working with Muzi in recent years and learning from his experience. I dedicate this book to him with my deepest appreciation and affection.

In the course of my research I was assisted by numerous individuals and bodies, not all of whom agreed to be mentioned by name. They included government agencies, organisations, company representatives, businessmen, academics and journalists. Of these I should like to thank the staff of all the Arab, Israeli, European and American archives to which I had access, and especially those of the Carter Presidential Library in Atlanta, Georgia and of the Public Record Office in London. Special thanks are also due to the senior officials at the Office of Antiboycott Compliance (OAC) of the US Department of Commerce in Washington DC, who made time for me; Dr Jess Hordes, Director of the ADL (Anti-Defamation League) office in Washington DC and ADL staff in New York, and Mr David Weinberg of the ADL in Jerusalem, for his analysis of the US Jewish policy toward the boycott and for providing me with much interesting documentary material; Mr Will Maslow of the American Jewish Congress in New York; Mr Daniel Lack of the World Jewish Congress in Geneva; the Anti-Boycott Committee in London and the *Centrum voor Informatie en Documentatie Israel* (CIDI), in the Netherlands and to the centre *Européen Juif d'Information* (EJI), in Brussels. I also had the honour of preparing a report on the L'Oréal boycott case for the late Prof. Jean-Louis Bismuth of the *Mouvement pour la Liberté du Commerce* (MLC) in Paris, in the course of which I was able to analyze many original boycott documents from the Central Boycott Office (CBO) in Damascus.

In the course of my work I had access to documents from Israel's Economic Warfare Authority in the Ministry of Finance, the Economic Department in the Ministry for Foreign Affairs and the Industrial Cooperation Authority under the Ministry of Industry and Trade, and should like to thank all the officials in these offices who assisted me – especially Mr Moshe Kobi of the EWA. I made extensive use of notes which I took while interviewing numerous persons connected in one way or another with the boycott in the course of the late 1980s and early 1990s. Not all the interviewees agreed to be exposed or quoted. I should, however, like to make special mention of the journalists Yuval Elizur and Eliahu Salpeter, who have been actively involved in Israel's anti-boycott efforts for over 20 years.

I should like to thank my academic home, the Middle East Business and Economic Research Institute at the Interdisciplinary Center in Herzliya, and the Begin–Sadat Center for Strategic Studies, for encouraging me to persist in my research on the boycott. I also owe special thanks to Prof. Efraim Karsh of King's College, London for his wise advice, and to IBM (Israel) for providing me with a grant which enabled me to begin this study.

Concerning the transition from boycott to cooperation, as director of Info-Prod Research (Middle East) Ltd, I have had first-hand experience in the setting up of quite a few joint ventures in Arab countries and the development of Israeli trade relations with them. I should like to thank the Info-Prod staff who are involved on a daily basis with this important work, and especially Dr Rahel Rimon, who helped me with the initial editing of the material for this book, and Joshua Zaretsky.

It was a great pleasure for me to have Dr Susan (Sheila) Hattis Rolef by my side in the course of the work on this project. Sheila contributed ideas and information to numerous chapters, let me use transcripts of interviews she carried out on the boycott in the late 1970s and early 1980s and was responsible for the final editing and polishing of the book, at the stage in which accuracy, patience and devotion are invaluable.

Finally, I should also like to thank my publisher, Mr Frank Cass, and Mr Robert Easton and Mr Andrew Humphrys, my editors at Frank Cass Publishers. Last, but not least, I am grateful to the significant women in my life, who have borne with me: my mother Ruth, my wife Lea, and my daughters Nitzan and Shahar.

Abbreviations

ABC	Anti-Boycott Committee (Britain)
ADL	Anti-Defamation League of B'nai Brith (Washington DC and Jerusalem)
AIPAC	American Israel Public Affairs Committee
AJC	American Jewish Committee
AJCongress	American Jewish Congress
ALC	*Association pour la Liberté du Commerce* (France)
AP	Associated Press
BBC	British Broadcasting Corporation
BIPAC	Britain Israel Public Affairs Committee
BOO	build–own–operate
BOOT	build–own–operate–transfer
BOT	build–operate–transfer
BR	*Boycott Report* (American Jewish Congress)
CBO	Central Boycott Office (Damascus)
CEJI	*Centre Européen Juif d'Information*
CEO	Chief Executive Officer
CIDI	*Centrum voor Informatie en Documentatie Israel* (Netherlands)
COFACE	*Compagnie Française d'Assurances pour le Commerce Extérieur* (France)
DISC	Domestic International Sales Corporations (US)
DoP	Declaration of Principles (Oslo Agreement – 13.9.93)
EAA	Export Administration Act (US)
EC	European Community
ECD	Commission on Economic Coercion and Discrimination (Canada)
ECGD	Export Credit Guarantee Department (UK)
EDC	Export Development Corporation (Canada)
EEC	European Economic Community
EJI	*Européen Juif d'Information*
EU	European Union
EWA	Economic Warfare Authority (Ministry of Finance, Jerusalem)
FBIS	Foreign Broadcast Information Service

FDI	Foreign Direct Investment
FEATT	Full Employment in America Through Trade Inc.
FICC	Federation of Israeli Chambers of Commerce
FO	Foreign Office (Britain)
G-7	Group of Seven – the seven major industrial states
GAO	General Accounting Office (US)
GATT	General Agreement on Tariffs and Trade
GCC	Gulf Cooperation Council
GDP	Gross Domestic Product
GHOURFA	German–Arab Chamber of Commerce
GNP	Gross National Product
HMG	Her Majesty's Government (Britain)
HMSO	His (Her) Majesty's Stationery Office (Britain)
ICAO	International Civil Aviation Organization
ICC	International Chambers of Commerce
IIC	The Israel Institute of Coexistence
IJA	Institute of Jewish Affairs
IMF	International Monetary Fund
IRS	Internal Revenue Service (US)
ITC	International Trade Commission
JETRO	Japanese Trade Relations Organization
JTA	Jewish Telegraphic Agency
KIIC	Kuwait International Investment Company
KUNA	Kuwaiti News Agency
LICRA	*Ligue contre le racisme et l'anti-semitisme* (France)
MEED	*Middle East Economic Digest*
MENA	Middle East News Agency
MENA	Middle East and North African (economic conferences)
MFN	'Most Favoured Nation'
MITI	Japanese Foreign Trade Ministry
MK	Member of Knesset
MLC	*Movement pour la Liberté du Commerce* (Paris)
NCM	*Nederlandsche Credietverzekering Maatschappij*
OAC	Office of Antiboycott Compliance (US Department of Commerce)
ODA	Organizational Development Assistance
OECD	Organization for Economic Cooperation and Development
PLO	Palestine Liberation Organization
PRO	Public Record Office (London)
REX	Committee on External Economic Relations (European Parliament)
SC	Security Council (UN)
SEC	Securities and Exchange Commission (US)
SWB	Summary of World Broadcasts (BBC)

UAE	United Arab Emirates
UAR	United Arab Republic
UK	United Kingdom
UN	United Nations
UNCTAD	UN Conference on Trade and Development
US	United States
USGPO	US Government Printing Office
USTR	US Trade Representative
WJC	World Jewish Congress (Geneva)
WTO	World Trade Organization

Foreword by Muzi Wertheim

IN 1977 the words 'No more war' echoed throughout the world. Until then, the Arab boycott against Israel was a legitimate means of war. In peace, or even on the road to peace, the boycott is a senseless and erroneous instrument in a conflict which the participants are striving to settle. It involves people, not armies. The casualties on both sides will be progress, economic growth, jobs, welfare. 'A la guerre comme à la guerre' – but political encounters, even political conflicts, are not war.

The ending of a war in the eyes of people on both sides, whether businessmen, professionals, workers or public servants, means that all are going to do their best in order to improve their lot, to advance their own economic interests. If that implies doing business elsewhere, rather than in Israel, it should be a business decision, inasmuch as doing business with Israel should be purely a business decision. If the barrier to trade is anything beyond that, it prevents free competition and the loser will be one's own people, unnecessarily, to no purpose.

We are businessmen, not politicians, we should have no inhibitions in admitting to ourselves all the facts, sensitivities, and traumas of the past. They are relevant to our doing business. The facts from a businessman's viewpoint are that Palestinians and Arab states, which are bound to the Palestinians by natural solidarity, have a valid case. Dr Chaim Weizmann, Israel's first president, who testified to the Royal Commission on Palestine in 1937, said: 'Gentlemen, you don't have to decide who is right or who is wrong, but what harm to what side (Jews or Arabs) can be considered as the "lesser evil".' We live in a world of facts. The State of Israel is a fact and the Oslo Agreement, conferring a 'pre-state' status to the Palestinians, is a fact. The business community on both sides, particularly the Israeli private sector, must open the necessary windows and offer its utmost in business opportunities to Palestinians and the neighbouring Arab states. What about the boycott? In my opinion, it is soon to be a ghost of the past, even if some militant leaders do not admit it yet and want to revive its heyday splendour. A generation of total boycott has not checked Israel's economic growth. The ability to inflict vital injury at present is unreal. From the start, it has been a weapon of spite rather than a serious threat to Israel's development. In many respects it served to stimulate and push Israel's economic progress by pitting it against advanced competitive markets in Europe and the US, therefore maximizing its own creative and competitive potential.

The boycott closed the Port of Haifa as a much-needed sea outlet in the Mediterranean to Jordan's agriculture and mineral exports; to Iraq's oil pipe; to Syria's, Lebanon's, and the West Bank and Gaza's (until 1967) agricultural produce, which were exported in great quantities to Mandatory Palestine and particularly to the Jewish sectors. These and other comparative advantages, if kept and cultivated, would not only have brought peace much earlier but could have triggered an economic reality of progress, welfare and prosperity for all concerned.

The boycott aggravated and perpetuated the tensions and interfered with Arab international economic intercourse. It runs against all international conventions, from the charter of the UN to the first bilateral agreements between Israel and its enemies in Rhodes in 1949.

Trade and commerce with the Western countries have traditionally been objectionable to Islamic countries and in particular to the Arab Moslems. What is most resented is the long array of manifestations of Western superiority in material, technological and organizational fields. These attainments are constantly visible or, as Arabs see it, are 'flaunted' by the West and make the West appear as a superior power, while spiritually, morally and in all social standards it is inferior to Islam and the Arabs in their own eyes.

The Arabs, whose culture (and armies) dominated parts of Europe in centuries past (Spain and eastern Europe), are brought up and conditioned to regard all the West's economic 'marvels' as secondary to Islam's values. When they nevertheless find that they are unable to resist imitating the Western way of living in many ways, they feel that involuntarily they adopt an inferior scale of values that is upheld in the West. This causes reaction and resentment, particularly among the religious leaders, and the result is quick escalation to hate, as clearly exhibited in Iran. Israel is regarded as the spearhead of the West, and is therefore a prime target for Arab feelings of frustration and hate.

It is not realistic to expect businessmen to succeed in dissolving and dissipating the convictions and prejudices of generations. What can be expected of us, however, is full appreciation and sensitivity to it. The affluent society is not an Arab ideal. Worldly goods come second to traditions and feelings and a sense of having been subjected to injustice. This is the environmental atmosphere in which we are operating at present. The anti-Western and anti-Israel stance will not change overnight. The myth of 'economic domination', which hides the fear of Western life styles, will not be dispelled instantly.

If we set our business priorities correctly, giving precedence to Palestinian and Arab needs in infrastructure, communications and labour, and to creating labour-abundant industries that provide jobs and outlets for the existing produce of Palestinians and Arab countries with whom we have concluded peace treaties, we shall be taking the first right step. If we present to our Arab parties a low profile, try to give them a 'first refusal' on produce that they sell, provide them with what we can offer at a comparative advantage in quality and price, then the fate of the boycott will be sealed. It may not 'die out with a bang', but it will slowly and surely fade away.

Introduction

THE LONGEST functioning example of economic sanctions being applied against any state – the Arab boycott of Israel – appears to be disintegrating. The boycott was always an integral part of the Arab–Israeli conflict, and, at least until the 1970s, was designed to help bring about the demise of Israel as a state.

The background to the boycott's gradual demise has been the Arab–Israeli peacemaking process, which opened with the Madrid Conference at the end of October 1991. However, the first cracks in the system started to appear earlier with some direct trade between Israel and the Arab world taking place across the Open Bridges on the River Jordan during the late 1960s, through the 'Good Fence' between Israel and Lebanon after 1975, through Egypt after the signing of the peace treaty between Israel and Egypt in 1979, and occasionally through third parties. Imposition of the secondary and tertiary boycotts – i.e. the refusal of the Arabs to have economic relations with companies which maintain economic contacts with Israel or with blacklisted companies – started coming across difficulties in several states, but especially the United States, which as of 1976 started passing effective anti-boycott legislation and regulations. Nevertheless, the Arab boycott remained a factor to be reckoned with, causing the Israeli economy certain difficulties, though never inflicting on it anything even resembling a fatal blow.

Many books and articles have been written about the Arab boycott of Israel. However, this is the first study which looks at all angles of the boycott issue, including the Arab perspective of the boycott, the highly problematic question of how to evaluate its effectiveness and cost, and the prospects for the boycott being replaced by regional economic cooperation. It is also the first study in English to extensively examine Arab sources on the subject, and archival material from a variety of sources.

The study opens with a review of the general theory of economic sanctions as reflected in the literature, and some of the practical experience of economic sanctions, showing how the specific case of the Arab boycott correlates with this theory and experience. Chapter 1 deals with what economic sanctions try to achieve and by what means, sanctions as a form of collective action in the twentieth century, how one measures the effectiveness of sanctions, and what makes for their success or failure.

Within the general framework of the study of economic sanctions, the Arab boycott is without doubt a fascinating case-study, though it is atypical in many respects. First, it is probably the only case of economic sanctions imposed on a state still in its embryonic stage, and consistently applied against it for over 50 years. In terms of its objectives and the extremely complicated mechanisms developed to apply it, it does not resemble any other case of economic sanctions in the twentieth century. The persistence of the Arab states in applying it, and of Israel's efforts to minimize its importance while adapting to the reality which it laid down – is unique in history, as were the boycott's original objectives. At least until recent years the goal of the boycott was not to change Israel's policies or conduct, but simply to try to destroy it, or at least make its life as difficult as possible.

Chapter 2 charts the history of the boycott and its development. Economic boycotts were used by the Arabs against the Jews in Palestine from the end of the nineteenth century. True, these endeavours were usually ineffective, and, since the Zionists sought to develop an independent Jewish entity in Palestine, frequently served Zionist interests more than the efforts of the Arabs to stop the Zionist development. However, the Arab boycott of Israel originated from a decision of the Arab League at the end of 1945 to institute a boycott against the Jewish community in Palestine. This boycott turned into the most institutionalized and comprehensive system of economic sanctions ever imposed against a people and a state.

We have attempted to follow the various stages in the development of this boycott, its institutions, its practices and its goals. One may discern three main periods in its evolution: (1) the period up to the 1973 oil crisis, in which the two sides played a relatively innocent cat-and-mouse game; (2) the period after 1973, when the vast economic power amassed by the Arab oil-producing states enabled the Arabs to implement the boycott more effectively than before in third states, causing Israel to make much greater efforts to counter its effects – at the same time, the first major cracks in the boycott started to appear in this period; (3) the period since 1991, when the current Middle East peacemaking process was embarked upon, accompanied by a widening of the cracks in the system, including the development of overt economic relations between Israel and a growing number of Arab states.

Chapter 3 deals with the legal aspects of the boycott. This chapter is divided into those legal considerations which apply to economic sanctions in general, and those relating to the Arab boycott of Israel in particular. The legal discussion on both levels deals with general principles of international law; multilateral and bilateral agreements, including the terms of the constitutions or covenants of international organisations; and domestic legislation in various countries relating to economic sanctions and discrimination in general, and the Arab boycott of Israel in particular.

Generally speaking, the application of economic sanctions in international relations is not illegal, though certain boycott practices, especially when they are forced on third countries not directly involved in the conflict between the sending and receiving states, may be. The legal argument turned into an integral part of the semantics and propaganda surrounding the boycott, but there was never the slightest chance that the problem would be resolved by legal means.

Chapter 4 deals with the Arab perspective of the boycott against Israel. An effort has been made here to show how the Arabs have perceived the boycott over the years – how they regarded its goals, its chances of success and its actual effect. This is in addition to what was said in the previous two chapters on Arab arguments regarding the legality of the boycott and its various practices, and the history of the boycott, which was to a large extent determined by what the Arabs chose to do and sought to achieve.

This chapter is based, to a very large extent, on Arab sources, which previous studies of the Arab boycott, published outside the Arab world, did not use. It is without doubt one of the most innovative sections of this study, even if somewhat problematic because we have no way of checking the accuracy of the information provided in the Arab sources.

Chapter 5 deals with loopholes in the application of the boycott.

Even in the years when the boycott was most strictly applied there were loopholes in the application of both the primary boycott and the secondary and tertiary boycotts, proving that where there is a will there is a way. It was not only Israeli businessmen who were interested in finding ways around the boycott, and showed a good deal of ingenuity in doing so, even in the Arab world there were businessmen who were interested in having dealings, even if only indirect ones, with Israel.

Chapter 6 deals with Israel's reaction to the boycott from its inception. Israel's constant dilemma was that, while it wanted to do whatever it could to stop the application of the secondary and tertiary boycotts in third countries, it neither wanted to give the boycott free publicity nor to give the impression that the boycott had a serious effect on the Israeli economy. This chapter deals with the various bodies established in Israel over the years to deal with the Arab boycott, the cooperation between these bodies and various bodies acting against the boycott abroad, and the approach taken *vis-à-vis* third countries in which the boycott was applied.

Chapter 7 deals with the measures taken in the US to counter the effects of the Arab boycott. The US was the only country which, as of the mid-1970s, had effective anti-boycott legislation, and in which the boycott issue was constantly raised in the legislature. This was due to a large extent to the determination and effectiveness of the major Jewish organizations – the Anti-Defamation League, the American Jewish Committee and the American Jewish Congress – which considered the boycott a central issue on their agendas. However, this was also in keeping with the American free-trade tradition and disapproval of interference with it. Since the Gulf War the US has also played a major role in trying to get the Arab states to rescind the boycott.

The attitude towards the boycott of six west European countries – France, Britain, Germany and the Benelux countries – is dealt with in Chapter 8. Though all these countries, except Britain, eventually passed some sort of anti-boycott legislation, compliance with boycott demands was always widespread in them. While the governments of these countries condemned the secondary and tertiary boycotts, they were not inclined to intervene to stop their application, despite the legislation passed in most of them. Formally, Britain was the worst culprit, though the issue was raised publicly from time to time, and in late 1978 a Select Committee in the House of Lords was appointed to deal with anti-boycott legislation.

Chapter 9 deals with the policy of the European Community towards the boycott. Over the years various EC officials tried to change their approach to the boycott, but, in practical terms, Israel was unsuccessful in getting the EC and its member states to either apply the anti-discrimination articles in the Treaty of Rome and in the agreements signed between the EC and various Arab states to the boycott, or harmonize their legislation, so that all the member states would have some sort of laws prohibiting cooperation with the boycott.

However, Japan was the industrialized country least willing to take any measures to fight the boycott, and until the early 1990s its economic relations with Israel were extremely limited as a result. Chapter 10 deals with the submission of the Japanese to the boycott – frequently even voluntarily (i.e. without being asked to comply by any Arab state). The Japanese attitude started to change after the Gulf War and the Madrid Conference, resulting in an expansion of trade between Japan and Israel, and, in the beginning, of Japanese investment in Israel. A similar situation existed with regards to South Korea. The situation in Australia and Canada was less drama-tic, though the attitude of the governments of these two members of the Commonwealth was probably typical of that of most of the industrialized world.

Chapter 11 deals with the effectiveness and cost of the boycott – i.e. the question of whether it achieved its goals, and its economic cost to Israel. Naturally, when one comes to deal with how effective the boycott has been, one must first clarify what the Arab states tried to achieve by imposing it. The Arab goals underwent change over the years, and the more realistic these goals became – moving from the aim of destroying Israel to that of merely influencing its policies – so the effectiveness, or at least the chance of attaining the goals set, grew. As to the economic cost to Israel, we have shown that it is extremely difficult to quantify this, though there is no question that the boycott had a major effect on the Israeli economy over the years. In this chapter an effort is made, for the first time, to grapple ration-ally and systematically with the issue of effectiveness and cost.

The gradual shift from confrontation to cooperation, and the development of positive, albeit limited, economic relations between

Israel and many of the Arab states is dealt with in Chapter 12. This transformation has been slow and problematic, and by mid-1998 the boycott had not yet vanished altogether, to a large extent because of difficulties in the peacemaking process.

This chapter deals specifically with where the primary, secondary and tertiary boycotts stand today, the various approaches to economic cooperation between Israel and the Arab world, the achievements of four Middle East and North African economic conferences held since 1994, joint ventures as a form of cooperation, the current state of proposed regional projects and the problem of financing.

1

The Theory and Practice of Economic Sanctions and the Arab Boycott

The Means and Goals of Economic Sanctions

ECONOMIC SANCTIONS in international relations may be defined as an attempt by a state or group of states (the sender states) to force another state (the target state) to change its policy on a particular issue or on a whole range of issues, its conduct or its orientation through the use of economic means designed to hurt it economically.

In his study of economic sanctions James Barber distinguished between three categories of objectives in the use of such sanctions: *primary objectives*, which are concerned with the actions and behaviour of the state or regime against which the sanctions are directed; *secondary objectives*, relating to the status, behaviour and expectations of the governments imposing the sanctions; and *tertiary objectives*, concerned with broader international considerations, relating either to the operation and structure of the international system as a whole, or to those parts of it which are regarded as important by the operating states. Barber concluded that when economic sanctions are applied over a lengthy period of time, the relative weight of the different categories of objectives may shift.[1] Kenneth W. Abbott, on the other hand, identified four rationales for applying sanctions: economic warfare, imposing costs, the denial of means and symbolic communications.[2]

In the case of unilateral sanctions imposed by major powers, these may come to demonstrate leadership in world affairs. The US, for example, imposed sanctions against countries abusing human rights, to eradicate apartheid in South Africa,[3] to enforce compliance with nuclear non-proliferation safeguards, in efforts to negotiate compensation for property expropriated by foreign governments, and as an anti-terrorism measure. It has been suggested that the rationale behind the imposition of sanctions by the US has not always been to attain well defined goals, but rather the result of a feeling by the Administration that in face of morally or politically repugnant behaviour by a potential target state, the US, as a super-power, could not afford to be passive.[4]

Another motive for imposing sanctions may be deterrence – where it is hoped that the target state will be discouraged from taking a particular action by increasing the associated costs.[5] But perhaps the most prevalent goal of states imposing economic sanctions – given the fact that the rate of success of such sanctions is not impressive – is their symbolic value, as a statement of disapproval.[6]

In his study of the short-lived sanctions imposed by the European Parliament on 9 March 1988 on Israel, when it refused to ratify three economic protocols, Ilan Greilsammer concludes: 'Sanctions may be ineffective with regard to their primary and official goal; however, that does not mean they are ineffective with regard to their symbolic or secondary goals.'[7] What the European Parliament did was to express its disapproval of Israel's reaction to the *Intifada*, and its refusal to allow the direct export of Palestinian merchandise from the West Bank and Gaza Strip to the European Community. The sanctions neither had much of an effect on the Israeli economy nor on the policies of the Israeli government, and by October the protocols were ratified.[8]

Irrespective of what the motive might be for the application of economic sanctions, their use as a foreign policy means is perceived as being a less risky and cheaper alternative to military force,[9] even though injudicious use of sanctions might cause as much economic damage to the sender states or certain economic sectors within them, as to the target state.[10]

In their major study on economic sanctions, Gary C. Hufbauer and Jeffrey J. Schott defined the economic means which can be used within the framework of economic sanctions as the 'withdrawal, or threat of withdrawal, of customary trade or financial relations', where 'customary' refers to 'economic contacts which would probably have occurred in the absence of sanctions'.[11]

Within the framework of international economic sanctions the Arab boycott of Israel has been unique both in its goals and in the way the sender states perceived it. The original purpose of the Arab states when they declared the boycott in December 1945 – two and a half years before the State of Israel was proclaimed – was to prevent its emergence as a state.[12] Later the boycott was one of the means used to try and destroy the Jewish state[13] – in other words, it was not an alternative to the use of military force, but a supplementary means.

It was in the course of the 1970s that the goals of the Arab boycott began to change, at first in trying to make Israel's economic life more difficult, and eventually as a *quid pro quo* for an Israeli withdrawal from all the territories it had occupied in the course of the 1967 Six Day War.[14] In other words, it is only at the current stage of the boycott that its goals have started to resemble those of the classical model of economic sanctions.

Sanctions as a Form of Collective Action

Since ancient times, individual states have used economic means, including sanctions of one sort or another, to try to attain their goals *vis-à-vis* other states. In the twentieth century the imposition of economic sanctions has frequently been associated with the concerted action, within the framework of collective security systems – first of the League of Nations and later of the United Nations – designed to be used against member states found to have broken the rules of the game. Sanctions have also been used by regional or ideological blocs against common enemies.

In the case of the League of Nations the most famous case of sanctions was of those imposed against Italy after its occupation of Abyssinia in 1935 – sanctions which proved a total failure. Among the reasons for this failure were the inability of the sender states to determine clear goals, loopholes in the imposition of the sanctions and the refusal of several key states to cooperate.[15]

When, after the Second World War, the UN was founded, an attempt was made to learn from the failures of the past, and devise a system which would be more effective. However, once again the results were not particularly impressive.[16] Though there were many recommendations by the UN General Assembly for the imposition of sanctions – against Franco's Spain, Salazar's Portugal, South Africa with its policy of apartheid and even Israel – mandatory UN economic sanctions have only rarely been imposed. The first case was that of the sanctions imposed against Southern Rhodesia on 16 December 1966.[17] The Rhodesian sanctions were only made possible because Britain, as the power still formally in control of Rhodesia, had adopted unilateral measures against the white minority government which had unilaterally declared independence, and no other permanent member of the Security Council had an interest in vetoing the imposition of sanctions.[18] Insofar as the sanctions, which were imposed until 1979, and other international pressure eventually led to a peaceful transition of Rhodesia into the independent Zimbabwe, with a black majority government – these sanctions were successful.[19]

The UN General Assembly proposed that economic sanctions be imposed on South Africa, against the background of its policy of apartheid as early as 1962,[20] but it was only on 14 November 1977 that the Security Council imposed such sanctions,[21] and these sanctions were officially in force for some 17 years.

Since 1990 the Security Council has resorted more frequently to the use of economic sanctions against rogue states. The main reason for this has been that since the cold war came to an end, the automatic Soviet veto on all proposals to impose sanctions also vanished, and thus economic sanctions, of one sort of another, have been imposed against Iraq (SC resolutions 661, 670 and 687), parts of the former Yugoslavia (SC resolutions 713 and 757), Somalia (SC resolution 733), Libya (SC resolutions 748 and 883), Liberia (SC resolution 788), Haiti (SC resolution 841), Angola (SC resolution 864).[22]

The sanctions against Iraq were imposed by the Security Council, on 6 August 1990, following the Iraqi invasion of Kuwait, and were further tightened after the outbreak of the Gulf War.[23] The sanctions were followed by the freezing of Iraqi financial assets in most of the Western countries. At first the sanctions came across the problem of 'holes' in its imposition, and later, loopholes were formally permitted in their application for humanitarian reasons. Despite the high cost of the sanctions to Iraq, they did not attain their initial goal of getting Iraq out of Kuwait by non-violent means, they were only partially successful in forcing Iraq to dismantle its chemical arsenal and the rest of its non-conventional capability, and did not manage to topple the regime of Iraqi President Saddam Hussein. In addition, it was noted that the economic cost to many of the sender states was extremely high.[24]

The sanctions against Libya were imposed by the Security Council in March 1992 after Libyan President Mo'ammar Qadhafi refused to cooperate in the investigation of the blowing-up of the Pan-Am aircraft over the Scottish town of Lockerbie in December 1988. While the sanctions were much more effective than those against Iraq, and the cost to Libya has been estimated at many billions of dollars, at the time of writing they have failed to achieve their goal.[25]

Though UN-sponsored sanctions appear highly attractive in theory, in practice the concept of the international community using sanctions to protect the collective interest has failed. The main reason for this failure has been the absence of a set of norms which may be defined as the 'collective interest'. Over the years the member states of the UN have been divided on ideological, economic and historical grounds. Even after the collapse of the communist bloc and the apparent emergence of a new world order, as defined by former US President George Bush in the early 1990s, it still seems highly unlikely that a sufficiently broad consensus will be established to impose US-sponsored economic sanctions. Two additional problems are that while dictators such as Mo'ammar Qadhafi and Saddam Hussein seem capable of taking a good deal of punishment without even approaching breaking point, the world is incapable of disregarding the misery caused by sanctions to the populations of the states against which sanctions are imposed.[26]

The Arab boycott of Israel is a classic example of a regional organization – the Arab League – acting against a common enemy within the region, but external to itself. Though the Arabs tried on at least one occasion to get the UN General Assembly to impose sanctions against Israel, this effort failed.

The Effectiveness of Sanctions

Much of the theory of international economic sanctions deals with their effectiveness. According to Hufbauer and Schott: 'The "success" of an economic sanctions episode – as viewed from the perspective of the sender country – has two parts: the extent to which the policy outcome sought by the sender country was in fact achieved, and the contribution made by sanctions to a positive outcome.'[27] In objective terms sanctions have been successful in quite limited contexts. Success has usually been scored in cases where what was sought by the sender states was modest policy changes, and the target states were friendly or neutral – not hostile states. In other cases, success has appeared regularly only in attempts to destabilize target governments where parallel measures, such as covert or even overt action, were employed,[28] and in efforts to disrupt the minor military adventures of allies or friendly, neutral states. Attempts to change major target policies, to impair target military potential and to disrupt the military adventures of hostile states, have generally been unsuccessful. Moreover, success usually occurs where the target states and governments are politically and economically weak.[29]

In an article on the effects of sanctions Johan Galtung tried to determine under what conditions the impact of sanctions will be maximized. The ideal situation, he concluded, requires that the exports from the target state are sent mainly to the sender state and that there are no easy substitutes for them; that the exports from the target state can easily be obtained elsewhere by the sender state; and that trade relations are easily supervised and even controlled. These conditions are most easily met in the case of a small economic satellite of a major economic power.[30]

According to Margaret P. Doxey there are two main determinants for success: the degree of the ability of the sender state(s) to ensure enforcement of the sanctions, and the success of the receiving state(s) to withstand them.[31] Ya'acov Bar-Siman-Tov has suggested six factors, which he considers most important in determining the effectiveness of economic sanctions. These are:

• the degree of control of the punishing state over the supply of the economic goods needed by the target state;
• the degree of need of the target state for those economic goods, and its ability to obtain them elsewhere or to forego them altogether;
• the ratio between the cost of compliance and the cost of doing without the supply of economic goods;

- the determination of the target state to carry out its policy;
- the political will and ability of the punishing state to persist with its coercive policy and the ability to gain domestic support for it;
- the degree of public support in the target state for the policy that leads to the imposition of economic sanctions, and the willingness of the public to bear the consequences of its government's actions.[32]

Time is one of the factors that, according to Hufbauer and Schott, determine whether sanctions will or will not work. 'The cases we have documented', they say, 'show a clear association ... between the duration of sanctions and the waning prospects of success. It is not the passage of time alone that undermines economic sanctions ... The reason is that other factors are correlated with the length of an episode ...'[33] It has also been observed from experience that sanctions have a greater chance of success when they are implemented as part of a broader strategy, including diplomatic efforts.[34]

In another study Gary Hufbauer and Kimberly Elliot checked the effectiveness of financial sanctions (usually involving the interruption of official development assistance) versus trade sanctions, concluding that whether used alone or supplemented by trade sanctions, financial sanctions were twice as likely as trade controls alone to be successful.[35]

The effectiveness of sanctions is occasionally affected by the fact that the type of sanction chosen is not always one designed to maximize economic damage in the target country, but rather reflects competitive interest-group pressure in the sender state(s). The result may even be that the sanction helps promote the interests of influential pressure groups in the sender state rather than imposing significant harm on the target state.[36]

Among the examples of economic sanctions in the last 20 years considered a success were those imposed by the US against Iran following the incident in which 52 Americans from the US Embassy in Teheran were taken hostage in November 1979,[37] and those imposed against Uganda in October 1978 due to 'the consistent pattern of gross violations of human rights'.[38] In the former case, where financial sanctions were imposed, success was attributed to the high degree of cooperation by other states and the fact that the sender state was in control of a large portion of the assets of the target state.

At the same time, the fact that after a while holding the hostages turned into an embarrassment to the Iranian government, and was considered an obstacle in its attempt to win UN support in the Iran–Iraq War, also contributed to the sanctions' success.[39]

In the case of the sanctions against Uganda, the high level of dependence of Ugandan coffee exports – Uganda's main export commodity – on the American market, and the low level of dependence of the US on Ugandan coffee, ensured that soon Uganda's President Idi Amin Dada ran out of funds for both military and economic purposes. An accompanying suspension of American oil shipments to Uganda, which resulted in oil shortages, also contributed to Idi Amin's eventual downfall.[40]

The obvious reason why so many, if not most, sanctions fail to change the behaviour of the target states in a significant way is that the conditions for success enumerated above are rarely fulfilled. In addition to the fact that most sanctions are simply inadequate to cause serious economic hardship to the target state, one of the phenomena observed is that the imposition of sanctions in itself usually causes the population of the target state to rally round its government and make special efforts to overcome whatever hardships the sanctions may cause.[41]

One of the cases in which sanctions seemed consistently to fail was that of South Africa. Economic sanctions were first imposed on South Africa by the UN General Assembly in 1962.[42] However, as long as a majority of the Whites in South Africa were determined to withstand outside pressure, because they felt that they had too much to lose and because the economy did not collapse, sanctions failed to achieve their main goal – namely the abolition of the policy of apartheid. The main reasons why the economy did not collapse, though the effects of the sanctions were certainly felt, were the great natural wealth of the country and the fact that the sanctions were never fully applied.[43] However, once the majority of Whites in South Africa came to believe that change was inevitable and that eventually the Blacks would have to be granted equal rights, there is no question that the economic sanctions speeded up the process, and as President De Klerk began dismantling apartheid, so the call by South African Whites for the sanctions to be lifted grew.[44] The economic sanctions were finally lifted in 1993, after a multi-racial Transitional Executive Council started to operate in South Africa.[45]

All in all the consensus in the literature seems to be that 'economic sanctions alone have been ineffective in the fulfillment of their primary objectives ... The point made by most authors is that it is a mistake to expect economic sanctions alone to achieve the desired primary objectives ... In terms of political achievements, sanctions must be regarded as a marginal instrument of influence.'[46]

In the case of the Arab boycott the sender states rarely had any difficulty in ensuring that the members of the Arab League upheld the primary boycott (involving the absence of any sort of direct economic relations between the Arab states on the one hand and Israel on the other). They were also generally successful in their efforts to impose the secondary and tertiary boycotts (getting third countries or companies in third countries to refrain from doing business with Israel or with companies doing business with Israel); especially after the 1973 Yom Kippur War, when the Arab oil-producing states made maximum use of the vast economic power which the world oil crisis placed in their hands.

The relative failure of the boycott[47] (according to a scoring system devised by Hufbauer and Schott to determine the degree of success of sanctions, on a scale of 1 (failure) to 4 (success) the policy result of the Arab boycott was 2) was thus not a function of the inability of the Arab states to ensure enforcement; it was rather in the ability of Israel to develop its economy despite the limitations placed on it by the Arab boycott. It might even be argued that the Israeli economy benefited from the boycott, insofar as it forced Israel's economic leaders to use their wits to work out unconventional solutions to the problems created by it.[48]

There is no doubt that the fact that the boycott of Israel became a permanent feature, made it easier for Israel to adapt to it. With the help of Jewish organizations abroad, and the cooperation of well-wishers in many foreign countries, Israel waged a persistent campaign to reduce the effects of the secondary and tertiary boycotts. Though this campaign was only partially successful, in its absence the negative effects of the boycott on the Israeli economy would undoubtedly have been much greater.[49]

It is self-evident that as long as the goal of the Arab boycott was to prevent the emergence of the State of Israel and later on its destruction, it failed – a classic example of over-ambitious goals, or what Hufbauer and Schott refer to as 'biting off more than you can chew'.[50]

Insofar as the goal evolved into trying to cause the Israeli economy as much damage and dislocation as possible, and to get companies from third countries to avoid trading with Israel, investing in it or having any direct economic dealings with it – it was partially successful.

As we shall see in Chapter 11 it is, however, extremely difficult to quantify the actual damage caused to the Israeli economy by the boycott.

Sanctions which are Counterproductive

Beyond the possibility that sanctions may fail to achieve their goals, there is the danger that they might cause more damage to the sender state, or particular groups within it, than to the target state, or that the wrong parties in the target state will be hurt. An example of the former was the grain embargo imposed by the US against the Soviet Union in 1980, in order to get the latter to change its policy in Afghanistan. The embargo, which was never meant to cause starvation in the Soviet Union, did cause major economic damage to American grain producers, and it was rescinded by President Reagan in 1982.[51]

An example frequently brought for the phenomenon of the wrong party being hurt by sanctions, is the sanctions formerly imposed against South Africa. According to numerous studies, these sanctions had more devastating effects on the Black population of the country. Their welfare and political status were the cause the sanctions had to serve, but they, rather than the White population, were victimized by them.[52]

In the case of the Arab boycott the only attempt to calculate the economic damage caused to the Arab states themselves concerned the early years of the boycott in the 1940s,[53] even though the Arab states undoubtedly payed a high price in their effort to implement it, both in terms of the loss to themselves of avoiding all economic contacts with Israel, and in terms of the business they lost as a result of foreign companies refusing to give in to boycott demands.

It may also be argued that the Arab boycott caused more damage to the Arab citizens of Israel than to its Jewish citizens, since for the former the adaptation to the new economic reality after 1948, and the total separation from their brethren in neighbouring countries, was particularly painful.

Notes

1. James Barber, 'Economic Sanctions as a Policy Instrument', *International Affairs*, 55, 3 (1979), p. 367.
2. Kenneth W. Abbott, 'Economic Sanctions and International Terrorism', *Venderbilt Journal of Transnational Law*, 29 (1987), p. 289.
3. See for example Winston P. Nagan, 'Economic Sanctions, US Foreign Policy, International Law and the Anti-Apartheid Act of 1986', *Florida International Law Journal*, 4 (1988), p. 85 and William S. Maddox, 'The Comprehensive Anti-Apartheid Act: A Case Study in the Legality of Economic Sanctions', *Washington and Lee Law Review*, 44 (1987), p. 1382.
4. For a discussion of the use by the US of economic sanctions and their association with security considerations see Richard J. Ellings, 'Embargoes and World Power: Lessons from American Foreign Policy', in *Westview Special Studies in International Relations* (Boulder, CO: Westview Press, 1985). See also Sydney Weintraub, ed., 'Economic Coercion and US Foreign Policy: Implications of Case Studies from the Johnson Administration', in *Westview Special Studies in International Relations* (Boulder, CO: Westview Press, 1982) which provides case studies of unilateral coercion with foreign aid as the principal instrument of threat, in relationships involving the US and third world countries, and Barry E. Carter, *International Economic Sanctions: Improving the Haphazard US Legal Regime* (Cambridge: Cambridge University Press, 1988).
5. Gary C. Hufbauer and Jeffrey J. Schott, *Economic Sanctions Reconsidered: History and Current Policy* (Washington DC: Institute for International Economics, 1985) p. 10 (the second edition of this book was published in 1990).
6. Anna Schreiber, 'Economic Coercion as an Instrument of Foreign Policy', *World Politics*, 25, 3 (April 1973), p. 406 and Margaret P. Doxey, 'Economic Sanctions: Benefits and Costs', *The World Today*, 36, 12 (December 1980), pp. 484–9.
7. Ilan Greilsammer, 'European Sanctions Revisited', *Policies Studies*, 31, Jerusalem, the Leonard Davis Institute for International Relations, the Hebrew University of Jerusalem (July 1989), p. 26.
8. Ibid., p. 1.
9. James Barber, op. cit.
10. For example, the grain embargo declared by the US on the Soviet Union in the mid 1980s following the Soviet involvement in Afghanistan was rescinded by the US Commerce Department on the grounds that they had not hurt the Soviets, but instead had weakened US suppliers.
11. Hufbauer and Schott, op. cit., p. 2.
12. See, for example, Dan S. Chill, *The Arab Boycott of Israel: Economic Aggression and World Reaction* (New York: Praeger Publishers, 1976), p. 1.
13. In an article published in 1954 Boutros Boutros-Ghali stated that the goal of the

18   *From Boycott to Economic Cooperation*

boycott, as interpreted by the Arab League, was 'to bring about the eventual economic collapse of the state of Israel' and to reveal that '[Israel] is not economically viable in the midst of a hostile world'. Boutros Boutros-Ghali, 'The Arab
League: Ten Years of Struggle', *International Conciliation* (May 1954), p. 421.
14. See also Chapter 4.
15. See Doxey, op. cit., pp. 47–58.
16. For the period until 1970 see ibid., pp. 59–88.
17. Security Council resolution 232 (1966), in *UN Resolutions, Security Council*,
    Series II, compiled and edited by Dusan J. Djonovich, Vol. VI (New York:
    Oceana Publications/Dobbs Ferry 1989), pp. 15-16 and Security Council reso-
    lution 253 (1968), ibid., Vol. VII (1990), pp. 15–17.
18. Margaret P. Doxey, *International Sanctions in Contemporary Perspective* (London:
    Macmillan Press; New York: St Martin's Press, second edition, 1996), p. 21.
19. See for example Harry R. Strack, *Sanctions: the Case of Rhodesia* (Syracuse, NY:
    Syracuse University Press, 1978), and by the same author, 'The Effectiveness of
    Rhodesian Sanctions: Symbolism and Influence', *Harvard International Review*,
    10 (1988), p. 23.
20. General Assembly resolution 1761 (XVII) (1962), in *UN Resolutions General
    Assembly*, Series I, compiled and edited by Dusan J. Djonevich, Vol. IX (New
    York: Oceana Publications/Dobbs Ferry, 1974), pp. 102–3.
21. Security Council resolution 418 (1977), in *UN Resolutions Security Council*,
    Series II, compiled and edited by Dusan J. Djonevich, Vol. X (New York:
    Oceana Publications/Dobbs Ferry, 1992) pp. 41–2.
22. Omar Al-Hassan, *Economic Sanctions and the Middle East in 1996* (London: Gulf
    Centre for Strategic Studies, 1996), p. 2 and Nico Schrijver, 'The Use of
    Economic Sanctions by the UN Security Council: An International Law
    Perspective', in H.H.G. Post (ed.), *International Economic Law and Armed
    Conflict* (Alphen aan den Rijn: Martinus Nijhoff, 1994), pp. 132–61.
23. Security Council resolution 661 (1990), Resolutions and Decisions of the
    Security Council, 1990, S/INF/46 (1991), pp. 19–20. See Doxey, op. cit. pp.
    36–9.
24. Ibid., pp. 15–30, and Amer al-Roubaie and Wajeeh Elali, 'The Financial
    Implications of Economic Sanctions Against Iraq', *Arab Studies Quarterly*, 17, 3
    (Summer 1993), pp. 53–68.
25. Ibid., pp. 10–13.
26. For the legal aspects of the UN provisions on sanctions, see Chapter 3.
27. Hufbauer and Schott, op. cit., p. 32.
28. This is believed to have been the case, for example, in the case of limited finan-
    cial sanctions imposed by the US against Panama in the effort of the US to
    topple Manuel Noriega. See for example, Joseph C. Lombard, 'The Survival of
    Noriega: Lessons from the US Sanctions Against Panama', *Stanford Journal of
    International Law*, 26 (1989), p. 269.
29. Ibid., pp. 42–7 and 82–3. See also the criticism of this study by Kenneth W.
    Abbott, 'Coercion and Communications: Frameworks for Evaluation of
    Economic Sanctions', *New York University Journal of International Law and
    Politics*, 19 (1987), pp. 781– 802.

30. Johan Galtung, 'On the Effects of International Economic Sanctions – With Examples from the Case of Rhodesia', *World Politics*, 19 (1967), pp. 384–5.
31. Margaret P. Doxey, *Economic Sanctions and International Enforcement* (London: Oxford University Press for the Royal Institute of International Affairs, 1971), pp. 89–137.
32. Ya'acov Bar-Siman-Tov, 'The Limits of Economic Sanctions: The American–Israeli Case of 1953', *Journal of Contemporary History*, 23 (1988), pp. 425–43.
33. Hufbauer and Schott, op. cit., p. 86.
34. See for example Alexander L. George, David K. Hall and William R. Simons, *The Limits of Coercive Diplomacy: Laos–Cuba–Vietnam* (Boston: Little Brown, 1971).
35. Gary Hufbauer and Kimberly Elliot, 'Qualified Success: Financial Sanctions and Foreign Policy', *Harvard International Review*, 10, 5 (1988), p. 8.
36. See for example, William H. Kaempfer and Anton D. Lowenberg, 'The Theory of International Economic Sanctions: A Public Choice Approach', *American Economic Review*, 78 (September, 1988), p. 786, and by the same authors, 'Sanctioning South Africa: the Politics Behind the Policies', *Cato Journal*, 8 Winter (1989), p. 713.
37. See for example Robert Carswell, 'Economic Sanctions and the Iran Experience', *Foreign Affairs*, 60, 2 (Winter 1981/2), pp. 247–65, and Doxey (1996) op. cit., pp. 28–32.
38. See for example Judith Miller, 'When Sanctions Worked', *Foreign Policy*, 39 (Summer 1980), pp. 118–29.
39. Carswell, op. cit., p. 247.
40. Miller, op. cit., pp. 122–3.
41. Peter Wallenstein, 'Characteristics of Economic Sanctions', *Journal of Peace Research*, 5 (1968), p. 265 and Miroslav Nincic and Peter Wallenstein (eds), *Dilemmas of Economic Coercion* (New York: Praeger Publishers, 1983).
42. General Assembly resolution 1761 (XVII) (1962), *UN Resolutions, General Assembly*, Series I, compiled and edited by Dusan J. Djonevich Vol. IX (New York: Oceana Publications/Dobbs Ferry, 1974), pp. 102–3.
43. Sir Patrick Moberly, 'Assessing Their Effectiveness: South African Sanctions', *Harvard International Review*, X, 5 (1989), p. 32; Edward Seaga, 'Impact of Economic Sanctions on the South African Economy', *Round Table*, 306 (1988), p. 136 and Nagan, op. cit., p. 85.
44. See for example Jose I. Fernandez, 'Dismantling Apartheid: Counterproductive Effects of Continuing Economic Sanctions', *Law and Policy in International Business*, 22 (1991), p. 571.
45. Doxey, op. cit., p. 25.
46. Barber, op. cit., pp. 373–4.
47. Ibid., p. 185.
48. For example, if it had not been for the Arab boycott Israel probably would not have developed various sophisticated industries in the military and civilian spheres.
49. See Chapter 6.
50. Hufbauer and Schott, op. cit., p. 81.

51. Keesing's Contemporary Archives 9 May (1980), p. 30229 and 24 September (1982), p. 31724.
52. See Charles M. Becker, 'The Impact of Sanctions on South Africa and its Periphery', *African Studies Review*, 31, 2 (1988), p. 61; Paul Lansing and Sarosh Kuruvilla, 'Business Divestment in South Africa: In Whose Best Interest?', *Journal of Business Ethics*, 7 (August 1988), p. 561; Haider Ali Khan, 'The Impact of Trade Sanctions on South Africa: A Social Accounting Marrix Approach', *Contemporary Policy Issues*, 6 (October 1988), p. 130.
53. See Chapter 4.

2

The History of the Arab Boycott and its Administration

The Arab Boycott before the Establishment of the Arab League

WHAT IS known today as the 'Arab boycott of Israel' was announced at the second meeting of the Arab League Council in October 1945, two years and seven months before the establishment of the state of Israel, and was directed against the Jewish community in Palestine – the *Yishuv*.[1] This was not, however, the first time that the Arabs used economic means in their effort to halt the development of the Zionist enterprise in what was known at the time as Palestine. As of the 1890s, numerous boycotts were declared against the Jews. These boycotts were apparently not very effective, and had greater declaratory rather than economic effect.

As already mentioned, in the 1890s, as the Arab inhabitants of the Palestinian districts of the Ottoman Empire became concerned about the growing flow of Jewish immigration, and called upon the Ottoman rulers to forbid land sales to Jews. Local newspapers started to advocate the boycott of goods produced and sold by Jews, while the population was urged not to rent homes to Jews or trade with them.[2]

According to one source, after 1909 an association was established in Jerusalem, whose objective was the boycotting of Jewish merchandise, in retaliation for an alleged Jewish boycott of Muslim and Christian goods and the refusal to hire Arab workers. At the end of 1910, the owner of the Haifa-based newspaper *al-Carmel*, Naguib Nazar, established an association to 'organize an economic boycott against the Jews by not purchasing from or selling to them, and not leasing properties to them'. In 1914 a large number of associations were set up in various parts of Palestine, all of which were intended to fight the Jewish boycott and encourage Arab industrial production.[3] The accuracy of this report was questioned by another source who claimed that the Jews in Palestine refrained from purchasing goods from Arab shops, and as far as possible from employing Arab workers only *after* the ensuing of the British Mandate.[4]

On 3 January 1919, an agreement was signed between the Emir Feisal, who had led the Arab Revolt against the Ottoman Empire during the First World War, and Dr Chaim Weizmann, as head of the Zionist Organization, regarding 'closest collaboration in the development of the (pan-) Arab State and (the Jewish national home in) Palestine' – the establishment of both of which had been promised by the British in the course of 1916–17. The agreement also called for economic cooperation between the two sides.[5]

However the Emir Feisal failed to establish the pan-Arab state he had dreamt of, briefly assuming the throne in Syria and then becoming King of Iraq.[6] Furthermore, his pragmatic approach towards the Zionists was totally unacceptable to the rest of Arab national movement, which opposed the Jewish National Home policy of the British Government as declared in the Balfour Declaration, and its inclusion in the terms of the Mandate for Palestine granted Britain by the League of Nations in 1922. Economic boycotts soon became one of the weapons used by the nationalists against the development of the Jewish community in Palestine.

In a meeting of the Muslim–Christian Committee, which convened in Nablus on 16 January 1920, a decision was adopted to boycott Jews completely, and prevent them from entering or living in Nablus and its suburbs until the last vestiges of Zionism were eradicated. Similar decisions were adopted by an organization in Jaffa, as well as by the Christian leadership of Jerusalem. Following the 1921 attacks by Arabs on Jews, the former declared an embargo on all Jewish goods. In August 1922, the Fifth Palestine Arab Congress, meeting in Nablus, passed a resolution calling on Arabs to boycott Jewish businesses and to forbid land sales to Jews.[7] This policy was applied with greater vigour after the outbreak of the August 1929 disturbances, when Arabs, who were found to have broken the boycott, were physically attacked by their brethren and their merchandise damaged.[8]

A pan-Arab meeting which was held in Jerusalem on 27 October 1929, called for a complete boycott of all Jewish merchandise, and resolved to compel compliance by Arabs everywhere. The Congress called upon every Arab to buy nothing from the Jews except land,

and to sell them everything except land.[9] At around the same time the Arab merchants of Jerusalem set up a committee to supervise the boycott of Jewish merchants and goods. This was accompanied by the removal of Hebrew signs from Arab stores. In Jaffa the city council adopted a decision regarding the boycotting of the Rutenberg Electric Corporation, and the lighting of the streets with gas lights.[10]

In 1931 the Arab Workers Committee published a black book, calling upon the Western and Islamic worlds to boycott Jewish goods and encourage local products and merchandise. At the end of September 1931, Jamal al-Husseini, Secretary of the (Palestine) Arab Executive, called on the Arabs of Palestine to boycott Jewish products, and a similar appeal was made by Mussa Kassem al-Husseini, President of the Arab Executive, two months later.[11] The World Islamic Congress, which convened in Jerusalem on 7 December 1931, following the publication of the MacDonald White Paper, with the participation of some 130 delegates from 22 Muslim countries, supported these moves by calling upon all the Muslim states to avoid any trade relations with the Jewish community in Palestine[12] One of the duties of the members of a youth organization formed by the Arab Executive in Palestine in 1932, was to enforce a boycott declared against the first Tel Aviv Levant Fair organized by the Yishuv.[13]

On 26 March 1933 the Arab Executive Committee convened a mass meeting in Jaffa which resolved to boycott both British and Zionist goods,[14] and in October 1934 the Arab Labour Federation decided to picket Jewish enterprises and to conduct an anti-Jewish boycott. A boycott of all Jewish shops and tradesmen was proclaimed by Haj Amin al-Husseini, the Grand Mufti of Jerusalem. Two British students of the history of the Arab boycott, Terence Prittie and Walter H. Nelson, have suggested that the Mufti, who during the Second World War served the Germans, might well have sought to emulate the Nazi model.[15]

In March 1937 the Arab Executive called on all the Arabs in Palestine and the Arab states to boycott the Levant trade fair in Tel Aviv,[16] and in September 1937 a pan-Arab congress, which convened at Bludan in Syria, passed *inter alia* resolutions demanding the repeal of the 1917 Balfour Declaration, the abolition of the mandate and the enforcement of an economic boycott against the Jews as a patriotic duty. The Congress also threatened to extend the boycott to British goods.[17] Even before the Congress at Bludan, the boycott appears to have been fairly successful, and in its report of July 1937 the Palestine Royal Commission stated that: 'There is little or no Arab shopping now at Jewish shops.'[18]

Almost two months after the outbreak of the Second World War, on 29 October 1939, the Arab Executive published an appeal to the Arab and Muslim world to boycott all Jewish products and stores.[19] However *de facto* the boycott was actually suspended during the War, when the Arab states neighbouring on Palestine became the main market for Palestinian Jewish produce.[20] In the course of the Second World War and in the immediate post-war period, the Jewish economy in Palestine developed at a rapid pace.[21] The Arab states viewed this development, which was accompanied by a sharp increase in imports from the West, with growing concern, realizing that it strengthened not only the economic but also the political base of the Zionist enterprise, and believing that it was detrimental to the development of the Arab economy in Palestine and of the Syrian and Lebanese economies, which were traditional sources of both agricultural and industrial goods to Palestine.[22]

However after the establishment in March 1945 of the League of Arab States, with the participation of Egypt, Lebanon, Syria, Transjordan, Iraq, Yemen and Saudi Arabia – the main purpose of which was to promote pan-Arab cooperation in the political, military, economic and social spheres[23] – the economic boycott of the Jews in Palestine was formally declared and institutionalized. In fact, the decision of the Arab League collectively to impose a boycott against the Jewish community in Palestine was part of the general process of the 'inter-Arabization of the Palestine issue'.[24]

The Arab Boycott from 1946–48

On 2 December 1945, the Council of the Arab League issued its first formal boycott declaration.[25] The declaration, contained in resolution 16, urged both member states and Arab countries not yet members, to prohibit the importation and use of the products of Jewish industry in Palestine, effective 1 January 1946. 'The products of Palestinian Jews', the resolution stated, 'are to be regarded as undesirable in Arab states. They should be boycotted and (use of them) prohibited, as long as their production in Palestine is liable to bring about the realization of the Zionist political goals.'[26]

The rationale behind this declaration was that since the Arab goal was to obstruct the development of a Zionist economy, capable of sustaining a Jewish state,[27] and since Jewish industry in Palestine was based on Zionist funds, collected in foreign countries to serve the establishment of a Jewish national home and state in Palestine,[28] the Arabs would be assisting this endeavour if they were to purchase Jewish products and manufactured goods, The terms 'Jews' and 'Zionists' were used in the declaration interchangeably.[29] The Jewish Agency reacted by lodging a protest with the UN on 4 January 1946, against the Arab League, on the grounds that its actions were contrary to the provisions of the UN Charter.[30]

In February the League started to create the apparatus for implementing the boycott. The first body established was the Permanent Boycott Committee, located in Cairo, to supervise the implementation of the boycott resolution.[31] The Committee presented a report to the League's Council in March which detailed the legal actions taken by each member state in pursuance of the League's December resolutions. The report also clarified the measures required to fill the gaps left by the cessation of all trade relations with the Jewish community in Palestine. The main solution proposed was the increase of imports from countries outside the region. The report also proposed placing strict restrictions on imports and exports which might prove useful to Jewish industry.[32]

On 12 June the Boycott Committee adopted a recommendation in resolution 70, which called on all the Arab states to set up national boycott offices to give effect to the previous resolutions. Subsequent measures adopted by the League with regards to the boycott included the requirement of those selling goods to the Arab states to provide certificates of origin which would ensure that these goods were not manufactured in Israel, the allocation of 50 per cent of the value of goods confiscated due to the boycott to customs officials, and the prohibition of the use by Arabs of Jewish banks, insurance companies, contractors and transport in Palestine. Resolution 68 of the League Council declared that propaganda should be carried out to make the boycott of Zionist goods a creed of the Arab nations, so that each Arab might preach it enthusiastically to all.[33]

Member states of the League soon started to implement these resolutions through national legislative and administrative measures. For example:

- special import licences were generally required to import goods of Palestine origin;
- Syria enacted legislation forbidding the importation, distribution, or smuggling of Zionist goods. Sanctions against those in breach of this law ranged from imprisonment with forced labour to capital punishment;
- Lebanon initiated legislation prohibiting trade in Zionist goods. Offenders were liable to get sentences of up to 15 years imprisonment for a first offence, and up to life imprisonment for repeated offences;
- Saudi Arabia requested the foreign petroleum companies operating in its territory not to employ Jews;
- Saudi Arabia, Bahrain and Kuwait agreed in August 1947 to prohibit the passage of Zionist goods through the Gulf of Bassrah and Arab ports under their control;
- Egypt prohibited the handling of Palestinian goods in transit at any Egyptian port or free zone;
- the Transjordanian Medical Association called on the public not to call on Jewish doctors or use Jewish medicines;
- Iraq prohibited export of any raw materials, whether or not of Iraqi origin, to Zionist factories;
- in Palestine itself the Arab Higher Committee established central and local boycott committees, which conducted propaganda campaigns within the Arab population and took active steps to prevent Arab customers from frequenting Jewish shops. Blacklists were compiled of offenders, and these suffered punishment at the hands of self-appointed guardians of the boycott.[34]

Despite the initial enthusiasm, the first annual report of the Permanent Committee, published in October 1947, made it clear that the Arab states had not complied with the council resolution calling for supervisory committees to oversee the implementation of the boycott. It was also reported that Jewish investment was taking place in the Arab states by means of non-Jewish cover operations, while goods produced by the Jewish community in Palestine were reaching the Arab states via Cyprus, Turkey and Greece.[35]

Following the passage of UN General Assembly resolution 181 of 29 November, 1947, that called for the partition of Palestine into Jewish and Arab states, the members of the Arab League, all of which rejected the partition plan, intensified the application of the boycott – first in a last-minute effort to prevent the establishment of the Jewish state, later in a continued effort to bring about its defeat and destruction.

It should be noted, however, that 'despite all these administrative activities' trade between the Arab states neighbouring on Palestine and Palestine (including its Jewish economic sector) continued to thrive, as indicated by the following figures:

Lebanon and Syria. In 1947 Palestine was the largest importer of Lebanese and Syrian products, purchasing from Lebanon and Syria £1.9m worth of food stuffs, and another £1.6m of other products – a total of £3.5m, up from 1.4 million in 1944 and 1.6m in 1945. Exports to these countries were relatively low: £250,000 in finished products and £540,000 in fuel products.

Transjordan. Palestine was traditionally Transjordan's largest customer for agricultural goods. In 1942, exports to Palestine comprised 90 per cent of Transjordan's total exports. In 1946, Palestine's share of Transjordanian exports reached £1.7m of a total of £2.44m – i.e. 83 per cent of total exports in that year. Exports from Palestine to Transjordan rose from £242,000 in 1942 to £616,000 in 1946. In 1947 these exports, a substantial part of which consisted of refined fuel products, fell to £429,000, which was at least partially the result of the newly imposed boycott. The fall of imports to Palestine from Transjordan to £522,000 was largely the result of the poor harvest in Transjordan in 1947.[36]

The Arab Boycott – The First Two Decades after the Establishment of The State of Israel

Following the proclamation of the State of Israel on 14 May 1948, the Arab League repeated its call for a ban on all commercial and financial transactions with Israel. Postal, radio and telegraphic communications were cut off and a land, sea and air blockade was imposed. Israeli goods, shipped through the ports of Alexandria, Port Said and Port Suez, were confiscated by Egyptian inspectors. A prize court, established in Alexandria in July 1949, authorized the seizure of cargoes with Israeli destinations. Later regulations, promulgated in 1950, allowed for the search of ships and aircraft and confiscation of Israeli-bound goods.[37] Upon the outbreak of the 1948/49 Arab–Israeli War, the Permanent Committee ceased to function.[38]

On 6 February 1950, Egypt issued a decree, in which article I stated: 'The searching of ships for purposes of seizing war contraband, shall take place in accordance with provisions hereunder.' Article III went on to say that 'Force may at all times be used against any ship attempting to avoid the search, where necessary by firing so as to force it to stop and submit to the search. Where the search subsequently reveals that the ship is not carrying any contraband, it shall be permitted to continue its voyage.' According to article IV 'If the crew of the ship resists the search by force, the ship shall be deemed to have lost its neutrality by reason of the hostile act'. In that event, a ship may be seized even if the search reveals that it was not carrying contraband and the cargo may be impounded for that reason. Under this decree Egypt started to prepare a blacklist of ships, having transgressed or been suspected of transgressing the Egyptian blockade practices, and denied their free use of the Suez Canal. By 1955 this list included 104 ships.[39]

Under the provisions of this law oil was declared among the strategic goods which should be denied to Israel. In order to prevent Iranian oil from reaching Israel's Red Sea port of Eilat, Egypt embarked on a blockade of the Straits of Tiran and the Gulf of Aqaba. Captains of cargo vessels and oil tankers were required to guarantee that their vessels would not ultimately discharge any of their cargo in an Israeli port, and submission of log books by tankers proceeding south through the Suez Canal became obligatory.

Violations of regulations by any ships were deemed to constitute hostile acts, and even if no contraband was found on board, the ship would be seized and the cargo impounded. On 22 July the Egyptian government issued a regulation requiring masters of northbound tankers passing through the Suez Canal, regardless of destination, to sign declarations stating that their vessels would proceed direct to the named port of destination after leaving Port Said. In addition, such masters were ordered to obtain a declaration from the customs officials at the port of destination certifying that their cargo was discharged there and that it was for local consumption. This document was to be countersigned by the local Egyptian consul. It was further decreed that agents of each vessel countersign the master's declarations. Production of such a certificate was required at Suez within one month after the vessel discharged its cargo. In addition, tanker owners and operators were being warned by Cairo officials that force would be used if necessary to detain tankers believed to be bound for Israel and without final clearance certificates. Masters, it was reported, would be fined an equivalent of from $5–56 if found without such required documents.[40]

In the summer of 1950 Britain, Norway and the US complained to the Egyptian government about the blacklisting of certain of their tankers, and not allowing them to use the Suez Canal, since they had previously called at Haifa port.[41] Following Israeli protests, the UN Security Council passed a resolution on 1 September 1951, demanding that Egypt terminate its restrictions on navigation through international waterways. However, that was to remain one of numerous UN resolutions which were ignored by the parties concerned.[42] On 28 November 1953, the term contraband was extended by Egypt to include 'foodstuffs and all other commodities likely to strengthen the war potential of the Zionists in Palestine in any way whatsoever'.[43]

In October 1956 another Security Council resolution instructed Egypt to lift the blockade on shipping in the Canal and end its state of belligerence with Israel, adding: 'The operation of the Canal should be insulated from the politics of any country.'[44] Nasser ignored these protests and except for the years 1957–59 (the two years following the Sinai Campaign and Suez War) the canal remained closed to Israeli ships and ships bound for Israel.[45]

The Egyptian decree of February 1950 signalled a change in the basic policy of the Arab League Council. Prior to the decree the boycott's immediate purpose had been to bar direct Arab trade with Israel. Now the Arab League embraced shipping services in an attempt to hinder the flow of Israel's trade relations.[46] On 8 April 1950 the League Council approved a decision by its Political Committee to the effect that from now on all ships carrying goods or immigrants to Israel would be blacklisted.[47] In other words, in addition to the primary boycott concerning direct economic and business relations between the Arab states and Israel (which the Arabs frequently referred to as the negative, or passive boycott), a secondary boycott relating to third parties was added, which was also referred to as the positive (or active) boycott.[48]

On 19 May 1951, the Arab League Council passed resolution 357 establishing the position of Boycott Commissioner, and providing for the appointment of his deputies, who were to act as liaison officers accredited by each member state. The Central Boycott Office (CBO) was set up in Damascus with branch offices in member states. The major task of the Damascus CBO – which rapidly became the central organizational instrument used by the Arab states in their economic war against Israel – was to maintain 'security of communications between the [affiliated] boycott offices in each country, and coordination of activities in the local offices'.[49]

The CBO, whose first director was Lou'a Ahmad Shoukri, was also instructed to report regularly to the Secretary General of the Arab League, and through his office to the Arab League Council.[50] Biannual meetings of the boycott liaison officers were held each year thereafter, in order to coordinate boycott policies and programmes, and to compile blacklists of individuals and firms that had violated the boycott. The boycott was provided with legal teeth through the enactment of appropriate legislation in each of the member states and the issuing of administrative regulations officially imposing the boycott on Israel. Finally the May meeting decreed that 'participation in regional conferences organized on the initiative of one country or by an international organization could not be attended if Israel were also invited'. The Arab states subsequently boycotted the Izmir Fair because of Israel's participation, refused to take part in congresses and seminars sponsored by specialized agencies of the UN and even shunned international sports events.[51]

By March 1952 all the regional boycott offices were established,[52] and at its October 1952 meeting the Arab League Council passed resolution 471, which established the Palestine Department in the League Secretariat, with power to supervise the CBO. Resolution 482 extended the boycott to foreign companies with branches in Israel.[53] By 1954 5.7 per cent of the Arab League budget – $57,800 – was allocated to the CBO in Damascus.[54]

It should be noted that throughout the years the secondary and tertiary boycotts were applied almost exclusively against companies in third countries rather than the countries themselves. There were, however, several episodes, in the early years, in which third countries became targets, at least temporarily, of the boycott. In 1952 there was a plan to boycott the Federal Republic of Germany after it signed the Restitution Agreement with Israel.[55] However, the boycott was never implemented. According to Arab sources, this was because of American and Zionist pressure.[56] In fact it was because of active diplomatic efforts by the Federal Republic itself in the Arab world, the promise of generous economic aid to Egypt and the fact that the Arabs stood to lose more from boycotting West Germany than the other way around.[57]

The following year, 1953, the Arab League Council recommended a wide range of restrictions on trade with Cyprus, which had become a centre for illicit Arab–Israeli trade.[58] International criticism of this attempt to extend the boycott to a third state, not directly connected with the Arab–Israeli conflict and not merely to an individual firm, led to a certain relaxation of the restrictions imposed, though not to their total elimination.

By 1953 the Arab boycott of Israel was a well-established feature in world trade relations. A memorandum prepared in 1953 by the British Foreign Office, described the boycott in the following terms:

> The general purpose of the boycott is … to harm Israel's economy and trade. The particular methods by which this is to be done … are broadly as follows:
>
> a) To prevent any trade between Israel and the Arab countries. By denying to Israel's manufacturers their natural markets and forcing Israel to purchase food and raw materials from afar, this aim, which has been effectively carried out, has achieved some success …
>
> b) To prevent the Israel economy receiving support or stimulus from other countries by refusing to allow firms which have branches or factories in Israel to trade with the Arab states. This is the point on which a number of concerns, notably Imperial Chemical Industries, have fallen foul of the boycott.
>
> c) To prevent strategic materials being imported into Israel. This objective accounted for the interference which has been experienced by some British ships calling at Arab ports en route to Israel carrying certain types of cargo.
>
> d) To limit the transport services available to Israel by refusing to allow ships or aircraft to call at Arab ports if they come from or are going to Israel. This is a recent development, hardly yet effective …[59]

The conclusions of the memorandum regarding the future of the boycott were as follows:

There is no likelihood that there will be any general improvement in the boycott situation so long as the present Arab–Israel position continues. The tendency is for the boycott to become increasingly widespread and for its organization to improve. Arab public opinion supports it. It provides the Arab League with a convenient and non-controversial outlet for its energies.[60]

In the beginning of 1953 there were also first reports about Arab attempts to get European and American airlines to boycott Israel, or at least avoid investing in Israel. Thus a report dated 29 April 1953, from the British Ambassador to Beirut to the Foreign Office in London, stated that the Lebanese Department of Civil Aviation had approached BOAC, Cyprus Airways, KLM, SAS, Air-France, Pan-American and TWA with such demands.[61]

On 11 December 1954 the Arab League Council passed resolution 849, which approved the Unified Law on the Boycott of Israel. The provisions of this resolution, which were subsequently incorporated into the national legislation of most of the Arab League members in the course of 1955, formalized the uniform application of the boycott by the Arab states. The new law prohibited Arab individuals and entities from dealing with agencies of persons working on behalf of Israel, or with foreign companies and organizations having interests, branches or agencies in Israel. Exports of Arab goods to countries re-exporting them to Israel were prohibited upon penalty of imprisonment with hard labour and heavy fines.[62]

In the mid-1950s boycott activities intensified, and gained the moral backing of the Soviet Union – the new and powerful ally of the Arab states with revolutionary regimes: Egypt, Syria, Yemen, Sudan and, towards the end of the decade, Iraq.[63] In 1957 the Arab League announced that its members would henceforth deny overflight and landing rights to Air France because it had allegedly invested in Israeli development projects and had produced 'propaganda films' for Israel. After holding out for 18 months, Air France finally capitulated to Arab demands towards the end of 1958.[64]

In 1958 the application of the boycott was extended to include all goods exported by a third state, if these were identical to goods imported by this state from Israel. This regulation included goods produced from Israeli raw materials or components.[65] Also in 1958 a boycott regulation was added to provide for the blacklisting of foreign ships, which had visited an Arab port and an Israeli port during the same trip. In 1964 the application of this regulation was modified to exempt 'universal cruise ships' which do not carry goods.[66]

In 1959 the General Union of Arab Chambers of Commerce, Industry and Agriculture adopted the rules declared by the CBO, and issued a list of the types of firms which were to be placed on the Arab boycott's blacklist:

- firms with branches in Israel;
- firms with assembly plants in Israel, including firms whose agents assemble their products in Israel;
- firms with general agencies or main offices for their Middle Eastern operations in Israel;
- firms that give their patents, trademarks or copyrights to Israeli companies;
- firms, and other public or private organizations, that purchase the shares of Israeli companies;
- consultants and technical firms that offer their services to Israel.

Firms found to be in breach of any of these conditions were offered the choice between closing down the prohibited operation, or being blacklisted.[67]

After 1959 new causes for blacklisting were added, and the CBO started to formulate boycott principles, which were intended to serve as guidelines for the member states while enabling each of them to decide whether or how to implement these guidelines in accordance with their individual requirements. Thus each of the members of the Arab League issued its own separate boycott instructions, tailored to meet its particular requirements.

In the course of the 1960s a growing number of American films were blacklisted because they allegedly contained Zionist propaganda, or because the actors (including Eartha Kitt, Edward G. Robinson and Marilyn Monroe) 'have shown pronounced pro-Israeli sympathies and have helped collect donations for Israel'. Louis Armstrong was banned because he had performed in Israel, and the records of numerous famous artists were also banned for similar reasons.[68]

In 1960 the Arab League opened its first information office in the Afro-Asian area in New Delhi. The task of the office was to explain the Arab position on the boycott of Israel and the question of the Palestinian refugees, and to promote cooperation in the spheres of oil and commerce.[69] In the mid-1960s a new boycott office was opened in the Gulf emirates, *inter alia* in order to prevent Israeli goods entering the Arab world via Iran.[70]

The Boycott at its Peak – The Oil Crisis and the Aftermath of the October War

The general boycott principles were amended from time to time, the last version being issued by the CBO in 1972. In 1977 a summary of the principles was published by the CBO, section (1) of which dealt with manufacturing and trading companies:

> Transactions with foreign companies are banned in the following cases if such companies insist on their attitude by carrying on such practices and not ceasing from performing them:
>
> a) If they have main or branch factories in Israel;
> b) If they have assembly plants in Israel. This also applies to foreign firms and companies whose agents assemble their products in Israel. The ban will be applied too in the case of assembly if it is proven that a certain Israeli company has assembled, on commercial scale, a unit of a certain product or goods from parts, the majority of which is produced by a certain foreign company or any of its branches/subsidiaries, unless such foreign company establishes its non-responsibility for such assembly and takes legal proceedings against the Israeli company which committed the assembly. This provision is applied if the parts used in producing the unit constitute more than 50 per cent of the parts of such unit or if the engine of the unit is of the foreign company's production;
> c) If they have in Israel, either general agencies or main offices for their Middle Eastern operations;
> d) If they give the right of using their names or manufacturing licences to Israel companies;
> e) If they hold shares in Israeli companies or factories;
> f) If they render consultative services and technical experience to Israeli factories;
> g) If the foreign company is engaged in the field of export-import and because of obstinate bias in favour of Israel, refuses to promote and sell Arab products while it promotes and sells Israeli products similar in price and quality;
> h) If they take part in searching for the natural resources of Israel such as petroleum drilling;

i) If they decline to answer the questionnaire addressed by the Arab authorities requiring them to explain the nature of their relations with Israel and whether they form a violation or not; the ban imposed on a certain company is applied against all of its parent and subsidiary companies.[71]

In the years 1963–79 Mohammed Mahgoub, a retired Egyptian General, headed the CBO in Damascus. He had some 20 employees, five of whom had diplomatic status.[72] Under Mahgoub's management the boycott apparatus assumed four levels of organization, which at least formally still exist today in those countries that continue to apply the boycott:

The general representation (or secretariat general) is located in Damascus. It is divided on a regional rather than functional basis, but does have functional sub-divisions. Special departments exist for following current cases, gathering information and research and preparing the agenda for the General Conference.

The local (or regional) units are supposed to function in the member states of the Arab League. The units serve as permanent inter-mediaries between the general representation in Damascus and the domestic governments. Each state may present its proposals and suggestions through the local unit, and is informed by the local unit of decisions adopted by the boycott apparatus after these have been approved by the General Conference of the Arab League. The local unit is frequently located in the central customs building. In the past the decisions and regulations passed by the CBO were usually auto-matically adopted as law in the various Arab states. The local units are supposed to engage in investigating specific cases, to participate in the decision making of the boycott apparatus at its various levels, and to ensure that resolutions adopted by the General Conference of the Arab League are implemented in the countries in which the units function.

The liaison officers are the representatives of the CBO stationed in third countries. They usually have the status of advisors or attachés in some Arab embassy. These officers are directly answerable to the general representation in Damascus, while administratively they are connected to the Arab League secretariat. Their task is to seek new cases, verify information, stand in close touch with all the eco-nomic advisors in the Arab embassies, and convene the local economic committee. This committee is a body made up of all the economic representatives in the various Arab embassies, and its function is to instruct the liaison officer what information to seek and to recommend cases to be brought to the economic representation in Damascus. When the liaison officer comes across a problem connected with the boycott which might have political or diplomatic ramifications, he is to report it to the Arab League administration.

The General Conference is the supreme institution of the Arab boycott, that used to convene twice a year, each time in another Arab capital, before meetings of the Arab League Committee. It adopted decisions regarding companies suspected of being in breach of the boycott, which were prompted by a liaison officer, a local unit or anonymous information. After adopting a decision, the General Conference drafted a report for the general meeting of the Arab League. The adoption of the report gave the decisions of the conference legal authority.

A decision adopted to act against a certain company was followed by research about the company, the sending out of a questionnaire, and should the answers to the questionnaire indicate breach of the boycott regulations, the dispatch of a warning letter and regular reminders. The target company was then required to break off its relations with Israel and to prove that it had done so. If a satisfactory result was not attained, the economic committee adopted a decision to boycott the company, and this decision was passed onto the Arab League for approval.[73]

It should be noted that, at least in theory, companies doing business with the Arab states were put through a rather long procedure of ensuring that they knew the rules of the boycott, and were then given ample opportunity to prove their acceptance of them. The procedure began with a letter informing the target company of 'the boycott law and its regulations' and that infringement of these would lead to its being boycotted. An authorized official of a company entering a business relationship in the Arab world for the first time, was asked to sign a sworn statement to the effect that the company was not in breach of, and would not in future break the boycott regulations.[74] In addition, companies sending goods to an Arab country had to fill a negative certificate of origin which declared *inter alia* that the origin of the said goods was not Israeli, and no Israeli materials or products were used in the process of its manufacture. After all this, companies suspected of carrying on business relations with Israel received a questionnaire, in which they were asked for detailed, confidential information on their business activities, and an undertaking to cease all economic contacts with Israel.[75]

In principle, on the basis of this system, if a company was black-listed, no private or public factor in the Arab world was to trade with it. Anyone found to have broken the regulations was liable to be fined, imprisoned or have boycotted goods confiscated. Nevertheless there were always exceptions in which companies or states were allowed to continue to trade with a blacklisted company.[76]

The 1973 'oil crisis', resulting in the rapid accumulation of petrodollars by the Arab oil producing states, led to a vast expansion in trade and investment deals between Arab countries and Western companies, and increased the power of the Arab states to impose the secondary and tertiary boycotts. Towards the end of February 1975 the Arab League adopted a resolution calling for the intensification of the economic boycott of Israel.[77] With the newly acquired power of the Arab oil-producing states, there seemed no limit to the economic difficulties that the Arabs could cause Israel, and Israel started preparing for the worst.[78]

Even in these years, which were the heyday of the boycott, observers noted that imposing the boycott was no simple task, especially in the financial sphere. In February 1975 the CBO published a list of the 14 banks which headed its blacklist: Rothschild (UK), Warburg (UK), London and Colonial (UK), Lazard Frères (US), American Bank and Trust (US), National Provincial and Rothschild (Canada), Banque Belge Centrale SA (Belgium), Banque Max Fisher (Belgium), Société Bancaire et Financière d'Orient (France), Union Financière de Paris (France), Bank für Gemeinwirtschaft (West Germany), Discount Bank (Overseas) Ltd (Switzerland), International Credit Bank (Switzerland). The principle was that no Arab bank should enter into any contractual arrangement with any blacklisted bank.

However, as explained by the *Middle East Economic Digest* *(MEED)*, this was not always easy to apply in practice, quoting the example of the Kuwait International Investment Company (KIIC).[79] In 1975 the KIIC was co-manager for two international bond issues: $25 million for the Swedish company Volvo, and $50 million for Mexico. The issues were underwritten, *inter alia*, by two blacklisted banks – Warburg and Rothschild. The KIIC replied to Arab critics of this arrangement by saying that 'The international banking business is a network which you cannot dissect to allow some and blacklist others.' Nevertheless, at least in this case the CBO finally got its way, and the KIIC eventually withdrew from the loan issue.

The boycott ruling that emerged from this case was that entering into an indirect contractual arrangement as co-manager with a blacklisted underwriter, constituted a violation of the boycott, but that it was permissible for both an Arab bank and a blacklisted bank to be ordinary underwriters, and appear together in the same newspaper 'tombstone' advertisements for the loan. 'In the words of one Kuwaiti banker: "that would be like travelling in the same bus innocently without shaking hands or kissing"'.[80]

This pragmatism also concerned 'normal trade' between third countries and Israel. The selling of completely finished foreign goods to Israel, other than those beneficial to its war effort, was not regarded automatically as contravening the Arab boycott regulations,[81] though such trade was included when the Arabs felt that the boycott would damage Israel.[82]

In fact the secondary and tertiary boycotts were always erratically enforced by the Arab states, each of which had its own blacklist.[83] Over the years some Arab states continued to trade with foreign companies that maintained open economic relations with Israel, when this served their own economic interests,[84] and there were even cases of direct links with Israel itself.[85]

The haphazard manner in which the boycott was applied, even in the years in which Arab economic power was at its peak, resulted in the issue being raised in various Arab forums. Thus the conference of the heads of Arab welfare and development agencies, which convened in 1977, decided that the boycott should be enforced more strictly and that Arab states which failed to comply with the boycott regulations should be deprived of all assistance.[86] Resolution 3553 of the Arab League council of 1977 called for the use of mass communications techniques and the offices of the Arab League throughout the Arab world, for the purpose of countering Israel's anti-boycott propaganda efforts.[87]

Towards the end of the 1970s six Arab League members – Algeria, Mauritania, Morocco, Somalia, Sudan and Tunis – complied only with the primary boycott,[88] while Iraq, Jordan, Kuwait, Libya, Oman, Qatar, Saudi Arabia, Syria, the United Arab Emirates (UAE) and the

two Yemens, adhered to the boycott on all levels, at least formally.[89]
Jordan traded informally with Israel across the open bridges (after
1967), just as Lebanon did through the 'good fence' (after 1975). On
the other hand, following the overthrow of the Shah in Iran in 1979,
the latter country joined the list of non-Arab Islamic states (some
with a large Muslim minority) which actively participated in the
boycott; these included Bangladesh, India, Malaysia, Mali, Pakistan
and Uganda.[90] In 1981 the Boycott office in Damascus was supplemented by an Islamic Office for the Boycott of Israel, which was
affiliated to the Islamic Conference Organization in Jedda.[91]

From the Signing of the Egyptian–Israeli Peace Agreements to the Eve of the Gulf War

The signing of the Camp David Accords between Egypt and Israel in
September 1978, followed by the peace treaty of March 1979, which
included an explicit Egyptian undertaking to cancel the boycott,
which was translated into Law 66 of 18 February 1980 lifting the
boycott of Israel,[92] created a problem for the boycotting states, since,
at least formally, a serious loophole was created in its application. In
reaction to Egypt's move, the Baghdad Arab Summit Conference of
March 1979 decided to impose economic sanctions against Egypt,
and as late as 1988, not long before Egypt was readmitted into the
Arab League, three Egyptian companies, which carried out direct
contacts with Israel, were blacklisted. These included the Royal
Trading Office, the Suez Canal Bank and Air Sinai.[93] The Baghdad
Conference also dealt with the Arab boycott against Israel, emphasizing that the boycott was a basic weapon in the Arab strategy, which
sought inter-Arab economic integration on the one hand, and prevention of Israeli penetration of the Arab world on the other. This was
accompanied by a call to strengthen the boycott apparatus, while fulfilling the boycott's principles and implementing its regulations more
stringently, in order to neutralize the effect of Egypt's defection.[94]

However, even after signing its peace treaty with Israel and the
rescinding of its 1955 boycott law the following year, *de facto* Egypt
continued to apply the boycott against Israel. In the following five
years nearly 500 requests for boycott compliance were received by
American companies alone wishing to do business with Egypt [95]

Israel's invasion of Lebanon in June 1982, in what it called Operation Peace for the Galilee, gave the boycott new impetus, as many companies in Western countries started boycotting Israel without any prodding from the Arab states, because of their disapproval of the Israeli policy. By 1987, 26 countries, in addition to the 22 member states of the Arab League, boycotted Israel economically, either completely or partially. These included Afghanistan, Albania, Bangladesh, Brazil, Bulgaria, Burundi, Cambodia, Chad, China, Congo, Cuba, Czechoslovakia, the German Democratic Republic, Guinea, Hungary, India, Indonesia, Iran, North Korea, Pakistan, Poland, Sri Lanka, the Soviet Union, Taiwan, Vietnam, Yugoslavia.[96]

In reaction to the outbreak of the *Intifada* – the Palestinian uprising against the Israeli occupation in the West Bank and Gaza Strip – in December 1987, the Commissioner General of the CBO in Damascus, Zuhair Aqil, stated at a meeting of the Arab boycott liaison officers that the boycott is 'one of the Arab weapons in confronting the Zionist entity, which we ought to maintain to prevent Israel's economic development and foil its ambitions'. He added that the deaths of Palestinians in the occupied territories should be 'a motive for all of us to tighten Arab Boycott measures and stand by our brothers in fighting Zionist aggression'. The goal of the CBO, he added was 'to give the boycott more momentum and effectiveness, facilitate its measures and speed up decision-taking'.[97]

Though the policy of the CBO seemed to be as rigid as ever, in fact, cracks could be observed in the boycott's implementation. Thus, though at the beginning of July 1988 the CBO refused to remove Coca-Cola from the blacklist, at around the same time the company, which claimed to be doing business with 11 Arab states, launched a TV advertising campaign in Bahrain, and opened bottling and canning plants in several Gulf states.[98]

In July 1989 the boycott commissioners from most of the 22 Arab League states met in Damascus. At this meeting the economic sanctions against Egypt, which had been readmitted to the Arab League two months previously, were lifted. On the same occasion 21 companies were removed from the blacklist, including General Motors, Jeep, Jeyes and L'Oréal. The partial boycott of the Japanese Sony and its affiliated companies was also ended, and settlements were reached with Chrysler, General Electric and the contracting firm GKN, all of whom had been threatened with blacklisting. Nevertheless, 15 new companies were added to the blacklist, including Iron & Gate, Keystone Camera Products, La Compagnie Financière and Delta Textile.[99]

A further meeting of the boycott commissioners in February 1990 once again updated the blacklist and banned the importation 'of goods which carry a boycotted name and a trade mark produced by any company regardless of nationality or source'.[100] The purpose of this measure was to prevent Israeli goods or goods bearing the brand names of boycotted companies from entering Arab markets indirectly.[101]

In July 1990, in reaction to the new wave of immigrants to Israel from the former Soviet Union, which began towards the end of 1989, the Arab foreign ministers, meeting in Tunis, decided to start boycotting companies and other institutions that help Jews migrate to Israel.[102] In October the CBO in Damascus specified that these companies would include airlines and shipping companies participating in bringing the immigrants to Israel.[103] By the beginning of 1991 several companies which had sold Israel prefabricated houses for the new immigrants, were also placed on the blacklist, and several other companies in the construction business and related industries received warnings from the boycott office that sales to Israel would result in their being blacklisted.[104]

The Arab Boycott after the Gulf War

The period between the Iraqi invasion of Kuwait in August 1990 and the end of the Gulf War in February 1991, had a profound impact on US–Arab and Arab–Israeli relations. In the war itself American troops fought side by side with British, French and Arab forces – including a token Syrian contingency force – to restore the Emir of Kuwait, Sheikh Jabber a-Sabakh, to his throne, and prevent a possible Iraqi takeover of Saudi Arabia. Israel was a passive partner in this coalition. At the end of the war Washington felt that the Arab Gulf states owed the US a debt of gratitude, and a responsibility to assist in building a more peaceful and stable Middle East.

In terms of the Arab boycott, the Gulf War was undoubtedly a watershed. Though an intensification of the boycott's application was observed in the course of 1991,[105] American pressure mounted on the Arab states to lift the boycott within the framework of a Middle East peace settlement.

The first indication that a change was to be expected came when it was announced at the beginning of 1991 that Pepsi-Cola – which, unlike Coca-Cola, which had entered the Israeli market in 1965, had always boycotted Israel – was seeking an Israeli bottler, and this was in addition to sales of its products in restaurants belonging to the Pizza Hut chain in Israel. All this came after Coca-Cola had started in 1989 to edge its way back into some Arab markets due to lax enforcement of the boycott.[106] However, if anyone thought that enforcement of the boycott would from now on start moving on a clear path towards cancellation, they were soon to be disappointed.

Between 27 April and 4 May 1991 the Arab boycott liaison officers, including officials from Saudi Arabia, Kuwait, and the other Gulf states, met for their 64th conference in Damascus. At this meeting, 110 companies were added to the blacklist, including 104 companies owned by the controversial Jewish businessman Robert Maxwell. On the other hand several others, including Coca Cola, the Home Insurance Company, Helen Curtis and the Phoenix insurance company, were removed.[107] Coca Cola was removed from the blacklist, having been on it for over 20 years.[108]

In May Ibrahim al-Ghanem, Director General of Kuwait's Customs Authority, informed Reuters that the Emirate would be applying the boycott less rigidly than before. Al-Ghanem's statement was quoted extensively around the world. However, Kuwaiti diplomats in Washington were quick to deny that any policy change regarding the boycott had been effected, pointing out that al-Ghanem was not authorized to issue definitive policy statements.[109]

In July 1991 there were rumours to the effect that the Gulf Cooperation Council (GCC) had adopted a decision to enable the sale of oil to Israel.[110] The following month the American Ambassador to Kuwait made a statement to the effect that the Kuwaiti authorities had decided to stop enforcing the secondary boycott, at least with regards to the American firms.[111] A similar reassurance was given by Kuwaiti government officials to the World Jewish Congress.[112]

It was the Europeans who towards the G-7 meeting in July 1991 first linked the removal of the boycott by the Arabs to the freezing of all settlement activities in the occupied territories by Israel. The Bush

Administration adopted the idea from the Europeans, even though the previous two years Secretary of State James Baker had led a campaign, supported by Congress, for a unilateral lifting of the boycott. Following a meeting between King Fahd of Saudi Arabia and Baker, the Saudis issued a statement to the effect that they would suspend their economic boycott of Israel if Israel would freeze its settlement drive in the territories.[113] The Saudi offer to end the boycott was soon followed by similar statements by the United Arab Emirates (UAE) and Oman. However, the idea was rejected out of hand both by the Israeli government on the one hand, and by the Arab League on the other. While the Shamir Government refused to stop the settlement activity at any price on ideological grounds,[114] the Arab League argued that the G-7 did not realize that by linking the cancellation of the boycott to Jewish settlements in the occupied territories, they were merely strengthening 'the Israeli stubbornness and hardline attitudes towards international peace'.[115]

In the hope of attracting more international companies to tender for post-Gulf War reconstruction contracts, Kuwait decided in November 1991 to somewhat relax its boycott of Western companies dealing with Israel. Nevertheless al-Ghanem (see above) added that firms in which Israeli capital was invested would still be barred from bidding in tenders. He added that 'the (primary) boycott of Israel will remain as it is. It is linked to the peace settlement. Ending the boycott is an important card which will be used as an incentive to push the peace process.' Another reason for the new Kuwaiti policy was the fact that while the PLO had supported Saddam Hussein in the course of the Gulf crisis and war, Israel had indirectly joined the anti-Iraq coalition.[116]

Throughout 1992 there were contradictory signals regarding Arab application of the secondary boycott. In July the Dutch weekly *Vrij Nederland* got hold of boycott documents sent by the Kuwaiti boycott office, headed by Ibrahim al-Ghanem. Companies tendering for the construction of the Az-Zour south power station in Kuwait, were asked to verify that they did not infringe boycott regulations.[117] On 29 October the Kuwait desk officer at the Department of State informed the American Jewish Congress, in a written reply to a query, that the Emirate still operated its boycott office, blacklisted companies and required boycott certificates for all bids on Kuwaiti projects.[118]

In October the Arab League convened a meeting of boycott commissioners in Damascus – the first such meeting in over a year. There still were at this time several thousand blacklisted European companies,[119] and probably as many from other continents, and there seemed to be no formal decision in sight to end the blacklisting. Nevertheless, by the beginning of 1993 boycott implementation had visibly weakened in most of the Arab countries, and it was reported that it was no coincidence that the CBO had difficulty getting a quorum for its meeting the previous October.

Throughout this period Kuwait and Saudi Arabia, which were still under heavy American influence following the Gulf War, continued to play cat-and-mouse games with the US Administration, indicating that they had ceased boycott enforcement while participating in Arab League boycott meetings and activities. Nevertheless one of the indications of the new times was that in January 1993 Israeli Foreign Minister Shimon Peres and FICC President Dan Gillerman were able, during a meeting of the World Economic Forum which convened at Davos in Switzerland, to talk directly to the president of the Saudi Chamber of Commerce and the chairman of the Kuwaiti Investment Office, and discuss with them the prospect of informal trade relations with Israel.

In February a State Department Near East desk officer informed the American Jewish Congress that the six GCC member states – Bahrain, Kuwait, Oman, Qatar, Saudi Arabia and the UAE – had informally agreed among themselves to remove more companies, both American and other, from their blacklists. The Gulf states were nevertheless 'anxious' not to publicize the decision. According to the State Department official they were becoming more lenient on a case-by-case basis, even though they were not yet intending to lift the boycott or take any steps towards its removal.[120]

The boycott statistics compiled by the Office of Antiboycott Compliance (OAC) of the US Department of Commerce for 1992 indicated, however, that boycott enforcement was still very current. At the beginning of February ADL Director Abraham H. Foxman wrote to Assistant Secretary of State Edward P. Djerejian that the statistics for FY 1992 indicated that Kuwait and Saudi Arabia continued to be the leading enforcers of the secondary boycott. In that year there were 2,934 restricted trade practice requests in 2,846 documents, and the largest number of boycott request documents

originated from Kuwait. Moreover, the greatest number of prohibited export transactions, 1,062, originated from Saudi Arabia.[121]

The UAE were also continuing to apply the Arab boycott as if
nothing had changed. While the UAE Ministry of Commerce made
it clear that the UAE had no plans to drop the boycott before the
Arab League decided to act, in January 1993 the UAE Central Bank
informed all the UAE banks in a memo that all documents certifying
that imported goods complied with the Arab boycott had to be
authenticated exclusively by UAE embassies, and for a fee.[122] Later
that year the boycott office of the UAE issued a circular which
reminded public and private institutions that negative certificates of
origin must not only be secured for any imported product, but also
authenticated in the exporting country and in the UAE, and that
imported products may not be transported on ships or shipping lines
blacklisted by boycott authorities. The circular added that 'bidders
for contracts in the UAE must also state in their tenders that they are
aware of the rules governing imports to the country'.[123]

In the middle of February Secretary of State Warren Christopher
visited Kuwait and raised the boycott issue with its ruler, Sheikh
Jabber a-Sabakh, pointing out to him that the US Ambassador to
Kuwait would be following the issue. The Emir, so it was reported,
did not respond.[124] Four months later the Kuwaiti Foreign Minister,
Sheikh Sabakh Ahmed Jabar a-Sabakh, drew headlines around the
world when he told reporters that his country had disengaged from
the 'indirect' boycott of Israel. 'The rules of the boycott allow this if
there are considerations related to the national interest of the state',
and 'other states are doing the same', he stated, adding that Kuwait
would, for the time being, continue to implement the primary boycott.[125]

In Syria and several other Arab countries there were angry reactions to the Kuwaiti announcement. The Syrian press attacked
Kuwait, charging that it would allow Israel to 'strategically infiltrate'
the Arab world. A senior Arab commentator, Adnan Kruma from the
Lebanese paper *al-Di'yar*, wrote that Kuwait's conduct endangered
the Arab world: 'It causes a division among the Arabs, because each
state will now need to struggle individually on the question of the
boycott. [In addition], Israel wants to separate the issue of the boycott from the peace process and Kuwait is helping [it] accomplish
this.'[126] Still in Lebanon, the Islamic Amal movement condemned the

Kuwaiti decision not for tactical reasons but as a matter of principle. 'We call on our people and brethren ... to boycott each company and store which does not adhere to boycotting the enemy', Hussein Musawi, leader of Amal stated in Beirut. 'Ending the direct or indirect boycott of the usurper Zionist entity is a grave damage and danger to all our interests ... The Jewish bulldozer will seek to sweep aside our economy.'[127]

Israel on the other hand was naturally delighted with the news from Kuwait. Israeli Foreign Minister Shimon Peres stated that 'the time has come for all the countries to put an end to this ugly politics' by embracing open economic borders and free trade. 'The Arabs should join the modern age like everybody else', he added.[128] While the Conference of Presidents of the Jewish organization meeting in New York also joined in welcoming the announcement, ADL National Director Foxman sounded more sceptical: 'We welcome this long-overdue Kuwaiti decision, but remain cautious in light of past Kuwaiti pledges in this regard.'[129]

Foxman's scepticism proved to be in place. On 20 July Kuwait quietly backtracked from its much heralded announcement. Kuwait's second Deputy Prime Minister and Finance and Planning Minister, Nasir al-Radwan, submitted a formal government statement to the Kuwaiti National Assembly, which explained its policy regarding the boycott of Israel:

> First: The Government of the State of Kuwait is still committed to the provisions of Law No. 21 for 1964 regarding the Unified Law on the Boycotting of Israel, and the General Principles that implement this law, and that originally were the recommendations and general principles issued by the Conference of the Liaison Officers of the Boycotting Offices in the Arab states, which were endorsed by the Arab League Council. In this connection it is noteworthy that Kuwait is regarded as one of the Arab states most committed to these decisions and principles. Kuwait will not allow itself to violate any of the laws that have been agreed on, but movement will be within the legal framework which is compatible with the national and pan-Arab interest.
>
> Second: With regard to the indirect boycott, the consequences of the Iraqi aggression demand that the rules governing the dealing with some of the companies in the boycott of foreign companies list be reexamined in the light of considerations that concern the national interest and Kuwait's dire needs for the products of those companies,

whether in the sphere of defence and reconstruction, or those that are linked to strategic aspects.

Third: If the new developments in the Arab–Israel conflict, including the Middle East peace conference, have prompted some countries of the world – for the sake of this new turning point – to call on the two sides in the Arab–Israeli conflict to take positive steps to push the peace negotiations toward progress by looking into lifting the Arab boycott and in return ending the Israeli policy of settlements building, the Government of the State of Kuwait confirms its full commitment to its pan-Arab responsibilities and its adherence to the provisions of the law and principles of the boycott in accordance with its belief in not taking unilateral steps outside the framework of the GCC group and the Arab group ...

It is worth mentioning that the Arab boycott of Israel is being carried out in three steps. The first step is the direct boycott of Israel in all aspects. The second is the special boycott of companies that are related to Israel. And the third step is the special boycott of foreign companies that have ties with other foreign companies that are linked with Israel. The second and third steps are called the indirect boycott ...

Therefore the Government hopes this statement will clarify this matter and will remove any ambiguities to confirm that the norm of national interest forms the basis of Kuwait's dealings with the issue of the indirect boycott. This is what many other Arab countries have done and it is a matter that does not clash with the law or principles of the boycott.[130]

In other words, the Kuwaiti minister denied that Kuwait had abandoned blacklisting, or renounced the secondary and tertiary boycotts. All that Kuwait had decided was to 'reexamine' (i.e. ignore) boycott restrictions as they might have applied to companies whose products and services were critical to Kuwait, and this was nothing new. Arab states had long disregarded boycott restrictions when it was in their interest to do so, especially with regard to arms manufacturers, hotel chains, key consumer product suppliers, etc.

A meeting of the CBO in Damascus on 29 April 1993 decided to blacklist two companies accused of helping Jewish settlement activities in the occupied territories. One was a Bulgarian company by the name of Electro-Impex, the other a Yugoslav company by the name of Jecho-Metal.[131]

Even though in May 1993 the US Department of State released a letter affirming a Saudi commitment to end the indirect boycott,[132] there was ample evidence to indicate that the commitments and practices were not positively correlated. In August the ADL charged Saudi Arabia with deceit about its promises to end enforcement in the secondary boycott. Statistics released by the OAC for the second quarter of 1993 indicated that Saudi Arabian requests for prohibited boycott information from US companies were actually up nearly 40 per cent over the same quarter in 1992, and were higher during the April–June 1993 quarter than they had been in any of the previous four quarters. 'In light of this', the ADL leaders stated in a letter to Secretary of State Christopher, 'we hope you will use the opportunity presented by the recent application of Saudi Arabia to join the GATT to obtain firm assurances that the Saudis will terminate the secondary and tertiary boycott.'[133]

In Saudi Arabia as elsewhere in the Arab world there was undoubtedly at this time some ambivalence regarding the boycott. While the leaders were wary of giving up the boycott as a negotiating card before a comprehensive Middle East settlement was attained, pressure from the US and the interests of Saudi businessmen were pulling in the opposite direction. Business interests were reflected in what certain Saudi newspapers were writing.

In the middle of October 1993 the London-based, Saudi-owned weekly *al-Majalla* published an article by its editor, Abd al-Rahman al-Rashid, in which he wrote: 'Keeping the boycott in focus is meaningless now that we have recognized Israel and are engaging in a political process with it, especially in view of the widespread smuggling of Israeli goods into the Arab world.' Al-Rashid noted that the boycott is 'a means, not an end in itself', and that while economic factors had affected Israel's approach to the peace process, the boycott was no longer needed. The benefits of free trade between Israel and the Arab world, he concluded, could have more influence on Israel's political political leadership, and failure to end the boycott could lead Israel to 'drag its feet' in the peace process.[134] Similarly the Saudi daily *al-Shark al-Awsat* published on 19 October an interview with a leading Saudi businessman, Abd al-Aziz al-Suleiman, in which he welcomed Arab trade with Israel after the establishment of peace.[135]

The application of more rigorous measures in various states in the world against the boycott in the first half of 1993, as well as a visible change in the Japanese attitude to the boycott led to a series of stories in the international press about the 'weakening' or 'crumbling' of the Arab boycott. 'Step-by-step, government officials and business leaders here [in Israel] say the decades-old Arab economic boycott of Israel has weakened to a point that many international companies now believe they can safely ignore it', wrote the *New York Times* correspondent in Jerusalem. Israelis, he wrote, feel that the momentum against the boycott is on their side. At the same time, quoting Israeli officials, the paper noted that the 'boycott is far from out ... it continues to scare away foreign businesses skittish about offending Arab countries, especially the oil-producing nations of the Persian Gulf'.[136]

The Arab Boycott after the Signing of the DoP

The signing of the Israeli–Palestinian Declaration of Principles (DoP) in Washington on 13 September 1993 raised high hopes in Israel that the boycott would very rapidly be cancelled, especially by those Arab states with no border conflicts with Israel. However, five days before the signing ceremony in Washington the Arab League already made it clear that no revolutionary changes were to be expected. On 8 September the Arab League denied reports that it was preparing to discuss ending the boycott. Arab League Assistant Secretary-General Adnan Imran issued a statement to the effect that no Arab state had placed the issue on the agenda of the League's Council. The boycott had been imposed because of Israel's occupation of Arab territories, the statement continued, and it would only be eliminated when the cause had been eliminated.[137]

Syria was also quick to dash any hopes of a speedy end to any part of the boycott. On 18 September Syrian Foreign Minister Faruq al-Shar'a stated that the boycott of Israel must continue for as long as the reasons that prompted Arab countries to introduce the boycott still stood,[138] and on 26 September Syrian state-controlled radio called for the intensification of the boycott.[139] Syria then called a meeting of Arab League boycott officials for 24 October to discuss expansion of the blacklist.

The Secretary General of the GCC, Fahim Bin Sultan al-Qassimi, pointedly told reporters that the boycott would not end. 'It is too early to talk about lifting the boycott', he argued. Jordanian Crown Prince Hassan added that ending the boycott would be 'Arab suicide'.

Arab League Secretary General Esmat Abdel Meguid also made a point of cooling off the enthusiasm emanating from the Israeli–Palestinian agreement, noting that any lifting or alteration of the boycott would have to be unanimous, 'and since unanimity is impossible, it will remain in force'.[140]

Nevertheless heavy American pressure brought about the cancellation of the boycott meeting called by Syria (see above), after only about half the Arab League member states agreed to participate in it. Several reports stated that it had been PLO urging that brought about the cancellation of the meeting, since the PLO feared that new blacklist activities would give the US Congress an excuse to hold up economic aid for the Palestinian Authority.[141]

The position of the PLO on the boycott issue in this period was, in fact, ambivalent. In the course of the European Parliament debate on its boycott resolution in November 1993[142] Ioannis Paleokrassas, representing the European Commission, drew attention to the $600 million aid package pledged by the European Union to the Palestinians, implying that the two – the lifting of the boycott and aid to the Palestinian authority – were somehow connected. He thus focused attention on a true dilemma faced by the Palestinians. On the one hand the continuation of the boycott for the Palestinians was an important bargaining chip. On the other hand Palestinian support for the boycott was not only contrary to the spirit of the peace process, but also counter-productive with regards to the development of the fledgling Palestinian economy.[143]

Already on 24 September, only 11 days after the signing of the DoP, a senior economist in the PLO, Samir Hulleilah, stated that the future Palestinian administration in the West Bank and Gaza Strip would bar Israeli firms from bidding for major public sector contracts, since the Palestinians did not want the Palestinian authority to 'become a Trojan horse for Israeli economic supremacy in the Arab world'.[144] Another senior Palestinian economist, Samir Abdallah, who headed the Palestinian delegation to the multilateral economic talks within the framework of the Madrid process, stated on 20 October that it was too early to call off the boycott, since convincing progress had not yet been made in the peace process.[145] Yassir Arafat himself, asked on 26 September whether he would encourage the Arab countries to lift the boycott, refused to commit himself in any way.

On 1 October 1993, on the occasion of the 'International Donors Conference' at which over 40 states pledged over $2 billion of aid for the Palestinian authority, Yassir Abed-Rabbo, a close associate of Arafat's in the PLO Executive Committee, indicated at a press conference that the boycott should not be lifted until 'complete Israeli withdrawal from the Palestinian and Arab occupied territories, including Jerusalem'. He added that he considered the boycott to be a 'final status issue' – in other words one to be raised when talks on the permanent settlement between Israel and the Palestinians would be negotiated. On the same day Syrian President Hafiz al-Asad stated in a TV interview broadcast in the US that he would not sanction lifting the boycott unless there was a 'comprehensive settlement' in the region.[146]

In October a delegation, including ten major American businessmen, was organized by the American Jewish Congress for an 'economics-of-peace' tour of Saudi Arabia, Egypt, Jordan and Israel. In the Arab states the members of the delegation pressed their hosts to act towards the cancellation of the boycott as a condition for joint ventures between American companies and Arab ones. According to Henry Siegman, Executive Vice-President of the American Jewish Congress, the businessmen with whom the delegation met in the various Arab countries had agreed that the boycott was an anachronism, and that it was anyway melting away. However few were willing to broach formal cancellation prior to a Syrian–Israeli settlement. 'They don't want to strip Syria of an important bargaining card', he explained.[147]

This position was confirmed by a meeting of the Arab League at ambassador level in Cairo on 22 November, which announced that the boycott would continue 'until Israel would withdraw from all the occupied territories, after Israel adopted all the international resolutions regarding the solution of the conflict, and after the establishment of a Palestinian state with Jerusalem as its capital'. Nevertheless it was reported that several representatives had called for the boycott to be lifted.[148]

Early in November US Senators Lautenberg and Grassley spearheaded a Senatorial letter to Arab League Secretary-General Esmet Abdel Meguid, expressing 'profound disappointment' in the Arab League's unwillingness to support a recision of the boycott. 'We had expected that, as a complement to the momentous breakthrough in

Israel–Palestinian reconciliation, the Arab nations would support the peace process with appropriate confidence-building measures, and put an end to the economic boycott', they wrote.[149] Meguid replied that 'the boycott is a legitimate and defensive instrument of diplomacy ... [it] is entirely linked to the "no peace" situation that exists between the Arab World and Israel ... I am astonished to witness your calls for ending the boycott *before* the ending of occupation of Arab territories ... as well as *before* the achievement of the national rights of the Palestinian people. Normalization cannot precede the accomplishment of substantive progress on all tracks.'[150]

At around the same time Meguid stated, at the end of an Arab League council meeting requested by Libya to urge Arab states to maintain the boycott: 'We want to end the boycott but the reasons that led to its imposition – the continuation of the occupation and the need for Palestinians to gain their rights – are still valid.'[151]

Even a call to Jordan to lift the boycott was rejected at the end of 1993. Jordan's Crown Prince Hassan stated on Abu Dhabi television that a gradual approach was required,[152] and this despite the fact that peace talks between Jordan and Israel were at this time at an advanced stage.

But as was the case in the previous few years, so now there were also developments regarding the boycott, which pointed in the opposite direction. In October a group of Moroccan industrialists attended a business conference in Israel – the first official delegation from Rabat to visit Israel. This was followed by a rapid development of economic ties at various levels, including investment by Israeli companies in Moroccan agricultural projects, and a number of joint ventures. Mutual banking arrangements and telephone connections were also instituted.[153]

In January 1994 a Saudi paper reported that Gulf leaders had decided [once again] on a gradual reduction in boycott restrictions.[154] Also in January Qatar admitted that it was engaged in extensive negotiations with Israel to ship and pipe natural gas via Israel to European destinations.[155] The following month the project was the subject of a discussion between the Foreign Minister of Qatar, Sheikh Hamad Bin Jassim al-Thani, and Israeli Foreign Minister Shimon Peres,[156] and a French company was engaged to carry out a feasibility study for its implementation. The three main alternatives being investigated by the French company were: a pipeline from the

Gulf, passing through Saudi Arabia and Jordan; a pipeline from the Nile Delta region in Egypt; the transport of gas from the Gulf in liquified form by tanker to the port of Eilat or to a terminal on Israel's Mediterranean coast.

During the visit to the Middle East of US Secretary of Trade Ron Brown in the third week of January 1994 it was reported that he had received a commitment by Meguid that the Ministerial Council meeting of the Arab League, which was to meet in late March in Cairo, would discuss the issue of the secondary and tertiary boycott.[157] However, not only did the Arab League fail to take action against the secondary boycott during the meeting, but the subject did not even appear on its agenda, and Syrian Foreign Minister Faruq Al'Shar'a issued a statement to the effect that 'The decision to boycott Israel came about as a result of the Israeli occupation and the existing state of war between the Arabs and Israel.' He added that, 'It is impermissible to lift the embargo before its causes are eliminated … If one or two states are trying to interpret some of the boycott classifications, it is wrong to engage in such classifications because the boycott law stipulates that the boycott should continue until its causes are eliminated'.[158]

The official Syrian paper *Tishrin* added, the following day, that the Arab boycott of Israel was a response to the hostile and criminal Israeli policies, which were in violation of the most basic rules of international law, the Geneva conventions and the UN Charter. 'Would it be out of place', *Tishrin* asked, 'if we asked those urging a revocation of the Arab boycott to put pressure on Israel to make it respect international law and human rights, and respond to the wishes for peace?'[159]

On 7 April economic and trade officials from 22 Arab countries recommended that the boycott be maintained until the legitimate rights of the Palestinians were restored.[160] Later that month Oman hosted the multilateral talks on water resources in the Middle East with the participation of Israeli officials and journalists. The Omani Minister of State for Foreign Affairs, Youssef Bin Alawi Bin Abdullah, stated in an interview to Israeli television, that the boycott would remain in force until Israel withdrew from the Arab lands it had occupied in 1967. 'No one can consider peace between you [Israel] and distant [Arab] countries at a time when there is no agreement on peaceful steps with the neighbouring states.'[161] Yet the mere fact that

Israelis were allowed into Oman and an Omani minister was willing to appear on Israeli television demonstrated the ambivalence and even non-coherence of the Arab position, in which many individual Arab states were willing to set the boycott aside while the Arab League took a conservative position.

On 30 September 1994 the Saudi Foreign Minister, Saud al-Faisal, announced in the name of the six Gulf states (Saudi Arabia, Bahrain, Qatar, Oman, Kuwait and the UAE), the cancellation of the indirect boycott on Israel.[162] The following day the GCC issued the following statement:

> The Cooperation Council of the Arab State of the Gulf, having actively supported the Middle East peace process ever since the launching of the Madrid Conference, and being fully aware of the important breakthroughs realized so far, particularly in the Palestinian and Jordanian tracks, which comprise agreements covering economic cooperation between the Israelis and both the Jordanians and the Palestinians, seriously recognize the importance of a review of the provisions of the Arab boycott of Israel, so as to take into consideration progress achieved and substantive future requirements of the peace process. The GCC member states have constantly reiterated their determination to enhance cooperation with their trading partners in various spheres. Concerning the application of the Arab boycott of Israel, necessary measures have been taken with a view to protecting the mutual interests of the GCC and its trading partners.As a result of these measures and for all practical purposes, the secondary and tertiary boycotts are no longer a threat to the interests of these partners. Whereas the Arab boycott of Israel was enacted by the League of the Arab States, and its review to take into consideration developments and requirements of the Middle East peace process must take place, the GCC member states will support all or any initiative for such review presented in the League of Arab States. Further, the GCC believe that a sponsorship of such an initiative by Arab parties directly involved in the bilateral negotiations, whether selectively or individually, shall facilitate the required review and ensure a greater chance of success.[163]

While Israel welcomed the statement, the Arab League in Cairo criticized the announcement, made at the the UN Security Council in New York, stating that since 'the Arab boycott of Israel was imposed by a decision taken by the Arab League Council ... it is up to the Arab League Council to call it off'.[164] In the beginning of October the head of the CBO, Zuhair Aquil, denied that the Arab League was considering closing down the boycott office, as had been reported in the Israeli press. He added that even the GCC, that had decided to lift the secondary and tertiary boycotts, were not considering lifting the primary boycott. The boycott, he said, had been begun because of Israeli encroachments on Arab territory, its displacement of Arab citizens and its depriving them of their rights. All these wrongs had to be undone before the boycott could be lifted.[165]

In the beginning of November Arab League Secretary-General Dr Esmat Abdel Meguid said in a meeting with Jan Kalicki, counsellor to the US Department of Commerce, that economic cooperation in the Middle East would only be possible after a comprehensive and just regional peace on the basis of international legality and UN resolutions was achieved, and real progress in the negotiations between Israel, Syria and Lebanon was made. The Arab boycott, he said, would continue because it was linked to the establishment of Arab–Israeli peace.[166] Egyptian Foreign Minister, Amer Musa, took a much more moderate position. During a visit to Cairo by Israeli Foreign Minister Shimon Peres in January 1995, Musa stated that it was up to the Arab League to deal with the Arab boycott issue. If the issue would be raised, Egypt would have no objection. He added that there was no boycott problem between Egypt and Israel.[167]

On 27 October 1994, Jordan signed a peace treaty with Israel that included the establishment of full economic relations between the two countries. On 26 July 1995 the Jordanian parliament cancelled the Jordanian boycott laws against Israel. Of the parliament's 80 members, 51 voted in favour of the cancellation, 21 against and eight were absent.

By mid-1995 it was noted that there was a clear weakening in the application of the boycott to shipping. According to a survey prepared by the World Federation of Independent Tanker Owners the change started to be felt in the latter part of 1993 after the signing of the DoP between Israel and the PLO. It was added that the countries that still applied the boycott in full were Libya, Syria and Yemen. Nevertheless, getting a ship off the blacklist, even after it has been sold to a new owner, usually still requires an official statement by the owners that it will not dock in future in Israel.[168]

A meeting of the CBO, which was to have taken place in Damascus at the beginning of October 1995, did not take place because the approval of two-thirds of the member states required to hold it could not be mustered. Officials in the CBO estimated that the problem arose from the fact that quite a few Arab states had cancelled the indirect boycott of Israel and were participating in various multilateral conferences, which started to convene after the Madrid Conference to deal with the normalization of relations with Israel.[169] The meeting was put off until April 1996, and then again to October, but failed to convene.[170] Nevertheless towards the end of the month the Saudi Defence Minister, Prince Sultan Bin Abdel Aziz, once again reiterated the position that the primary boycott would only be removed after peace agreements were signed between Israel, Syria and Lebanon.[171]

On 1 January 1996 Oman declared that it would cancel the primary boycott against Israel,[172] and in the beginning of 1997 the US Office of Antiboycott Compliance reported that Qatar had closed its office responsible for administering the boycott.[173] Thus by the end of 1996 there were 14 Arab states which had developed economic relations with Israel, while eight were still fully applying it.[174]

The Boycott after the Israeli Election of May 1996

The Arab reaction to the victory of Likud leader Binyamin Netanyahu in the first direct elections for Prime Minister in Israel was one of great concern, and Syria announced on 19 June 1996 that it would propose that the Arab Summit of 23 June reapply the Arab boycott against Israel.[175] This statement was somewhat misleading since the boycott had never been formally lifted. However, the Arab Summit chose to issue a relatively mild and vague statement saying that: '[The Arab leaders] emphasize the need to respect the economic obligations towards the [Arab] League.'[176]

Nevertheless, by the end of 1996 Israel was once again feeling the effects of the boycott as the peace process seemed to enter a state of stalemate. Even though Israeli companies were present at the Cairo Economic Conference, which was held in November, the atmosphere towards Israel was much cooler than at the Casablanca Conference of 1994 and the Amman Conference of 1995.[177] In December 1996, the Director General of the Israeli shipping company Zim, Matti Morgenstern, explained that while the gradual lifting of the secondary boycott after 1991 had benefited Israeli trade, *inter alia*, because foreign shipping companies were no longer afraid to stop over at Israeli ports, the stalemate in the peace process was having the opposite effect.[178]

At the end of March 1997, in reaction to the Israeli decision to build in Har Homa in Jerusalem, the continued building in the Jewish settlements and the general stalemate in the peace process, the Arab foreign ministers, meeting in Cairo, recommended that the various Arab states stop the process of normalization in their relations with Israel and formally continue to preserve the primary boycott against Israel, until such time as a comprehensive and just peace is attained in the region.[179] The following month an authoritative source in the CBO in Damascus announced that the Bureau's activities had been neither suspended nor frozen, even though there were difficulties in getting a quorum together to convene a meeting.[180]

Though, by mid-1998, the CBO had not managed to get the boycott apparatus to function as it had before the Madrid Conference, there were indications that both the primary and the secondary boycotts were still being implemented by some members of the Arab League. Thus, for example, officials of the Ministry of Economy and Trade in Beirut announced that they were acting to implement the boycott with regards to the sale in Beirut of liquor produce by Seagrams – a blacklisted company – and several companies recently acquired by it.[181] In February 1998 it was reported that the German company Siemens was having difficulties regarding a contract to construct two telecommunications substations in Syria, which are to serve the grid interconnection with Jordan, because it was being asked to attest that it is complying with the provisions of the Arab boycott of Israel.[182] The following month, the Saudi Ministry of Commerce announced that it had opened an investigation regarding the appearance of Israeli-manufactured goods on the Saudi market, contrary to the Saudi policy of rigorously applying the Arab boycott of Israeli goods. A ministry official stated that there 'are severe penalties for those who deal with Israeli companies, including a three-year prison term, fines and the confiscation and destruction of the products'.[183]

Notes

1. Robert W. MacDonald, *The League of Arab States – A Study in the Dynamics of Regional Organization* (Princeton, NJ: Princeton University Press, 1965), p. 348.
2. Aaron J. Sarna, *Boycott and Blacklists – A History of Arab Economic Warfare against Israel* (Totowa, NJ: Rowman & Littlefield, 1986), p. 3.
3. Ja'far Tah Hamza, *Al-Muqata'a al-'Arabiyya li-Isra'il* (Arabic) (The Arab Boycott of Israel) (1973), pp. 27–33.
4. Juzif Mughayzal, *Al-Muqata'a al-'Arabiyya wal-Qanun al-Dawli* (Arabic) (The Arab Boycott and International Law) (Beirut: M.T.F. Markaz al-Abhath, 1968), pp. 55–6.
5. See Yaàcov Shimoni, *Political Dictionary of the Arab World* (New York: Macmillan, 1987), pp. 183–4.
6. Ibid., pp. 182–3.
7. ESCO Foundation for Palestine, *Palestine, a Study of Jewish, Arab and British Policies* (New Haven, CT: Yale University Press, 1947), p. 480.
8. Sarna, op. cit, p. 4; Hamza, op. cit, pp. 33–41; Mughayzal, op. cit, p. 56.
9. Sarna, op. cit., p. 6. Also Shafiq Ahmad Ali, the sixth of a series of articles on the Arab boycott in *Al-Wattan* (Qatar), 6 January 1997. Ali gives the date of this meeting as 27 November 1929, but Sarna's source is the *New York Times* of 28 October 1929.
10. Shafiq Ahmad Ali, the sixth of a series of articles on the Arab boycott in *Al-Wattan* (Qatar), 6 January 1997.
11. Susan Hattis Rolef, 'Israel's Anti-Boycott Policy', *Policy Studies*, 28 (Jerusalem: The Leonard Davis Institute for International Relations at the Hebrew University of Jerusalem, February 1989), p. 7.
12. See Yehoshua Porath, *From Riots to Rebellion – the Palestinian–Arab National Movement 1929–1939* (London: Frank Cass, 1977).
13. ESCO Foundation for Palestine, op. cit., p. 766.
14. Ibid., p.769.
15. Terence Prittie and Walter Henry Nelson, *The Economic War Against the Jews* (London: Secker & Warburg, 1978), p. 9.
16. Shafiq Ahmad Ali, the sixth of a series of articles on the Arab boycott in *Al-Wattan* (Qatar), 6 January, 1997.
17. R. G. Woolbert, 'Pan-Arabism and the Palestine Problem', *Foreign Affairs* (January 1938), p. 317.
18. *Palestine Royal Commission Report* (London: HMSO, 1937), p. 146.
19. Shafiq Ahmad Ali, the sixth of a series of articles on the Arab boycott in *Al-Wattan* (Qatar), 6 January 1997.
20. Rolef, op. cit., p. 8.
21. Yossi Beilin, *Hata'asiya Ha'ivrit – Shorashim* (Hebrew) (Roots of Israeli Industry) (Jerusalem: Keter Publishing House, 1987), pp. 67–89.
22. See for example the Alexandria Protocol of 7 October 1944.
23. See Shimoni, op. cit., p. 80.
24. Shalom Schirman, 'The History of the Arab Boycott, 1921–1975', *Middle East*

Review (Winter 1975/76), p. 40.

25. Dan S. Chill, *The Arab Boycott of Israel – Economic Aggression and World Reaction*, Praeger Special Studies in International Economics and Development (New York: Praeger Publishers, 1976), p. 1. See also Shafiq Ahmad Ali, the seventh of a series of articles on the Arab boycott in *Al-Wattan* (Qatar), 7 January 1997.
26. MacDonald, op. cit., pp. 118–19.
27. Kennan Lee Teslik, *Congress, the Executive Branch, and Special Interests: the American Response to the Arab Boycott of Israel* (Westport, CT: Greenwood Press, 1982), p. 8.
28. Sarna, op. cit., p. 7.
29. Prittie and Nelson, op. cit., p. 10.
30. Rolef, op. cit., p. 9. For a discussion of the legality of economic sanctions under the UN Charter, see Chapter 3, p. 66.
31. James H. Bahti, *The Arab Economic Boycott of Israel* (Washington DC: The Brookings Institute, 1967), p. 1.
32. Mughayzal, op. cit., pp. 56–62, and Hamza, op. cit., pp. 42–7.
33. Sarna, op. cit., p. 8.
34. Marwan Iskandar, 'Arab Boycott of Israel', *Middle East Forum* (October 1960), p. 27. See also Shafiq Ahmad Ali, the seventh of a series of articles on the Arab boycott in *Al-Watta* (Qatar), 7 January 1997.
35. Ibid.
36. Gershon Maron, *'Haharem Ha'aravi Verishumo Hakalkali'* (Hebrew) (The Arab Boycott and its Economic Impact), *'Riv'on Lekalkala'* (January 1954).
37. Sarna, op. cit., p. 9.
38. Mughayzal, op. cit., and Hamza, op. cit.
39. Abba Eban, *Voice of Israel* (New York: Horizon Press, 1957), pp. 258–9.
40. *The New York Times*, 28 July 1950.
41. Ibid. 26 August 1950.
42. The resolution called upon Egypt: 'to terminate the restrictions on the passage of international commercial ships and goods through the Suez Canal, wherever bound and to cease all interference with such shipping beyond that essential to the safety of shipping in the Canal itself and to the observance of the international conventions in force' (Eban, op. cit., p. 267).
43. Ibid., p. 258.
44. *UN Resolutions, Security Council*, Series II, compiled and edited by Dusan J. Djonovich, Resolution No. 118 S/3675, passed on 13 October 1956.
45. Prittie and Nelson, op. cit., p. 13.
46. Chill, op. cit., p. 3.
47. Yosef Schechtman, *Haherem Ha'arvi Velikho* (Hebrew) (The Arab Boycott and its Lessons), *Ha'umma*, 4, 13 (June, 1965), pp. 5–6.
48. Shafiq Ahmad Ali, first of a series of articles on the Arab boycott in *Al-Wattan* (Qatar), 1 January 1997.
49. Arab League Council Resolution 357, 19 May 1951, as cited in Egyptian Society of International Law, *Egypt and the United Nations* (New York: Manhattan Publishing, 1957).

50. Teslik, op. cit., p. 8. See also Shafiq Ahmad Ali, the first of a series of articles on the Arab boycott in *Al-Wattan* (Qatar), 1 January 1997.
51. Oded Remba, 'The Arab Boycott: A Study in Total Economic Warfare', *Midstream* (Summer 1960), p. 44.
52. Mughayzal, op. cit., pp. 62–4 and Hamza, op. cit. pp., 47–51.
53. MacDonald, op. cit., p. 356.
54. Ibid., p. 144.
55. See Nicholas Balabkins, *West German Reparations to Israel* (New Brunswick, NJ: Rutgers University Press, 1971), pp.147–8.
56. Hamza, op. cit., pp. 192–7.
57. See Lily Gardner Feldman, *The Special Relationship between West Germany and Israel* (London: George Allen & Unwin, 1984), pp. 195–6.
58. See Chapter 5, p. 119.
59. PRO, FO 371/104206 XC13782.
60. Ibid.
61. PRO, FO 371/104213A E1124/1.
62. Schechtman, op. cit., p. 9.
63. Prittie and Nelson, op. cit., p. 17.
64. MacDonald, op. cit., p. 120.
65. Schechtman, op. cit.
66. *Davar*, 11 January 1965.
67. Chill, op. cit., p. 4.
68. Remba, op. cit., p. 46.
69. *New York Times*, 29 October 1960.
70. *Ma'ariv*, 17 June 1965.
71. This summary appeared in a paper presented by the Economic Warfare Authority of the Israeli Ministry of Finance to the Seminar on Freedom of Trade with Israel, which took place in Brussels on 24–5 June 1984.
72. Yuval Elizur, *'Aflayat Yisrael Biydey Britania – Hukit'* (Hebrew) (Discrimination by Britain against Israel is Legal), *Ma'ariv-Asskim* (1 April 1986).
73. Based on CBO documents.
74. An example of such a statement was published in the paper presented by the Economic Warfare Authority of the Israeli Ministry of Finance to the Seminar on Freedom of Trade with Israel, which took place in Brussels, op. cit. The wording of the statement was as follows:
    1) We don't have a branch of our firm in Israel;
    2) We have no assembly factory in Israel, neither directed by us nor by other concern [*sic*] on our behalf;
    3) There are neither general agents nor control offices representing us in the Middle East for Israel;
    4) We don't grant the right or use of our name in Israel;
    5) We have no participation in Israeli factories or companies in or out of Israel;
    6) We don't give advice nor export opinion to Israeli companies;
    7) We have no other relations with Israel in any form or manner.
75. Schechtman, op. cit.

76. Based on interviews held by the author.
77. *Jerusalem Post*, 25 February 1975.
78. See Chapter 6.
79. *Middle East Economic Digest (MEED)*, 16 January 1976, p. 4.
80. Ibid.
81. This was stated in evidence given to the Select Committee on the Byers Foreign Boycotts Bill in the British House of Lords in 1978, by the Commissioner of the CBO – Mohammed Mahgoub. See report of the Select Committee on the Foreign Boycotts Bill, House of Lords, 1 (Report and Minutes of Proceedings), HMSO, London (July 1978), p. 34.
82. Ibid. 2 (Minutes of Evidence), HMSO (July 1978), p. 151.
83. Ibid, pp. 95–100 and 128.
84. Hamza, op. cit., pp. 63–9, and symposium on the Arab Boycott, *Shu'un Falestiniyya*, 46 (June 1975).
85. See Chapter 5, p. 119–22.
86. Hamza, op. cit.
87. Mohammed Mahgoub, memorandum on 'The Nature of the Arab Boycott of Israel'.
88. Teslik, op. cit., p. 11.
89. Holly L. Feder, 'US Companies and the Arab Boycott of Israel', Texas Women's University, U.M.I. (1988), p. 9.
90. Ibid., p. 10.
91. Sarna, op. cit., p. 32.
92. Lufti El-Khouri, 'Form over Content', letter from Cairo, 89 (1–3 May 1997), by courtesy of *Al-Ahram* weekly.
93. Reuters, 4 February 1988.
94. Lieutenant Colonel Yosef, *Halohama Hakalkalit Ha'aravit Neged Yisrael* (The Arab Economic Warfare against Israel), *Ma'archot*, 275 (August 1980), p. 31.
95. Ibid, p. 8.
96. Publication 391 of the Israeli Customs Authority of 1 June 1987.
97. Reuters (Damascus), 30 January 1988.
98. Reuters 10 July 1988.
99. Reuters (Damascus), 6 July 1989.
100. Boycott Report 13/9, November/December 1989 and 14/4, April 1990, and *Middle East Economic Digest (MEED)*, 23 February 1990.
101. Reuters, 22 February 1990.
102. Reuters (Tunis), 16 July 1990.
103. Reuters (Damascus), 18 October 1990.
104. *Yedi'ot 'Aharonot*, 1 April 1991.
105. See for example Gil Feiler, 'Arab Boycott Getting Worse', *Israel Business Today*, 6, 255 (13 December 1991), p. 1.
106. *The Jerusalem Report*, 24 January 1991.
107. *Hadashot*, 6 May 1991 and Burt Keimach, 'The Arab Boycott of Israel – An Exercise in Failed Economic Warfare', *Focus*, published by BIPAC (May 1991).
108. *The Jerusalem Post*, 6 May 1991.
109. Ibid., 10 May 1991.

110. *Misr al-Fatat*, quoted by *Ma'ariv*, 29 July 1991.
111. *The Jerusalem Post*, 8 August 1991.
112. World Jewish Congress *Intelligence Report*, 14 September 1992.
113. *The Jerusalem Post*, 21 July 1991.
114. See for example *Ma'ariv*, 18 July 1991.
115. Reuters (Cairo), 17 July 1991, quoting Adnan Omran, the Assistant Secretary General for Political Affairs at Arab League headquarters.
116. Reuters (Kuwait City), 15 November 1991.
117. World Jewish Congress, *Intelligence Report*, 14 September 1992.
118. *Boycott Report*, 17/1, January 1993.
119. A brief by the European Jewish Information Centre, 'The Arab Boycott and its Impact on the European Community', 3 June 1992.
120. *Boycott Report*, 17/3, March 1993.
121. Letter dated 4 February 1993.
122. Reuters (Abu Dhabi), 28 January 1993.
123. AP report from Abu Dhabi, quoted in *Ha'aretz*, 2 November 1993, and BBC *Summary of World Broadcasts*, 3 November 1993.
124. *Wall Street Journal*, 23 February 1993.
125. *Ha'aretz* and *The Jerusalem Post*, 9 June 1993, Reuters from Kuwait, 8 June 1993, Jewish Telegraphic Agency (JTA), 9 June 1993.
126. *Ha'aretz*, 9 June 1993.
127. Reuters (Beirut), 10 June 1993.
128. JTA, ibid. *Ha'aretz*, 23 June 1993.
129. Ibid.
130. KUNA (Kuwaiti news agency), 20 July, 1993, quoted in the FBIS, 21 July 1993.
131. Reuters (Damascus), 29 April 1993.
132. Julia Schöpflin, 'The Arab Boycott of Israel: Can it Withstand the Peace Process?', London, Institute of Jewish Affairs, *Research Reports*, 4 (March 1994), p. 5.
133. ADL press release, 17 August 1993.
134. *The Jerusalem Post*, 20 October 1993.
135. Ibid.
136. Clyde Haberman, 'Though still in Effect, Arabs' Economic Boycott of Israel Weakens', *New York Times*, 11 May 1993.
137. MENA, Cairo, 8 September 1993.
138. MENA, 18 September 1993.
139. SWB, 27 September 1993.
140. Chris Hedges, 'Despite US Urging, Arab Lands Hold firm to their Israel Boycott', *New York Times*, 6 October 1993.
141. MEED, 1 November 1993, and Schöpflin, op. cit., p. 4.
142. Chapter 9.
143. MEED, op. cit., pp. 10–11.
144. *Near East Report*, 4 October 1993.
145. *Near East Report*, 11 October 1993.
146. Schöpflin, op. cit., p. 3.

147. *Ha'aretz*, 28 October 1993.
148. *Ma'ariv*, 23 November 1993.
149. US Senate letter, 4 November 1993.
150. *MEED*, 29 November 1993.
151. Reuters (Cairo), 22 November 1993.
152. Reuters (Abu Dhabi), 26 December 1993.
153. *Israel Business Today*, 18 April 1994, and *Boycott Report*, 18/1.
154. *Al-Sharq al-Awsat*, January 1994.
155. *Yedi'ot 'Aharonot* and *The Jerusalem Post*, 28 January 1994.
156. *MEED*, 25 February 1994.
157. *MEED*, 11 February 1994.
158. BBC Monitoring Service, 28 March 1994 quoting Syrian Arab Republic Radio.
159. Ibid., 29 March 1994.
160. Reuters (Qatar), 7 April 1994.
161. Reuters News Service, 18 April 1994.
162. Reuters (Jerusalem), 30 September 1994.
163. Published by the Israel Information Service Gopher Information Division, Israel Foreign Ministry.
164. Reuters (Cairo), 2 October 1994.
165. BBC Monitoring Service, 8 October 1994.
166. Arab Republic of Egypt Radio, the BBC Monitoring Service, 5 November 1994.
167. Ibid., 5 January 1995.
168. *Al-Sharq al-Awsat* (Arabic), 21 June 1995, p. 9.
169. *Al-Hayat* (Arabic) of London, 16 October 1995.
170. Shafiq Ahmad Ali, the first in a series of articles on the Arab boycott in *Al-Wattan* (Qatar), 1 January 1997.
171. *Ha'aretz*, 30 October 1995, quoting *Al-Hayat*, of 29 October 1995.
172. *Mabat Lahadashot* (the evening news magazine on the first Israeli TV channel), 1 January 1996.
173. OAC, 1997, pp. 11–124.
174. Shafiq Ahmad Ali, the first of a series of articles on the Arab boycott in *Al-Wattan* (Qatar), 1 January 1997. Ali argues that Egypt, Jordan the Palestinian Authority and the Comoros islands had cancelled the application of the boycott, another ten, including Morocco, Djibouti, Mauritania, Eritrea and Oman, had established trade relations with Israel. Among the states still maintaining the boycott were Syria, Lebanon, Iraq, Sudan and Libya.
175. *Ha'aretz*, 20 June 1996.
176. Ibid., 24 June 1996.
177. See Chapter 12, pp. 293–7.
178. *Ha'aretz*, 13 December 1996.
179. *Ha'aretz*, 1 April 1996, and Heb Keinon, 'Biteless Boycott', *The Jerusalem Post*, 4 April 1997.
180. *Al-Sharq al-Aswat* (London), 23 April 1997.
181. *Daily Star* (Beirut), 15 December 1997.
182. *MEED*, 13 February 1998.
183. *Saudi Gazette*, 23 February 1998.

3

The Legal Debate around
Economic Sanctions

General Principles of International Law

THERE ARE two levels at which one may discuss the legality of economic sanctions – the level of customary international law and that of existing international agreements. According to Stephen C. Neff of Edinburgh University, there are three main approaches to the question whether economic sanctions are sanctioned by international law outside the enforcement provisions of the UN Charter. The first, which he terms 'the state-sovereignty school', holds that there is no general rule of customary international law forbidding the waging of economic warfare. The second, which he terms 'the neutrality school', holds that direct economic warfare is not unlawful but that belligerent economic measures, that impinge upon neutral third parties, are contrary to international law. The third, which he terms 'the prohibitionist school', holds that the waging of economic warfare is generally unlawful.[1]

The International Court of Justice in the Hague dealt with the issue in 1986, in the case of *Nicaragua v. United States*, In this case the question of the legality of the total trade boycott imposed by the US against Nicaragua in 1985 was reviewed. The Court concluded that as a matter of general customary international law the US action could not be condemned, and that there was no obligation on states to maintain trade relations with other states in the absence of treaty commitments to the contrary, or other specific obligations.[2]

The general legal conclusions which one may draw from this case are however limited, and according to Stephen C. Neff, while broad international consensus probably exists to the effect that as a general rule economic warfare is impermissible, if it came to translating this consensus into a principle of customary international law, many exceptions would be permitted, especially in the case where economic sanctions are resorted to as a form of reprisal.[3] Thus, if economic sanctions as a form of non-forcible reprisals are designed to counteract violations of the law on the part of their target, international law appears to sanction them.[4]

Among the more specific legal questions which have been asked in connection with economic sanctions are those related to the freezing of the assets of the target state abroad – in other words the extraterritorial effect of sanctions,[5] and the effect of such sanctions on the constitutional rights of the citizens of the sending country.[6] As we shall see below, in the case of the Arab boycott the question of what the general principles of international law have to say on the issue have been much more extensively explored.

International Agreements and Treaties

There are two sides to the question whether economic sanctions conform to existing international agreements. On the one hand there are agreements which implicitly or explicitly permit the imposition of such sanctions under certain circumstances. On the other there are agreements whose goal is to do away with any form of economic discrimination, and it may be argued that since sanctions are a form of deliberate negative discrimination, they run contrary to such agreements.

The League of Nations and United Nations

Both within the framework of the League of Nations in the inter-war period, and that of the United Nations following the Second World War, economic sanctions were accepted as a form of collective action that members may use against other members that have been accused of aggression, and in the case of the UN, also of violations of human rights. However it was only under the UN Charter that sanctions were explicitly mentioned, as a means that the Security Council is authorized to order to meet a threat to or breach of the peace, or in response to an act of aggression (article 39), and which members are bound to carry out (article 25). The Security Council can also recommend sanctions.

In contrast to the narrow basis for sanctions in the League Covenant, the grounds for UN sanctions are potentially very wide. The prerequisite for the use of sanctions is agreement among all permanent members, and at least four non-permanent members of the Security Council (article 27). The decision to impose sanctions is taken by the Security Council after it has determined, under article 39 of the Charter, that there exists a 'threat to the peace, breach of the peace, or act of aggression'. Once authorized, sanctions introduced under article 41 of the Charter create a mandatory obligation with which all states can comply, and afford complying states complete legal justification for their implementation.[7] The General Assembly also has the power to recommend sanctions by a two-thirds majority vote.[8] Such sanctions are mandatory, and have only rarely been acted upon, as in the case of Rhodesia,[9] in the case of the arms embargo against South Africa,[10] and in the case of the economic sanctions against Iraq in the aftermath of its invasion of Kuwait in August 1990 and the Gulf War which followed.[11]

On 24 October 1970, the General Assembly adopted the 'Declaration of Principles of International Law Concerning Friendly Relations and Cooperation among States in Accordance with the Charter of the United Nations'. *Inter alia*, this Declaration states that 'No State may use or encourage the use of economic, political or any other type of measures to coerce another State in order to obtain from it the subordination of the exercise of its sovereign rights, and to secure from it advantages of any kind.'[12]

Other Organizations

Formally, under the UN Charter, regional organizations do not have the right to impose economic sanctions against other states without the specific approval of the Security Council, and must at least inform the Council once such measures have been taken.[13] While the League of Nations Covenant and the UN Charter allowed for economic sanctions under certain circumstances, it has been argued that sanctions are in total contradiction to article 11 in the General Agreement on Tariffs and Trade (GATT), which has recently transformed into the World Trade Organization, which prohibits economic discrimination. Nevertheless article 21 of the agreement does allow each contracting party to take 'any action which it considers necessary for the protection of its essential security interests', as long as such action is taken in time of war or some other international relations emergency.[14] In October 1982 Argentina invoked the GATT against the European Community when the latter applied sanctions against it in connection with the Falklands War. Argentina expressed concern at 'the worrisome tendency of certain industrial countries to adopt trade restrictions in order to exert coercive or political pressures by taking advantage of their dominant position in the world market, thereby adding an element of injustice and insecurity in international trade relations'.

The Legality of the Arab Boycott

The Arab states always used legal arguments to justify their total war against Israel in general, and the Arab boycott in particular,[15] while Israel as well as Jewish and pro-Israel lobbies in various countries have used legal arguments to prove the opposite point of view. In addition to arguments relating to international law and the provisions of international treaties – including the foundation treaties and charters of international organizations – the domestic anti-boycott legislation in third countries where the Arabs have attempted to apply the boycott also became an issue.

The Arab Boycott and General Principles of International Law

Among the principles of international law which the Arabs have accused Israel of violating, have been: the illegal migration of Jews to Palestine since the nineteenth century in face of the objections of its Arab inhabitants; 'expulsion of the people from the land of their forefathers'; violation of the rights of the Palestinians; the 'continued war of extermination against the Palestinian People'; annexation of Arab lands; the establishment of Jewish settlements on Arab lands; the destruction of Arab villages and the confiscation of Arab property; deportation of Arab residents from occupied territories; the denial of the right of return of refugees and deportees to their homes; improper conduct towards Arab detainees; collective punishments.[16]

Mundar Anabtawi pointed out in 1975 that the laws or war provide that a state is entitled not only to impose an economic boycott

on a state with which it is in a state of war, but also to take discriminatory measures against third parties which do not fulfil the duty of
neutrality in this war. According to Anabtawi, by refraining from
applying this law in full the Arab states had acted with restraint
towards foreign countries, though he admitted that this was done
due to lack of ability and self-confidence, and the strong ties between
certain Arab states and the US.[17]

The Secretariat General of the Arab League explained, in a document supplied to the British House of Lords Select Committee on the
Foreign Boycott Bill in 1978, that the boycott 'is also considered legal
in a state of peace if used for punishment'. Thus, 'Boycotting is a procedure which can be used by a state to face the harm that it suffered
by illegal action performed by some other state. The purpose is to
make the violating state respect international law and thus stop the
illegal action. In other words, to face illegality by "legality".' The
conclusion of this line of argumentation was that '[even] if the
armistice [the agreements which concluded the 1948/49 Arab–Israeli
War – GF] puts an end to the state of war, the Arab boycott will
remain legal according to international law and to the opinion of
the big majority of legal experts, on the basis that this boycott is a
punishment for an illegal action.'[18]

All through the years the Arabs argued that respect for the boycott
regulations constituted a sovereign right of the Arabs, whose realiza-
tions did not involve interference in the internal affairs of foreign
countries (forbidden by the UN Charter), and that therefore the
western countries had no right to interfere in internal Arab affairs.
They defined the boycott as a legitimate means of self-defence according to international law and legal principles, and vehemently denied
that it was religious or racist by nature, since it was being applied
against an enemy state and its institutions that serve its military and
economic potential. Thus they regarded it as a weapon which they
intended to use until such time as they could defeat Israel militarily.[19]

Another general legal argument which the Arabs used was that the
Arab boycott does not infringe upon the current international trade
rules, since it conforms with the legal norm which applies to any
contract, which grants each contracting party the right to set whatever terms and conditions it deems consistent with its own interests,
as long as the other party remains fully free either to accept or to
reject them. Pursuant of this norm the Arab states attached specific

conditions to the economic or trade contracts they concluded with foreign partners, with the view to ensuring that no Israeli products enter Arab markets, and that attempts to boost Israeli economic capacities, that are perceived by the Arabs as aimed against them, are foiled.[20]

What the Arab argument finally boiled down to was that in trade agreements, as in any other contractual agreement, each contracting party has the right to lay down whatever terms and conditions it deems consistent with its interests. They argued that as long as both remained fully free either to accept or reject the terms and conditions offered by the other side, the application of the boycott rules in their trade relations with foreign partners was not in breach of the accepted legal norms.[21] In a related argument, trade boycotts were described by Arab spokesmen as legitimate instruments of national policy from a legal point of view, because trade itself is seen as a function which states are not obliged to carry out. Thus Leila Meo relied on the following passage to legitimize the boycott: 'Foreign trade has traditionally been a matter of national sovereignty. Its establishment has been a matter of sufferance, diplomatic negotiation, or conquest rather than legal right.'[22]

Seen from the Israeli perspective, as long as a state of war existed between the Arab states and Israel, no one questioned the legal right of the Arabs to refuse to have any economic dealings with the Jewish state. Thus the question was not whether the primary boycott was legal, but whether the Arab states were legally justified in trying to force third countries, or companies in third countries which were not in a state of war with Israel, to cooperate with the Arab boycott. A panel of eminent international jurists held a mock-trial on the issue in Washington in October 1975. The panel found that economic boycotts and embargoes levelled against third countries not directly involved in a conflict for political reasons are illegal under international law, and that countries imposing economic boycotts and embargoes must pay reparations to third countries financially injured by the discriminatory actions.[23]

Legal Arguments around Specific Boycott Practices

In addition to the use of legal arguments in the debate about the boycott as such, legal arguments were also used in the debate about specific boycott practices. Thus in the course of the 1950s, Israel kept pointing out that the Egyptian closure of the Suez Canal to Israeli and Israel-bound shipping was contrary to the 1888 Constantinople Convention, which had provided that the Suez Maritime Canal 'shall always be free and open in time of war as in time of peace to every vessel of commerce or war without distinction of flag'. Egypt argued that articles IX and X of the convention enabled it to take measures for the security of its own forces and for the defence of Egypt. However, article XI stated that 'the measures which shall be taken in the cases provided for in articles IX and X of the present treaty shall not interfere with the free use of the Canal'.

Egypt also argued that though the 1888 Convention provided for free passage through the Suez Canal even in time of war, for both belligerents and non-belligerents, this freedom applied only to belligerents that were at war with countries other than Egypt – not Egypt itself. Israel refuted this argument by pointing out that article IV of the Convention spoke of belligerents being allowed to use the canal 'even though the Ottoman Empire should be one of the belligerent powers', foreseeing a situation in which Egypt and the Ottoman Empire might be at war with each other.[24]

On 28 September 1954 the Israeli ship *Bat Galim*, which was bound from Eritrea to Israel with a cargo of meat, plywood and hides, was detained in the Canal, its cargo was confiscated, and its crew thrown into jail under a fictitious charge. The crew was finally set free, but the ship and its cargo were confiscated. 'It is difficult to think of a larger aggregate of offences against international law and maritime tradition than those which Egypt compressed into the single episode of the *Bat Galim*', Israel's Permanent Representative to the UN, Abba Eban, wrote in 1957. 'There is obstruction of free navigation; piratical seizure of a ship in an international waterway; physical violence against the persons of mariners exercising innocent passage; fabrication of charges against sailors in transit; unlawful imprisonment; the bearing of false witness from the highest tribunals of international security; dishonourable nonfulfilment of a pledge given by a member nation at the table of the Security Council.'[25]

In 1953 the British Foreign Office examined the legal implications of the interference with British trade and transport caused by the boycott. The conclusion was that such interference 'would only be justified if the Arab states enjoyed belligerent rights. In fact', it was argued, 'they do not claim such rights and ... would be unable to establish such a claim'.[26] In the memorandum that it prepared, the Foreign Office pointed out that 'The ground on which we have been resisting discrimination against British interests are not primarily legal.'[27]

In later years Israel argued about the legality of negative certificates of origin. The negative certificates of origin issued by various Arab states demanded that foreign companies with which they did business would declare that the products they were selling were not manufactured in Israel, no components in them were manufactured in Israel etc. The Arabs argued that such certificates were as legitimate as ordinary certificates of origin, and that they were a means for putting the Arab states' right to decide with whom they wished to trade into effect.[28]

A separate legal debate developed around the question of the legality of the oil embargo imposed by the Arab oil-producing states in 1973–74. The embargo was not formally part of the Arab boycott, but rather a corollary to it. It was directed especially against the Netherlands, Canada, Great Britain, Japan and the US, and expressed dissatisfaction with these states' policies vis-à-vis Israel and the Yom Kippur War.

As was only to be expected, the Arab view was that the embargo was perfectly legal, going so far as to describe it as 'an instrument for the respect and promotion of the rule of law'.[29] The Arabs likened the oil embargo to Western, particularly American, legislation imposing special export controls over individual commodities, as well as to multilateral efforts aimed at giving a wide base to the strategic export controls and articles 20 and 21 of GATT.[30]

Others took the view that the Arab stategy constituted the 'deliberate employment of an economic instrument of coercion against other states and peoples in order to place intense pressure upon their freedom of choice', which, with the interrelated use of diplomatic and ideological instruments as well as the coordinated use of military forces against the State of Israel, is in violation of international law.[31]

International Treaties and Organizations

In the legal debate over the boycott, Israel and its allies usually concentrated on trying to show that the application of the secondary and tertiary economic boycotts contradicts existing international agreements – especially the UN Charter, articles 85 and 86 of the Treaty of Rome, the EC's agreements with the Maghreb and Mashreq states, articles 11 and 12 of GATT, etc.

As early as 1946 the Jewish Agency argued, in representations to the British Colonial Office, that the Arab boycott was contrary to non-discrimination clauses in existing commercial treaties and agreements between Palestine on the one hand and Syria and Lebanon on the other, and the Anglo-Egyptian Agreement, which included Palestine.[32]

The United Nations Charter and Resolutions

Very soon after the Arab boycott went into force on 4 January 1946, the head of the Jewish Agency Political Department, Moshe Shertok (later Sharett), argued in a letter that he sent the UN Secretary General, which was based on a legal analysis prepared by Dr Nathan Feinberg (who was later to become one of Israel's foremost authorities on public international law), that 'the Jewish Agency for Palestine begs to submit that [the] decision to wage an economic war against a section of the population of a neighbouring country ... is inconsistent with the purpose and the whole spirit of the UN. The maintenance of international peace and harmony and the protection of the freedom of all peace-loving peoples to engage in all legitimate activities, are the very essence of the new world order.' Shertok invoked the Preamble of the UN Charter, as well as articles 1(2) & (3), 55, and 56.[33]

In defending the legality of the Arab boycott the Arabs have frequently cited article 16 of the UN Charter which, they argue, approves of economic embargoes as a sanction against states declaring war on other states. Articles 51 and 52, they add, recognize the inherent right of states, individually and collectively, to exercise the right of self-defence, which according to them may be exercised by economic means.[34]

In justifying the oil embargo which the Arab oil-producing states imposed on the Netherlands, Canada, Great Britain, Japan and the US in the aftermath of the 1973 October War, the Arabs argued that it could be justified as falling within the right of a belligerent state to apply economic sanctions against third-party states that violate their obligations of neutrality, and within the pertinent resolutions of the UN and its agencies. In particular they cited UN General Assembly resolution 1515 (XV) of 15 December 1960, which dealt with 'Concerted action for economic development of economically less developed countries' and upheld 'the sovereign right of every state to dispose of its wealth and its natural resources', [35] as well as a resolution by the UN Conference on Trade and Development (UNCTAD) on permanent sovereignty over natural resources, of 19 October 1972, and UN General Assembly resolution 3175 (XXVIII) of 17 December 1973, affirming 'the right of the Arab states and peoples whose territories are under foreign occupation, to permanent sovereignty over all their natural resources'. It was pointed out, however that the actual wording of General Assembly resolution 3175 also stated that the General Assembly 'deplores acts of states which use force, armed aggression, *economic coercion* [author's emphasis] or any other illegal or improper measures in resolving disputes concerning the exercise of the sovereign rights (over natural resources)'.[36] Furthermore, article 1(2) of the 1966 International Covenant on Economic, Social and Cultural Rights states that the free disposal of natural wealth and resources must not prejudice 'any obligations arising out of international economic cooperation, based upon the principle of mutual benefit and international law'.[37]

Israel and its allies in the battle against the Arab boycott naturally relied on different resolutions. Already in 1951, in connection with the Egyptian prohibition on the passage of Israeli ships and cargoes through the Suez Canal, the UN Security Council passed a resolution to the effect that 'the restrictions on the passage of goods through the Suez Canal to Israel ports are denying to nations, at no time connected with the conflict in Palestine, valuable supplies required for their economic reconstruction, and that these restrictions together with sanctions applied by Egypt to certain ships, which have visited Israeli ports, represent unjustified interference with the rights of nations to navigate the seas and to trade freely with one another – including the Arab states and Israel'.[38]

The Declaration on Principles of International Law Concerning

Friendly Relations and Cooperation among States [2625 (XXV)] which was adopted by the UN General Assembly on 24 October 1970 was also cited.[39] *Inter alia* this declaration stated that 'it is the duty of states to refrain in their international relations from military, political, economic or any other forms of coercion aimed against the political independence or territorial integrity of states' in conformity with the UN Charter obligation of Article 2(4), requiring member states to refrain from the threat or use of force in their international relations. Another General Assembly resolution cited was one adopting the Charter of Economic Rights and Duties of States [3281 (XXIX)], passed on 12 December 1974, of which article 32 proscribed means of coercion, in terms which would also apply to boycott operation.[40]

The Arab states have also used the argument that they have been justified in applying sanctions against Israel as a punishment due to Israel's refusal to comply with numerous resolutions by the UN Security Council, General Assembly, Economic and Social Council, Commission on Human Rights and other specialized agencies. Since Israel ignored these resolutions, they argued, and the UN did not respond as it had done in the cases of other countries such as Rhodesia and South Africa, the Arabs had a right to act unilaterally to protect themselves and take retaliatory measures against Israel.[41] In a paper which it presented to the British House of Lords Select Committee on the Foreign Boycott Bill in July 1978, the Secretariat General of the Arab League, went so far as to state that in light of the Israeli violations 'the Arab states not only find themselves entitled to exercise their right of self-defence *but that it is also their national and international duty to do so'*. [42]

The General Agreement on Tariffs and Trade (GATT)[43]

The General Agreement on Tariffs and Trade was first signed on 30 October 1947 after the establishment of an International Trade Organization failed to materialize. The GATT framework, whose goal was to liberalize world trade by reducing tariffs and other trade barriers, and to eliminate discrimination in international trade relations, continued to exist until April 1994, when it was replaced by the World Trade Organization. Israel acceded to GATT in 1962; Egypt, Kuwait and Tunisia joined later on. Several other Arab states, which were not members of GATT, nevertheless applied its terms *de facto*; these included Algeria, Qatar, the United Arab Emirates (UAE) and North Yemen.

According to Israel and its partners in the battle against the Arab boycott, the primary and secondary boycotts are incompatible with the provisions of GATT – in particular article 11, which provided for the elimination of quantitative restrictions, and article 13, which provided for the non-discriminatory administration of quantitative restrictions.[44] However the states that signed the GATT had the option of waiving the basic principle of non-discrimination, and this on the basis of article 21, which enabled the contracting parties to exclude from the scope of their obligations any action that they considered necessary for the protection of their essential security interests. The Arabs argued that this article provided legal support for their boycott of Israel.[45]

Israel and its allies replied that article 21 had to be subject to the rule of reasonable interpretation. Any exception to the performance of a non-discrimination obligation based on the ground of essential interests, would have to be interpreted in good faith and in accordance with the ordinary meaning given to the definition of this term.[46] It was further pointed out that the concept of 'essential security interests' would have to be interpreted in terms of GATT's objectives. In particular it was suggested that article 21 was intended to refer to measures of economic coercion decided upon by the Security Council under Chapter VII of the UN Charter in cases of a threat to the peace, breach of the peace and acts of aggression, as provided for in article 50 of the Charter, as in the case of the UN sanctions against Rhodesia.[47] Another argument has been that article 21 is not in accord with the provisions of the UN Charter, and especially article 2(4), which prohibits more than the use of armed force.[48]

In addition, article 35 stipulated that the GATT would not apply as between one contracting party and any other contracting party, if either of them at the time of accession refused such application in its relations with the other. This article was invoked by Egypt to justify the boycott against Israel, at the time of its accession to GATT in 1970. Egypt did agree, however, to examine complaints regarding the operation of the secondary boycott and to consult with the contracting parties concerned within the framework of GATT.[49] Israel on the other hand challenged the Egyptian practices of blacklisting, and the request for negative certificates of origin from firms in third countries as being contrary to article 11. It should be pointed out that Egypt revoked the article after signing the Peace Treaty with Israel in 1979.

Since so few Arab states were members of GATT, there was little point invoking the agreement against these states. However Israel maintained that since the secondary boycott was directed against firms and individuals in third states, the governments of these states had an obligation, under the terms of GATT, to create conditions in which the trading community can function freely and efficiently by taking measures against the application of the secondary boycott in their territory. However when in the mid-1990s several Gulf states applied for admission into GATT, the Clinton Administration, which was campaigning for the lifting of the boycott within the framework of the Middle East peace process, informed the states concerned that 'the secondary and tertiary boycotts are in conflict with some of the basic principles of GATT'.[50]

The Treaty of Rome and Agreements of the EC with the Maghreb and Mashreq Countries[51]

There are two articles in the Treaty of Rome – articles 85 and 86 – that have been cited by Israel and its allies as prohibiting the application of and compliance with the secondary and tertiary boycotts within the European Community. These articles fall within the framework of the rules of competition that constitute part of the basic policy of the European Community. Article 85 deals with the prohibition, as incompatible with the basic principles of the Common Market, of 'all agreements between undertakings, decisions by associations of undertakings and concerted practices which may affect trade between Member States and which have as their object or effect the prevention, restriction or distortion of competition within the Common Market'. These include the application of dissimilar conditions to equivalent transactions with other trading partners, thereby placing them at a competitive disadvantage, and making the conclusion of contracts subject to acceptance by the other parties of supplementary obligations, which by their nature or according to commercial usage, have no connection with the subject of such clauses ('tie-in' clauses).[52]

Article 86 deals with the prohibition of 'any abuse, by one or more undertakings of a dominant position within the Common Market or in a substantial part of it ... insofar as it may affect trade between Member States'.[53]

In addition, the agreements signed by the European Community with the Maghreb and Mashreq countries in 1975 and 1976 all contained non-discrimination clauses that appeared to exclude the application of the secondary and tertiary boycotts by the relevant Arab states in the EC member states.

The Arabs rejected the claim that articles 85 and 86 could be applied to the secondary and tertiary boycotts, arguing that these articles only applied to circumstances which were anticipated to have a significant effect on the trade between the member states of the EC. Regarding the agreements between the Community and the Arab states, the Arabs pointed out that all these agreements include clauses enabling the signatories to take any measures they deem vital to protect their security in time of war or international tension, which, they argued, applied to the Arab–Israeli conflict.[54]

Domestic Anti-Boycott Legislation

Since originally few states had any sort of legislation which might be used to try to combat the Arab boycott, part of Israel's battle against the Arab boycott, especially after 1975, focused on trying to convince friendly states to pass anti-boycott laws, that would make submission to the secondary and tertiary boycotts a punishable offence.

The United States[55]

The only country that has extensive anti-boycott legislation is the US. This resulted from the free-trade and human rights traditions of the country on the one hand, and systematic pressure of American Jewish organizations and pro-Israel Congressmen on the other.

The American legislation is not a single law but a combination of federal and state statutes, regulations, guidelines, executive orders and common law interpretations thereof.[56] The oldest piece of legislation, adapted for use against the tertiary boycott, was the 1870 Sherman Antitrust Act. The US Justice Department's Antitrust

Division interpreted the law in a manner that had anti-boycott implications in the Bechtel case of 1976/77, which ended in a consent decree.

The civil action against the Bechtel Corporation, one of the World's largest construction firms, was filed by the Department of Justice in January 1976. Bechtel was accused of violating Section 1 of the Sherman Act by entering into agreements and understandings with certain unnamed co-conspirators, and taking action jointly with them to refuse to subcontract with persons blacklisted by the Arab boycott in connection with major construction projects in Arab League countries. Bechtel originally contested that the Arab boycott of Israel was political by nature, and therefore beyond the scope of the antitrust laws. However, within a year the Department of Justice and Bechtel agreed upon a consent decree that articulated certain permitted and prohibited activities by Bechtel deemed to be boycott-related. The Bechtel Decree and its interpretation by the Justice Department were significant guidelines to future enforcement policy on boycott related activities by the Department's Antitrust Division. *Inter alia*, this policy prohibits American companies from performing or implementing any agreement, even one entered into within an Arab country, to refuse to deal or to require others to refuse to deal with any US person blacklisted pursuant to the Arab boycott. The policy also prohibits assisting an Arab client in the selection of subcontractors, where that client refuses to deal with US companies on the blacklist. An American company also may not maintain or use in the US any blacklist in connection with major construction projects.[57]

Section 717 of Title VII of the 1964 Civil Rights Act makes discrimination in employment practices of federal agencies unlawful, while Executive Order No. 11478 prohibits discrimination in federal agency employment practices, and directs the Civil Service Commission to enforce this prohibition. Both specifically state that they are not applicable to aliens employed outside the limits of the US. Some commentators argue that they are applicable, however, to American citizens wherever such individuals are employed, including employment for work in Arab countries notwithstanding local law restriction in such Arab countries. If a boycott-related violation of Title VII is found, a country's powers in providing remedies are varied. The employer can be enjoined from further discrimination, portions of the contracts or agreements calling for the discriminatory employment practices can be declared void or unenforceable, and finally, courts can award damages, including back-pay, as well as require affirmative hiring to rectify the past discrimination.[58]

In 1976 several provisions were added to the Internal Revenue Code, within the framework of the Tax Reform Act of that year. These provisions, known as the Ribicoff amendment, denied certain tax benefits to taxpayers who participated in, or cooperated with international boycotts. The tax benefits affected by the boycott provisions were: (a) the foreign tax credit; (b) the deferral of tax on the earnings of foreign subsidiaries; (c) the deferral of tax on the earnings of Domestic International Sales Corporations (DISC).

Under the Tax Reform Act, as amended in 1986, a company or individual is deemed to have participated in or cooperated with a boycott if it refrains from: (a) doing business with or in a boycotted country or with the government, companies or national of that country; (b) doing business with any US person engaged in trade in a boycotted country or with the government, companies or nationals of that country; (c) doing business with any company whose ownership or management is made up, all or in part, of individuals of a particular nationality, race or religion, or to remove (or refrain from selecting) corporate directors who are individuals of a particular nationality, race or religion; (d) employing individuals of a particular nationality, race or religion; (e) shipping or insuring products on a carrier owned, leased or operated by a blacklisted person. An agreement to cooperate with a boycott may be indirect, and need not be with the boycotting country itself but may be required by a third party.

The two exceptions to these prohibitions are that one may comply with a boycotting country's prohibition on the importation into that country of goods that are produced in whole or part in a boycotted country, or on the exportation of its products to a boycotted country. The Treasury Guidelines applying to this provision go into great detail in determining what does and what does not constitute 'participation in or cooperation with' an unsanctioned foreign boycott.[59]

In 1977 anti-boycott provisions were added to the Export Administration Act (EAA) of that year. The intention of these provisions was to discourage and, in certain circumstances, prohibit American companies and individuals from taking or agreeing to take certain actions to comply with, further or support economic boycotts fostered or imposed by foreign states against countries friendly to the US, and which are not the object of any form of embargo by the US. They particularly focused on preventing US residents from discriminating against or refusing to do business with other US residents at the request of foreign governments.

The EAA and Export Regulations specifically prohibited many actions that had been routinely undertaken by American firms trading in the Middle East prior to 1977. These fell under four general categories:

- A refusal to do business with or in a boycotted country, with any business concern or national or resident of a boycotted country, or with any other person, where such refusal was pursuant to an agreement with, requirement of, or request from or on behalf of, a boycotting country;
- A refusal to employ or otherwise discriminate against any individual who is a US person on the basis of race, religion, sex or national origin of such person or against any US business concern on the basis of the race, religion, sex or national origin of any owner, officer, director or employee of such business concern;
- The furnishing of personal or business information, either requested or volunteered, that would assist an unsanctioned foreign boycott, unless this was 'normal business information in a commercial context';
- The paying, honouring, confirming or otherwise implementing a letter of credit that contained a condition with which a US person may not comply.

The EAA and Export Regulations specifically provided for certain exceptions to otherwise prohibited actions. Thus, a US person was permitted to comply with:

- The laws of a boycotting countries that prohibited imports of specific goods or services provided either by a boycotted country, businesses within a boycotted country, or nationals or residents of a boycotted country;
- Shipping requirements of a boycotting country that prohibited shipment of imported goods on a carrier of the boycotted country, or by a route not prescribed by the boycotting country or recipient of the shipment;

- 'Unilateral and specific selections' made by nationals or residents of a boycotting country with respect to choice of carriers, insurers, providers of services to be performed within a boycotting country, or suppliers of certain goods;
- Export requirements of a boycotting country restricting shipments or trans-shipments to a boycotted country or any business or concern, national or resident of a boycotted country;
- Any immigration requirement of a boycotting country, including the provision of requested information about himself or a member of his immediate family;
- The laws of the boycotting country governing his activities exclusively within that country, including any import laws, even though compliance with such laws may involve boycott-based refusal to deal, in the event that he is a *bona fide* resident of that country.

The Act and Regulations included an anti-evasion provision, the key element of which was whether or not there was the requisite 'intent to evade' the restrictive provisions of these laws. However, the most important aspect of the legislation was its reporting requirements. A US person who received a request to take any action that is boycott related and has the effect of furthering or supporting a restrictive trade practice or boycott unsanctioned by the US was obliged report such request to the Department of Commerce, either in writing or orally. Violations of the EAA or any regulation, order or licence issued thereunder, or an attempt to evade complying with the law, may result in criminal, administrative and/or civil sanctions. Sanctions include fines, the suspension, revocation, or denial of export privileges conferred under the EAA, or exclusion from practice before the International Trade Administration.[60]

In addition to the legislation mentioned above, the Securities and Exchange Commission played a role in inhibiting boycott conduct by firms subject to the SEC's jurisdiction, even though the federal securities laws enforced by the SEC were not specifically designed as deterrents to boycott participation.[61] Several states have also enacted anti-boycott laws.[62]

Some Arab spokesmen have argued that the constitutionality of the American anti-boycott legislation should be tested, and that the secondary and tertiary boycotts are not illegal under the Civil Rights

Act, since it is not discriminatory on the basis of religion, sex, race or ethnic origin.[63]

France[64]

France was the first European state to pass an anti-boycott law, though the application of the law was greatly modified by various government directives. In November 1976 legislation was initiated in the National Assembly, entitled 'various economic and financial provisions', within the framework of which article 32a aimed at the suppression of all racial discrimination in trade and economic affairs.[65] Article 32a was formulated as an amendment to a law of 1 July 1972, that sought to eradicate all forms of discrimination based on origin, nationality, race or religion, following ratification by France of the 1966 UN Convention on the Elimination of all Forms of Racial Discrimination.

As finally enacted on 7 June 1977,[66] article 32a amended the Penal Code by adding to it two new provisions: clauses 187–2 and 416–1, which made it a punishable offence for any public official, individual person or company, by any act or omission and without just cause, to contribute under normal circumstances to making more difficult the exercise of any economic activity by (a) a physical person, by reason of his national origin, or his real or supposed membership of a specific ethnic, racial or religious group or (b) any legal entity, by reason of the national origin or the real or supposed membership or non-membership of a specific ethnic, racial or religious group of all or any of its members or of any or all of its executive officers. According to these provisions offenders are liable to imprisonment of two months to one year and a fine of FF 200–20,000, or one of these penalties. At the same time article 32(3) stipulated that these penal provisions would not apply if the commercial activities to which they referred were in conformity with government directives adopted within the context of the French government's economic and commercial policy, or as a result of its international commitments.[67]

Another law, passed on 16 July 1980, dealt with the communication of documents and information of an economic, commercial or technical nature to foreign individuals or legal entities. Article 2 of the law provided that 'Save as provided in treaties or international agreements, it is forbidden for any individual of French nationality or usually residing on French soil, and for any head, representative, agent or employee of a legal entity having its head office there ... to communicate in writing or orally or in any other form, anywhere, to foreign public authorities, documents or information of an economic, commercial, industrial, financial or technical nature, the communication of which may undermine the sovereignty, security, or the essential economic interests of France or the public order ...'.[68] Penalties include either a two to six months' imprisonment or a fine of FF 10,000–120,000, or both. The object of the 1980 law was to prevent pressure being exerted on companies having their headquarters in France, with the intention of prejudicing the interests of France in the development of its international economic exchanges.

Benelux Countries[69]

On 29 June 1981, the Netherlands introduced an amendment to article 429 of the Dutch Penal Code, making it a criminal offence for anyone to discriminate in the course of practising a profession or trade, against a person on grounds of race. The provision was not to apply to cases of positive discrimination in favour of persons belonging to particular ethnic or cultural minorities. What it achieved was to do away with the certificates of religious affiliation ('non-Jew certificates').

In May 1984 the legislation was extended, making it mandatory to register all foreign boycott-related requests within a specific period, their nature and the identity of those making such requests. Further information could also be required by the authorities, and the measure established an independent commission to which injured parties domiciled in the Netherlands could turn.

On 9 August, 1980, amendments were introduced to the Luxembourgian Penal Code, *inter alia*, making it an offence, under article 454, to discriminate against any person on grounds of race, national or ethnic origin in the course of trading or offering to tender goods or services, to announce one's intention to refuse to provide goods or services, or to practise discrimination in the aforementioned circumstances. Article 455 of the Code, made it an offence, for anyone to carry out acts of incitement, by writing, printing or any other form of public communication, to commit the offences mentioned in article 454, or to commit acts of incitement to hatred or violence against any person, group of community or against any of its members on any of the aforementioned grounds. It is also an offence to belong to any organization whose aims or activities are for the purpose of committing such acts.

A similar amendment to that enacted in Luxembourg was passed in Belgium on 30 July 1981. Article 1 of the Belgian law made punishable certain acts of incitement specified under article 444 of the Penal Code – namely, incitement to discrimination, hatred or violence against a person, by reason of his race, colour, national or ethnic origin. The same offence is committed if directed against a group or community, or against certain members of such a group or community on the aforementioned grounds. Article 3 of the law makes it an offence for anyone committing a discriminatory act against any person on grounds of race, colour, national or ethnic origin when tendering or offering to tender goods or services in a public place.

Germany[70]

On 23 July 1992 Germany passed an anti-boycott law forbidding German firms to honour Arab requests to isolate Israel economically by including clauses in commercial transactions for the sale or purchase of goods, which would have the effect of giving in to or complying with the Arab boycott.

The Arab Reaction to Domestic Anti-boycott Laws

While the Arabs never denied the right of third states to pass anti-boycott legislation, they perceived of it as part of a 'Zionist counter-attack',[71] which they had every legal right to fight because it interfered with the sovereign right of the Arab states to implement the boycott in the first place. Thus the Arab League declared that its member states would not enter into any contracts with companies that claimed that they could not abide by the boycott because the laws of their own country forbad it. In a statement issued by the 41st Conference of the liaison officers of the regional Arab boycott offices, they declared that 'the Arab states ... completely insist that the laws in force in the Arab countries should be respected. They also announced that they would never deal ... with firms and companies, American or otherwise, which fail to respect Arab laws and regulations, using the medium of laws issued in their countries.' The statement went on to say that 'the Arab boycott did not and will never interfere in the internal affairs of any foreign country, but, at the same time, it will never permit, in any case, that foreign laws interfere in its business and will meet such interference with unyielding firmness'.[72]

This rather tortuous line of argumentation was used again nine years later in June 1987 when the Secretary General of the Arab League, Chedli Klibi, stated in a symposium on boycotts and economic measures in international conflicts held in Geneva, that the Arab boycott did not violate the national legislation of countries desirous of doing business with the Arab world, but that the Arab world expected their foreign partners to respect Arab legislation, including that regarding the boycott of Israel, in full.[73]

Israel[74]

Though the idea of some form of anti-boycott legislation came up in Israel in the course of the 1980s, such legislation was opposed by Israeli manufacturers who preferred to be left to their own devices in coping with the boycott, only occasionally turning to the authorities – after 1975 the Economic Warfare Authority of the Ministry of finance – when requiring outside intervention. Thus while Israel kept pressing other countries to pass anti-boycott legislation, it was only at the end of 1994 that it passed such legislation itself, as part of amendment 7 to the Tenders Obligation Law.

According to article 3b of the law, 'The Government is entitled to instruct by order, with the approval of the Knesset Foreign Affairs and Security Committee, that the state or a government association will not enter into a contract to perform a deal under article 2 with a certain foreign country or a certain foreign supplier for foreign policy reasons. Such an instruction will be published in the official gazette ...'.[75]

What the legislator had in mind was that the government should not be obliged to purchase a product from a company that in any way gives in to the Arab boycott, even if it has made the lowest offer in a tender. The government had sought to keep the reason for a decision not to accept an offer because of boycott considerations secret, but the Knesset Constitution, Law and Justice Committee insisted on the reason being published.[76] This article was opposed by several members of the opposition, who argued that a company participating in a public tender in Israel could not be regarded as one which had given in to the Arab boycott.[77] This disregarded the fact that some foreign companies were willing to sell certain products to Israel, but refused to sell other products, purchase goods from Israel or invest in Israel because of boycott considerations.

Notes

1. Stephen C. Neff, 'Economic Warfare in Contemporary International Law: Three Schools of Thought, Evaluated According to an Historical Method', *Stanford Journal of International Law*, 26 (1989), p. 67.
2. Military and Paramilitary Activities in and against Nicaragua (Nicaragua v. United States of America), *International Court of Justice Reports* (1986), p. 138.
3. Stephen C. Neff, 'Boycott and the Law of Nations: Economic Warfare and Modern International Law in Historical Perspective', *The British Yearbook of International Law* (1988), p. 115.
4. Ibid. pp. 147–8, *inter alia* citing Derek William Bowett, 'Economic Coercion and Reprisal by States', *Virginia Journal of International Law*, 13 (1972).
5. See, for example, the case of the American freezing of Iranian assets in the US following the rise to power of the Ayatollah Khomeini in Iran in 1979 (Robert Carswell, 'Economic Sanctions and the Iran Experience', *Foreign Affairs*, 60, 2 (Winter 1981/82), pp. 249–50; the case of Libyan assets frozen in 1987 (Henry Weisburg, 'Unilateral Economic Sanctions and the Risks of Extraterritorial Application: the Libyan Example', *International Law and Politics*, 19 (1987), p. 981; and the case of the American freezing of Iraqi and Kuwaiti assets in the aftermath of the Iraqi occupation of Kuwait in August 1990 (Welu and Zaucha Chaudhri, 'Sanctions against Iraq and Occupied Kuwait', *Middle East Executive Report*, 13, 1990).
6. See for example Leonard B. Boudin, 'Economic Sanctions and Individual Rights', *International Law and Politics*, 19 (1987), p. 803.
7. James O.C.Jonah, 'Sanctions and the United Nations', *Harvard International Review*, X, 5, (1988), p. 13, and Nico Schrijver, 'The Use of Economic Sanctions by the UN Security Council: An International Law Perspective', in H.H.G. Post (ed.) *International Economic Law and Armed Conflict* (Alphen aan den Rijn: Martinus Nijhoff, 1994), p. 144.
8. UN Document A/1775.
9. Security Council resolution 232 (1966), UN Resolution, Security Council, series II, compiler and editor Dusan J. Djonovich, Vol. VI (New York: Oceana Publications/Dobbs Ferry, 1989) pp. 15–16 and Security Council resolution

253 (1968), ibid., Vol. VII (1990), pp. 15–17.

10. Margareth Doxey, 'International Sanctions: The Lessons of Experience', *Harvard International Review*, 10, 5 (1988).

11. On the Iraqi sanctions see several articles on the issue in *Middle East Report* (March/April 1995), pp. 2–22.

12. General Assembly resolution 2625 (XXV), in *UN Resolutions, General Assembly*, Series I, compiled and edited by Dusan J. Djonovich, Vol. XIII (New York: Oceana Publications/Dobbs Ferry, 1976), p. 337.

13. Article 53 in the Charter of the United Nations. See Louis L. Snyder (ed.) *Fifty Major Documents of the Twentieth Century* (Princeton, NJ: D. Van Nostrand, 1955), p. 169.

14. See, for example, M.A.G. van Meerhaeghe, *International Economic Institutions* (London: Longman, second edition, 1971), pp. 112–13.

15. See for example Address by Dr Muhammad Aziz Shukri, 'Misconceptions Concerning the Arab Boycott of Israel', 26 July 1989.

16. Leila Meo, ed., *The Arab Boycott of Israel* (Detroit: Association of Arab-American University Graduates, 1976), pp. 4–6.

17. Mundar Anabtawi in Hani al-Hindi, coordinator of a symposium on the Arab Boycott, *Shu'un Falestiniyya*, 46 (June 1975), pp. 133, 135.

18. Statement of the Secretariat General of the Arab League, House of Lords Select Committee on the Foreign Boycotts Bill, Vol. 1, Report of Proceedings, HMSO, 28.7.78.

19. Lieutenant Colonel Yosef, *Halohama Hakalkalit Ha'aravit Neged Yisrael* (The Arab Economic Warfare against Israel), *Ma'archot*, 275 (August 1980), p. 31.

20. Address delivered by the Secretary General of the Arab League, Chedli Klibi, at the opening of the International Symposium on Boycott and Economic Measures in International Conflicts, held in Geneva in June 1987.

21. Ibid. It should be noted that the 'legal norms' argument loses much of its force when the states involved are members of international agreements based on the principle of non-discrimination and are thus not completely free to agree to discriminatory terms.

22. Leila Mao, op. cit., p. 7, citing J. Dupray Muir 'The Boycott in International Law', *The Journal of International Law and Economics*, 9, 2 (1974), p. 188.

23. *Jerusalem Post*, 19 October 1975.

24. Abba Eban, *Voice of Israel* (New York: Horizon Press, 1957), pp. 258, 262–3.

25. Ibid., pp. 160–1.

26. Memorandum prepared by the British Foreign Office, quoting a minute by Mr Fitzmaurice of 1 April 1953, PRO FP371/104207 XC13782.

27. Ibid.

28. Ja'far Tah Hamza, *Al-Muqata'a al-'Arabiyya li-Isra'îl* (Arabic) (The Arab Boycott of Israel) (1973) pp. 110–17.

29. See, for example, Ibrahim F.I. Shihata, 'Destination Embargo of Arab Oil: Its Legality under International Law', *The American Journal of International Law*, 68 (1974), pp. 591–627.

30. See below, pp. 74–6.

31. Jordan J. Paust and Albert P Blaustein, 'The Arab Oil Market – A Threat to

International Peace', *American Journal of International Law*, 68 (1974), pp. 410–39.

32. See minutes of a meeting between Jewish Agency representatives and Colonial Office officials on 22 May 1946, Central Zionist Archives, S8–356.
33. Susan Hattis Rolef, 'Israel's Anti-Boycott Policy', *Policy Studies*, 28 (Jerusalem: The Leonard Davis Institute for International Relations at the Hebrew University of Jerusalem, February 1989), p. 9.
34. See for example *Sada Alwatan*, 8 September 1989.
35. *UN Resolutions, General Assembly*, Series I, Vol. VIII 1960–62, compiled and edited by Dusan J. Djonovich (New York: Oceana Publications/Dobbs Ferry, 1974), p. 134.
36. *UN Resolutions, General Assembly*, Series I, Vol. XIV 1972–74, compiled and edited by Dusan J. Djonovich (New York: Oceana Publications/Dobbs Ferry, 1978), p. 425.
37. Shihata, op. cit.
38. Rolef, op. cit., p. 13.
39. *UN Resolutions, General Assembly*, Series I, compiled and edited by Dusan J. Djonovich, Vol. XIII (New York: Oceana Publications/Dobbs Ferry, 1976), p. 337.
40. Ibid., Vol. X.
41. For a detailed review of the Arab argument, see Juzif Mughayzal, *Al-Muqata'a al-'Arabiyya wal-Qanun al-Dawli* (Arabic) (The Arab Boycott and International Law) (Beirut: M.T.F., Markaz al-Abhath, 1968) pp. 9, 31–54; Hamza, op. cit., pp. 22–6; Muhammad 'Abd al-'Aziz Ahmad wa-Muhammad al-Jabali, *Al-Difa' al-Iqtisadi Didda al-Atma' al-Istighlaliyaa al-Isra'iliyya* (Arabic) (The Economic Protection from Israel's Ambitions to Exploit the Region), pp. 13–14.
42. Statement of the Secretariat General of the Arab League, House of Lords Select Committee on the Foreign Boycotts Bill, Vol. 1, Report of Proceedings, HMSO, 28 July 1978.
43. Unless otherwise indicated this section is based on a paper prepared by the Economic Warfare Authority in the Israeli Ministry of Finance at the end of 1982 and on M. Shaton, 'GATT and the Arab Boycott', in Susan Hattis Rolef (ed.) *Freedom of Trade and the Arab Boycott* (Jerusalem: The Anti-Defamation League of B'nai B'rith in cooperation with the Israel Institute of Coexistence, 1985), pp. 109–13.
44. WJC publication 'Consequences of Arab Measures of Economic Coercion, with Particular Reference to Boycott Practices, from the Standpoint of International Law, International Trade Law, and the Law of Certain European Institutions' (October 1975), p. 12.
45. Shukri, op. cit.
46. Daniel Lack, 'Developments in the Field of Anti-boycott Measures at Regional and National Levels' (15 June 1978), p. 5.
47. WJC publication op. cit., pp. 13–15.
48. Paust and Blaustein, op. cit., p. 424.
49. GATT Working Party's Report, 7 February 1970, L/3362, paragraph 25.
50. *Arab News*, 3 February 1994.

51. See also Chapter 9.
52. *Treaties Establishing the European Communities, Treaties amending these Treaties, Documents Concerning the Accession* (Luxembourg: Office for Official Publications of the European Communities, 1973), pp. 245–6.
53. Ibid., pp. 246–7. See also Daniel Lack, 'Note on Identifying Potentially Actionable Cases of Boycott under EEC Competition Rules', December 1975.
54. Shukri, op. cit.
55. See also Chapter 7.
56. Nancy Jo Nelson, 'The United States Legal Response to the Arab Boycott – A Quagmire for the Innocent', *The Palestine Yearbook of International Law* (Nicosia: Al-Shaybani Society of International Law, 1989), p. 131.
57. Ibid., pp. 158–9.
58. Ibid., pp. 162–3.
59. Ibid., pp. 152–5.
60. Ibid., pp. 135–51.
61. Ibid., pp. 160–2.
62. Ibid., pp. 131–3.
63. Shukri, op. cit.
64. See also Chapter 8, pp. 201–9.
65. WJC, 'Recent Anti-Boycott Developments in France and the EEC', Geneva (10 June 1977). See also Jean-Louis Bismuth, *Le boycottage dans les echanges economiques internationaux au regard du droit* (Paris: Economica, 1980).
66. Law No. 77–574 of 7 June 1977.
67. Bismuth, op. cit.
68. Law No. 80–538.
69. See also Chapter 8, pp. 223–7.
70. See also Chapter 8, pp. 215–23.
71. Hamza, op. cit., p. 3.
72. Statement of the Secretariat General of the Arab League, op. cit.
73. Opening of the International Symposium on Boycotts and Economic Measures in International Conflicts, Geneva (June).
74. See also Chapter 6.
75. Law No. 1495, which went into effect on 22 December 1994.
76. See explanation by chairman of the Knesset Constitution, Law and Justice Committee, MK Dedi Zucker, in the Knesset debate on the second and third reading of amendment No. 7 to the Tenders Obligation Law, held on 20 December 1994.
77. See, for example, speech by MK Dan Meridor, ibid.

4

The Boycott of Israel –
The Arab Perspective

The Goals of the Boycott

THE BASIC Arab approach to the boycott was first and foremost that
it constituted a legitimate and effective tool in the campaign against
the realization of the Zionist goals and its 'invasion of Palestine' on
the one hand,[1] and the survival of the Jewish state in the Middle East
on the other.[2] 'Since the establishment of the State of Israel', the
introduction to a Boycott Office publication stated in 1956, 'the Arab
Governments have adopted various means for liberating the plun-
dered land. The economic boycott against Israel has been and still is
one of those means.'[3]

This approach stemmed from the premise, which lay at the base of
the policies of all the Arab states towards Israel at least until the
1970s (and is still current in certain circles and regimes in the Arab
world today), that Israel is a thorn (or knife) in the Arab flesh, which
should and can be removed.[4] Furthermore, they argued that they
were legally justified in pursuing this goal, since Israel was an illegal
state which had come into existence by illegal means.

However, side by side with the more extreme goals of the boycott
which were concerned with principles, one could also discern pragmatic ones based on more immediate interests. For example, in the
years before 1948 the fear of Syrian and Lebanese producers that
they might lose markets to their Jewish competitors in Palestine,
played a major role in their support of the boycott.[5] In the 1960s
there were also indications that the goal of the boycott was perceived
not so much as a means of destroying Israel, but rather as a means of
causing Israel economic hardship. In 1961 the Arab League defined
the goals of the boycott as follows:

1. to prevent the flow of capital or technological know-how which might contribute to the strengthening of the Israeli economy or military force;
2. to follow developments in the Israeli economy and Israel's industry, and prepare a plan for obstructing them;
3. to follow the penetration of Israeli economic, financial, trading and industrial activities in third countries, especially in Asia and Africa, in order to obstruct them, and to compete with Israeli exports;
4. to block Israel's anti-boycott campaign in third countries and explain the boycott's purposes;
5. to acquire information relating to all of Israel's activities vital for the growth of its economy.[6]

Four years later the Commissioner of the Central Boycott Office, Mohammed Mahgoub, was quoted as having said that 'the sole purpose (of the boycott) is to disrupt trade relations with Israel, to weaken the Israeli enemy in this way, and to stop foreign investors from establishing ties with Israel, by means of economic pressure'.[7] In 1979, the Baghdad Arab Summit Conference, which convened in order to deal with the problem created by the Egyptian–Israeli Peace Agreement, emphasized that the boycott was a basic weapon in the Arab strategy, which sought inter-Arab economic integration on the one hand, and to prevent Israeli penetration of the Arab world on the other.[8] Following the outbreak of the *intifada*, the Palestinian uprising against the Israeli occupation in the West Bank and Gaza Strip, in December 1987, the Commissioner General of the CBO in Damascus, Zuhair Aquil, stated at a meeting of the Arab boycott liaison officers that the boycott is 'one of the Arab weapons in confronting the Zionist entity, which we ought to maintain to prevent Israel's economic development and foil its ambitions', and proposed that the boycott be tightened in sympathy with the victims of the *intifada*.[9]

However it was not until the early 1990s that they started to perceive of the boycott not only as a negative means, but as a positive means for forcing Israel to comply with certain Arab demands, such as a full Israeli withdrawal from all the Arab territories occupied by it,[10] or its recognition of Palestinian rights.[11] Explaining his country's policy towards the primary boycott in November 1991, Ibrahim al-

Ghanem, Director General of Kuwait's Customs Authority, stated that 'the (primary) boycott ... is linked to the peace settlement. Ending the boycott is an important card which will be used as an incentive to push the peace process'.[12]

Two years later the Secretary General of the Arab League, Esmet Abdel Meguid, wrote to US Senators Lautenberg and Grassley, in reply to a letter expressing 'profound disappointment' at the Arab League's unwillingness to lift the boycott, that 'the boycott is a legitimate and defensive instrument of diplomacy ... [it] is entirely linked to the "no peace" situation, that exists between the Arab World and Israel ... I am astonished to witness your calls for ending the boycott *before* the ending of occupation of Arab territories ... as well as *before* the achievement of the national rights of the Palestinian people. Normalization cannot precede the accomplishment of substantive progress on all tracks.'[13]

In other words it was only in the early 1990s that the Arabs started to perceive their boycott of Israel in the way other sender states perceive economic sanctions which they impose against target states – namely as a means of getting the latter to change or modify their policies.[14]

Justification of the Boycott as a Defensive Measure

After 1948 the Arabs started to justify the boycott of Israel on the grounds that, since the aim of the Jewish state (in their view) was to dominate the Middle East, politically, economically and culturally, for the attainment of which purpose it used a 'systematic policy of force' accompanied by a 'systematic rejection of international law', a state of war existed in which the boycott was one of the means used by the Arabs to defend themselves.[15] Some actually regarded the boycott as the most important weapon in the Arab arsenal.[16]

The 'Principles of the Arab Boycott of Israel', as published in 1961, *inter alia* stated that 'The Arab boycott is a defensive measure meant for the protection of Arab security and economy against the aggressive means and economy of Israel.'[17] Some Arab commentators attributed to it even greater importance, claiming that it influenced Arab life politically, economically and psychologically.[18]

Arab writers explained that the aim of 'Zionist industry' was to flood the Arabs' markets with its products, thereby destroying the development of Arab industries and achieving economic dominance within these markets. In total disregard of the Labor-Zionist ethos and much of both the pre- and post- 1948 reality, one writer claimed that: 'the Jews came to Palestine with the hope of turning it into an industrial and a financial centre which would control the economies of the Middle East, and thereby making profits of millions ... No Jew came to Palestine in order to work, but just to become a work overseer.'[19]

Totally innocent statements by Israeli leaders and diplomats were brought as 'proof' for the existence of a Zionist plot of economic domination. One such statement was made by Dr Chaim Weizmann, the first President of Israel, who spoke of Israel becoming the 'Switzerland of the Middle East', and supplying the needs of all the far-flung markets of the Middle East. Another was a speech given in 1952 by Abba Eban, the Israeli Ambassador to the US and permanent representative to the UN, in which he called for an end to the Arab boycott, and the establishment of trading links between Israel and the Arab states, involving Israeli purchases of raw materials from the Arabs and sales of industrial goods to them. The Arabs found further support for their contention in a declaration issued by the Rand Corporation in the US to the effect that Israel had ambitions to attain economic superiority in the Middle East, and that this superiority would turn the questions of political borders and the size of the country into secondary issues.[20]

A statement widely circulated in the US by the General Union of the Arab Chambers of Commerce in the 1950s, on the purpose and regulations of the Arab boycott, expressed this approach in the following terms: 'The Arabs are certain that the aggressive and dynamic Zionist State of Israel is planning to expand further at the expense of Arab lands, and to turn more Arabs into refugees. This State even hopes to dominate economically wherever it finds itself unable to dominate politically ... The Arabs are determined to frustrate this plan of aggression. They are determined to defend themselves, their homes and their normal living. They are therefore doing no more than trying to deny Israel that economic power which might enable it to realize a new step in its attempt to achieve its distorted dream of domination.' The boycott is further described as a 'legitimate and purely defensive measure'.[21]

Israel did not usually try to convince the Arabs that such fears were totally unfounded, under the assumption that it was nothing but propaganda which the Arabs themselves did not really believe. However, on the rare occasions when it did try to influence Arab public opinion, the efforts proved futile. Thus, in 1956 an Egyptian journalist, Ibrahim Izzat, invited to spend two weeks in Israel as a guest of the Israeli government, reported after leaving Israel that Israel's aim was economic domination of the Middle East, and that if peace were to be concluded between the Arabs and Israel, the latter would flood the Arab markets with goods to such an extent that most Arab industries would perish.[22]

On 9 June 1960 President Gamal Abdel Nasser of Egypt declared at a press conference, held at the conclusion of a state visit to Greece, that Israel's goal of increasing its population to four million must inevitably lead to the continuation of its expansionist policy. In fact in the early years every Israeli move – such as the utilization of Jordan River waters for irrigation, the struggle for the right of passage through the Suez Canal and the Gulf of Aqaba, or the establishment of diplomatic and economic relations with Asian and African countries – were perceived by the Arabs as constituting part of an Israeli masterplan for expansion, and the boycott as a means of thwarting Israel's ambitions.

In 1970 a Palestinian researcher in Beirut followed a similar line of argumentation. 'It is, perhaps, not generally realized that the Zionist invasion of Palestine does not aim only at the military and political domination of Palestinian territory but also at the regional economic domination which alone, in the long run, can secure the final consolidation of the usurpation of Palestinian territory', Amer A. Sharif wrote. 'Having at their disposal all the material and technological superiority of Western capitalism, the Zionist hope – through the *"pax Israeliana"* they want to impose on the Middle East – to conquer large Arab markets which are still widely under-exploited. Only thus can the huge investments made in Israel, thanks to Western aid, become really profitable. It is in this context that we can explain the yearly conferences of pro-Zionist Jewish millionaires which have been regularly convened in Israel since the June 1967 war, the war having given the hope of seeing military conquest eventually turned into economic domination.

'To resist this aggressiveness, which was already obvious even before the creation of the state of Israel, the Arabs have developed a general boycott, economic, financial, and commercial, prohibiting all relations, not only with Israeli interests, but also with firms of any type, whatever their geographical location, which conduct business with Israel.'[23]

The fear of Israeli economic domination is still prevalent, and those opposed to the lifting of the boycott and enabling Israel to join a Middle East economic grouping, invoke this fear to justify their position. Just before the signing of the Declaration of Principles between Israel and the PLO an Arab League official expressed the following opinion: 'Israel is much more advanced than Arab countries and its industrial production is huge compared with that in Arab states. Ending the boycott means that Israel will find a vast outlet for its products, and Israeli companies or firms related to Israel can set up industrial projects in Arab states. This will hit Arab industries as they will be less competitive. I think Arabs will pay the price of removing the boycott.'[24]

Half a year later the chairman of Saudi Arabia's Federation of Chambers of Commerce and Industry, Abdul Rahman Bin Ali al-Juraisi, stated that the Gulf states should reject the idea of a Middle East common market, which was being advocated by Israel after the Madrid Conference, since such a common market would only work to Israel's advantage. A leading Kuwaiti economist, Jassim al-Sa'adoun, reconfirmed in a lecture in Abu Dhabi that a Middle East economic grouping that would include Israel would result in Israel dominating Arab trade and replacing business centres such as Dubai, Bahrain and Lebanon.[25]

But not all the Arab economists fear Israeli domination. Thus the Egyptian economist Sa'id al-Najar explained in a paper written in the beginning of 1994 that the fear that Israel will dominate the Arab economies had no basis in economic realities. On the contrary, he argued, it was Israel that had reason to fear a take-over of the Israeli economy by the Gulf states. However, he too objected to the establishment of a Middle East common market, which he felt was not in the interest of the Arab states.[26]

The Legality of the Boycott

The Arab states have always found it of the greatest importance to justify the boycott on legal terms. The specific arguments used by them have been dealt with in great detail in Chapter 3 which analyzes the legal aspects of the boycott. Briefly, however, it may be noted that the basis for the arguments in favour of its legality are the general principles of international law, the Charter of the UN and various international agreements, and the main argument is that the Arabs are defending their legitimate rights against Israeli aggression, illegal acts and refusal to comply with various UN resolutions.

The Arab Denial of the More Objectionable Aspects of the Boycott

One of the curious aspects of the Arab boycott of Israel has been that despite its aggressive and non-compromising nature, Arab spokesmen have gone to a lot of trouble to make it sound less threatening and objectionable. For example Fuad K. Suleiman argued in 1976 that the boycott was not a blockade, quarantine or embargo, pointing out that no Israeli ports had been blockaded by Arab ships or armed forces.[27]

However, the strongest Arab denials regarding the true nature of the boycott concerned accusations that the boycott was directed as much against the Jews as it was against Israel. Jewish businessmen would only be hurt, the Arabs argued, if they supported Israel. In February 1975, in an interview with the *Middle East Economic Digest*, Mohammed Mahgoub stated that 'We don't differentiate between one race or nationality and the other. A company is blacklisted because it plays a role in helping Israel's economic, industrial or military efforts ... To prove my point there are many firms owned by Jews that operate freely in the Arab world, while there are others owned by Moslems or Christians that are blacklisted because they deal with Israel.'[28]

In a letter dated 31 August 1975, sent to the New York office of the National Association of Securities Dealers Inc., Mahgoub once again stated that 'the boycott authorities do not discriminate among persons on the basis of their religion or nationality, they rather do so on the basis of their partiality or impartiality to Israel and Zionism ... [the boycott's] purpose is to protect the security of the Arab states from the danger of the Zionist cancer ... to prevent the domination of Zionist capital over Arab national economics, and to prevent the economic force of the enemy... from expansion at the expense of the interests of the Arabs'.[29] A year later Mahgoub further elaborated on this point stating that if the owners or those controlling foreign companies or firms 'have Zionist inclinations, such as continuous contributions of large amounts to Israel or other Zionist organizations, or such as joining Zionist organizations or societies, or such as working openly against Arab interests and promoting the interests of Israel or world Zionism ... no relations will be established with such companies, because it was actually proved by experience that such companies take advantage of those relations in order to damage Arab interests and propagate world Zionism'.[30]

As proof for their claim that the Arab boycott was not anti-Jewish, Arab sources constantly cited statements to this effect made by American officials in the years 1975–76. For example, in a statement he made on 11 December 1975 to the Subcommittee on International Trade and Commerce, James Baker, who at the time was Under-Secretary of Commerce, accepted the Arab claim that the boycott was not discriminatory on religious grounds, and on this basis expressed opposition to proposed amendments to the Export Administration Act (EAA), that would have prohibited American compliance with the boycott.[31] Some of the other statements quoted were one by Secretary of the Treasury William Simon on 6 September 1976 to the effect that: 'According to the principles underlying the Arab boycott of Israel, this boycott is not based on discrimination against foreign companies and American citizens on account of religion or race', and one by Secretary of Commerce Juanita Drepps on 11 June, 1976 that: 'The Arab boycott is one of the aspects of the Middle East conflict. It is not in its present form, based on religious or ethnic criteria.'[32]

While denying that the Arab boycott was anti-Jewish, some Arab analysts had an explanation for why Israel claimed that the boycott was motivated by racism. They argued that in economic terms Israel had no chance of winning its battle against the Arabs, and that therefore it resorted to propaganda in which claims of anti-Semitism played a major role.[33] Other Arab analysts countered the accusations about the anti-Jewish nature of the boycott by arguing that it was Israel that was a racist state, invoking Israel's Law of Return and Nationality Law, which clearly discriminate in favour of Jews, as proof for their claim.

In objective terms, however, it was impossible to deny that the boycott was far from partial to Jews. The Arabs appeared to take it for granted that every Jew was automatically an active supporter of Israel, unless he proved otherwise, and the request for 'non-Jew' certificates from companies with which they did business, was a common practice. In its August 1957 issue *Fortune* magazine reported that companies were receiving questionnaires from Cairo seeking information on whether their firms had Jewish owners or shareholders, the extent of Jewish ownership, relations with Jewish contractors, membership of Jews on company boards and the number of Jewish employees and the position held by them.[34] Had the Arabs honestly made a distinction between Jews in general and supporters of Israel in particular, they should have requested non-Zionist declarations, not non-Jew certificates.

In the US there were numerous cases of firms, that were targeted by the Arab boycott for no other reason than the Jewish religious affiliations of their directors. According to an editorial dated 14 February 1975 in the *Wall Street Journal*, which had been written against the background of a banking scandal involving the boycotting of Jewish owned banks participating as underwriters in international loan syndicates, 'the blacklisting of these firms appears less to be an attempt to undermine Israel than an attempt to inject anti-semitism into Western business practice ... The Arabs have had trouble distinguishing these two purposes throughout their 30-year old economic boycott of businesses with ties to Israel.'[35]

The most frequently cited case of the boycott's anti-Jewish undertones occurred in Great Britain in 1963 when Lord Mancroft, a prominent Jewish director of the Norwich Union Insurance Company who had served in the British government in the 1950s, was forced to resign his post as chairman of the Norwich Union Board as a result of Arab pressure.[36] In the Netherlands the demand for 'non-Jew' certificates was so common that submission to such demands was outlawed in 1981.[37]

It should be noted that Saudi Arabia and some of the other Gulf states never concealed their anti-Jewish biases. Companies working on contract in Saudi Arabia were told not to bring in either Jewish personnel or products made by Jewish firms,[38] and Jews were generally unwelcome, even as US servicemen, or as diplomats.

Another common Arab claim was that the boycott was directed at Israel only and not at other states. If foreign firms were boycotted, they argued, it was only to the extent that they strengthened the Israeli aggression. Ordinary trade with Israel did not necessarily fall within this definition, or lead to the firms involved being boycotted.[39] Appearing in 1978 before the British House of Lords Select Committee, which was established to consider the passing of a Foreign Boycotts Bill, Mahgoub emphasized that 'the Arab boycott does not apply to normal trade with Israel, i.e. selling completely finished foreign goods to Israel other than those beneficial to Israel's war effort'. Only companies that performed 'any action in Israel, which might support its economy, develop its industry or increase the efficiency of its war effort', were liable to be blacklisted.[40]

The Arab Reaction to Anti-boycott Measures taken by Third States and to Israel's Anti-boycott Campaign

Since the Arabs believed that their boycott of Israel was perfectly justified, they regarded any interference by foreign governments in the implementation of the boycott as an outrage, and efforts to limit the economic and political effects of the boycott by means of legislation in foreign countries in general and in the US in particular, as a 'Zionist counter attack'.[41]

When the British government made its displeasure known with regards to successful Arab efforts to get Lord Mancroft to resign from the board of directors of the Norwich Union in 1963 because of his religion, the Arab League announced that British 'interference' with the boycott would force Arab countries to reconsider their economic ties with the United Kingdom. It added that a Foreign Office statement, which had been issued against the background of the Norwich Union affair to express displeasure with Arab interference in domestic British affairs, constituted 'support of the Zionist viewpoint against a system dictated by the legitimate right of self-defence against Zionist aggression'.[42]

Fifteen years later, against the background of the Foreign Boycotts bill, which was being considered in Parliament, the Commissioner General of the CBO in Damascus warned that enactment of the bill would 'jeopardize the interests of the UK because the long-lasting, excellent and developing economic and financial relations between the UK and the Arab world will face a great relapse'. The Secretary General of the Joint Arab–British Chamber of Commerce went further, stating that if enacted the bill would 'effectively put an end to all trade between the UK and the Arab world'.[43]

In the case of the US the Arabs were inclined to attribute to Israel demonic powers. For example, Muhammad 'Abd al-'Aziz Ahmad and Muhammad al-Jabali argued that the decision as to who would be the presidential candidates in the US is determined in Tel Aviv.[44]

Even though the Arabs regarded the 1965 amendment to the US Foreign Aid law, which expressed congressional disapproval for the Arab boycott,[45] as a Zionist success, Arab sources commented at the time that the wording of the amendment was moderate.[46]

However, by the mid-1970s the legislation being considered by Congress was much more serious. Now the Arabs argued that the Zionists were determined to disrupt the development of economic ties between the US and the Arab states, which had gained great economic power in the aftermath of the 1973 oil crisis. According to certain Arab sources, the Zionists were spreading the misconception that the Arabs were so dependent on the US economically, that the latter had no reason to fear any retaliation from the Arabs in reaction to its passing anti-boycott legislation. President Carter had been sufficiently influenced by this, they added, that during his 1976 election campaign he had promised to put an end to the boycotting of American companies by the Arab states.[47] Dr Mohammed Aziz Shukri, Legal Advisor to the Secretary General of the Arab League, even suggested that the constitutionality of the American anti-boycott legislation should be tested.[48]

According to some Arab spokesmen the American anti-boycott legislation of the mid-1970s had an adverse effect on the level of US–Arab trade, and one source even predicted that by the end of the 1970s it would decrease by 50 per cent.[49] US trade figures indicate that trade with the Arab world actually rose in the years following the implementation of the legislation.[50] One reason for this, as suggested by the Arabs themselves, was that it was due to the fact that since the legislation was not enforceable outside the US, the subsidiaries of American-owned multinational corporations were not bound by its provisions and ignored it.[51] Another explanation might be that, had the legislation not existed, trade between the US and the Arab oil-producing states would have risen even more sharply in those years.

Curiously enough supporters of the Arab boycott were still arguing against the American anti-boycott legislation in the 1990s. Commenting on a new anti-boycott bill which had been tabled in the House of Representatives in the beginning of 1993, *Arab News* argued that if the legislation, which proposed penalizing countries that gave in to the secondary boycott, was passed, this would be tantamount to the US declaring a 'secondary boycott against countries that followed the secondary boycott against Israel. This', the paper concluded, 'is just another example of the false logic that the Israeli lobby is able to sell to Congress.'[52]

In the late 1980s Arab observers were still arguing that anti-boycott and anti-discriminatory legislation passed in Europe was part of the Zionist anti-Arab campaign carried out with the aid of Jewish wealth, and described such legislation as anti-Arab and in itself discriminatory.[53] However, the Arab analysis of the policies of the various European governments towards the boycott concluded that even those states that expressed reservations about it, were not inclined to intervene in order to prevent its implementation, and some, including Norway, Sweden and Britain, were even actively involved in trying to get the names of companies owned by their nationals off the blacklist.[54]

Not surprisingly, the Arabs were pleased with the policies of those states that were not only unwilling to take effective moves against the boycott, but were not even willing to express their reservations, such as Japan or (until the late 1980s) the countries of the Eastern bloc.[55]

The Effectiveness of the Boycott

To what extent did the Arabs really believe that the boycott was an effective means in their attempt to liquidate the Jewish state? The evidence indicates that for many years they did. This belief rested on the premise that Israel is an artificial state, supported by foreign funds, and that the boycott would serve to bring about its speedy economic collapse. In 1956 an Egyptian monthly, which reflected government positions, wrote that as long as the boycott would continue to be applied, the collapse of the state of Israel was inevitable.[56] Three years later the official journal of the Egyptian police wrote that 'Israel cannot be destroyed by force and therefore must be destroyed economically. If the Arabs can prevent Israel's economic expansion', it concluded, 'they will hasten its end.'[57]

In 1965 this was still an accepted line of argumentation. In the preface to his book published in that year, 'Ali 'Abd al'Rahman 'Awf noted that the Arab boycott would bring about the collapse of the State of Israel. 'Our economic siege of Israel', he wrote, 'is slowly strangling it ... If the [boycott] is enforced carefully ... it will lead to [Israel's] destruction.'[58]

While one may argue that the Arab expectation that the boycott would help destroy Israel was not realistic, they certainly had reason to believe that the boycott would cause it economic hardships. The Arab states believed that the primary boycott, which they regarded as a passive boycott, hurt Israel by cutting it off from its natural sources for raw materials and foodstuffs, and from the closest markets for its products, which resulted in both Israeli exports and imports being more expensive owing to transportation costs. This they argued made Israel less competitive on world markets and increased the cost of living in Israel.[59] In other words they attributed Israel's balance of payments and inflation problems to the primary boycott.

The secondary and tertiary boycotts, which they regarded as active boycotts, were designed to block the development of economic relations between Israel and companies from third countries and prevent the flow of foreign capital and know-how to Israel. This was to be achieved primarily by blacklisting offending companies, and here the Arabs relied on these companies' profit motive, and the much greater potential of the Arab market.[60] The fact that many foreign companies gave in to the boycott proved that the Arabs were at least partially correct in their expectations. Two early examples from the 1950s were those of the Dutch electrical appliances manufacturer Philips and the French car manufacturer Renault, both of which backed off from investments in Israel.[61] Nevertheless, Ja'far Tah Hamza, who wrote about the boycott in 1960, claimed that in terms of money flowing into Israel the secondary and tertiary boycotts benefited it. While not denying that the boycott managed to keep a good deal of foreign investment away from Israel, he argued that contributions from world Jewry and foreign aid, which were encouraged by the boycott, outweighed the loss to Israel of foreign investment.[62]

Over the years many of Israel's diplomatic initiatives were perceived by the Arabs as stemming from its efforts to break loose from the effects of the Arab boycott. In the early 1960s it was Israel's economic and technical aid program in Asia and Africa that caught their attention. Egyptian President Nasser defined this program as 'a new form of colonialism', and 'the biggest hoax of our time', for which he blamed the former colonial powers.[63] The Cairo daily *Al-Akhbar* wrote that: 'Israel's penetration into the new states ... is a means to break (the Arab) blockade and to reduce its effect. If Israel will succeed in bolstering its relations with these states and these peoples, it will find a way to undermine our boycott. Thus we would have a useless and ineffective measure against Israel. This is a very grave matter in our eyes.'[64]

The Arabs also viewed Israel's efforts in the course of the 1960s to become associated with the European Common Market as a means of extricating itself from the effects of the boycott. Though Israel's chances of attaining associate status in the Community were negligible (for reasons unrelated to the Arab–Israeli conflict), the Arabs took the prospect very seriously, and appeared to believe that if Israel became affiliated with the Community most of its economic problems, including unemployment, insufficient investment and inflation – all problems which Arab observers were inclined to attribute to the boycott – would be resolved. They were also concerned that such affiliation would result in the European states being more inclined to support Israel in the Arab–Israeli conflict. It was for this reason that the Arab states made great diplomatic efforts to convince the Community to prevent Israel's becoming an associate.[65]

The 'open bridges' policy implemented by Israel following the Six Day War, which enabled goods and persons to cross the Jordan River between the West Bank and Jordan over two bridges, was similarly perceived by the Arabs, though here their dilemma was between preventing Israel from circumventing the primary boycott and the economic welfare of the Palestinians in the territories.

Israel's peace initiatives over the years were also presented by the

Arabs as a reaction to the economic problems that the boycott caused it.[66] Hamza enumerated the economic benefits that Israel could gain from the cancellation of the boycott, as follows:

• profits from intra-regional trading which would be attracted to Israel as a trading centre;
• transit trade;
• the removal of many of the barriers from Israel's trade with the rest of the world;
• contracts and commercial relations previously denied it;
• the flow of foreign capital for investment purposes, including investment by major corporations which would decide to construct subsidiaries or regional centers in Israel.[67]

Writing in 1970, Amer A. Sharif, a Palestinian researcher, had no doubt that the boycott had 'considerably hampered the development of the Israeli economy'. However, he admitted 'there is as yet no precise knowledge of the extent to which the boycott is effective. We do not know how great are the losses and distortions caused to the Israeli economy, the importance of its dissuasive effect on firms maintaining relations with Israel or intending to do so, or the side effects, positive or negative, which it has occasioned to Arab economies.' His proposal was that the Arabs conduct extensive statistical studies in order 'to gather the necessary data to gauge the effectiveness of present Arab boycott methods and thereby to increase the power of this economic weapon and make it both more costly still for Israel and its foreign partners, and more beneficial to the Arab economies – i.e. more of an incentive to their industrial development.'

Sharif proposed that this be accompanied by two measures. 'firstly, there must be a gradual escalation of boycott activities, an advance from the concept of boycotting foreign firms dealing with Israel to the more comprehensive one of boycotting the economies of countries which maintain relations with Israel. Secondly, inter-Arab economic cooperation must be developed much more rapidly. This will strengthen the economic independence of the Arab countries and consequently make it easier for them to advance from the first type of boycott to the second.'[68]

However, by mid-1975 Arab observers were having serious doubts as to whether the boycott was an effective strategic weapon, for which they blamed the fact that it played a relatively limited role within the context of global Arab policies, and at the same time was not an integral part of these policies. The 1973 oil embargo was presented as a rare example of where the boycott had been used as an effective strategic weapon.[69]

Arab Thoughts on How to Make the Boycott More Effective

Clearly, all the activities of the CBO in Damascus and the meetings of the Arab League which dealt with the boycott of Israel were constantly directed towards making its application more effective. However after Israel embarked on its major campaign against the boycott following the 1973 October War,[70] new ideas were considered, especially in the sphere of information.

During the 31st conference of the Arab League, it was suggested that in order to make the boycott more effective Arab information efforts abroad regarding the boycott be increased, and that the Arab public at home be encouraged to cooperate with its implementation. The Conference recommended that delegations be sent to the Maghreb, the Gulf States and the Eastern Arab states to implement the latter goal.

In 1977 the Arab League Council adopted resolution 3553, which called for the use of all means of mass communications to explain the Arab position to counteract Israel's anti-boycott campaign. All the regional offices of the Arab League were used for this purpose, as were Arab diplomats and other Arab representatives, who met with senior officials in various countries where the Israeli campaign was being felt. In these meetings the Arabs both explained their point of view and tried to convince their interlocutors that if they would insist on fighting the boycott, as Israel was trying to get them to do, their country's economic interests would suffer.[71]

Those observers who felt that the problem with the Arab boycott was that it did not constitute part of a complete strategy, pointed out that the oil embargo in 1973/74, and the threat of moving petro-dollars from one Western financial centre to another for political reasons thereafter, constituted a 'correct' use of the boycott weapon. It was suggested that in order to make more effective use of the boycott as a strategic weapon, the Arab states should establish new institutions, with the authority to take political decisions; reduce the size of the existing boycott apparatus; avoid attempts to apply the boycott to new regions; examine the influence of Israeli activities in the spheres of banking, commerce and marketing; employ professional propaganda to explain the boycott; and formulate an investment policy which would take political as well as economic factors into account.[72]

Cracks in the Boycott

It was not, however, Israel's efforts to break loose of the effects of the boycott that worried the boycott's staunch supporters most. They were more concerned with cracks in the determination of various Arab states to continue to implement it.

How did the Arabs explain these cracks? Hamza argued that the profit motive among the Arab oil-producing states would finally neutralize the boycott's effect.[73] In 1989 the Legal Advisor to the Secretary General of the Arab League, Mohammed Aziz Shukri, argued that the boycott definitely was not intended to harm the Arab states economically. What he was speaking about was the reason for why the Arabs applied the boycott more leniently in certain spheres such as hotels, oil, nuclear power, shipping and airlines.[74] There is no doubt that Arab businessmen frequently felt that the boycott was adversely affecting their interests, which explains many of the breaches.

While Hamza considered the Arab oil-producing states to be those most likely to want their governments to ignore the boycott, in fact it was usually businessmen in less prosperous Arab states who felt most harmed by its application. Thus, for example, five months before the outbreak of the Six Day War, the Lebanese paper *Al-Hayyat* reported that the representatives of the (Christian) Falange parties in the Lebanese parliament had confronted their government with the following analysis:

   a. The boycott of Israel is a principle accepted by the Lebanese, and it is not subject to debate. Thus, any discussion about the boycott does not question the principle of the boycott, and evolves only around the means for implementing it and its results, both with regards to Lebanon and to the Palestinian problem;

b. The goal of the boycott is to tighten the noose around Israel's neck, and not that of the sender states – especially Lebanon. The boycott has lost much of its effectiveness, and the damage caused to Lebanon frequently surpasses that caused to Israel;

c. Trade and services constitute a major source of income for every country, and in the case of Lebanon they constitute the backbone of the economy. The boycott of Israel causes Lebanon special economic problems. At the same time it is impossible to implement its principles effectively, because the Boycott Office (in Lebanon) has a staff of only one official, and no matter how great an expert he is, he cannot possibly deal with the issue alone;

d. As a member of the Arab League Lebanon has undertaken various obligations with regards to the boycott, but Lebanon has rights as well and thus far only the obligations have manifested themselves. As a result Lebanon has been has been forced to sacrifice some of its basic interests, without any return.[75]

As indicated elsewhere,[76] there were always some cracks in the implementation of the boycott, which gradually increased following the Six Day War when Israel implemented its 'open bridges' policy towards the East, then in 1975 when it opened the 'good fence' to the North, and finally as a natural consequence of the various stages of the Middle East peace process. These growing cracks were clearly not viewed with favour by those who objected to the boycott being lifted, either before a satisfactory settlement with Israel was attained, or absolutely. Thus, for example, Israel's open bridges policy following the Six Day War raised a serious discussion in Arab quarters. On the one hand it was argued that the West Bank had traditionally been attached economically to Jordan and it was not desirable that these ties should now be severed. However, there was also the fear that Israel would take advantage of the opening to Jordan to export Israeli goods to the Arab world. The change in the make-up of the products moving from the West Bank eastward seemed to indicate that this was indeed the case.[77] The outcome was a call to strengthen the supervision of the bridges to prevent Israel's profiting from this policy,[78] but not to cause the collapse of the West Bank economy by closing the bridges altogether.[79]

There is no doubt, however, that the peace agreement between Egypt and Israel, which included an Egyptian undertaking to lift the boycott and cancel its boycott legislation, was the first really serious blow to the boycott. In his series of articles on the boycott in the Qatari daily *Al-Wattan* in January 1997, the Egyptian writer Shafiq Ahmad Ali made it clear that in his eyes it was the Camp David Accords which 'constituted the first nail in the coffin of the boycott'.[80] Ali, representing those in the Arab world who continue to object to any reconciliation with Israel, describes Sadat as 'one of the most questionable persons in the world', the friend of 'Israeli and American agents'. Despite the activities of these agents, he added, 'the people in Egypt did not buy the agreement, and the proof is that 20 years after the agreement was signed, the people in Egypt still object to any effort to normalize the relations'.[81] In other words, Ali argues simultaneously that the boycott is dead (because of what Sadat did), and that is not (because the people object to normalization).

The reaction of those forces within the Arab world responsible for the implementation of the boycott to the growing cracks in its application has, not surprisingly, also been ambivalent, and they have frequently denied that such cracks were actually visible. As late as 1994, when there was already a significant amount of trade going on between Israel and numerous Arab states, the CBO in Damascus denied that there was any weakening in the application of the boycott. On 16 September 1994 Zuhair Aquil, the Boycott Commissioner, stated on Damascus radio that no Arab state has any form of trade exchange with Israel, and that despite reports in the international media 'the Arab boycott of Israel is still effective'.[82]

Nevertheless, in face of growing evidence that various Arab states were not implementing the boycott as stringently as previously, and statements by the Gulf States that they would no longer apply the secondary and tertiary boycotts, the Arab League issued a statement in Cairo on 2 October 1994 to the effect that 'the Arab boycott of Israel was imposed by a decision taken by the Arab League Council and it is up to the Arab League Council to call it off'.[83]

Cancellation of the Boycott

Clearly, as long as the goal of the boycott was to destroy Israel, the Arabs never considered the conditions for cancelling it. However, much more interesting was the fact that those Arab leaders who were willing to make peace with Israel did not view the boycott as a problem, and if it had not been for Israel's insistence, the boycott would not have been mentioned in the various peace agreements signed between Israel and its neighbours. Thus, when Egyptian President Anwar Sadat was asked about the boycott by an Israeli journalist during his visit to Jerusalem in November 1977, he noted that the boycott was a secondary issue which would be automatically resolved once the primary issues were resolved.[84] Nevertheless, on Israel's insistence, the Egyptian Parliament cancelled the boycott law of 1955 in 1980.[85]

In fact all the agreements reached between Israel and its neighbours were followed by the development of direct economic relations of one sort or another, which simply made the boycott redundant in these particular cases. The issue of the cancellation of the boycott did however come up in the statements of the spokesmen of Arab states and organizations which were already willing to accept the peace process in principle, but were either still arguing that the conditions for making peace with Israel were not yet ripe, or had not yet reached the point of actually accepting the practical implications of peacemaking.

When, following the Gulf War of January/February 1991, the G-7 proposed that the boycott be cancelled in return for an end to Jewish settlement activities in the West Bank and Gaza Strip, this approach was embraced by several Arab states, including Egypt, Syria, Lebanon and Saudi Arabia. On 20 July 1991 Riyadh announced that it would suspend its boycott of Israel if Jewish settlement of the occupied territories, including East Jerusalem, was frozen.[86]

Arab League officials rejected this formula. Soon after the G-7 proposal was issued Adnan Omran, Arab League Assistant Secretary General for Political Affairs, sharply criticized the proposal. 'There is no balance in the G-7 statement, which does not realize the importance or reason behind the Arab boycott', he said, adding that 'the boycott resulted from a cause which is the state of occupation by Israel of Arab lands. With the end of the cause, there will be no reason to continue the boycott and any change in this equation will lead to Israeli rejection of peace efforts and will not achieve peace.' He presented the traditional Arab position that the economic boycott was the 'Arabs' legal method of defending themselves against an occupation, which continued to defy and challenge the international community'. His conclusion was that 'linking the Jewish settlements with the Arab Boycott will only strengthen Israeli stubbornness and hardline attitudes towards international peace efforts'.[87]

Nevertheless, even some of the most rigid Arab League spokesmen were apparently willing to accept the proposition that once Israel fulfilled certain conditions the boycott could be cancelled. For example, the 37th Conference of the Arab boycott liaison officers concluded from the fact that both Israel and the US included the cancellation of the boycott among their conditions for a Middle East peace, that the boycott was one of the most important cards that the Arabs had to achieve political gains in the process.[88]

On 8 September 1993, several days before the signing of the DoP between Israel and the PLO, the following analysis was offered by an Arab boycott official in Abu Dhabi: 'Israel should not expect the boycott to be removed altogether just because it recognizes the Palestine Liberation Organization and grants self-rule to Palestinians in Gaza and Jericho', he said. 'However I expect the indirect boycott to be eased gradually, not under a collective decision, but as an individual initiative. I think this will encourage Israel to relax its position and offer more for peace. I do not think there will be any decision to end the direct boycott until its cause – the Israeli occupation of Arab land – disappears ... As was the case with South Africa, I believe the taboo of dealing with Israel will break gradually.'[89]

Towards the end of September the Secretary General of the Gulf Cooperation Council, Sheikh Fahim Bin Sultan al-Qassimi, stated that normal ties with Israel, including an end to the Arab boycott, would be possible only when Israel withdrew from occupied Arab lands. This was also the position expressed by the Secretary General of the Arab League, who said that the ending of the Arab boycott would have to be balanced by the achievement of a just and comprehensive peace on all Arab fronts.[90]

Tishrin, a Syrian state-owned paper, adopted a more rigid position, even though it too seemed to accept the premise that the boycott could be abolished if Israel fulfilled all of the Arabs's just demands. In an editorial on 26 September 1993, it wrote that 'The Arabs are requested to tighten rather than abolish the boycott against Israel because two years of [peace] talks on the Middle East in Washington produced nothing due to Israeli rejection of the basis of just and comprehensive peace.'[91]

In Cairo Tala'at Hamed, an Arab League official, told a Reuters correspondent that the boycott's goals 'are political before they are economic ... As long as Israel occupies Arab lands and continues its non-humanitarian practices against the Arab citizens there and does not implement the UN resolutions on their rights, the boycott will continue'. He added that it would be possible to review the indirect boycott 'if there is progress achieved on all levels in the peace talks'.[92]

It should be noted that even though American pressure on the Arab states by the Clinton Administration to lift the boycott of Israel has hastened the process of its being less stringently applied, these states have resisted its complete removal with the argument that the boycott is one of the last cards left in their hands to force Israel to withdraw from occupied territories.[93]

Three years later this was still the position held by most of the Arab states. Thus on 31 March 1997 the Arab foreign ministers, meeting in Cairo, decided that the normalization in the relations of the Arab states with Israel should be stopped until such time as Israel abided by the principle of 'land for peace', and that the primary boycott against Israel should be preserved until a comprehensive and just peace was attained in the region.[94]

The Palestinians in the territories, who as a result of the objective conditions are almost totally dependent on the Israeli economy and consequently cannot afford to boycott Israel,[95] have nevertheless also conditioned the cancellation of the boycott by the Arab states on Israel's fulfilling certain conditions. Thus for example Samir Abdallah, a Palestinian delegate to the multilateral talks on economic development, explained at a press conference on the economic implications of the DoP in Jerusalem, which took place in October 1993, that 'From our side why we can't ... ask the Arabs or the Arab countries to remove the boycott [is because] it will be badly understood.' The problem, he explained was that the closure imposed by Israel on the territories since March 1993 (as a reaction to a wave of stabbings of Israelis by Palestinians), constituted a boycott which effectively prevented trade with Israel and Palestinian workers working in Israel, and under these circumstances there was no reason why the Palestinians should fight against the boycott of Israel.[96] In other words, if Israel would avoid what the Palestinians viewed as a boycott of the territories, they would support the lifting of the Arab boycott of Israel.

Writing in the beginning of 1994 the Egyptian economist Sa'id al-Najar suggested that three conditions should be fulfilled before the Arabs agreed to cancel the boycott:

1) The Gaza–Jericho Agreement must enable the Palestinian people, after an interim period, to return to itself its rights, including the right of self-determination. This means success in the negotiations for all four problems mentioned above (Jerusalem, Jewish settlements in the West Bank and Gaza Strip, refugees and borders).

2) All the standing problems on the Syrian, Lebanese and Jordanian course must be settled, especially Israel's withdrawal from the Golan Heights and what is called the 'security strip' in Southern Lebanon, and the occupied Jordanian lands. [The paper was written before the signing of the Jordanian–Israeli peace agreement – G.F.].

3) The cancellation of the boycott must take place simultaneously by all the Arab states, and it is preferable that this will be done on the basis of a decision by the Arab League, that imposed the boycott in the first place.

Al-Najar added, however, that the three conditions did not have to be fully fulfilled before the lifting of the boycott would begin. 'It is enough if the parties concerned will agree on the principles that will shape the settlement and the time-table for the various stages', he wrote. 'In addition, this should not prevent immediate negotiations on the framework for regional cooperation on specific issues, such as water and the environment, as long as the plan will be implemented after the boycott is cancelled.'[97]

In face of growing evidence that various Arab states were not implementing the boycott as stringently as previously, statements by the Gulf States that they would no longer apply the secondary and tertiary boycotts and the convening of the Casablanca Conference on Economic Cooperation with the participation of Israel and representatives of numerous Arab countries, the Arab League issued a statement in Cairo on 2 October 1994 to the effect that 'the Arab boycott of Israel was imposed by a decision taken by the Arab League Council and it is up to the Arab League Council to call it off'.[98]

There were however individuals and groups who continued to object to the cancellation of the boycott on principle. One of the reactions to the Casablanca Conference was the convention of an unofficial conference in Beirut under the title: 'The Permanent

Conference for Combatting the Zionist Cultural Invasion', with the participation of some 500 delegates. What the organizers believed was at stake was the Arab culture, identity, language, history and civilization, and the Islamic heritage. After two days of discussions, the Conference passed resolutions which *inter alia* declared that 'the Arab–Zionist conflict is about existence – not borders', and rejected the 'principle, details and outcome' of the current peace negotiations, adding that 'all Arab individuals, groups, organizations and institutions that deal or promote dealing with the Zionist entity, must be condemned and ostracized'.[99]

Reporting on the event the Lebanese press argued that the establishment of economic links among all the countries of the region, including Israel, before a comprehensive and lasting peace settlement was achieved between Israel and its Arab neighbours was 'obviously unrealistic'. The reports also expressed the fear that by normalizing economic relations with Israel, the Arabs would begin the process of cancelling their own identity.[100]

Notes

1. See comments by Hani al-Hindi, coordinator of a symposium on the Arab Boycott, *Shu'un Falestiniyya*, 46 (June 1975), pp. 132-60.
2. One Arab writer stated in 1965 that 'if the [boycott] is enforced carefully ... it will lead to [Israel's] destruction ... It is clear that the boycott is the most efficient weapon against Israel, and that not war and not appeals to the UN will lead to the quick collapse of Israel, but rather the economic siege and the boycott ...' ('Ali Abd Al-Rahman 'Awf, *Isra'il wal-Hisar al-'Arabi* (Arabic) (Israel and the Arab Blockade) (Cairo, 1965), p. 7.
3. Introduction to *The Boycott of Israel – Its Principles and Objectives* (Arabic), Damascus, Central Boycott Office, August 1956, in Meron Medzini (ed.) *Israel's Foreign Relations. Selected Documents 1947–1974* (Jerusalem: Ministry for Foreign Affairs, 1976), p. 280.
4. In the first in a series of article on the boycott published in the Qatari paper *Al-Wattan*, on 1 January, 1997, Shafiq Ahmad Ali wrote: 'In early papers and documents of the Arab League on the boycott issue it was written ... that there was an intension to bring about a freezing of the Israeli economy and its suffocation, and thus bring about a deterioration in the situation of the Jewish state, and then *to pull out the knife, that had been stuck in the back of the Arab nation.*'
5. See, for example, the Alexandria Protocol of 7 October 1944, which was *inter alia* designed to weaken the development of the Jewish economy.

114   *From Boycott to Economic Cooperation*

6. Mundir Sulayman al-Dajani '*Al-Muqat'a al-'Arabiyyha li-Isra'il: Ahdafuha wa-Fa'aliyyatuha*' (Arabic) (The Arab Boycott of Israel: Its Goals and Activities), *Al*-Nadwa (February 1990), pp. 41–2.
7. Article by *Washington Post* correspondent Alex Morris, quoted by *Ma'ariv*, 17 (June 1965).
8. Lieutenant Colonel Yosef, *Halohama Hakalkalit Ha'aravit Neged Yisrael* (The Arab Economic Warfare against Israel), *Ma'archot*, 275 (August 1980), p. 31.
9. Reuters (Damascus), 30 January 1988.
10. It should be noted however that it was never quite clear what they meant by 'Arab territories occupied by Israel' – whether they meant the territories occupied by Israel in 1967, those occupied by it in 1948/49 beyond the territories allotted the Jewish state by the UN partition plan of 1947, or the whole territory of mandatory Palestine.
11. As in the case of the territories, so here it was usually left unclear what rights the Arabs had in mind – whether it was a right to a state, the right to return to the territory of Israel, or the right to sovereignty over the whole of mandatory Palestine.
12. Reuters (Kuwait City), 15 November 1991.
13. *MEED*, 29 November 1993.
14. See for example statement by Syrian Foreign Minister Farouq al-Shar'a at the Arab League Ministerial Council, which met in Cairo at the end of March 1994 (BBC Monitoring Service, 28 March 1994).
15. Other means included the armed conflict, as well as diplomatic and communications boycotts. The diplomatic boycott extended 'to international conferences and organizations where Arab delegates have no contacts with Israeli delegates', and involved the refusal to grant visa or entry permits 'to Israeli delegates attending conferences held in Arab states', or to 'attend regional conferences if Israel is also invited'. The communications boycott involved the prohibition of any air, land or sea communications with Israel, the denial of permission to Israeli aircraft to overfly Arab territory and of flight information, as well as of radio, telephone and postal services (Fuad K. Suleiman in Leila Meo (ed.) *The Arab Boycott of Israel* (Detroit: Association of Arab-American University Graduates, 1976), pp. 24–7).
16. Hanni al-Hindi, op. cit.
17. Al-Dajani, op. cit.
18. Preface by Anis Cha'i, director of the PLO Research Center in Beirut to Juzif Mughayzal, *Al-Muqata'a al-'Arabiyya wal-Qanun al-Dawli* (Arabic) (The Arab Boycott and International Law) (Beirut: M.T.F., Markaz al-Abhath, 1968).
19. 'Awf, op. cit., pp. 7–8.
20. Ja'far Tah Hamza, *Al-Muqata'a al-'Arabiyya li-Isra'il* (Arabic) (The Arab Boycott of Israel) (1973), pp. 215–16.
21. Oded Remba, 'The Arab Boycott: A Study in Total Economic Warfare', *Midstream* (Summer 1960), pp. 48–9.
22. Ibid., p. 49.
23. Amer A. Sharif 'A Statistical Study on the Arab Boycott of Israel', *Monograph Series*, 26 (Beirut: The Institute for Palestine Studies, 1970), p. ix.

24. BBC Monitoring Service (Abu Dhabi), 10 September 1993.
25. Reuters (Abu Dhabi), 30 March 1994 quoting the paper *Al-Khaleej*.
26. Sa'id al-Najar, *Likrat Estrategyat Shalom Aravi* (Towards an Arab Peace Strategy) (Tel-Aviv: The Tami Steinmitz Centre for Peace Research, *Translation Series*, 1), 1994.
27. Fuad K. Suleiman, op. cit., p. 34.
28. Peter Kellner, 'The Boycott – A Two-edged, Fexible and Powerful Weapon', *MEED*, 16 January 1976, p. 4.
29. *The American Boycott and American Business*, Report by the Subcommittee on Oversight and Investigations of the Committee on Interstate and Foreign Commerce, with additional and minority views, House of Representatives, 94th Congress, Second Session, US Government Printing Office (Washington, September 1976), p. 2.
30. Press statement by Mohammed Mahgoub, 'The Nature of the Arab Boycott of Israel', issued in 1976.
31. Roy M. Mersky (ed.), *Conference on Transnational Economic Boycotts and Coercion*, 19–20 February 1976, University of Texas Law School, papers presented at the Conference, Vol. 1 (New York: Oceana Publications, 1978), p. 193. See also Chapter 7, pp. 158–63.
32. These three statements were quoted in an address delivered by the Secretary General of the Arab League, Chedli Klibi, at the opening of the International Symposium on Boycott and Economic Measures in International Conflicts, held in Geneva in June 1987.
33. Mundar Anabtawi, Symposium organized by *Shu'un Filastiniyya* (June 1975), p. 160.
34. Remba, op. cit., p. 46.
35. Mersky, op. cit., p. 348.
36. Terence Prittie and Walter Henry Nelson, *The Economic War Against the Jews* (London: Secker & Warburg, 1978), pp. 60–3. See also Chapter 8.
37. See Chapter 8, pp. 223–6.
38. Sol Stern, 'On and Off the Arabs' List', *The New Republic* 27 (March 1976), p. 9.
39. Mughayzal, op. cit., p. 65.
40. House of Lords Select Committee on the Foreign Boycotts Bill, Vol. 1, Report of Proceedings, HMSO, 28.7.78, paragraph 34. See also Chapter 8.
41. Hamza, op. cit., p. 3.
42. Prittie and Nelson, op. cit., p. 61.
43. Aaron Sarna, *Boycott and Blacklist – A History of Arab Economic Warfare against Israel* (Totowa, NJ: Rowman & Littlefield, 1986), pp. 148–9.
44. Muhammad 'Abd al-'Aziz Ahmad wa-Muhammad al-Jabali, *Al-Difa' al-Iqtisadi Didda al-Atma'al-Istighlaliyaa al-Isra'iliyya* (Arabic) (The Economic Protection from Israel's Ambitions to Exploit the Region), p. 16.
45. See Chapter 7, pp. 155–6.
46. Al-Dajani, op. cit., pp. 42–3.
47. Hamza, op. cit., pp. 92–109.
48. *Sada Alwatan*, 8 September 1989.

49. Hamza, op. cit., p. 110.
50. Official American trade figures show that in 1976 US imports from the Arab states amounted to $14,529 million and exports to the Arab states to $10,075 million. In 1979 the figures were $36,267 million worth of imports and $12,556 million of exports (See IMF, *Direction of Trade*, October 1977 and May 1980). See also Sarna op. cit., pp. 108–9, and Carry E. Carter, *International Economic Sanctions: Improving the Haphazard US Legal Regime* (Cambridge: Cambridge University Press, 1988), p. 180.
51. Al-Dajani, op. cit., p. 43.
52. *Arab News* (Dammam), 24 May 1993.
53. Address by Dr Muhammad Aziz Shukri, 'Misconceptions Concerning the Arab Boycott of Israel', 26 July 1989.
54. Hamza, op. cit., pp. 76–85, 118–29.
55. Ibid. pp. 86–91, 137–40.
56. *The Egyptian Economic & Political Review* October/November, 1956.
57. *Al-Bulis*, 30 August 1959.
58. 'Awf, op. cit., pp. 3–4.
59. Hamza, op. cit., pp. 141–5.
60. Ibid., pp. 51–62.
61. See Al-Dajani in Hani al-Hindi, (ed.), op. cit., pp. 140–1. Philips had opened a small plant for electric bulbs in Israel in the early 1950s, and after being blacklisted closed its operation in 1952; Susan Hattis Rolef, 'Israel's Anti-Boycott Policy', *Policy Studies*, No. 28 (Jerusalem: The Leonard Davis Institute, 1989), p. 13. The case of Renault occurred in 1959. Renault, a French government-owned company, was blacklisted after agreeing to assemble cars in Israel. It subsequently terminated its Israeli operation; Prittie and Nelson, *The Economic War Against the Jews* (London: Secker & Warburg, 1978), p. 139.
62. Hamza, op. cit., p. 180.
63. Remba, op. cit., p. 52.
64. *Al-Akhbar*, 5 April 1960.
65. Ahmad and al-Jabali, op. cit., pp. 89–91.
66. See for example, 'Awf, op. cit., pp. 12, 15–18.
67. Hamza, op cit., pp. 170–4 and al-Dajani in Hani al-Hindi (ed.), op. cit., pp. 145–7.
68. Sharif, op. cit., pp. ix–x.
69. Hamdan, in Hani al-Hindi (ed.), op. cit., p. 157.
70. See Chapter 6, p. 134.
71. See, for example, Mohammed Mahgoub, 'The Nature of the Arab Boycott of Israel', press statement, 1976.
72. Hamza, op. cit., pp. 192–7.
73. Ibid., p. 168.
74. Shukri, op. cit.
75. *Al-Hayyat*, 7 January 1967.
76. See Chapter 5.
77. Dagani, op. cit., p. 45.

78. Fu'ad Hamdi Basisu, *'Al-Watan al-Muhatall Bayna Mutatallabat Da'am al-Sumud wa-Iltizamat al-Muqata'a al-'Arabiyya li-Isar'il'* (Arabic) (The Occupied Homeland between the Demands of the 'Sumud' and the Commitment to the Arab Boycott of Israel), *Shu'un 'Arabiyya*, 42 (June 1985), pp. 31–2.

79. Hamza, op. cit., pp. 197–212.

80. Shafiq Ahmad Ali, 13th article in a series on the Arab boycott in *Al-Wattan* (Qatar), in January 1997.

81. Ibid.

82. *Riyadh Daily*, 18 September 1994.

83. Reuters (Cairo), 2 October 1994.

84. Hamza, op. cit., pp. 216–19.

85. Holly L. Feder, 'US Companies and the Arab Boycott of Israel', Texas Women's University, U.M.I. (1988), p. 8. It should be noted, however, that despite the cancellation of the boycott law, between 1980 and 1985 close to 500 boycott requests were received by US companies from Egyptian trading partners.

86. *The Sunday Times*, 21 July 1991.

87. Reuters (Cairo) 17 July 1991.

88. Statement issued by the 37th Conference of the Liaison Officers of the Arab Boycott of Israel.

89. BBC Monitoring Service (Abu Dhabi), 10 September 1993.

90. *Gulf Times*, 30 September 1993.

91. Reuters (Damascus), 26 September 1993.

92. Reuters (Cairo), 26 September 1993.

93. *Al Ahram*, 27 January 1994.

94. *Ha'aretz*, 1 April 1997.

95. It should be noted, however, that soon after the outbreak of the *intifada* in December 1987 there was a decision, which was not fully implemented, not to purchase from Israel luxury goods or goods that could be manufactured in the territories.

96. Reuters (Jerusalem), 20 October 1993.

97. Al-Najar, op. cit., pp. 18–19.

98. Reuters (Cairo), 2 October 1994.

99. See, for example, *Saudi Gazette*, 5 December 1994.

100. Ibid.

5

Loopholes in the Application of the Boycott

EVEN THOUGH the Arab boycott of Israel has probably been the longest lasting and most rigorously implemented example of economic sanctions ever imposed by a group of states against a target state, it was never air-tight. That there should be cracks in the secondary and tertiary boycotts was perhaps to be expected, since these aspects of the Arab boycott concerned companies in third states which were in no way directly involved in the Arab–Israeli conflict, and only companies with special commercial interests in the Arab world were even willing to consider cooperating with it. However, over the years there have also been cracks in the primary boycott, stemming from certain Arab commercial interests and, as of the mid-1970s, from the first steps towards a rapprochement between Israel and at least part of the Arab world. Various techniques developed by Israeli companies to circumvent the boycott have also played a role in creating cracks in the Arab boycott wall.

Cracks in the Primary Boycott

Though the boycott was rigorously implemented by the Arab states over the years, there was always some trade being carried out between Israel and some Arab states, usually indirectly but after 1967 also directly across the open bridges via Jordan, after 1975 through the 'good fence' via Lebanon, and after the signing of the 1979 Egyptian–Israeli peace treaty, and the promulgation in Egypt of Law 66 on 18 February 1980 calling for the lifting of the boycott against Israel, via Egypt.[1]

Soon after the implementation of the boycott and before the establishment of the State of Israel, it was reported that the Arabs were buying Jewish produced goods from Palestine via Cyprus, Turkey and Greece.[2] In 1952 the policy committee of the CBO in Damascus claimed to have discovered a loophole in the boycott involving Cyprus, and that Israeli products – especially pharmaceuticals and toiletries – had reached Lebanon and Syria. Its reaction was to demand that Arab companies with offices in Cyprus, which used them in order to trade with Israel, close these offices, and to call upon the Arab governments to boycott Cyprus economically because it served as a centre for unofficial trade between Arab merchants and Israel.[3] According to the British Foreign Office at the time a 'complete interdiction of trade with the colony [Cyprus] has been threatened at one time or another by most Arab governments, but it appears that the Boycott Office have now decided to cease action against Cyprus. A letter to this effect from Brigadier Mansour, the head of the Office, was received not long ago by the colony's Chamber of Commerce. Most of our difficulties have arisen with Saudi Arabia which applied a total ban on trade with Cyprus in December 1952.'[4]

Forty-three years later Cyprus was still considered a venue for illicit trade between Israel and the Arab countries, even after direct contacts started being established. Thus, on 23 January 1996, the Qatari Foreign Minister, Hamed Bin Jasem al-Thani, announced that Israel was exporting $2 billion worth of goods to the Gulf states, and that this trade was going through Cyprus.[5] In the mid-1960s a new boycott office was opened in the Gulf emirates, *inter alia*, in order to stop Israeli goods entering the Arab world via Iran.[6]

The 'open bridges' policy introduced by Israeli Defence Minister Moshe Dayan in the aftermath of the Six Day War, which enabled the passage of persons, goods and money between the occupied territories and Jordan across the bridges over the Jordan River, was ostensibly designed to enable the Palestinian population of the occupied territories, many of whom were Jordanian citizens, to maintain contacts with Jordan.[7] In fact it established a means for some direct trade between Israel and the Arab world. In 1971 it was estimated that Israel's trade with the Arab world which crossed the bridges reached $20 million.[8]

The final destination of Israeli products crossing the bridges was, so it was alleged, not only the Jordanian market, but those of several Gulf states as well.[9] This trade is believed to have consisted primarily of agricultural products – especially citrus fruit, bananas, cucumbers and potatoes. As early as 1968 Lebanese citrus growers started complaining of competition from Israel. Complaints also came from Lebanon about Israeli products reaching Arab markets in the guise of goods allegedly manufactured in the Gaza Strip and West Bank.[10] The figures brought to prove this argument showed these imports to have risen from IP (Israeli pounds) 43 million in 1966 to IP 107 million in 1972.[11] Another source claims that the value of merchandise crossing the bridges eastwards was $10.4 million in 1968 and $75.2 million in 1981.[12]

On 31 January 1968 the CBO sent all the regional offices a circular stating that Jordan was buying goods produced in Israel via the bridges. On 7 February 1968 Syria started barring the entry of products from Jordan, arguing that even if they did not originate in Israel, those manufactured in the West Bank contained Israeli inputs. The matter was raised at the 16th meeting of the regional boycott officers, which convened in Beirut. One of the recommendations made by this meeting was to stop various products from the Gaza Strip, especially citrus fruit, crossing the bridges. The committee also recommended limiting imports from the West Bank. Jordan, however refused to comply with these recommendations. What many Arabs found disturbing about the 'open bridges' policy was not only the fact that it constituted an open breach of the primary boycott, but that it helped Israel dispose of surplus agricultural products.[13]

After 1975 a new channel for Israeli products reaching Arab markets developed through southern Lebanon, especially after an official crossing point – the 'good fence' – was opened not far from the Israeli town of Metulla.[14] Israeli products not only entered Lebanon in this way, but Syria as well. In the peak year of 1982 – the year of the Lebanese War – Israeli trade with Lebanon was estimated at $100 million.[15]

The signing of the Egyptian–Israeli peace treaty in March 1979 resulted in official economic ties being established between the two countries, and the formal cancellation of the boycott by Egypt. Trade, however, remained limited, consisting primarily of the sale of Egyptian oil from the Sinai to Israel and, on a much smaller scale, of such products as Israeli beer.[16] While the Egyptian government did not encourage the development of economic contacts with Israel, many Egyptian companies continued to boycott it.[17] Five years after the signing of the peace treaty the annual Israeli–Egyptian trade (oil excluded) ran at no more than $2 million though, according to Prof. Seev Hirsch of the Department of Economics at Tel Aviv University, another $18 million was probably getting through unofficially.[18] Export channels were also opened in the late 1970s using straw companies set up by Israel in Cyprus, Greece and Spain. [19]

Israeli exports to other Arab markets – particularly the Gulf states – grew at an impressive rate. An article published in *Forbes* by Hesh Kestin, on 22 October 1984, gave a figure of $500 million as an estimate for the annual volume of trade between Israel and the Arab world. Eliezer Sheffer, a lecturer in economics at the Hebrew University in Jerusalem, gave a more careful estimate, stating that anywhere between 1 and 10 per cent of Israeli exports totalling about $10 billion at the time, could be finding their way to Arab destinations, but that no one really knew.[20]

Kestin based his observations on a large number of interviews with academics, officials and businessmen, and had the following to say: 'Israeli manufacturers, working with Arabs in Israeli-administered territories and with sympathetic European and American traders abroad, have found ways to penetrate even the most hostile countries in the lucrative Arab market, selling everything from renowned drip irrigation systems to ouds [an Eastern musical instrument].' These exports included a large variety of goods, including fresh and frozen fruit and vegetables, processed food, seed,[21] textiles, office equipment, furniture,[22] cosmetics, medicine, raw materials, agricultural equipment, solar water-heating systems, electronic and communications equipment. According to Kestin, anywhere from 10–20 per cent of Israel's $700 million worth of exports of agricultural equipment – primarily drip irrigation systems – found its way to Arab countries, and that the 'distinctive black piping of Israeli drip systems can be seen on either side of the Jordan River, and as far away as Saudi Arabia'.

By 1990 – more than a year before the Madrid Conference – some Arab buyers openly attended the Agritech Exhibition in Tel Aviv. In October 1991, on the eve of Madrid, Prof. Gad Gilber of Haifa University estimated that Israeli exports to the Arab states had reached somewhere between $500 million or $1 billion – 5–10 per cent of total Israeli exports.[23]

However, the major breakthrough occurred following the signing of the DoP between Israel and the Palestinians. In 1994 the Casablanca Economic Conference, which convened at the end of October, was the meeting place for Israeli businessmen and businessmen from many Arab countries under official auspices. The Amman Economic Conference in October 1995, the Cairo Economic Conference in November 1996 and the Doha Conference in November 1997 served the same purpose.

There are many good economic reasons why Israeli products managed to break through the barriers of the primary boycott. In the case of certain agricultural and electronic equipment the qualitative advantage of Israeli goods and their compatibility with local needs encouraged sales. In the case of food-stuffs and many finished products, the advantages of 'border trade' – consisting of relatively low packing, transport and insurance costs – was an important factor.

Nevertheless, it should be pointed out that while Israeli products have fared well in Arab markets, Arab exports to Israel remain extremely low, except for Israeli oil purchases from Egypt which in the years 1979–89 were worth $3.9 billion (in current prices).[24]

Cracks in the Secondary Boycott

Though the central boycott authority and the boycott authorities in individual Arab states were, over the years, extremely active in approaching companies believed to be in breach of the boycott regulations, demanding that they cease all business contacts with Israel and threatening to blacklist them if they did not, in themselves these efforts did not guarantee success. Thousands of foreign companies continued to do business with Israel even in the period when the Arab economic power was at its zenith following the 1973 oil crisis, usually directly but occasionally also by means of straw companies or other manipulative practices. A typical example in the course of the 1980s was that of the West German conglomerate Höchst. There were certain sections within Höchst which would have no dealings with Israel altogether, others which dealt with Israel indirectly and at least one section which had open relations with it.[25] In Israel there were export and import firms that specialized in offering companies abroad means of circumventing the boycott.

The lack of effective control by the boycott authorities on companies in third states was not, however, the only reason for the cracks in the implementation of the secondary and tertiary boycotts. Another reason was that the boycott authorities did not always choose to threaten companies maintaining economic contacts, and even when such threats were made, they were not automatically acted upon, especially if this was seen to be contrary to Arab economic interests. In the mid-1960s, an Israeli observer had already pointed out that, despite the efforts of the boycott authorities, most of the west European airlines maintained regular flights to Israel without this affecting their business in the Arab world. He added that especially in cases where boycott threats by the CBO in Damascus were not accompanied by a decision by specific Arab states to implement them, or when a counter-boycott could be effectively implemented by pro-Israel factors, these threats remained a dead letter.[26]

This pragmatic approach was publicly admitted in 1989 by Dr Shukri, the legal advisor to the Secretary General of the Arab League, who stated that one of the factors affecting the implementation of the boycott was 'not to harm the Arab economy. This calls for a very lenient interpretation of the conditions regarding, for example, hotel, oil, nuclear, shipping and air service corporations.'[27]

An often quoted example of an American company openly doing business with Israel and not being blacklisted was that of General Electric, even though in the course of the 1980s it helped Israel in its development of the Lavi fighter plane before the project was scrapped.[28] Back in 1977 General Electric (as well as several other major North American firms, including the Bank of America and Westinghouse) was released from the fear of being blacklisted after the commissioner general of the CBO, Mohammed Mahgoub, announced in Cairo at the end of a conference of Arab boycott officials, that they could continue to do business with Israel, 'so long as they do not have plants in Israel that use Israeli labour and thus help the economy ... If they want to trade, that does not affect us. The point is a company should not have a plant there.'[29] It was only in 1992 that General Electric, acting through a Dutch subsidiary, opened its first plant in Israel. The plant it set up dealt in the production of plastic products by means of special recycling techniques.[30]

How Israeli Exporters got around the Boycott[31]

As already indicated above, throughout the years Israel managed to create cracks both in the secondary and tertiary boycotts and in the primary boycott. To a certain extent this was done by means of all sorts of tricks and business manoeuvres, the main goal of which was to conceal the origin of Israeli manufactured products.[32] In the sphere of textiles, for example, Israeli exporters were in the habit of not putting 'made in Israel' labels in their products, frequently at the request of their customers abroad.[33]

Other means of concealing the origin of Israeli-manufactured products, included working through brokers or straw companies located outside Israel, packaging products in a manner which suggested that their origin was other than Israel, and in some extreme cases even falsifying certificates of origin. These practices resulted in an increase in the cost of Israeli goods to the final purchaser, and many of them bordered on the illegal. Exporters were naturally wary of reporting such practices.

However, some of Israel's larger manufacturers found, in the late 1970s, a less problematic means of getting around the boycott, even though getting around the boycott was not the only cause for what they did. The foreign exchange liberalization which followed the formation of the first Likud-led government in Israel in 1977, encouraged several major Israeli companies to purchase existing European companies which were in financial difficulties, together with their trade-marks. The managing directors of several of these Israeli companies, interviewed at the end of 1978 and the beginning of 1979, gave the boycott and other political trade barriers (such as the difficulty of selling to the countries of the East bloc which had broken off diplomatic relations with Israel in the aftermath of the Six Day War), as one of several reasons for this move.[34]

Notes

1. Lufti El-Khouri, 'Form over Content', Letter from Cairo, No. 89 (1–3 May 1997).
2. Marwan Iskandar, 'Arab Boycott of Israel', *Middle East Forum*, (October 1960), p. 27
3. PRO, FO 371/98275 E1123/22 and FO 371/104207 XC13782.
4. Ibid.
5. *Al-Jumhuriya* (Egypt), 24 January 1996.
6. *Ma'ariv*, 17 June 1965.
7. See entry 'open bridges' by Meron Benvenisti in Susan Hattis Rolef (ed.) *Political Dictionary of the State of Israel*, second edition (Jerusalem: The Jerusalem Publishing House, 1993), pp. 233–4.
8. *Time* magazine, 19 July 1971, p. 18
9. Fu'ad Hamdi Basisu, '*Al-Watan al-Muhtall Bayna Mutatallabat Da'm al-Sumud wa-Iltizamat al-Maqata'a al-'Arabiyya li-Isra'il*' (Arabic) (The Occupied Homeland Between the Demands of the 'Sumud' and the Commitment to the Arab Boycott of Israel), *Shu'un 'Arabiyya'*, 42 (June 1985), pp. 8–9.
10. Ibid., pp. 20–2
11. Halal Ga'mil, quoted in Ja'far Tah Hamza, *Al-Muqata'a al-'Arabiyya li-Isra'il*, (Arabic) (The Arab Boycott of Israel) (1973), p. 207
12. Dagani, op. cit.
13. Hamza, op. cit., pp. 197–212.
14. Gad Gilber, '*Lo Bodkim Taviyot*' (Labels Aren't Being Checked), *Ha'aretz*, 26 April 1991.
15. Hesh Kestin 'Israel's best-kept secret', *Forbes*, 134 (22 October 1984), pp. 50–5.
16. It is said that even before the peace between Egypt and Israel an Israeli manufactured beer called OK was available in Egypt (Hesh Kestin, op. cit.).
17. See, for example, Gil Feiler, *Scientific and Technological Cooperation Between Israel and Egypt: Possibilities and Achievements*, Tel Aviv University, The Armand Hammer Fund for Economic Cooperation in the Middle East (January 1991).
18. Kestin, op. cit.
19. For example a straw company was set up by Koor Industries in Barcelona in 1979 to sell 'metal' to most of the Arab countries.
20. Kestin, op. cit.
21. According to Professor Ezra Sadan, director of the Vulcan Institute and a former Director-General of the Ministries of finance and Agriculture, seeds have sold well throughout the Arab world, and 'if the Arab boycott is eliminated, we shall be able to sell them even better.' *Globes*, 2 November 1993, p. 29.
22. According to a former senior employee of the Jerusalem-based furniture company Rim, in the early 1980s (apparently in the period when Binyamin Netanyahu, today Israel's Prime Minister, was employed at Rim as sales manager), this company had a line of furniture designed especially for sale in Saudi Arabia.
23. Arye Aplatoni, '*Milliard Dollarim*' (A Billion Dollars), *Ma'ariv – Assakim*, 29 October 1991.

24. Gad Gilber, op. cit.
25. Transcript of interviews carried out by Susan Hattis Rolef in the early 1980s.
26. Yosef Schechtman, *Haherem Ha'arvi Velikho* (The Arab Boycott and its Lessons), *Haumma*, 4 (13 June 1965), pp. 8–10. Schechtman brought the example of an American company, Red Fox, which chose to disregard boycott threats in 1961 after being approached by its Arab business contacts with suggestions on how to circumvent the boycott. Boycott threats were effectively thwarted in the case of the Brown and Williamson tobacco company, where the Jewish organizations threatened to boycott its products in the US unless it refused to give in to threats from Damascus.
27. Address by Dr Muhammad Aziz Shukri, 'Misconceptions Concerning the Arab Boycott of Israel', 26 July 1989.
28. Inge Deutschkron, '*Hama'avak Neged Haherem Ha'aravi Be'artzot Habrit*' (The Struggle against the Arab Boycott in the United States), *Ma'ariv-Assakim*, 18 February 1986.
29. Letter from Arnold Forster, General Counsel of the ADL, to the group counsel of the International and Canadian group of General Electric Vincent Johnson, dated 21 June 1977.
30. *Globes* (Hebrew), 24 July 1992.
31. Unless otherwise indicated, this section is based on the transcript of interviews carried out by Dr Susan Hattis Rolef in the late 1970s and early 1980s with senior Israeli manufacturers and exporters, who for obvious reasons asked to remain anonymous and for their companies not to be mentioned by name.
32. FICC report, 21 January 1993.
33. In 1982 the Israeli Ministry of finance initiated a questionnaire which was sent to all the Israeli exporters of textile goods asking them how a new European Community regulation regarding the requirement for all non-community manufacturers to indicate the country of origin of their products. One of the questions asked was whether previously they had sold their products without origin tags, and why. About 40 of those who replied to the questionnaire admitted that the reason they sold their products without origin tags was boycott related, and that it was the buyers who requested that the fact that the textiles were manufactured in Israel be concealed.
34. '*Yitzur Yisraeli Be'europa*' (Israeli Production in Europe), *Hashuk Hameshutaf* (The Common Market) (January 1979), p. 2

6

Israel's Anti-boycott Campaign[1]

FROM THE Arab perspective the success of the boycott of Israel largely depended on the willingness of other states to cooperate with the Arab policy, especially insofar as the secondary and tertiary boycotts were concerned. However, since at least in the case of the Western democracies it was highly unlikely that any state as such would cooperate with it on ideological grounds, the Arabs adopted the tactic of placing pressure on companies in these countries to refrain from doing business with Israel. These companies in turn were expected to place pressure on their governments not to implement an anti-boycott policy, even though the boycott clearly went against the principle of free trade and non-discrimination in trade relations, which have been the basic principles in the declared policies of all the Western democracies since the Second World War.

The Jewish community in Palestine until 1948, and the State of Israel thereafter, tried at first to get the primary boycott cancelled, but soon discovered that this particular battle was hopeless as long as the state of war between Israel and its Arab neighbours continued. Thus Israel concentrated on developing an economy in total detachment from the region of which it constitutes a geographical part, but which refused to accept it either politically or economically, and on the battle to counter the secondary and tertiary boycotts.

Fighting the secondary and tertiary boycotts involved trying to get third states and international organizations to adopt explicit measures to prevent their implementation on the one hand, and to convince foreign companies not to give in to the boycott, or at least to find ways to circumvent it, on the other. As of the mid 1970s, Jewish and pro-Israel groups and organizations in various Western countries – but especially the US – joined in the campaign, *inter alia*, seeking allies among the political leaders of their respective countries.

The Period up to 1948

Following the decision of the World Islamic Congress of December 1931 to avoid any trade relations with the Jewish community in Palestine,[2] Dr Haim Arlosoroff, Head of the Jewish Agency Political Department, was informed that there was in fact very little compliance by the Palestinian Arabs with the boycott, and it was consequently decided that no action was required. However, five years later, in the midst of the Arab general strike in Palestine, which included the boycotting of Jewish businesses, Arie Shenkar, President of the Jewish Manufacturers' Association of Palestine, proposed that the Jewish community should react by becoming increasingly independent of the local Arab economy, which is what actually started happening by force of circumstances rather than as a deliberate policy.

After the Arab boycott was formally declared by the Arab League in October 1945, the official Zionist leadership and representatives of Jewish industry in Palestine tried to the get the Palestine Government and the UN to force the Arabs to cancel the boycott. Nothing concrete was, however, achieved. The reaction of the British authorities to Jewish appeals was reminiscent of the reaction of the British government some 30 years later when Israel, and organizations supporting it, tried to get it to take concrete action against the implementation of the boycott in Britain. On 25 February 1946 for example, the Chief Secretary of the Government of Palestine, John Shaw, wrote to the head of the Political Department of the Jewish Agency, Moshe Shertok, stating that 'His Majesty's Government, as the mandatory Government, disapproves of any discriminatory measures instituted by foreign governments adversely affecting the welfare of the Palestine population, irrespective of race or religion ...'

On a later occasion Shaw advised the Jewish Agency Executive against a counter-boycott, which was being considered in Jewish economic circles. In fact, the British authorities kept rejecting as likely 'to do more harm than good' all practical proposals made by the Jews, including the abrogation of Palestine's trade agreements with two of the Arab states, that had declared the boycott – Lebanon and Syria. In addition, Jewish efforts were made to prevent certain American and British firms from moving their local agencies from Jewish to Arab hands as a result of the boycott.

In addition to trying to get third countries to act, the Jewish Agency made an effort to get at least one of the Arab states, Egypt, to break the boycott. In the summer of 1946 Eliahu Sasson, one of the top officials in the Political Department, was sent to Cairo in an attempt to reach an agreement with the Egyptian government. According to David Horowitz, who was head of the Economic Department at the time (he later became the first governor of the Bank of Israel), it was felt that for economic reasons Egypt might find it beneficial to cooperate economically with the Yishuv (the Jewish community in Palestine) rather than fight it. However, when Sasson came to Cairo for a second visit, he realized that the task was hopeless.[3]

Nevertheless, 'the boycott was perceived [by the Jews] in this period as temporary – as something which the neighbouring Arab states would be unable to keep up. Those who believed that the future of [Jewish] industry in Palestine lay in the expansion of exports to the countries of the Middle East could not reconcile themselves to a situation in which the markets of all the states in the region were closed to them. Reports on the failure of the Arab boycott were published from time to time in the press by the leaders of the economy.'[4]

1948–60 – Muddling Through

After Egypt issued a decree on 6 February 1950 to the effect that it would search ships on their way to Israel for purposes of seizing 'war contraband',[5] Israel decided to react in kind, and in April tried to stop a British ship which was anchoring at Haifa with a consignment of railway tracks for Egypt on board, until receiving an Egyptian guarantee that products whose destination was Israel would be allowed through Egyptian ports. However, Israel finally stepped down, after harsh reactions were received from both London and Washington.[6]

The boycott issue was first raised by Israel at the UN in connection with the right of Israeli ships and cargoes to pass through the Suez Canal. The issue was brought up in the Security Council by Israel's Ambassador to the UN, Abba Eban, on 26 July 1951. As a result of this initiative Israel scored what proved to be little more

than a declaratory victory, when the Security Council passed a resolution on 1 September, which expressed reservations about Egypt's
boycott practices insofar as passage through the Suez Canal was
concerned.[7]

In 1953 the first formal machinery to contend with the effects of
the boycott was set up in Israel in the form of a special desk within
the Research Department at the Ministry for Foreign Affairs. This
desk functioned from March 1953 until the late 1950s. An inter-
ministerial committee was also formed under the Director General of
the Ministry, to coordinate the government's anti-boycott policy.
However, it was the Economic Department in the Ministry which
was most active on the issue in these years.

From the very beginning there were differences of opinion within
the Ministry as to whether Israel should take an aggressive stand on
the boycott issue, and especially whether counter boycott measures
were desirable. The predominant line was, however, a minimalist
one, and what worried the Israeli authorities was less the damage to
Israeli trade caused by boycott activities, than the atmosphere of
terror which the Arabs were trying to create around investments in
Israel.

Means of action included approaches to the UN and various
foreign governments, as well as organizations such as the International Chambers of Commerce (ICC) and the International Civil
Aviation Organization (ICAO). The most Israel derived from its
efforts vis-à-vis governments and inter-governmental organizations,
were mild declarations condemning the boycott. The responsiveness
of non-governmental international organizations was, in this period,
usually more positive.

In 1956 first efforts were made to mobilize Jewish organizations
around the world to participate in the anti-boycott efforts. This
Jewish activity involved establishing an apparatus in the US to be
directed by the Israeli economic consul in New York, and a department for anti-boycott warfare within the Secretariat of the World
Jewish Congress (WJC) in London, under the guidance of the Israeli
Embassy there. The boycott issue was also raised at the 24th Zionist
Congress which convened in Jerusalem in April/May 1956. The
outcome of the latter effort was an attempt to institutionalize co-
operation between the External Relations Department of the Jewish
Agency and the Ministry for Foreign Affairs. This effort resulted in

the setting up of an anti-boycott committee, in August 1957, with the participation of these two bodies, as well as representatives of private industry, agriculture, commerce and other economic branches.

1960–73 – Institutionalization

At the end of 1959 Foreign Minister Golda Meir finally decided to set up a special department within the Ministry for Foreign Affairs to deal with the boycott issue. This decision resulted from two significant developments. The one was the seizure by Egypt of an Israeli cargo on board the Danish ship *Inge Toft* on 21 May 1959, which was followed by intensive but unsuccessful Israeli diplomatic efforts to stop the Egyptian application of the boycott to ships passing through the Suez Canal.[8] The second was the the submission of the French car manufacturer Renault to the boycott in August.[9]

The new department – *Matmach* (Hebrew acronym for *Mahlaka letichnun medini vekalkali* – department for political and economic planning) – was formed in January 1960, and superseded the activities of the committee which had been set up to deal with the issue within the Jewish Agency. Nevertheless for a certain period the External Relations Department of the Jewish Agency continued to dabble with the issue, even though it had no real control over events.

From the very beginning the *Matmach* faced a paradox, which to a certain extent continued to bedevil the Israeli anti-boycott policy for many years to come. On the one hand, Israel did not want to create the impression that the Arab boycott was more than a minor irritant, by giving publicity to its successes. On the other hand, one could not ignore the real economic damage and dislocation which the boycott was causing the Israeli economy – the real cost of which was never really discerned.[10]

It was in this period that the Norwich Union Insurance Company in Britain gave in to Arab League pressure and forced a Jewish member of its board, Lord Mancroft, to resign.[11] This was the first case in which the Israeli authorities actually opened a major public campaign abroad, including a press campaign, against the boycott, and succeeded. Lord Mancroft was invited by the Norwich Insurance Company to rejoin its board – an invitation which he declined.[12]

In the 1960s most of Israel's anti-boycott activities were concentrated in the US. The first representative of the *Matmach* in the US, Shlomo Argov, was appointed in 1960, and served as Political Consul in the Israeli Embassy in Washington, so that the time he could devote to boycott affairs was limited.[13] It was only in June 1962 that Argov's replacement, Binyamin Navon, was assigned exclusively to deal with boycott matters, and was stationed in New York. Besides trying to convince American businessmen to invest in Israel, Navon concentrated great efforts in trying to get the American authorities to act against the tertiary boycott, invoking the 1870 Sherman Antitrust Act.[14]

Strangely enough, the government in Israel did not show any enthusiasm towards Navon's activism. When Navon started dealing with the specific case of an American firm called Tecumseh, which had given in to tertiary boycott pressures, he was told by the Israeli Ambassador to Washington, Abe Harman, to drop the issue, since his involvement was liable to irritate the Department of State. At the same time both the purchasing mission of the Israeli Ministry of Commerce and Industry and that of the Ministry of Defence refused to avoid dealing with companies which cooperated with the boycott.

The one official Israeli body which did not seem wary of touching the boycott was the newly founded Investment Authority within the Ministry of finance. Under Dr Zevi Dienstein, who was appointed head of the new body as well as of the Investment Centre within the Ministry of Commerce and Industry, the Authority started systematically approaching all the major corporations in the US about investments in Israel. This activity soon created a more or less complete picture regarding the corporations which were giving in to boycott demands. However, when the Authority approached the US Administration with a request that it protect American investors in Israel against the boycott, the response was unsympathetic.

Nevertheless it was in this period that the major Jewish organizations in the US – the Anti-Defamation League of B'nai Brith (ADL), the American Jewish Committee (AJC) and the American Jewish Congress (AJCongress) started to cooperate among themselves on the boycott issue. This cooperation developed, in the mid-1970s, into an effective anti-boycott coalition, which played a major role in the passage of the various pieces of anti-boycott legislation in the US.

In 1964 Navon was replaced by the journalist Yuval Elizur, who, unlike his predecessor who was attached to the Israeli Consulate, was attached to the Israeli Economic Mission in New York, pointing to the growing involvement of the Ministry of Finance in the issue. The emphasis was now placed on managing to get individual companies, which had given in to the boycott, to reverse their decision. Among the American companies involved were the tyre manufacturer Goodyear, the car manufacturer Ford and Coca-Cola. The following year Elizur together with the American Israel Public Affairs Committee (AIPAC) and the American Jewish organizations, and the cooperation of congressmen from both the Democratic and Republican parties, managed to get Congress to pass an amendment to the Export Administration Act (EAA) which obliged American exporters to report to the Department of Commerce the receipt and nature of any boycott-related requests, which had the effect of furthering or supporting the Arab boycott.[15]

In February 1965 the Ministry of Commerce and Industry published a list of foreign companies which were known to cooperate with the Arab boycott. The idea behind the publication of the list was that special permits would be required to import products from the companies involved. Foreign Minister Abba Eban denied that publication of the list constituted a counter boycott. 'The Government of Israel ... does not boycott companies that maintain commercial relations with Arab countries', he wrote in an article for the *Israel Year Book* for 1966, 'but Israeli importers are entitled to know the identity of companies that discriminate against Israel in compliance with the Arab boycott.'[16]

The years between the 1967 Six Day War and the 1973 October War were years of unprecedented economic prosperity in Israel. Although some attention was given to the boycott in the form of (unsuccessful) attempts to prevent Egypt's accession to GATT without its giving up its boycott practices *vis-à-vis* Israel, and, in the words of Minister for Foreign Affairs Abba Eban in a reply to a parliamentary question, 'to prevent the EEC from signing documents which might, even indirectly, be interpreted as approval of the Arab boycott', most of the focus was directed at fighting Arab terror rather than the Arab boycott.

In 1971 the director of the *Matmach*, Tuvia Arazi, was quoted by *Time* magazine as having said that 'The boycott does us infinitesimal harm now. It is so inefficient and ineffective that we simply don't need this division (the *Matmach*) any more.'[17] In 1973, just before the October War, the *Matmach* actually ceased to exist as a separate department in the Ministry of Foreign Affairs, and the boycott issue was returned to the Economic Department.

1974–79 – The Charge Forward

Towards the end of February 1975 the Arab League adopted a resolution to intensify the economic boycott against Israel. Strangely enough within Israeli government circles there was no inclination to change the manner in which the problem was being dealt with. Pressure for a change came from outside government circles, from a body calling itself, 'The Israel Institute of Coexistence' (IIC).

The IIC was founded at the beginning of 1974 by a group of prominent figures in the Israeli economy led by two journalists and a well known chartered accountant, who became deeply concerned by the prospect of the Arabs using their newly acquired economic power to destroy the Israeli economy. One of the IIC's goals was to persuade the government to set up a body to prepare an economic warfare strategy for Israel. The fact that the then Director General of the Ministry of Finance, Avraham Agmon, was a member of the group that founded the Institute, and the advisor to the Minister of Finance, Danny Halperin, was an enthusiastic supporter of its views, resulted in the establishment of the Economic Warfare Authority (EWA) within the Ministry of Finance in July 1975. The EWA was established at about the same time as a seminar was organized by the IIC at Christ Church College, Oxford on 'Oil Wealth, Discrimination and Freedom of Trade', which came out with detailed proposals for action.[18]

To the EWA, which had a small permanent staff, was attached to a public committee, which was made up of representatives of industry and other economic sectors as well as representatives of the Minister for Foreign Affairs, in which the boycott issue was now handled within the framework of the newly formed Energy Department, and the Ministry of Industry and Trade. The attempt to involve the Manufacturers' Association and the Export Institute (a body associated with the Ministry of Industry and Trade, whose job is to promote Israeli exports) failed, primarily because both bodies felt that excessive dabbling in the boycott issue might be counter-productive to Israel's export drive. Interestingly enough none of Israel's prime ministers, finance ministers or foreign ministers in the years which followed was especially interested in the boycott issue, but each gave the Authority their full backing and cooperated with it when requested to do so.

One of the first things which the EWA did was to deal with definitions. It was in this period that the distinction was made between the primary, secondary and tertiary boycotts. With the help of information gathered by the IDF intelligence services it was very soon realized that there was no such thing as 'the boycott', but rather separate boycotts by the various Arab states, which were loosely coordinated by the Central Boycott Office (CBO) in Damascus. Special attention was also given to the so-called 'loopholes' in the application of the boycott.

In terms of the target of the anti-boycott campaign, it was decided to start in the US, and to mobilize all three major American Jewish organizations, which were already involved one way or another in the issue, despite having been previously discouraged from doing so by the Israeli government. 'A variety of methods and techniques were developed over the years', a representative of the ADL explained in 1984. 'These ranged from fact finding to lawsuits, to press conferences, to corporate shareholder campaigns. Allegations of US government and corporate misconduct were made, and the corrosive effects of the Arab boycott uncovered. The boycott issue was presented as a domestic American concern involving the protection of American sovereignty and free trade principles from Arab economic blackmail. Although Israel would certainly benefit from tough anti-boycott laws in the US', it was argued, 'it was US self-respect and interest that would be vindicated. In part, because of this orientation, AIPAC did not play a significant role in this effort.' On the same occasion Danny Halperin, at that time Economic Minister at the Israeli Embassy in Washington, and previously head of the EWA, stated very bluntly that 'the precondition for the success (of the anti-boycott action in the US) was that it should not be perceived as an Israeli issue, but as an American one. Thus, while Israelis have been very visible in the anti-boycott campaigns in other countries ... we kept out of the limelight in the US.'[19]

As it turned out the first piece of anti-boycott legislation to be passed in this period in the US – the Ribicoff Amendment to the Tax Reform Act of 1976 – was not initiated by the Jewish organizations.[20] The next piece of anti-boycott legislation in the US, in the form of an amendment to the EAA, was passed in 1977, after Jimmy Carter had become President, and this after he had, under the influence of the Jewish organizations, taken a stand against the boycott in the 1976 presidential elections.[21]

The second country in which intensive action was taken, though with much less success than in the US, was Great Britain, where an organization called the Anti-Boycott Committee (ABC) was established to increase public awareness concerning the Arab boycott. It was, to a certain extent, as a result of the work of the ABC that Lord Byre proposed a bill on foreign boycotts in 1978, and a Select Committee of the House of Lords carried out a serious investigation on the issue. However, nothing of any practical importance emerged.[22]

In France the Israeli Embassy was instrumental in getting a group of French public figures and lawyers, both Jewish and non-Jewish, to form the *Movement pour la Liberté du Commerce* (MLC), which in turn played a major role in getting the French National Assembly to include an anti-boycott provision in a law dealing with a miscellany of economic measures passed on 7 June 1977.[23] In the Netherlands the body which started to act on the boycott issue was the *Centrum voor Informatie en Documentatie Israel* (CIDI), and in October 1979 the Dutch government agreed to a series of anti-boycott measures. In Canada a Commission on Economic Coercion and Discrimination (ECD) was founded in 1976, having a marginal effect on Canadian policy.

All in all Israel's anti-boycott campaign in those countries where local organizations, either purely Jewish, or including both Jews and non-Jews, seemed by the late 1970s to be bearing some fruit, even if primarily on the declaratory level. However, the EWA in the Ministry of Finance did not only rely on action in foreign countries. It also started dealing with specific complaints by individual Israeli firms which had come across problems in their foreign economic relations due to the secondary, tertiary or voluntary boycotts.

As might have been expected, the cases reaching the EWA almost invariably involved small Israeli firms. Large firms and conglomerates such as Koor (the Histadrut-owned industries) usually managed on their own, and preferred not to approach the govern-ment.[24] The EWA usually dealt with particular cases through the anti-boycott organizations in the various countries, or the economic attachés in Israeli embassies abroad, who approached the boycotting companies abroad. Efforts were also made to get the governments in whose countries these companies were situated to intercede. The approach to foreign governments was carried out by the Ministry for Foreign Affairs or the economic attachés.

Another form of activity in which the EWA was engaged, in full cooperation with the Ministry for Foreign Affairs, was getting foreign governments to issue anti-boycott declarations. Foreign governments were also asked to stop indirectly cooperating with the boycott authorities, as for example in the case of the authentication of signatures on negative certificates of origin. The idea of trying to organize a counter-boycott was never seriously considered, since it was clear that the economic balance of forces doomed such an attempt to failure. Experience had also taught the Israeli authorities that not even American Jews were willing to cooperate with such a move, if it involved any real economic inconvenience to them.

1979–89 – The Years of Inertia

By the late 1970s much of the enthusiasm concerning the struggle against the Arab boycott waned. This was due to several factors. First of all, it became apparent that the success which had been scored in the US would not be repeated in Europe and that any progress in the European states would be slow and hesitant. Second, the fear that the Arabs would act effectively to destroy the Israeli economy – by buy-ing it up, through the boycott, and by other means – proved to be totally unfounded, while the peace treaty signed with Egypt in 1979 not only weakened the application of the boycott by that country, but gave rise to hopes that a change was imminent in Israel's relations with other Arab states as well.

By 1979 the staff of the EWA had greatly shrunk, and its new head, Ephraim Davrath, who was also head of the Ministry's Inter-national Affairs Department, spent more time dealing with other issues. Nevertheless, largely out of inertia, the Authority and all the organizations abroad continued to function, more or less along the same lines as previously.

Among the successes of the Israeli government's anti-boycott policy after 1979 was the passing of legislation in France. After assuming the presidency in France, François Mitterrand fulfilled his pre-election promise of reactivating the defunct 1977 legislation and removing all the obstacles from its application.[25] Progress was also made in the Netherlands,[26] and Belgium.[27] At the same time the Lebanese War (1982–85) and the measures which Israel took after December 1987 to suppress the *intifada*, resulted in a rise in the application of a voluntary boycott of Israel by foreign companies, and a growing reluctance by foreign governments to take measures which might be interpreted as explicitly pro-Israel.

As already pointed out the EWA continued to collaborate with the various organizations abroad involved in anti-boycott activities. However, whereas until 1979 it was the EWA which activated the foreign groups, after 1979 it was increasingly the foreign groups which pushed for Israeli action. This emerged very clearly at the June 1984 Brussels Seminar on 'Freedom of Trade with Israel' where some of the non-Israeli participants complained about the apparent lack of interest in the subject in the Israeli government. One of the specific complaints was that, whereas Israel had been pushing foreign countries to pass anti-boycott legislation, none had been passed in Israel itself.

In 1988 an inter-ministerial committee, made up of the EWA and representatives of the Ministry of Industry and Trade and Ministry for Foreign Affairs, started to consider anti-boycott legislation, which would enable the government to take measures against foreign companies that had given in to the boycott of Israel. However, nothing came of this initiative, primarily because of the opposition of the industrial sector to such legislation.

As a result of the proddings of the American Jewish organizations, and to a lesser extent the ABC in Britain, two initiatives were embarked upon following the Brussels seminar, and a follow-up meeting in London in March 1985. The first concerned the problem of Japan, the second the establishment of a documentary centre to disseminate up-to-date information concerning the boycott.

Japan had always been the worst offender in terms of giving in to the Arab boycott.[28] Following the London meeting the International Steering Committee to Combat the Arab Boycott was set up with the participation of the official Israeli bodies concerned and the foreign

organizations dealing with the boycott issue, with the goal of starting an anti-boycott campaign in Japan. the International Steering
Committee enjoyed some cooperation from the US Administration,
and the full cooperation of the then Israeli Ambassador to Tokyo,
Dr Ya'acov Cohen and the Israeli Manufacturers' Association.

Though progress was made on this front, it was probably less due
to the campaign than to a decrease in the Japanese dependence on
Arab oil and Arab customers for Japanese goods. Japanese industry
had also become more aware of commercial opportunities in Israel,
and of the advanced stage of scientific and technological developments in Israel in certain spheres of interest to Japanese industry,
such as bio-chemistry.

In November 1985 the International Steering Committee met with
the Luxembourgian Foreign Minister, M. Jacques F. Poos, who was
President of the EC Council at the time, in an effort to gain his
support for the harmonization of the anti-boycott legislation within
the community. The Steering Committee was, however, unsuccessful in its endeavour, and was told by Poos that the Arab point of
view, which maintained that the boycott was a political weapon
which they were exercising within the context of a right of belligerency, had to be considered. The members of the Committee
replied that the primary boycott could be justified on grounds of the
right to belligerency, but not the secondary and tertiary boycott, but
did not manage to convince their interlocutor.[29]

As to the establishment of a documentary centre, a boycott information centre was finally set up within the framework of the ADL
offices in Jerusalem in October 1987.

In May, 1988 an inter-ministerial committee, in which the
Ministries of Finance, Foreign Affairs and Industry and Trade were
members, was set up to formulate and coordinate the government's
policy regarding the boycott.[30] However, by the middle of August
1989 the committee had not yet been convened.[31]

1989–91 – The Awakening

In August 1989 there was a joint initiative by Minister of Industry
and Trade, Ariel Sharon, and Minister of Finance, Shimon Peres, for
a renewed inter-ministerial committee to deal with the Arab boycott

more effectively than in the past. But once again there was little follow-up to this decision as a result of the crisis within the government around progress in the peace process – especially in talks with the Palestinians – which finally resulted in the breakup of the National Unity Government in March 1990.

In November 1989 the American and European organizations active in the anti-boycott effort, met in London, together with Israeli officials. The consensus strategy that emerged from the meeting was to 'make the anti-boycott struggle international', i.e. to intensify pressure on European Community and Asian states to act against the application of the secondary boycott in their countries, and to enlist the US Administration and Congress in this effort. There were discussions about founding a European Jewish political lobby attached to the European Community headquarters in Brussels, in order to advance the concept of EC-wide anti-boycott legislation. As a result the *Centre Européen Juif d'Information* (CEJI) was founded in 1991.

Also discussed was the targeting of public pressure on specific Japanese and South Korean companies, that were flagrant boycott participants, and the possibilities of using international economic forums, such as the G-7, GATT and the OECD, to advance the anti-boycott effort.[32] Thus by the time Iraq invaded Kuwait in August 1990, the groundwork for, and basic outlines of a carefully thought out anti-boycott effort had already been laid down, even though observers of the boycott scene in Israel were complaining that few of the London decisions had actually been implemented.[33]

Nevertheless efforts were underway to strengthen the existing anti-boycott legislation in the US, in order to apprehend and demonstratively punish companies participating in the boycott, and pressure was exerted on the Administration by Congress to make the boycott a priority issue and to link the battle against it to international trade agreements.

A multi-faceted political education effort was underway within the EC aimed at stimulating consideration of anti-boycott legislation. Research mechanisms were introduced, within Jewish groups in particular, to monitor the scope and impact of intrusive Arab boycott activities, and to highlight international trade opportunities in Israel. The *Boycott Report*, published by the American Jewish Congress, was especially effective in this respect. In addition to reporting on boycott and anti-boycott activities, the *Boycott Report* regularly published news of Israeli trade gains. This included lists of American and other foreign companies doing business with Israel, Israeli participation at international trade fairs and economic conventions, lists of the countries and companies participating in trade fairs in Israel, news of favourable IMF and Wall Street reports on the Israeli economy, etc.

Whereas in the past there had been a certain ambivalence in the way the boycott was approached inside Israel, now it became an issue openly mentioned in relevant forums. Thus for example at a meeting of the Economic Forum of the Association of the Self-Employed, Minister of Industry and Trade, Ariel Sharon, stated that 'the Arab boycott impairs the willingness of large companies in the US and Europe to purchase Israeli products. In the last year we have exported $3.2 billion to Europe, but our imports from there totalled $6.5 billion. Our entire balance of trade deficit is with the European countries ... One reason for this is that as a result of the Arab boycott there hasn't been a significant growth in our exports [to Europe].'[34]

Since 1991

In the aftermath of the Gulf War the Israeli government concluded that the political climate was suitable for opening a direct campaign against the Arab boycott, since many of the countries leading the boycott now owed their independence to the US.[35] Though little came of the grandiose plans of Minister of Economics and Development, David Magen, for the establishment of a ministerial committee to deal with the issue, and for the passage anti-boycott legislation in Israel,[36] there is little doubt that 1991 saw the first signs of a change in the Arab attitude on the subject, and towards the end of April there were reports that there was a noticeable change in that of Kuwait and Saudi Arabia, the two Arab states which owed most to the US[37] – reports which later proved to be premature.

In May 1991 the Federation of Israeli Chambers of Commerce (FICC) and the ADL established a joint task force to monitor and combat the Arab boycott, in which senior representatives of Israeli banking, business and industry were involved. Together the two groups set out to educate and mobilize the Israeli business community to confront the boycott; to collect data and engage in fact-finding regarding specific instances of boycott discrimination against Israeli businesses; and to lobby European business leaders to support the adoption of anti-boycott legislation in their countries. '[Our] long-term goal is to break the chilling effect of the Arab boycott on foreign investment and joint ventures in Israel', FICC President Dan Gillerman told the press.[38]

One of the great hopes of those campaigning against the boycott following the Gulf War was that the G-7 meeting which was to take place in London on 15–17 July 1991 would condemn the Arab boycott in no uncertain terms. However, even though the G-7 did mention the boycott in their final communiqué, the manner in which this was done was disappointing to Israel. What was done was to link the call for an end to the boycott to a call for the suspension of all Israeli settlement activities in the West Bank and Gaza Strip.[39]

According to Israeli spokesmen, by proposing this *quid pro quo* formula (settlements for the boycott), the G-7 had essentially taken the pressure off the Arab states, and had thus squandered the anti-boycott momentum that had built up since the end of the Gulf War.[40] Shamir's government objected to the linkage between the boycott and the settlements on principle, and government spokesmen stated that the boycott was illegal and had nothing to do with Israel's settlement activities.[41] On 19 July 1991 Deputy Foreign Minister Binyamin Netanyahu stated that there was no connection between the two issues.[42] Two days later, as US Secretary of State James Baker was about to arrive in Israel, the Israeli government issued a statement to the effect that while the boycott was illegal and should be cancelled, other issues could be raised in the course of peace talks.[43]

Anti-boycott activists in the US were disappointed that the G-7 had failed to distinguish between the primary boycott, which indeed many considered to be a matter for Middle East peace talks, and the secondary and tertiary boycotts which involved interference in the affairs of third states and were therefore intolerable. The response of those supporting the approach of the G-7 was that the *quid pro quo* was fair, since just as one could argue against the legality and fairness of the secondary and tertiary boycotts so one could argue against the legality of Jewish settlements in what most of the nations of the world regarded, and continue to regard, as occupied territories.

The disappointing conclusion of the G-7 meeting resulted in a slowdown of all anti-boycott activity over the summer and winter of 1991, and very little change in the implementation of the boycott. Nevertheless, the Israeli business community, which for many years had consistently counselled a do-nothing approach to the Arab boycott, started undergoing a change of heart, feeling that perhaps the time had come to confront the boycott rather than seek ways to circumvent it.

In the beginning of August 1991 Minister of Economics and Development David Magen took an additional initiative towards a more active Israeli policy in combating the Arab boycott, and in February 1992 the Government held two discussions on the issue, following which the first ever formal resolution by any Israeli government on the boycott was adopted. The resolution instructed the Foreign Ministry to raise the boycott issue 'in all public and private diplomatic and economic meetings and forums between Israeli officials and those of other countries around the world'. Israeli diplomats were instructed to push for anti-boycott legislation in Western countries in a 'concerted and aggressive fashion'.[44]

However, a real relaxation in the application of the boycott only started to occur after the 1992 Israeli elections and the formation of a Labor-led government in July 1992, headed by Yitzhak Rabin. Though the new government accepted neither the *quid pro quo* of stopping settlement activities in the territories in return for relief in the boycott, or in return for American loan guarantees, it did freeze construction activities in the settlements for ideological reasons, believing that since in any case Israel would be returning most of the West Bank and Gaza Strip to Arab sovereignty within the framework of a permanent peace agreement, it was folly to continue to invest in civilian settlements in these territories.

Soon after becoming Foreign Minister in July 1992, Shimon Peres allegedly stated in an interview to the Egyptian weekly *Al-Musawar* that Israel would be willing to stop all the settlement activities in the territories, if in return the Arab states would remove the boycott from Israel.[45] Assuming that the report of what Peres had said is accurate, one may comment that since it was the new government's policy to stop all settlement activities in any case, Israel was not really offering a *quid pro quo*.

Soon after the formation of the new government Dan Gillerman called upon Rabin to demand that 'the US act to bring about an end to the boycott before the start of the next round of peace talks'. 'In the current situation [of peace talks], Israel must not reconcile itself to continuation of the secondary boycott even for one more day', Gillerman told reporters, 'and this issue must be put on the top of the agenda before the talks resume'. The FICC President also stated that calculations made by his organization had come up with the figure of $45 billion as the losses incurred to the Israeli economy as a result of the boycott in the previous 40 years.[46]

Gillerman himself, along with the President of the Israel Manufacturers' Association, Dan Propper, began to raise the boycott issue at many business forums, including meetings of the EEC–Israel Chambers of Commerce, and international Chamber meetings around the world. The emergence of an Israeli business anti-boycott lobby, after so many years of relative passivity, may be attributed largely to difficulties which Israel was having in its attempts to integrate more fully in the international business community in general, and that in Europe, in particular. Furthermore the wave of immigration to Israel from the Soviet Union as of 1989, which brought over half a million new immigrants to Israel, added new urgency to the need for foreign investment in the country, something that the Arab boycott had managed to impede for years.

The new Israeli policy, progress in the peace process (especially vis-à-vis the Palestinians and Jordan), and the declared Israeli willingness to return the Golan Heights to Syria within the framework of a full and comprehensive peace involving normalization in the relations between the two countries, resulted in significant breakthroughs in its relations with foreign countries. This involved the establishment of full diplomatic relations with many countries with which Israel had never previously had relations (including China and India), and the renewal of relations with the states of East Europe, which had severed relations in 1967, and with the black African countries, which had severed them in 1973. This new diplomatic reality made it much easier for Israel to convince other countries that under the circumstances the boycott was becoming archaic, and limitations on trade and investment in Israel by third countries was an anomaly.

However, if anyone had hoped that the boycott would simply melt away, this did not happen. In January 1993 Israeli business representatives and government officials held a press conference in which they denounced the boycott. Reversing a long-standing Israeli approach, Foreign Ministry and Finance Ministry officials and trade association representatives described the impact which the boycott had had on the Israeli economy, emphasizing the 'shadow effect' it had had on foreign investment in Israel. FICC President Dan Gillerman went so far as to say that the abolition of the boycott was 'more important to Israel than the agreement of the US government to provide Israel with $10 billion worth of loan guarantees'.[47]

In May 1993 Israel launched a quiet lobbying campaign among the G-7 countries, aimed at ensuring a strong anti-boycott statement at its meeting, which was to take place in Tokyo, and this after the meeting of the G-7 the previous year had refrained from mentioning the boycott altogether. Peres, Deputy Foreign Minister Yossi Beilin and Foreign Ministry Director General Uri Savir began to raise the boycott issue in all their diplomatic encounters. Peres wrote a letter on the subject to many European foreign ministers.[48] Jerusalem also flexed its muscles in negotiating foreign trade agreements. Minister of Transportation Israel Kessar refused to approve a contract between Mitsushita and El-Al for the supply of Panasonic video screens for El-Al jets, unless the Japanese firm agreed to spend 25 per cent of the contract value in reciprocal purchases in Israel. In the boycott's heyday, Israel simply could not have afforded to be so discriminating.[49]

On 6 July the Governor of the Bank of Israel, Prof. Jacob Frenkel, called upon the G-7 to appeal for an ending of the boycott, lauding Kuwait's announcement of the previous month that it would be easing its application of the secondary and tertiary boycotts.[50] In the US the Jewish organizations exercised pressure on the Administration in the same vein.[51] This time the statement issued by the G-7 was more satisfactory than that issued in 1991, since it did not condition the ending of the boycott on any Israeli concessions.[52]

There were great expectations in Israel that the signing of the DoP with the Palestinians in Washington on 13 September 1993 would lead to a rapid cancellation of the Arab boycott. This, however, did not happen, and in the beginning of October the presidents of Israel's six major economic and trade organizations demanded that the Israeli government 'insist that the Arab boycott be cancelled altogether, already during the present round of negotiations'. The

Israeli businessmen wrote to Rabin that 'it is inconceivable that international organizations will begin to channel large sums of money to the region for the implementation of a peace economy, without there being an immediate end to the Arab boycott'.[53]

Following the signing of the DoP the Israeli government rejected the policy, supported by various American Jewish leaders, of linking American aid to the Palestinian autonomy on the Palestinians' willingness to condemn the Arab boycott of Israel.[54] Rabin reiterated Israel's desire to have the international community provide the economic aid necessary to put the Palestinian autonomy on its feet, and rejected any linkage between the boycott and autonomy negotiations. 'Israel cannot at present demand the lifting of the boycott as a condition for talks with the Palestinians', he stated, adding that this would merely lead to deadlock. Rabin even expressed understanding for PLO unwillingness to support an immediate termination of the boycott. 'They do not want to do it prior to the beginning of the implementation of the accord. In their place, I wouldn't commit myself in this way – prior to implementation – either.'[55]

On 21 February 1994 Peres explained the Israeli policy to the Knesset Economics Committee. In its war against the Arab boycott, he said, Israel is not seeking to take over the Arab world. Through the peace process, Israelis are trying to bring about an economization of politics instead of a politicization of economics.[56]

Curiously enough, after no anti-boycott legislation had been passed in Israel for over several years, in December 1994 the Knesset passed an amendment to the 'Obligation for Tenders Law', which enabled the government to discriminate against companies 'connected with the Arab boycott'.[57] What the legislator had in mind was that the government should not be obliged to purchase a product from a company that in any way gives in to the Arab boycott, even if it has made the lowest offer in a tender.[58]

Though the Arab boycott has not vanished, its effects have certainly greatly weakened since 1994, and the issue has stopped preoccupying the Government of Israel and Israeli manufacturers and businessmen, the latter being much more concerned about the high interest-rate policy of the Bank of Israel than the last vestiges of the boycott.

Notes

1. Unless otherwise indicated, this chapter is based on Susan Hattis Rolef, 'Israel's Anti-Boycott Policy', *Policy Studies*, 28 (Jerusalem: The Leonard Davis Institute for International Relations at the Hebrew University of Jerusalem, February 1989).
2. See Chapter 2, p. 23.
3. David Horowitz, *Hayim Bamoked* (Hebrew) (In the Heart of Events) (Tel Aviv: Masada, 1975), p. 33.
4. Yossi Beilin, *Hata'asiya Ha'ivrit – Shorashim* (Hebrew) (Roots of Israeli Industry) (Jerusalem: Keter, 1987), p. 64.
5. See Chapter 2, p. 28.
6. Correspondence between the British Embassy in Tel-Aviv and the Foreign Office in April 1950, PRO, FO 371/82580.
7. See above Chapter 2, p. 29.
8. See for example report by the British Ambassador to Israel on a meeting with Israeli Foreign Minister Golda Meir in PRO 371/98275 1261/22.
9. See Chapter 8, p. 202.
10. See Chapter 11.
11. See above Chapter 8, p. 211.
12. Terence Prittie and Walter Henry Nelson, *The Economic War against the Jews* (London: Secker & Warburg, 1978), p. 62.
13. Twenty-two years later it was the shooting of Shlomo Argov – now Israel's Ambassador to Great Britain – which was the formal excuse for Israel's opening of the war in Lebanon in June 1982.
14. See Chapter 7, pp. 153–4.
15. See Chapter 7, pp. 155–6.
16. Meron Medzini (ed.) *Israel's Foreign Relations. Selected Documents 1947–1974* (Jerusalem: Ministry for Foreign Affairs, 1976), p. 283.
17. *Time* magazine, 19 July 1971, pp. 17–19.
18. Document prepared at the conclusion of the Oxford Seminar on Oil Wealth, Discrimination and Freedom of Trade which took place on 7–9 July 1975. The document included committee reports and a summary of high-priority actions.
19. J. Hordes, talk given at the Seminar on Freedom of Trade with Israel, held in Brussels in June 1984, on 'The History of Anti-Boycott Legislation in the US', in Susan Hattis Rolef (ed.) *Freedom of Trade and the Arab Boycott* (Jerusalem: The Anti-Defamation League of B'nai Brith, 1985), pp. 65–6 and D. Halperin, talk given on 'Combatting the Arab Boycott – An Historical Survey', ibid., p. 42.
20. See Chapter 7, pp. 162–3.
21. Ibid., p. 163.
22. See Chapter 8, pp. 214–15.
23. Ibid., pp. 202–3.
24. There is no written evidence on this subject since most Israeli firms refused, and continue to refuse, to discuss their boycott-related problems, preferring to deal with them *ad hoc*, not always by totally legal means.
25. See Chapter 8, p. 205.

26. Ibid., pp. 223–5.
27. Ibid., p. 227.
28. See Chapter 10, pp. 249–51.
29. Daniel Lack, 'Visit to President of the EEC Council, Luxembourg, 20 and 21 November, 1985', 28 November 1985.
30. Letter addressed by the Minister of Finance, Moshe Nissim, to the head of the EWA, the Deputy Director General for Economics at the Ministry for Foreign Affairs, and the Director of the Industrial Cooperation Authority at the Ministry of Industry and Trade, dated 17 May 1988.
31. Letter from the Director General of the Industrial Cooperation Authority to the Director General of the Ministry of Foreign Affairs, dated 15 August 1989.
32. Third Conference of the International Steering Committee on Freedom of Trade with Israel. See *Boycott Report*, 14/9 November/December 1990, and an internal ADL memorandum.
33. Eliahu Salpeter, '*Hifkiru et Haherem*' (The Boycott Has Been Neglected), *Ha'aretz* 14 June 1990.
34. Yossi Ben-Aharon, *Eretz Yisrael 1951* (1989), p. 4.
35. Oded Shorer, *Ma'ariv Assakim*, 16 April 1991, p. 5.
36. Ibid.
37. See for example briefing to the foreign press by Professor Mordechai Abir of the Hebrew University of Jerusalem, *Ma'ariv*, 30 April 1991.
38. ADL press release, 6 June 1991.
39. The final communiqué said the following: 'We urge all the parties to the dispute to adopt reciprocal and balanced confidence-building measures and to show the flexibility necessary to allow a peace conference to be convened on the basis set out in this initiative. In that connection we believe that the Arab boycott should be suspended as should the Israeli policy of building settlements in the occupied territories.'
40. American Jewish Congress Boycott Report newsletter editorial and *Boycott Report*, 15/8, September/October 1991.
41. Reuters (Israel), 20 July 1991.
42. *The Guardian*, 17 July 1991.
43. Reuters (Tel-Aviv), 21 July 1991.
44. See *Ha'aretz*, 16 February 1992, and Cabinet decision No. 2449 of the same date.
45. *Davar*, 30 July 1992.
46. FICC press release, 5 August 1992; *Hadashot*, 6 August 1992.
47. *Boycott Report* 17/3, March 1993.
48. *Ha'aretz* and *The Jerusalem Post*, 28 May 1993.
49. *Ma'ariv*, 13 April 1993.
50. Reuters, 6 July 1993.
51. See for example letter sent by Congressman Charles E. Schumer to fellow Congressmen on 28 April 1993 urging them to approach President Clinton on the issue.
52. Reuters (Jerusalem), 8 July 1993.
53. *Ha'aretz*, 6 October 1993.

54. The issue was hotly debated at two meetings of the International Steering Committee on Freedom of Trade with Israel held on 14 October and 3 November 1993 in New York.
55. *Ha'aretz*, 12 October 1993.
56. BBC Monitoring Service, 23 February 1994, quoting *Kol Yisrael* (the Israel radio broadcasting service).
57. *Globes*, 14 December 1994.
58. See Chapter 3, pp. 85–6.

7

The Policy of the United States

OUTSIDE ISRAEL, the country in which the greatest efforts were made to combat the Arab boycott and its effects was the United States. This was partially due to the American free-trade tradition, but was also the result of the work of the strong Jewish lobby, which operated in Washington and the pro-Israeli sentiments of many American Congressmen and members of the Administration, though Congress was usually more sympathetic towards the struggle against the boycott than the Administration.

The American Policy until 1975

Already in the early 1950s there were two categories of American companies insofar as the Arab boycott was concerned. First there were those which refused to submit to the boycott, some of which were subsequently blacklisted by the boycott authorities. These included corporations such as Studebaker, Ford Motor Company, General Motors, Hilton Hotels, Chase Manhattan and eventually also Coca-Cola. Others gave in to boycott requests or voluntarily submitted to the boycott, in order to avoid being placed on the blacklist.[1]

In 1952 the British Foreign Office received a report from Washington to the effect that according to State Department officials there was no pressure on them from American companies to take any action with regards to the boycott, and that they felt that particular problems should be dealt with on an individual basis.[2] According to a British Foreign Office memorandum written in 1953, the policy of the American Administration was to give in to commercial interests and comply with boycott regulations rather than try to stand up to them. '[T]he American exporting and manufacturing firms apparently do not attempt to carry on business in both Israel and the Arab states. The official representatives of the United States Government apparently concur in this line of conduct and our numerous efforts to stimulate the State Department to cooperate with us in particular instances, have so far led to nothing.'[3] In May 1956 the Public Service Division in the US State Department issued a statement regarding the boycott which said: 'We are obliged to recognize that any attempt by this country to force our views on a foreign national would be considered intervention in the domestic affairs of that national and therefore greatly resented.'[4]

It was only after several cases in which the anti-Jewish nature of the boycott became apparent, that resulted in such major companies as Aramco excluding Jews from jobs directly connected with their work in Saudi Arabia,[5] that a shift started taking place in the position of Congress, and later of the Administration. It was the Anti-Defamation League of B'nai B'rith (ADL) which was largely responsible for bringing the anti-Jewish nature of the boycott to light. The ADL, which continued in the coming decades to stand at the forefront of the anti-boycott campaign in the US, scored an early success when it managed to get both American Express and the cigarette manufacturer Brown & Williamson to refrain from a total boycott of Israel, by threatening to use the Jewish purchasing power against them.[6]

In July 1956 the Senate adopted a resolution confirming that attempts by foreign nations to discriminate against US citizens on grounds of religious affiliation, were incompatible with the relations that should exist among friendly nations, and that in all negotiations between the US and foreign states, every reasonable effort should be made to maintain the principle of non-discrimination.[7]

In January 1960 it was disclosed that since the spring of 1958 the US Navy had virtually foreclosed bidding on oil cargo shipping contracts to US-flag ships that had previously done business with Israel. In a standard clause, known as the 'Haifa clause', included in all contracts of the Military Sea Transport Service, the Navy reserved the right to cancel the charter, without liability for costs, if an Arab country refused to let the ship load or unload because it had previously carried Israeli cargoes or called on an Israeli port. The adoption of the clause had been prompted by the refusal of port officials at Ras Tanura in Saudi Arabia, to permit the loading of a vessel, that had at one time touched at an Israeli port. The Navy rescinded the clause less than a month after the disclosure, following considerable criticism in Congress that the clause seemed to support the Arab boycott of Israel.[8]

Another revelation at about the same time concerned the two government agencies that administered the sale of US agricultural surpluses to friendly nations. It was argued that the two approved charter contracts containing the following provision: 'Vessel is prohibited to call at Israeli waters or ports. Transshipment is prohibited. Vessel has not traded to [sic] Israeli ports.' An Agriculture Department spokesman defended the practice by saying, on 2 March 1960, that shipping contracts were made between the Arab country doing the purchasing and the American exporter or shipowner, and that the 'terms and conditions are of no concern to us'.[9]

On 13 April 1960 the Seafarers' International Union (SIU) decided to picket the Egyptian ship *Cleopatra*, in protest against harassment and mistreatment of American seamen in Arab ports and the loss of jobs for many American seamen as a result of the Arab policy of blacklisting ships, which had intensified in the beginning of 1960 following the formation of the short-lived union between Egypt and Syria (the United Arab Republic – UAR). This followed similar steps taken by the Finnish dockworkers in February, and the Swedish Transport Workers' Federation several days earlier. The SIU had decided to embark on this means of action after appeals to the President and the State Department failed to result in any decisive action.[10] The picketing ended only after the Acting Secretary of State, Douglas Dillon, issued a statement of policy that expressed US support for the principle of freedom of the seas and free access to foreign ports. It asserted that the US 'neither recognizes nor condones the Arab boycott', and that every opportunity would be utilized to reemphasize this fundamental position to the governments concerned. It vowed that the US would continue to pursue, by all appropriate and effective means, every avenue whereby private American interests in international trade would be fully safeguarded and restored.

The State Department publicly acknowledged for the first time that American seamen had been harassed at Arab ports and concluded by saying that it would 'renew its efforts to protect the interests of our shipping and seamen now being discriminated against by the Arab boycott and blacklisting policy', and would give full consideration to all communications from the Seafarers' International Union, other affected maritime unions and other interested groups.[11]

On 28 April 1960, over the objections of Senator James William Fulbright and pro-Arab groups in Congress, a 'Sense of Congress' resolution was adopted by the Senate condemning economic warfare, including boycotts.[12] The resolution gave the President authority, to be exercised at his discretion, to withhold mutual security aid as well as surplus food assistance to the UAR, as long as the ban on the passage of Israeli ships and cargoes through the Suez Canal remained in effect.[13] Despite the Dillon statement (see above), President Dwight David Eisenhower termed the amendment 'regrettable', and indicated that he would not use the discretionary authority. Reports were also being circulated to the effect that the State Department felt there was virtually no chance that new pressures would induce the Egyptian President to lift the Suez blockade or to alter his blacklisting policy.[14]

In May 1960 Congress also passed an amendment to the Mutual Security Act. The amendment condemned the boycott and stated that the US 'favours freedom of navigation in international waterways and economic cooperation between nations'. It added that the purposes of the Act 'are negated and the peace of the world is endangered when nations, which receive assistance under this Act wage economic warfare against other nations assisted under this Act, including such procedures as boycotts, blockades, and the restriction of the use of international waterways'.[15] While Fulbright was successful in getting the Senate to drop an anti-boycott clause from the Mutual Security Bill passed at the end of June 1961,[16] Congress added a preamble to the 1962 Foreign Assistance Act to the effect that 'it is the policy of the US to support the principles of increased economic cooperation and trade among countries – without discrimination as to race or religion'.[17]

The following year Binyamin Navon, a staff member of the Israeli consulate in New York assigned to deal with the Arab boycott,[18] was involved in an effort to try and question the legality of the application of the tertiary boycott in the US by invoking the 1870 Sherman Antitrust Act.[19] The particular case which was chosen was that of an American company called Tecumseh, which manufactured 80 per cent of the compressors used for refrigerators and air-conditioners in the US. For many years Tecumseh had worked with the Israeli refrigerator manufacturer Amcor without a contract, then a contract was finally drawn up and signed. Following the signing of the contract, Philco, a subsidiary of Ford, and another American firm started to press Tecumseh to cancel its contract with Amcor due to Arab boycott pressure. Tecumseh decided to revert to its original arrangement with Amcor, i.e. working without a contract. Navon, after consulting legal experts, pressed to have the issue taken to court on the basis of the Sherman Antitrust Act. However he was stopped by the Israeli Ambassador to Washington, Abe Harman, who feared that this activity would anger the State Department.[20]

In September 1964 Senator Harrison A. Williams from New Jersey revealed that 164 American companies appeared on the blacklists of one or more Arab states.[21] A lot of information on the boycott was gathered in this period by outfits such as Business International, and these occasionally published advice on how to cope with it.[22]

There were several ways in which blacklisted companies reacted. Some, such as General Tire and Rubber Co. of Akron, Ohio, which was placed on the blacklist because it held a one-third equity share in the Israeli tyre company Alliance, sold all its shares in 1963, and around 1970 hired the services of a Lebanese-based company, Triad Financial Establishment, headed by the Saudi businessman Adnan Khashoggi, which for a sum of $150,000 promised to get the company off the blacklist.[23]

A company refusing to give in to the boycott in this period was the recording company RCA. RCA was blacklisted in 1966 for granting a licence to an Israeli record company Hed Artzi to use the RCA label. Until that time RCA had been selling about $10 million worth of records annually to the Arab world. As a result of the blacklisting it lost over 90 per cent of that business. Furthermore, RCA was routinely cut out of contracts by other companies trying to observe the boycott rules. RCA could have manœuvred its way off the list, but its officials refused to deal.[24]

The Chase Manhattan Bank represented a third manner of reaction to the boycott. In July 1964 the Central Boycott Office (CBO) in Damascus issued a press release announcing that Chase had been blacklisted because it handled Israel's bond issues in the US, and thus was, according to the Commissioner General of the CBO, Mohammed Mahgoub,[25] the 'chief fiscal agent for Israel'. Mahgoub gave the Arab states six months to settle their accounts with the bank. Shortly thereafter the Syrian government issued instructions for all banks operating in the country to begin liquidating their transactions with Chase Manhattan. Mahgoub then announced that Kuwait was calling off plans to deposit $200 million with Chase, though the Kuwaitis denied any knowledge of such a proposed deposit. Chase Manhattan reacted with a diplomatic campaign at the highest levels in the more moderate Arab states and, since Egypt had a $10 million outstanding loan from Chase that it was eager to increase, the Egyptians were willing to help. In January 1965 the boycott council met again and Mahgoub was forced to announce that the action against Chase Manhattan had been suspended because of some certified documents submitted by the bank. No one knows what these documents said, but Chase continued to handle Israel's bond issues, in violation of section 18b of the boycott rules, and at the same time increased its financial dealings with such countries as Saudi Arabia and Kuwait.[26]

In 1964–65 the American Israel Public Affairs Committee (AIPAC), with the full cooperation of the American Jewish organizations and the encouragement of Yuval Elizur of the Israeli Economic Mission in New York,[27] started pressing for legislation barring boycott compliance, which was intended to prohibit compliance with the discriminatory stipulations of the Arab boycott.[28] Several such bills were reviewed by the Banking and Currency Committees of both the House of Representatives and the Senate. The proponents of the bills raised three main arguments in their favour: that the boycott involved religious discrimination; that the US ought to support Israel; and that foreign interference in the decisions of American business ought to be stopped.[29]

The legislation which was finally passed was initiated by a minor official in General Electric by the name of Parke W. Masters, a supporter of Senator Williams, who felt that such an initiative would help gain for Williams Jewish support.[30] The legislation formally recorded US opposition to restrictive trade practices and boycotts fostered or imposed by foreign states, and requested domestic companies to refuse to comply with them. However, it refrained from turning application of and submission to the boycott in the US into illegal acts. The legislation took the form of an amendment to the 1965 Export Control Act, which was proposed by Senators Harrison

A. Williams and Jacob Javits. Section 3(5) of the amended Act stated that:

> It is the policy of the US to oppose restrictive trade practices or boy-
> cotts fostered or imposed by foreign countries against other countries
> friendly to the US, and to encourage and request domestic concerns
> engaged in the export of articles, materials, supplies or information to
> refuse to take any action, including the furnishing of information or
> the signing of agreements, which has the effect of furthering or sup-
> porting restrictive trade practices, or boycotts fostered or imposed by
> any foreign countries against any country friendly to the US.[31]

Regulations issued subsequent to the amendment in September 1965 required the reporting of all boycott requests within 15 business days of their being received, to the Office of Export Control in the US Department of Commerce. The Department of Commerce was also to receive copies of the boycott questionnaires, while the Secretary of Commerce was given authority under the law to act upon reports of boycott requests in such manner 'as he may deem appropriate to carry out the purposes of the law'.[32]

Even though the passage of the amendment was regarded as a major breakthrough, the legislation remained limited. One of the reasons for this was that the Administration was afraid that anti-boycott legislation would have a negative effect on the American policy of economic denial directed against Communist states,[33] while Assistant Secretary of State Douglas MacArthur II admitted that the Administration did not wish to harm American commercial relations with Kuwait and Saudi Arabia.[34] An additional argument against the US taking more effective measures against the Arab boycott was that in the final reckoning it did not really hurt the Israeli economy.

In 1969 a further attempt was made to make compliance with the boycott illegal under American law by extending the Export Control Act (renamed the Export Administration Act – EAA). However, once again the attempt failed, owing to opposition by the Departments of State and Commerce. Among the arguments now used against the legislation: that it would favour foreign over American exporters to Arab markets; that it would disrupt the trade of the many American companies doing business with both Israel and the Arab world; that it would constitute an interference in the corporate decisions of American businessmen; and that the US would appear to take sides in the conflict. It was not just new legislation which failed to get through. Even the legislation which had been passed in 1965 was not being fully implemented. The Department of Commerce admitted that although 22,964 boycott request reports had been filed by American exporters from October 1965 to March 1969, no action had been taken to prevent compliance, and no penalties had been imposed on firms that failed to report the receipt of boycott requests. At the same time officials were undermining congressional intent by informing exporters that reporting to the Department of Commerce was not mandatory.[35]

Despite the poor record of the Department of Commerce on this issue, the Director of the Bureau of International Commerce in the Department of Commerce, Harold Scott, stated on 30 July 1970 that 'It has been the consistent policy of the US Government not to afford the Arab boycott official recognition. We have opposed it, sought to have some of the more objectionable features revised or eliminated, and have extended every possible assistance to US companies requesting help in protecting their business interests against the boycott. The Department of Commerce also has repeatedly reminded US exporters that under the Export Administration Act of 1969 (formerly the Export Control Act of 1949), they are encouraged to refuse to cooperate with such boycotts and that they must promptly report any boycott requests to the Department.'[36]

Yet, Scott's statement did not herald a new era, and in the five years 1970–74, when 44,709 transactions involving Arab boycott requests were reported without any penalties being imposed, the record of the Department of Commerce did not improve.[37] As late as September of 1976 the House Interstate and Foreign Commerce Committee's Subcommittee on Oversight and Investigations, chaired by Representative John E. Moss, still found that the Department of Commerce had been doing in the period 1970–75 the 'bare minimum' to carry out the provisions of the EAA, and that by early 1975 not a single firm had been charged with failing to comply with the reporting requirements despite ample evidence that noncompliance was rampant.

The Moss report went so far as to state that 'By actions such as distributing to US businesses "trade opportunities" containing boycott clauses, the Commerce Department actually furthered the boycott by implicitly condoning activity declared against national policy by Congress 11 years [earlier]', and that Commerce had deliberately misled Congress about the extent of compliance, and had even encouraged companies to comply 'by looking the other way'. As a result of the report, the Department of Commerce finally changed its regulations, so that firms reporting boycott requests were now obliged to notify the Department as to whether they intended to comply with them.[38]

In fact until 1974 the US, like most other countries, made only perfunctory attempts to curb the Arab boycott,[39] one of the reasons being that until that time submission to boycott threats was much more limited than it became afterwards, as a result of the 1973 oil crisis and the accumulation of billions of petro-dollars in Arab hands.

In 1974 the pro-Israel lobby in Washington intensified its activity in Congress and started lobbying more actively for effective anti-boycott legislation and its implementation.[40] Two main events encouraged the pro-Israeli lobbyists to intensify their activity. The first was the 1973 oil crisis which increased the Arab economic leverage in the US as elsewhere, and with it concern over the use which the Arabs might make of their newly found power.[41] The second involved an overt manifestation of anti-Semitism by Arab investment companies against Jewish-owned banks participating as underwriters in international loan syndications. In one case, that of the Intra Investment Company, the Administration was directly involved, and hastily sold its equity in the company.[42]

Introduction of more Serious Anti-boycott Measures 1975–79

The high-profile campaign embarked upon by the Jewish organizations, started in earnest in February 1975. Three major Jewish organizations were involved – the ADL, the American Jewish Congress and the American Jewish Committee (AJC), which had started to accumulate and analyze the implications of the massive transfer of wealth to the Arab oil-producing states resulting from the oil crisis. By the beginning of 1975 the three organizations concluded that, of the myriad of issues that flowed from the accumulating Arab economic power, they ought to focus their efforts on combating the boycott. They decided to place special emphasis on raising the issue, getting it before the public, creating a sense of urgency about it and building support for action by means of legislation.[43]

On 26 February 1975, Senator Frank Church, chairman of the Senate Foreign Relations Subcommittee on Multinational Corporations, made public a Saudi Arabian edition of an Arab boycott list of more than 1,500 American companies and the regulations of the CBO in Damascus.[44] It is not known who supplied Church with this information, but it is not unlikely that it came from the Jewish organizations.

The Ford Administration was not particularly happy about this campaign, preferring quiet diplomacy. In the course of a hearing before Frank Church's Subcommittee on 26 February, Harold H. Saunders, Deputy Assistant Secretary of State for Near Eastern and South Asian Affairs, testified that the lifting of the boycott was linked to the resolution of the Arab–Israeli territorial dispute, expressing the view that the boycott could best be dealt with through quiet diplomacy and persuasion[45] Both the Department of Treasury and the Department of Commerce made it known that they preferred that the Administration avoid intervention, by means of legislation, in the economic decisions of firms based on their own business interests,[46] avoiding the question why the Arab states should be allowed to intervene in these decisions by applying what amounted to blackmail on these firms.

Nevertheless, on 20 November 1975 the Administration announced an anti-boycott package, which was aimed at preventing 'any discrimination against Americans on the basis of race, color, religion, national origin or sex that might arise from foreign boycott practices'. The package included the following new rules:

- federal agencies making overseas assignments were forbidden to take into account any exclusionary policies of a host country based on discriminatory factors;
- the State Department was to be informed whenever a visa was rejected as a result of such exclusionary policies, and was to take diplomatic action on behalf of the individual concerned;
- the Department of Labor was ordered to instruct companies working for the government to refrain from any job discrimination connected with work in or for a foreign state;
- the White House would support anti-discriminatory legislation;
- the Commerce Department was ordered to prohibit exporters and related service organizations to answer or comply with any boy-

cott requests which could cause discrimination against US citizens or firms.[47]

The vagueness of the package was exemplified, however, when, on 11 December 1975, Under-Secretary of Commerce James Baker stated before the Subcommittee on International Trade and Commerce that the Department of Commerce did not view the boycott as being discriminatory on religious grounds.[48] The future Secretary of State stated that while the Administration was concerned about the restrictive trade practices imposed on US companies by the boycott, this had to be balanced by the need to support 'legitimate US interests in the Middle East'. These interests included US exports to the Arab countries, which were expected to reach $10 billion by 1980, where each billion of such exports represented 40–70,000 jobs for American workers. For this reason, Baker concluded, the Administration was opposed to all attempts to legislate against compliance with the boycott because it 'could result in the loss of significant trade opportunities by US interests and business concerns'.[49]

While the Administration was opposed to legislation, certain government agencies nevertheless tried to act in accordance with the spirit of the declared anti-boycott package. In December 1975, Federal Reserve Board Chairman, Arthur Burns, sent out a letter to all member banks warning them about the practice of issuing letters of credit containing boycott provisions. Such practices, he argued, were 'a misuse of the privileges and benefits conferred upon the banking community'. Banking circles were not happy about the ruling, which was liable to seriously affect the whole pattern of boycott conditioned trade with the Arab countries. The Departments of State and Commerce, also had reservations, and in January 1976 Burns bowed to the pressure and issued a clarifying letter in which he stated that the previous letter 'was not intended to create any new legal obligations for banks'. It added that the primary responsibility for implementing and enforcing US policy on the boycott issue rested with the Department of Commerce.[50]

On 16 January 1976 the Department of Justice also took an initiative in the spirit of the anti-boycott package and filed a civil action against the giant construction firm Bechtel Corporation for breach of the Sherman Antitrust Act.[51] Secretary of State Henry Kissinger was displeased with this initiative. According to a senior State Department source, Kissinger was worried that the antitrust action 'could be seen by the Arabs as a deliberate US government decision to act against their policy. Thus it could have had an adverse effect on the peace-making process.' However, the Attorney General, Edward H. Levi, held his ground, and the action was filed.[52]

Also in 1976 the Securities and Exchange Commission (SEC) filed a complaint against the General Tire and Rubber Company, alleging violations of federal securities laws through failures to disclose the payments it had made to buy itself off the Arab League blacklist.[53]

The campaign of the Jewish organizations lasted until June 1977.[54] In addition to the Administration's package, it resulted in several legal actions against the Department of Commerce, six congressional investigations into the operations of the boycott, legislative action in 22 states to prohibit compliance with the boycott within their jurisdiction, and the introduction of over 22 congressional bills to combat the boycott.[55]

In two suits brought against the Department of Commerce in this period it was charged with cooperation with the boycott by publishing 'boycott tainted trade opportunities' in foreign tenders. These tenders stated among other things that the transaction in question was subject to the rules of the contracting company's boycott of Israel. Another legal issue which came up concerned the withholding by the Department of information regarding the reporting forms filed by firms which had been approached with boycott requests. The issue came up in several boycott-related civil actions. The Department argued in its defence that the reports were filed under a 'statutorily-based government pledge that reported information would be handled on a confidential basis [and that] although it is in [the Secretary's] authority to reverse the determination that withholding these reports is not contrary to the national interest, there are substantial reasons of equity and policy for not doing so'. However, the Assistant Attorney-General, Barbara Babcock, stated in a letter dated 27 July 1977 to President Carter's Counsel, Robert Lipshutz, that withholding reporting forms was inconsistent with the President's clear policy statements on the boycott issue.[56]

Throughout the boycott debate in this period, there were differences in emphasis between the House of Representatives and the Senate regarding legislation. While the House viewed the issue as falling within the domain of foreign policy, and expected action to be taken to counter the boycott, the Senate regarded it primarily as a domestic issue, involving the protection of US sovereignty and the rights of American citizens. The Senate's approach was well represented by an anti-boycott bill drafted by Senator Stanley J. Marcuss (S. 953). Initially the bill outlined increased reporting requirements for firms receiving boycott requests and gave the President discretionary authority to curtail economic transactions with boycotting countries – authority that had already been granted by the 1969 EAA. The bill was strengthened and eventually passed by the Senate in August 1976.[57] On the other hand, the principle bill brought to the House of Representatives by Representative Jonathan B. Bingham (HR 4967), attempted to end compliance with the boycott, whatever the consequences.

However, the first substantial piece of anti-boycott legislation came in the form of the Ribicoff amendment to the 1976 Tax Reform Act, which, not surprisingly, was opposed by the Ford Administration.[58] The anti-boycott provisions introduced by Senator Abraham Ribicoff (S. 3138) amended the Internal Revenue Code of 1954 by denying a number of tax benefits to firms participating in or cooperating with the Arab boycott, but did not prohibit compliance with boycott requests.[59]

The amendment directed the Secretary of the Treasury to issue every three months an updated list of the countries found to participate in the implementation of the secondary and tertiary boycotts. Section 999 required every taxpayer who had any business operations in any of the boycotting countries to report that fact in form No. 5713 which was to be attached to his annual tax return to the Internal Revenue Service. He was also required to report any boycott participation or cooperation. The sanction for such a violation was the loss of foreign tax credits and benefits, including credit for foreign taxes and deferral of the taxes on the earnings of foreign subsidiaries.[60]

The Ribicoff amendment was not part of an overall anti-boycott strategy, nor was it coordinated with any of the other groups fighting the boycott. Nevertheless, opposition to it, both from the Administration and from the business community, proved ineffective.[61] The business community, which was afraid of adverse publicity that would result from an aggressive campaign against the anti-boycott legislation, was inclined to rely on the Ford Administration's opposition to it, and thus failed to organize adequately in the face of an active and energetic anti-boycott lobby.[62]

It was only in late 1976 that the American business community finally grasped the full implications of the anti-boycott legislation to their Middle East operations, and in 1977 came out in full force against it, even though this threatened to lead to an open confrontation with the Jewish community.[63] A major part of the campaign against the anti-boycott legislation was generated by oil companies such as Mobil, Exxon, Texaco and Continental Oil, while lobbying activities were initiated by Caterpillar Tractor Co., Bechtel Corporation, Standard Oil of California, American Cyanamid, as well as bodies such as the National Association of Manufacturers, the US Chamber of Commerce, the Emergency Committee for American Trade, and the US–Arab Chamber of Commerce.[64] The main thrust of this campaign was that the legislation was liable to result in the loss to American business of major business contracts in the Arab world, which would result in the loss of some 400–500,000 American jobs.[65]

Another group which was active on the anti-legislation front was one sponsored by the National Association of Arab-Americans, which was called Full Employment in America Through Trade Inc. (FEATT). The membership of this organization included persons known for their anti-Jewish sentiments, members of the Liberty Lobby and of the United Muslim Relief Incorporated.[66]

The boycott issue came up in the 1976 presidential election campaign, with Democratic presidential candidate, Jimmy Carter, announcing his support for legislation barring US compliance with secondary and tertiary Arab boycott requirements.[67] Carter's victory in November raised hopes among the American Jewish organizations that his Administration would be committed to the legislative efforts in Congress.[68] And, indeed, intensive negotiations carried out between January and May 1977 among the Administration, the ADL and the Business Round Table (an organization made up of 170 chief executive officers of the major American corporations) resulted in a 'Joint Statement of Principles', which set out in general terms areas in which it was agreed boycott compliance should be prohibited. It also laid down exceptions to the prohibitions, which recognized certain Arab rights in the sphere of regulating their own trade and immigration policies These principles were eventually included in the amendments to the Export Administration Act passed by Congress in 1977.[69]

The signing of the consent decree between the Bechtel Corporation (see above) and the Department of Justice in January 1977, which established the general principle that compliance with the tertiary boycott constituted a violation of US antitrust laws, also hastened the passing of the legislation, but failed to deal with wider aspects of the boycott or even repeated violations.[70]

On 22 June 1977 President Carter approved the amendments to the 1977 EAA.[71] The amendments required American firms and individuals to report to the Department of Commerce any request made to them to take boycott-related actions, and as later amended, prohibited the furnishing of the sort of information requested by boycotting states to help them impose their boycott. The amendments also prohibit dealing with letters of credit containing boycott requirements. Any person who failed to report boycott requests, or agreed to comply with boycott requests, which were considered a violation of the law, was liable to be fined.

The EAA aimed at limiting the reach of the secondary boycott by emphasizing the importance of territorial sovereignty. At the same time it applied extraterritorially to overseas subsidiaries of American firms, if they were 'controlled in fact' by their American parent companies, and their activities were within the 'interstate or foreign commerce of the United States'. What was meant by 'controlled in fact' was that either 50 per cent of the voting shares were owned or controlled by a US firm, over 25 per cent were so owned or controlled and no other firm had an equal share, or that most of the directors and executives of these overseas subsidiaries were appointed by US firms. In addition, the EAA provisions applied to such companies if they used US origin goods in boycott-tainted transactions.[72]

At the same time, domestic firms were allowed to provide positive certificates of origin for exported goods and even comply with the ban on blacklisted sub-contractors – the tertiary boycott – if the choice of subcontractors was 'unilateral and specific' on the part of the boycotting country or a resident therein. The EAA's application was also limited with regards to the activities of American subsidiaries functioning in boycotting countries.[73] Thus, subject to carefully limited exceptions, the EAA prohibited a US entity to refuse to do business with any Israeli business or national pursuant to an agreement with or a request from an Arab country; to refuse to employ or otherwise discriminate against any US person on the basis of religion or national origin; to furnish information about whether any person having had or proposing to have any business relationship with Israel; and to pay, confirm or otherwise implement a letter of credit that contained any of the prohibited conditions or requirements. Exceptions, designed to protect the legitimate interests of the Arab states, allowed compliance with requirements of an Arab country barring imports of Israeli goods or services; requirements barring the use of Israeli carriers; or certain requirements for import and shipping documents, such as information about country of origin and the name of the carrier.[74]

Enforcement of this complex law relied chiefly on the provision that required any US person who received a boycott-related request to report that request to the Department of Commerce. Such reports were now to be made available to the public. Boycott requests were reportable even if the action requested was not illegal because of one of the exceptions in the law. Failure to file such reports was punishable by a fine of up to $10,000.[75]

During the signing ceremony of the Act, President Carter emphasized the moral issues involved in outlawing the secondary and tertiary boycotts, and discriminating against American businessmen on religious or national grounds. 'My concern about foreign boycotts', Carter said, 'stemmed from our special relationship with Israel, as well as from the economic, military and security needs of both our countries. But the issue also goes to the very heart of free trade among all nations ... The Bill seeks ... to end the divisive effects on American life of foreign boycotts aimed at Jewish members of our society. If we allow such a precedent to become established, we open the door to similar action against any ethnic, religious or racial group in America.'[76] The President went on to pledge the Administration's effective enforcement of the legislation, and expressed his confidence that the 'enforcement of this legislation will help lessen the tensions in the Middle East and hopefully lead to a permanent peace there'.[77]

Following the passing of these two major pieces of anti-boycott legislation, the Jewish organizations introduced a monitoring programme to follow their implementation. In March 1977 the

American Jewish Congress started to publish a monthly newsletter, *Boycott Report*, which after 1979 started dealing with issues related to Arab influence in the US, in addition to boycott-related issues. The American Jewish Congress also instituted a programme of filing complaints with the appropriate federal agencies, sensitizing government officials to the boycott issue, and briefing reporters and journalists on the issue.[78]

On 23 September 1977 the Department of Commerce proposed regulations for the implementation of the anti-boycott provisions of the EAA. These came under severe criticism in Congress, which believed that the Department was attempting to undermine the stringent provisions of the statute. In the final version of the regulations, which came into force on 18 January 1978, a number of loopholes were eliminated. The regulations as finally approved met with the general approval both of the business community and the Jewish organizations.[79]

The attitude of the Department of Treasury towards the 1976 Ribicoff amendment, was similar to that of the Department of Commerce to the EAA, and the original regulations issued had to be revised in August 1977, January 1978 and finally in November 1979.[80] The two different sets of regulations under the TRA and the EAA caused confusion within the American business community. In the case of the TRA all efforts to get the act repealed failed.[81]

The Commerce Department regulations, enacted pursuant to the 1979 EAA, which fully incorporated the anti-boycott provisions of the 1977 EAA, prohibited US firms to furnish information about their business relationships with a boycotted country. The prohibition included information regarding business relationships with any business concerns organized under the laws of the boycotted country, any national or resident of the boycotted country, or any person known or believed to be blacklisted by the boycotting country. The prohibition did not apply to the furnishing of 'normal business information in a commercial context'. Such information could not be supplied either upon the direct or indirect request of another person or upon the initiative of the US firm. The prohibitions only applied to acts undertaken with intent of complying with, promoting or supporting an unsanctioned foreign boycott.[82]

Predictions by opponents of the anti-boycott legislation as to its dire consequences regarding the American economy proved to be unfounded. 'Last year's gloomy prediction that passage of the foreign boycott provisions of the Export Administration Amendments would cost thousands of US jobs and severely damage US–Arab trade, have not materialized', said Deputy Assistant Secretary of Commerce, Stanley J. Marcuss, on 14 September 1978. 'On the contrary, since the passage of the law, there has been a significant increase in US exports to the 14 Near East/North African boycotting nations.'[83]

Implementation of the Anti-boycott Legislation during the Reagan Administration – 1981–88

During the eight years of the Reagan Administration, which began in 1981, there were no changes in the provisions of the EAA. The 1977 legislation was reenacted verbatim in the 1979 EAA and continued to constitute the basis for all enforcement procedures. The Office of Antiboycott Compliance (OAC) was established within the framework of the Commerce Department, and started levying fines from US firms and their foreign subsidiaries that complied with boycott demands, while imposing penalties on firms that failed to report receipt of boycott requests. Its tasks are defined as: enforcing the anti-boycott regulations, assisting the public in complying with the regulations and compiling and analyzing information regarding international boycotts. Compliance officers enforce the regulations through investigations and audits. The Compliance Policy Division provides advice and guidance to the public concerning application of the regulations and analyses information about boycotts.[84] Special attention was soon directed at the banking community and the multinational corporations.[85]

In the case of tax benefits denied because of US companies' participation in or cooperation with an international boycott', Department of Treasury figures showed the sums to have fallen from $11 million in 1978, to $4 million in 1985, and $2.8 million in 1986. The explanation for the fall was that the offending companies managed to adjust their operations to avoid Treasury anti-boycott penalties.[86]

At the end of December 1987 the Houston-based Saudi-owned Al-Zamil trading company was fined a record $450,000 for 40 alleged violations concerning the company's refusal or agreement to refuse

Table 1: Enforcement of the Anti-boycott Provisions of the EAA since the
Beginning of the Reagan Administration

Financial year	No. of investigations	No. of settlement agreements	Total sum of civil penalties
1981	140	20	$385,000
1982	124	43	$548,750
1983	290	53	$1,378,750
1984	226	59	$1,647,500
1985	457	38	$518,500
1986	507	37	$425,500
1987	523	46	$1,349,750
1988	540	33	$3,993,500[a]
1989	117	23	$1,117,500
1990	83	21	$335,000
1991	96	18	$227,900
1992[c]	118	32	$4,000,000
1993[c]	80	37	$6,817,450[b]
1994[c]	78	31	$1,432,700
1995[c]	89	23	$1,826,850
1996[d]	35	20	$887,600

Notes:
[a] This sum includes the settlements with Safeway Stores Ltd and Sara Lee
Corporation (Source: Feder, op. cit., pp. 50–68).
[b] This sum includes $6.1 million paid by Baxter International and related parties;
Baxter also paid a $500,000 criminal penalty.
[c] The information for the years 1992–95 was kindly provided by Dr Jess Hordes of
the ADL in Washington DC.
[d] OAC (1997), pp. 11–116.

goods from suppliers on the boycott list, and a further alleged violations concerning the provision of prohibited information about the
blacklist status of various suppliers. On 15 January 1988 the Bank of
America agreed to pay $220,000 to settle claims that it had violated
legal provisions prohibiting US banks to act on international letters
of credit that require American companies to carry out boycott-
related activities.[87]

In March 1988 Safeway Stores Ltd paid a record fine of $995,000
in settlement of 449 (!) alleged violations of the anti-boycott laws. A
few months later, in August 1988, Sara Lee Corporation of Chicago,
settled a similar claim in respect of 235 alleged violations for
$725,000, thus avoiding what would have been the first criminal
charges brought against an American firm by the OAC.[88]

However, the case of the Dover Corporation – a manufacturer of elevators and other machinery which was trying to get itself removed from the Kuwaiti blacklist in violation of anti-boycott regulations – demonstrated that the Department of Commerce had to be careful in the understandings it reached with offenders or potential offenders. After being told explicitly by the OAC that the action it was planning to take to be removed from the blacklist would be a violation of the law, but that it would not face criminal prosecution for the offence, Dover nevertheless committed it. Commerce was left with the option of assessing a civil penalty for a wilful violation of the law.[89]

Though, as described above, there were some major settlements with offending companies, most of the enforcement activities of the OAC involved relatively small settlements, which varied from year to year. Attempts by penalized firms to claim that the US anti-boycott legislation was unconstitutional, since it infringed on their rights of free speech and association, were time and again rejected by the courts.[90] Other challenges to the EAA were directed at the extra-territorial application of export controls, and the President's authority to issue a blanket freeze of export licenses and to control international payments and financial transactions.[91]

Despite its many limitations, the anti-boycott legislation was generally believed to be fairly effective. In addition to having some deterrence effect, it forced the boycotting states to modify some of their boycott practices.[92] It became apparent that the attitude of the Arab oil producing states towards the US was much more a function of their immediate economic interests, than of the boycott and American efforts to ward off its effects. Thus, in 1981 – a year in which oil income was at its peak – US exports to boycott-observing countries reached $12.9 billion, while in 1986 with the decline of oil revenues – they dropped to $6.2 billion. In 1983 direct Arab investment in the US was estimated at $78 billion, of which some $44 billion were in government securities.[93]

The Bush Administration – 1989–92

Early in the Bush Administration, which began in 1989, the new Secretary of Commerce, Robert Mosbacher, promised 'vigorous enforcement of the anti-boycott legislation, using appropriate sanctions'.[94] In one of his early Middle East policy speeches, Secretary of

State James Baker also called upon the Arab states to 'end the boycott'.[95]

At the same time, with the encouragement of the American Jewish organizations, Congress once again started calling upon the Administration to intensify its activity against the boycott. In June 1989 Congress passed the 1990 Foreign Aid Authorization Act, which was accompanied by a request that the Secretary of State prepare a report concerning the policies of Arab states towards 'ending the economic boycott of Israel'. The purpose of this request, as in the case of other Congressional anti-boycott resolutions and legislative amendments which followed, was to put the boycott on the agenda, and force both the Administration and US trading partners to respond.

In 1990 a boycott scandal came up in connection with Baxter International – a giant Chicago-based medical supplies corporation. A former Baxter employee, Dr Richard Fuisz, made allegations to the effect that Baxter had engaged in an intensive effort, which had lasted for many years, to get itself off the Arab League blacklist, using means considered illegal under the anti-boycott laws. These allegations led to the opening of an investigation into Baxter by the OAC, which was later to expand to the Department of Justice, and become the longest and most extensive prosecution in American anti-boycott history.

Baxter had been doing business with Israel since the early 1970s. In 1971 it built a manufacturing plant in Ashdod in Israel, which employed 240 workers. In the early 1980s it was placed on the boycott list for owning a factory in Israel. It subsequently sold the facility to Teva Pharmaceutical Industries, Israel's largest pharmaceutical company,[96] and at their June 1989 meeting the Arab boycott commissioners decided to remove it from the blacklist. The effect of the Baxter case was to dramatize the far-reaching and distorting effect of the Arab boycott on the business decisions of American corporate executives, and to demonstrate that further action against the boycott was necessary.[97] In February 1991 the Department of Commerce referred the Baxter case to the Justice Department for the first-ever investigation of a company for possible criminal violations of US anti-boycott legislation, including export control provisions of the EAA.[98]

In 1989 there was a drastic fall in the number of investigations opened and the sums of the penalties collected by the OAC, despite evidence that Arab requests to American companies for boycott compliance, and the percentage of compliant responses, had not decreased. The explanation offered by the Jewish organizations for this phenomenon was that the salaries offered by the OAC were insufficient to attract staff of the quality and experience necessary to pursue effective commercial investigations, and that the size of the staff had consequently decreased. Penalties meted out to companies fined for infractions of the law were usually $10,000 per offence or less. These sums in no way constituted a deterrent to companies hoping to earn millions from Arab business.

As a result, several Congressmen, together with the Jewish organizations, initiated a campaign aimed at securing the agreement of the Department of Commerce to increase the budget and staff of the OAC, raising the mandatory fines that the OAC could impose, and encouraging the use of tougher penalties, such as a denial of export privileges to offending companies.

In addition the Treasury had not released a report on its administration of the anti-boycott provisions of the Internal Revenue Code since 1985, despite numerous requests from the Jewish organizations, and available reports covered tax returns only through 1982.[99] Senator John Heinz (R – PA) ordered a General Accounting Office (GAO) study of IRS application and enforcement of the tax code anti-boycott provisions.

Another element of increasing importance at this time in the accelerating anti-boycott effort, was a renewed focus on submission to the boycott by other Western governments and companies. It was felt that the willingness and freedom of European and Japanese companies to comply with Arab boycott requests, put American businesses at a disadvantage, and American businessmen were eager to have the Administration get foreign governments to cease authentication of boycott-tainted documents and adopt anti-boycott legislation.

In late 1989 Representative Robert Torricelli (D – NJ) introduced an amendment to the Foreign Aid Authorization bill, which required the Secretary of Commerce to report to Congress on the boycott compliance and/or anti-boycott policies of countries party to the General Agreement on Tariffs and Trade (GATT).[100] In the same winter, 100 Representatives also wrote to the Japanese and south

Korean prime ministers, protesting the flagrant compliance of these countries with the Arab boycott.

On 26 September 1990 a rule went into force which prohibited US persons to furnish certain types of information, in order to clarify that the anti-boycott provisions apply to the 'transmission' of prohibited information to another by a US person who has not authored such information.[101]

Developments Following the Gulf War – 1991–92

The Gulf War of January/February 1991 was a watershed insofar as the prospects for a settlement of the Arab–Israeli conflict were concerned, and thus for a modification and eventual lifting of the Arab boycott. This whole development was due to a large extent to the determination of the US to take advantage of the new circumstances to get the Middle East peace process off the ground.

Even before the outbreak of the Gulf War, American Congressmen raised questions about the policies of both Kuwait and Saudi Arabia towards American companies, which maintained economic ties with Israel. But it was only after the war was over that concerted efforts began to get a change in the policy of these states towards the boycott. As reconstruction works began in Kuwait, the American Jewish Congress wrote to the Director of the Middle East Division of the US Army Engineer Corps, who was in charge of coordinating the work in Kuwait, asking for assurances that contracts for the reconstruction of Kuwait and Saudi Arabia, signed by the Corps, would not contain boycott provisions.[102]

At the same time, Senators Joe Lieberman (D – CT) and Carl Levin (D – MI) initiated a letter to the Emir of Kuwait, Sheikh Jabber a-Sabakh, which was signed by 82 Senators, and was personally delivered by a delegation of Senators who visited the Gulf in the middle of March. The letter stated:

> [The] reconstruction [of Kuwait] also provides an historic opportunity to make an important move towards peace in the region by ending your nation's participation in the boycott of American companies which do business with Israel. This lifting of the secondary boycott would constitute an important gesture toward peace in the region and would eliminate a significant source of friction between our two

countries. Israel's restraint in the face of repeated Iraqi attacks should not go unrecognized by the allied coalition … We urge you to announce that Kuwait will no longer participate in the Arab boycott of Israel and that help from any American company in the reconstruction of your nation is welcome.[103]

Sixty-eight Senators signed a similar letter to King Fahd of Saudi Arabia. Secretary of Commerce Mosbacher personally raised the matter with the Emir of Kuwait, when they met on 16 March. Representative Mel Levine (D – CA) also obtained the signatures of Congressmen on a series of letters, that were sent to the Saudi and Kuwaiti ambassadors in Washington, and delivered to the King and Emir in person. The letter to the Emir read as following:

> In the process of granting contracts to American companies to rebuild Kuwait, we would hope that no American company would be discriminated against because it conducts business with Israel. We urge you to terminate your government's procedure of sending out boycott requests to American companies … The United States invested approximately $47.5 billion, and 304 Americans sacrificed their lives in an effort to bring peace and stability to the region. It is vital now that our Arab coalition partners also make a meaningful contribution to those efforts to secure the peace by ending their acts of war against Israel. As a modest first step, we urge you to lift the secondary boycott against firms that conduct business with Israel. This would provide a gesture of good faith and a confidence building measure between your country and Israel, and would avoid conflict between the United States and the Kuwaiti government on this issue.[104]

Congress also took out a full-page advertisement in the *New York Times*, entitled 'An Open Letter to the Arab Members of the Coalition', calling for an end to the boycott.[105] While neither the Kuwaitis nor the Saudis responded directly to any of these approaches, Administration officials indicated that Gulf leaders had pledged, off the record, to cease enforcing the boycott against American companies.[106] A Department of Commerce survey of US companies active in Kuwait indeed concluded that, for the moment, Kuwaiti contracts did not include boycott language.[107] But no one could extract a public declaration of any sort on the boycott, even regarding American companies, from either the Kuwaitis or the Saudis.

It was in these months that Representatives Charles Schumer (D – NY) and Ileanna Ros-Lehtinen (R – FL) established a 28-member 'task force to end the Arab boycott'. The force was designed to co-ordinate legislative efforts aimed at the Arab boycott of Israel, and US and foreign corporate compliance with the boycott. The group's first act was to send a joint letter to President George Bush, urging him to make the boycott a high-priority item on the US agenda for the approaching July meeting of the G-7 in London. The meeting was viewed as an opportunity to focus international attention on the boycott, and to codify Western expectations of the Arabs. Over 80 American US Senators wrote to Secretary of State James Baker on 19 April, and then again to the President on 10 July, asking that the US place pressure on its G-7 allies 'in the strongest terms possible to end their compliance with the boycott', and that, as a group, the G-7 should issue an unequivocal call on Arab nations to end the secondary boycott:

> While the US has enacted strict laws which prohibit US firms to com-ply with the boycott, our major trading partners have taken no such action. Accordingly, US firms vying for contracts are put at a dis-advantage with foreign companies because of the boycott restriction. We must implore our trading partners to examine their own policies toward the boycott, and urge them to pass legislation which prohibits private sector compliance ... In order to effectively stifle the coercive effects of the Arab boycott, we need the cooperation of our allies.[108]

In addition to the efforts to get the Arabs and the major industrial-ized powers to change their approach towards the boycott, efforts continued to be made in Washington to to get the OAC and other authorities dealing with the boycott, to enforce the existing laws more stringently, and improve the anti-boycott legislation. In July the House Foreign Affairs Sub-Committee on International Economic Policy and Trade, chaired by Representative Gedjenson, held hearings on the operations of the OAC.

Heading off the expected criticism of the OAC at these hearings, following a meeting, on 16 May 1991 between senior representatives of the AJC, the American Jewish Congress, the ADL and AIPAC with six senior officials of the Department of Commerce, Secretary of Commerce Robert A. Mosbacher pledged to support a five-fold increase in the levels of penalties the OAC could impose (from $10,000–50,000), and to increase OAC funding and staffing. On 30 October 1991 the House of Representatives passed a bill to increase the civil penalty for anti-boycott violations. These legislative measures were accompanied by the publication of new policy guidelines by the Department of Commerce. Two months later the Under Secretary for Export Administration of the Commerce Department issued new 'Guidelines for the Imposition of Penalties under the Anti-Boycott Regulations', committing the OAC to rigorous enforcement standards. The guidelines called for:

- the review of each case that the OAC investigated for potential criminal violations in consultation with the Department of Justice;
- the denial of export privileges when the violations were aggravated, e.g. discrimination on religious or ethnic grounds, refusal to do business and informing on other persons in boycott questionnaires. This category included use of a 'white list' of suppliers not on an Arab blacklist or of a blacklist of boycotted suppliers;
- the increase of the general level of penalties proportionally to the statutory maximum of $50,000 (exclusive of criminal violations), so that even penalties for 'routine' violations (such as late reports) would increase;
- the continuation of the policy of 'parsing' (considering each answer to a boycott question as a separate violation, even if the answers were all given on a single sheet of paper, and delivered in one transmission), and 'stacking' (regarding each furnishing of information as a separate violation).[109]

The problem which these moves sought to address was the fact that the low rate of penalties failed to deter many corporations from giving in to the boycott, as occurred in the case of the Dover Corporation. (See above) The situation regarding the enforcement of the anti-boycott provisions of the Internal Revenue Code was no more satisfactory, and the General Accounting Office actually released a report extremely critical of the IRS on this count.

During the period March–July 1991 eight new anti-boycott bills were introduced and over 15 House and Senate resolutions concerning the boycott were passed, in which the Arab states were called upon to recognize Israel, end the state of belligerency, enter direct negotiations with it and end the boycott, and the Secretary of State was called upon to report to Congress on progress in this sense.[110] Most of the anti-boycott provisions which were proposed never got through.

Among those that did was an amendment to the Defense Appropriations Bill, introduced by Senator Timothy E. Wirth (D – CO) in June 1991, which prohibited the Department of Defense to sign contracts of over $25,000 with foreign persons, companies or entities that complied with the secondary boycott. Foreign firms competing for Pentagon contracts were required to provide certification to this effect.[111] However the bill, which was signed into law by President Bush on 26 November 1991, included several loopholes. The first was that it allowed the Department of Defense to waive the non-boycott certification requirement, if the national security interests of the US made this necessary. Also exempted were Defense Department contracts for consumables, provisions and services contracted for US and allied military forces in foreign countries.[112]

Nevertheless, this law was regarded as highly significant by the anti-boycott lobby since Department of Defense contracts amounted to $300 billion annually, of which 20 per cent went to foreign contractors – mostly European and Japanese multinationals.[113]

Senator Ernest Frederick Hollings (D – SC) also successfully introduced a provision into the Commerce, Justice and State Appropriations Act, which was signed into law on 28 October 1991. The amendment included a provision – section 502 – that prohibited any State Department contracts with foreign or US firms that complied with the boycott or discriminated on the basis of religion. However, on 10 December, Secretary of State James Baker declared a waiver to the Hollings provision with regards to 19 of the 23 member states of the Arab League, and a few additional Muslim states, stating that even though the Department of State was opposed to the boycott of Israel and, 'in the context of the historic negotiations underway between Israel and the Arab States, is actively exploring means and opportunities for ending the boycott ... it would be impracticable at this time for our diplomatic posts to function if they could obtain essential services and goods only from firms willing to certify that they do not comply with the Arab League boycott of Israel or discriminate in the award of subcontracts on the basis of religion ...'.[114]

The House Appropriations Bill on Foreign Operations for FY 1992/93 included a provision, introduced by Representative Bill Green (R – NY) requesting the State Department to prepare a semiannual report describing those countries receiving US aid and/or arms, which were complying with the boycott of Israel, and detailing State Department efforts to encourage nations to end the boycott.[115]

In the meantime the OAC turned over the material of its investigation on Baxter International (see above p. 170) to the US District Attorney in Chicago for criminal investigation. This was the first time in the 14-year history of US anti-boycott legislation that a criminal indictment against an American firm was being considered. The preliminary investigation had uncovered a series of letters written by Baxter's Vice-President and General Counsel, Marshall G. Abbey, to Syrian military and boycott officials, suggesting that Baxter had not only assured the Syrian officials that it had ended all business in Israel, but had actually considered paying several million dollars in bribes to certain officials, in order to grease the path towards being taken off the blacklist, and being allowed to construct an intravenous fluid manufacturing plant in Syria.[116]

Under American prodding, the G-7 meeting, held in London in July 1991, issued a statement regarding the boycott, though it was not to the liking of Israel and the American Jewish organizations. The communiqué, issued by the G-7 at the end of their meeting, linked the lifting of the boycott to the cessation of Israeli settlement activities in the occupied territories.[117] This policy was strongly supported by President Bush, though he admitted in a letter to Representative Charles E. Schumer (D – NY) that the only common denominator between the boycott and the settlements was that he opposed both. The linkage, he added, merely reflected a 'widely shared political judgement'.[118] Since the Likud-led government of Yitzhak Shamir in Israel had no intention of stopping its settlement activities in the West Bank at any price, the G-7 communiqué had little practical significance, beyond the novelty of the seven major economic powers actually calling for the boycott to be lifted.

Following the convention of the Madrid peace conference at the end of October 1991, the US Administration continued to press Israel to freeze all its settlement activities in the territories, but now what was being offered was not the cancellation of the boycott, but American loan guarantees for a sum of $10 billion over five years to assist Israel in the absorption of the new wave of immigrants from the former Soviet Union. Though the Israeli government rejected the *quid pro quo*, towards the end of 1991 there was another burst of

Congressional activity around the boycott issue, aimed primarily at reducing or eliminating boycott participation by foreign companies. The intention was to reduce the competitive advantage of foreign firms over US firms seeking to penetrate Arab markets.

In the course of 1992 a major effort was required by the Jewish organizations to consolidate the legislative gains of the previous year. This was done, as in the past, by monitoring and prodding the enforcement of the new anti-boycott regulations. The result was that in fiscal year 1992, the civil penalties levied by the OAC increased almost nineteen-fold over the previous year's totals (see Table 2).

Table 2: Enforcement of the Anti-boycott Provisions of the EAA during the Bush Administration

Financial year	No. of investigations	No. of settlement agreements	Total sum of civil penalties
1989	117	23	$1,117,500
1990	83	21	$335,000
1991	96	18	$227,900
1992	118	32	$4,000,000

Source: Feder, op. cit., pp. 50–68. Information for the year 1992 kindly provided by Dr Jess Hordes of the IDL in Washington DC.

In June 1992 the OAC sent the American Jewish Congress a list of large firms investigated and fined over the years for violations of the anti-boycott laws. The list included such major banks as Bank of America, Chase Manhattan, Chemical, Citibank, Continental, Mellon, Security Pacific and Wells Fargo, as well as industrial giants such as A.R.J.R., Chrysler, Deere, Dresser, Ford, General Electric, Grand Union, Hewlett Packard, Honeywell, Hughes Aircraft, Nabisco, Raytheon, Rockwell, 3M, Safeway Stores, Sara Lee and Xerox. Most of the settlements reached with these companies involved the offending company paying a money fine. Safeway, for example, agreed to pay a penalty of $995,000 and Sara Lee agreed to pay $725,000. Xerox, on the other hand, consented to a six-month suspension of its export licence for trade with the Arab world.[119]

Despite the cooperative atmosphere, in February 1992 the Administration tried to repeal the Hollings amendment (see above), and to cancel the prohibition to issue 'Israel-only' passports, from the State Department's 1993 budget proposal.[120] Both Congress and the Jewish organizations reacted sharply. Representative Bill Green, who had first made public the proposed deletions, charged that the State Department 'couldn't do more to sanction the Arab League boycott of Israel than if the Arab League had written [the boycott deletion] itself'. The American Jewish Congress accused the State Department of trying to 'undo by stealth those advances in the fight against the Arab boycott which had been won in open Congressional debate'. The repeal attempt failed.[121]

The Defense Department was very slow to move in adopting the procedural regulations necessary for the implementation of the Wirth amendment (see above). Only after Representative Sam Gedjenson, chairman of the House Subcommittee on International Economic Policy and Trade, ordered a public hearing to challenge the Pentagon, did the Director of Defense Procurement issue a ruling, which brought about the immediate implementation of the amendment. The ruling cited the anti-boycott provision of the EAA in defining the prohibited compliance with the secondary boycott.

Towards the G-7 meeting at Munich in July 1992 the American Jewish Congress tried to convince the Department of State to get the seven to denounce the secondary boycott. However, when it became apparent that the State Department officials were unwilling to go any further than the declaration of the previous year, it informed the officials that it was preferable that no declaration be made.[122]

Soon after the G-7 meeting Secretary of State James Baker conferred with Egyptian President Hosni Mubarak, and raised with him the boycott issue, proposing the cancellation of the boycott in return for an Israeli freezing of settlement activities in the territories. Baker, who was apparently convinced that the newly elected Israeli government did not object to this formula,[123] was reported by Radio Monte Carlo as having made the following five-point proposal:

1. the Arab countries would formally announce the cancellation of the Arab boycott that prohibits Arab companies and organization to trade with Israel, in reaction to Israel's decision to stop construction in the settlements;
2. meetings would be arranged between Arab and Israeli economists in order to discuss means of cooperation between Israel and the Arab states;
3. limited exchanges of goods and trade deals would begin between Israel and the Arab states, in order to demonstrate good inten-

tions insofar as the continuation of the peace process and economic cooperation were concerned;

4. the US would provide appropriate loans to set up joint economic projects between Israel and the Arab states;
5. if Israel should renege on its commitment to stop settlements activities, the agreement would be cancelled, but this would not affect the continuation of the bilateral and multilateral talks or existing arrangements between Egypt and Israel.[124]

Just before the presidential and Congressional elections of November 1992, anti-boycott provisions were added to two important bills and signed into law. Senator Al Gore (D – ARK), who was soon to be elected Vice-President, had a provision added to the Defense Authorization Bill, which reenacted the Wirth amendment. At the same time Senator Frank Lautenberg (D – NJ) had a provision added to the Foreign Aid Bill, which called upon the President:

• to take more concrete steps to encourage vigorously Arab League countries to renounce publicly the primary boycott of Israel and the secondary and tertiary boycotts of American firms, that have commercial relations with Israel as a confidence-building measure;
• to report to Congress on the specific steps being taken by the President to bring about a public renunciation of the Arab primary boycott of Israel and the secondary and tertiary boycotts of American firms that have commercial ties with Israel;
• to encourage the allies and trading partners of the US to enact laws prohibiting businesses from complying with the boycott and penalizing businesses that do comply.[125]

During the presidential campaign Jewish groups were successful in getting both the Republican and Democratic parties to insert strong anti-boycott planks into their platforms. They were, however, unsuccessful in conditioning a $9 billion Saudi purchase of F-15 fighter jets on a formal Saudi agreement to end the blacklisting of American firms. Neither President Bush nor Democratic presidential candidate Bill Clinton was prepared to support linkage of the jet sale to Saudi action on the boycott, since 10,000 jobs in Texas and Connecticut were on the line. Nevertheless, both candidates, either directly or indirectly, promised tougher-than-ever anti-boycott activity if elected.

Deputy Secretary of State Lawrence Eagleburger sent a letter to the Conference of Presidents of the major American Jewish organizations pledging a 'renewed effort to lift the boycott', and describing a 'new US initiative' in this regard aimed at US trading partners and Arab countries. Governor Clinton told a B'nai B'rith convention that 'illegal' Arab 'economic warfare' against Israel 'must end, now'.[126]

As the Washington talks, which followed the Madrid Conference got under way, many American firms, that had previously been wary of any contacts with Israel, started to change their attitude. On 29 October 1992, in response to a query, the Kuwait desk officer at the Department of State. informed the American Jewish Congress that though Kuwait was still implementing the boycott, US companies 'had been advised' to ignore boycott requests, adding that 'we have received no complaints from any US firm to the effect that their refusal to supply [boycott] certificates has hindered their bidding efforts'.[127] Nevertheless, when the OAC released figures for boycott-related requests received by US firms in fiscal year 1992, the number of such requests was found to have increased to 9,912 from 6,812 the previous year, and of these 2,934 were from Kuwait – more than from any other country.[128]

The Clinton Administration

In the middle of February 1993, during a visit to Kuwait, Secretary of State Warren Christopher raised the boycott issue with its ruler, Sheikh Jabber a-Sabakh, pointing out to him that the US Ambassador to Kuwait would be following the issue. The Emir did not respond.[129] Reporting on the Secretary's visit to the National Director of the ADL, Abraham H. Foxman, Assistant Secretary of State, Edward Djerejian, stated:

> Secretary Christopher left a clear message ... that more needs to be done [in dismantling the boycott]. I can assure you that the boycott will continue to be a part of our high-level diplomacy with Arab countries ... With the Saudis and Kuwaitis, who have pledged to lift the secondary and tertiary aspects of the boycott from US firms, we are stressing the need for specific actions, such as ceasing the practice of soliciting boycott-related information and removing all references to the boycott in their legal and commercial language. We are following up on the Secretary's visit and emphasizing the need for early

actions. We too are concerned by the statistics on Saudi and Kuwaiti boycott practices during fiscal Year 1992 ... We have seen positive movement on this issue since the Gulf War and I am hopeful we will see more in the coming months.[130]

Despite the official American optimism, both Kuwait and Saudi Arabia participated in an Arab League boycott meeting which took place in late April 1993 in Damascus, at which 13 companies, including the American plastics giant Rubbermaid Inc. and General Dynamics Corp., were added to the blacklist, and seven, including Gerber Products, were crossed off the list.[131] The ADL, which had uncovered the fact, stated that it was outraged and called upon the Secretary of State to hold the two states accountable for their pledges.[132]

In the beginning of 1993 Representative Schumer introduced two new pieces of anti-boycott legislation. One required the US government to hold certain discussions and report to the Congress with respect to the secondary boycott. It called for the US ambassador to the OECD to monitor compliance with the boycott among member states, and to formulate guidelines for the organization to eliminate compliance with the boycott. It also called on US Trade Representative (USTR) Mickey Kantor to apply similar monitoring and guidelines to GATT members. According to the bill the two representatives would then have to report to the Secretary of Commerce, in consultation with the Secretary of State and Secretary of Treasury, on their results. The Secretary of Commerce would, in turn, report to Congress on all foreign countries which 'encourage or fail to discourage compliance with the boycott of Israel by the Arab countries'. The second bill denied 'most favoured nation' (MFN) status to companies that participate in, or cooperate with the boycott.[133]

Towards the G-7 meeting which was to meet in Tokyo in July 1993, the Jewish organizations and pro-Israeli Congressmen once again started to campaign for an unequivocal statement regarding the Arab boycott.[134] This time the G-7 issued a declaration which was much more pleasing to Israel. On the boycott issue the declaration read: 'We reiterate that the Arab boycott should end. We call on Israel to respect its obligations with regard to the occupied territories.' No mention was made of the settlements.[135]

Despite the G-7 declaration, in the course of 1993 the number of boycott requests coming from Saudi Arabia increased, and the ADL tried a new tactic. Since Saudi Arabia had applied for membership in the General Agreement for Tariffs and Trade, the ADL sought to get the US to condition its acceptance on 'firm assurances that the Saudis would terminate the secondary and tertiary boycotts'.[136] The same demand was repeated in a resolution tabled in Congress.[137]

Soon after the signing of the Declaration of Principles (the DoP) between Israel and the Palestinians in Washington on 13 September 1993, Christopher issued a public call to the six members of the Gulf Cooperation Council (GCC). The reply which he received was not encouraging. On 26 September the Secretary General of the GCC, Sheikh Fahim Bin Sultan al-Qassimi, responded to Christopher's call with the following statement: 'It is premature to speak about normal ties with Israel ... We have not yet reached the stage of normalization ... Why don't you ask Israel to destroy its nuclear arsenal? ... We think the nuclear threat is much more dangerous than the economic boycott.'[138]

On 1 October 1993 – the day on which over 40 nations pledged, with the encouragement of Israeli Minister of Foreign Affairs Shimon Peres, over $2 billion in direct assistance to the Palestinian Authority at the International Donors Conference in Washington – a senior member of the PLO Executive Committee, Yassir Abed-Rabbo, stated during a press conference at the State Department that the boycott should only be lifted after a 'complete Israeli withdrawal from the Palestinian and Arab occupied territories, including Jerusalem'. His statement was immediately criticized as 'anachronistic' by a US government official, who pointed out that 'when Israel and the Palestinians are talking about joint economic development – it doesn't make any sense to maintain the Arab boycott'. Also, when in the middle of October the Arab boycott officials convened in Damascus and once again demonstratively added several more companies to the blacklist, Djerejian responded by telling the Senate Foreign Relations Committee that the Arab blacklist was 'totally unacceptable' in the new situation, and that adding companies to the blacklist 'was obviously a step in the wrong direction'.[139]

On 8 October Representatives Alcee Hastings (D – FL), Peter Deutsch (D – FL) and Howard Berman (D – CA) proposed that the lifting of the US boycott of the PLO be conditioned on the PLO renouncing the boycott of Israel, urging the nations of the Arab League to renounce the boycott, and cooperate with the efforts of the

President to end the boycott.[140] In the Senate Senator Connie Mack introduced a bill which sought to link US aid to the Palestinian authority to a requirement that PLO chairman Yassir Arafat denounce the boycott (S. 1487). Senator Mack and Senator Joseph Lieberman had previously initiated a letter to President Clinton, signed by 50 Senators, urging him to freeze the $500 million US contribution to the aid package for the West Bank and Gaza, until the Palestinians agreed to renounce the boycott.[141]

Senator Mack's bill was opposed by Israel and the main Jewish organizations, and Secretary of State Warren Christopher, giving testimony to the Senate Committee on Foreign Operations on 2 March, termed the measure 'not a good idea'. In general, both Congress and the American Jewish community were divided over the wisdom of linking progress on the boycott issue to US economic support for the Palestinian autonomy. A debate also took place on whether American Jewish support for the removal of US statutory restrictions on the PLO should be conditioned on the willingness of the PLO to condemn the boycott. Kenneth Bialkin, one of the senior American Jewish leaders, and some AJC officials initially supported such a linkage, even though Israel did not.[142]

In the beginning of 1994 another 'arms sales linkage' provision was introduced by Senators Brown and Moynihan, and Representatives Tom Lantos (D – CA) and Benjamin A. Gilman (R – NY), which would prohibit US arms sales to countries that had approached US companies with requests to cooperate with the boycott (S. 1625 and HR 3656). Although the measure contained broad presidential waiver authority, Administration officials lobbied heavily against it, arguing that it would be awkward for Clinton to have to take advantage of the waiver loophole. Nevertheless, a senior US official explained that 'We can't completely ignore the concerns of the Congress, especially in circumstances where we support the objectives of the legislation.'[143]

In the middle of October 1993 the American Jewish Congress led a ten-member group of major US businessmen on an 'economics-of-peace' tour through Saudi Arabia, Egypt, Jordan and Israel, meeting with the leaders of these countries. *Inter alia* the group pressed the Arab leaders whom they met to end the boycott, making various ventures conditional on this being done. 'We discussed the boycott in the context of it impeding American joint ventures with Arab firms', the President of American Jewish Congress, Robert K. Lifton, explained. 'We reminded them that the existence of the secondary boycott and the anti-boycott legislation in the US were major impediments to increased American business involvement in the Arab region.'[144] 'They thought the American Jewish community would rush in with all [its] money to support the [peace] process, and they were shocked to find us say that's not going to happen', added the Executive Vice-President of the AJC, Henry Siegman, of the Arab leaders whom the group met with. 'No American CEO will take the risk – [and] no corporate counsel in America will advise a client to get involved in a venture that would risk violating US anti-boycott laws.'[145]

That a change was finally starting to take place within the American business community was best exemplified when in November 1993 Deloitte & Touche, one of the Big Six accounting firms in the US, listed Israel in its annual brochure describing the firm's international services. Previously, none of the 'Big Six' had listed Israel in their directories, despite the fact that all had working relationships with leading Israeli accounting firms. This change in the attitude of the six took place after the Jewish organizations had led a campaign to force such a change. Following Deloitte & Touche, KPMG Peat Marwick also announced that it would name its Israeli contact in the company's international directory.[146]

On 21 November the House of Representatives passed a resolution condemning the boycott of Israel and calling it an impediment to Middle East peace. The non-binding resolution, passed by a 425–1 vote, urged the Arab League and the US to work to end both primary and secondary boycotts.[147] Also towards the end of 1993 the International Trade Commission (ITC), prompted by Mickey Kantor, launched an investigation into the effects of the Arab boycott on US business. The ITC declared that it might have to go beyond the primary areas of concern cited by the USTR to assess 'the scope of the boycott, the degree of enforcement on a country-by-country basis, and the degree of compliance with the boycott by US businesses'. The main investigation was to focus on:

(a) lost sales and business opportunities in Arab countries or in Israel arising from the blacklist;

b) increased costs of doing business, including the acts of com-
    pliance with anti-boycott laws;
c) distorted investments or those not made in either Arab or Israeli
    markets.[148]

To conduct this study the ITC issued a public call in December
1993, directed especially at US businessmen, requesting confidential
information about commercial transactions and trade affected by the
boycott. But by the late Spring of 1994 the Commission had received
only a few submissions (including those of Jewish groups), and no
US company had agreed to testify in open hearing.

The year 1993 saw the most significant enforcement action in the
history of the anti-boycott program. This involved the consent agree-
ment with Baxter International, Inc., two of its subsidiaries, Baxter
AG and International Medical Technology, Ltd, and its General
Counsel Marshall G. Abbey. Baxter and its related parties together
paid $6.1 million in civilian fines, and another $500,000 as a crimi-
nal penalty. Even though the handling of the case by the Commerce
Department generated some controversy, ultimately the Justice
Department and the Office of Export Enforcement joined with the
OAC in the massive settlement with Baxter.[149]

However, if one leaves Baxter out, the total amount of fines
imposed in 1993 was on the low side – only $717,450 spread over 36
companies, of which over $80,000 were suspended. Of these, two
were charged with refusal to do business – a rare charge because of
the difficulty in proving that business had actually been turned
down. Another interesting case was that of American Express Bank,
Ltd. While letters of credit handled by the bank did not contain
illegal boycott terms, the documents provided to the bank by the
beneficiary did. For this infringement American Express paid
$103,000 for 13 violations and 26 reporting infractions.[150]

On 2 February 1994, two French Jewish businessmen – Jean and
David Frydman – filed a $100 million civil action suit in the New
York State Supreme Court against the American licensee and distri-
butor of the French cosmetics company L'Oréal – Cosmair Inc. The
Frydman brothers alleged violation of US anti-boycott laws, accusing
'Cosmair' of conspiracy, fraudulent misrepresentation and bribery.
They also filed a complaint against L'Oréal with the OAC, which the
American Jewish organizations had previously done in December
1991.[151]

Table 3: Enforcement of the Anti-boycott Provisions of the EAA during the
Clinton Administration

Financial year	No. of investigations	No. of settlement agreements	Charging letters	Warning letters	Closed	Total sum of civil penalties
1993	80	37	1	13	29	$6,817,450
1994	78	31	3	17	27	$1,432,700
1995	89	23	0	34	32	$1,826,850
1996	35	20	3	2	10	$887,600
Total	282	111	7	66	98	$10,964,600

Source: Information for 1993–95 kindly provided by Dr Jess Hordes of the ADL in Washington DC Information for 1996, the Office of Antiboycott Compliance, 1997, pp. 11–116.

Nine months previously Jean Frydman's son, Gilles, had supplied the US Department of Commerce with an exchange of letters between L'Oréal and the CBO, which indicated that L'Oréal had been willing to go to some length to comply with Arab demands, which included shutting down its Helena Rubinstein manufacturing operations in Israel, removing the Helena Rubinstein brand name from all subsidiaries worldwide, and replacing their boards of directors. Frydman argued that the founder of Cosmair, Jacques H. Corrze – a former Nazi sympathizer and war criminal, who had served a prison sentence in France in the years 1945–50 – had participated in the efforts to get L'Oréal off the blacklist,[152] and was thus in violation of the EAA.[153]

The Commerce Department, acting on the information supplied by Frydman, contended that transmitting the documents violated the American anti-boycott law, which bars companies from 'furnishing information about their business dealings with Israel'. Despite its protestations of innocence,[154] L'Oréal reached a settlement with the US Department of Commerce in August 1995, amounting to $1.4 million.[155] In addition, its Chairman, Lindsay Owen-Jones, apologized in a letter to the ADL, which had picked up the issue, for asking its US affiliate to send information to its Paris office to help the company's efforts to be removed from the Arab blacklist. 'I believe an international company like L'Oréal should have refused to place itself in such an unacceptable position and should not have replied to boycott inquiries'.[156]

In the middle of January 1994 Secretary of Commerce Ron Brown made a Middle East tour. During this visit Brown called, in each of Arab capitals which he visited, for an end to the boycott. 'The boycott is counter-productive to economic development in the entire region', he told reporters in Cairo on 21 January. 'We oppose the boycott and think it has become an anachronism as we move closer to peace.'[157] In Jordan Brown said that new American investments in Jordan depended on the removal of trade barriers and the lifting of the boycott against Israel,[158] while in Saudi Arabia he informed the Saudi of the bill pending in Congress which would impose sanctions on countries involved in the boycott, and which called for the banning of countries which adhere to the boycott from international agreements such as GATT.[159]

After meeting Arab League Secretary-General, Esmet Abdel Meguid, on 20 January in Cairo, Brown thought that he had received a commitment that recission of the secondary and tertiary boycotts against Israel would be considered at a ministerial meeting of the Arab League, which was to take place towards the end of March. But in the beginning of February Meguid explained that his commitment to Brown related only to specific projects. 'This matter has been put to me at the request of Secretary Brown concerning the secondary and tertiary boycott [affecting] American companies that would like to deal with some projects in Jericho and Gaza', he stated. 'I told him it would be OK for me to submit that request to the Council of Foreign Ministers due to meet in Cairo at the end of March.'[160]

Secretary of State Christopher let it be known that he would travel to the Middle East in March in connection with the peace process, and remain in the area for the Arab League meeting which was to convene on the 27th of the month, in order to further pressure Arab states for a favourable decision on the rescission of the boycott. Christopher finally cancelled his visit in view of the difficulties that had developed in the Israel–PLO talks and lack of progress in the negotiations between Syria and Israel following the massacre of Muslims in prayers at the Cave of the Patriarchs in Hebron by a Jewish settler. Some observers also suggested that Christopher realized that there was little chance for any movement regarding the boycott emerging from the Arab League meeting.

Though over 60 members of Congress signed a letter addressed to Meguid in which they sought assurances that the boycott would be discussed at the forthcoming League meeting, the issue was not raised, much to the disappointment of the US Administration and leaders of the Jewish organizations.[161] Meeting in Dokha in Qatar a week later, the Federation of Arab Chambers of Commerce re-iterated its commitment to uphold the boycott.

In early January 1994 the Jewish organizations once again started to prepare for the G-7 summit which was scheduled to meet in July in Naples in Italy. There was broad agreement that the Administration should be encouraged to press for another G-7 anti-boycott statement. This time, however, the statement desired would make a clear distinction between the primary and secondary boycotts, would call directly on the Arabs to unconditionally end the blacklist, and stay clear of any linkages to other issues associated with the peace talks.[162]

On 24 August, in an address to an ADL conference, President Clinton urged an end to the Arab economic boycott of Israel declaring that it was harmful to the Palestinians as well as the Israelis in view of the new economic relationship between the two. He added that ending the boycott was justified, given the progress being made on in the talks between Israel and Syria within the framework of the efforts to reach a comprehensive peace in the Middle East.[163] The following week, after a meeting with Secretary of State Warren Christopher at UN headquarters in New York, the six GCC foreign ministers announced that their countries would end the secondary and tertiary boycott of Israel, and support any move within the Arab League to end the primary boycott. The announcement was the result of direct American pressure which sought to end the discrimination against US companies which are obliged to comply with the American anti-boycott legislation.[164]

On 16 November 1994 USTR Mickey Kantor cited a US International Commission study, which concluded that the Arab boycott cost American business about $410 million in 1993. In addition, in the same year, the cost to American firms of complying with the US anti-boycott legislation was $160 million.[165]

However, despite the positive atmosphere, there was still wide-scale application of the boycott in the US. Of 31 consent agreements entered into by the Commerce Department in 1994, 11 involved banks, emphasizing the continuing importance of the role played by banks in implementing the boycott in commercial transactions in the Arab world, despite the gradual decline of the boycott. Two actions were against Chemical Bank, for which the bank paid a total of $44,000 for nine violations. In both cases the bank's violations had to do with the way letters of credit were handled rather than the actual violation of the letter of credit prohibition of the law. The most spectacular example of this involved 104 violations by the Italian Banca Nazionale del Lavoro, which resulted in payment of a $475,000 fine. Of the 104, 93 involved charges of furnishing prohibited information and 11 failures to report.[166]

In 1995 the situation in terms of number of investigations and sums of civil penalties collected actually showed a slight rise over 1994, but in 1996 there was once again a decrease.[167] Nevertheless a highly bizarre settlement case – all the more bizarre because two government agencies were involved and was apparently a case of the so called 'voluntary boycott' (compliance with the boycott without being requested to do so) – was reported by the Bureau of Export Administration in the Commerce Department on 26 February 1997. The case involved a company called CACI of Virginia employed back in 1991 on behalf of the Department of Justice and US Air Force to microfilm documents in Saudi Arabia connected with a lawsuit brought by Boeing against the Administration, having to do with military sales abroad. The conditions set by the Air Force and approved by the Department of Justice of the contract with CACI included the provision that 'No Jews or Jewish-surnamed personnel will be sent as part of the Document Acquisition Team because of cultural differences between Moslems and Jews in the region.' The settlement with CACI involved a $15,000 fine. The $20,000 fines imposed on the Air Force Officer and the Justice Department official who had proposed and approved the provision were cancelled because the two had been unaware of the law.[168]

Towards the end of 1996 the US was still conditioning the membership of Saudi Arabia, and other countries, in the World Trade Organization, on its cancellation of primary boycott against Israel.[169]

Notes

1. See Aaron J. Sarna, *Boycott and Blacklists – a History of Arab Economic Warfare against Israel* (Totowa, NJ: Rowman & Littlefield, 1986), pp. 19–25.
2. PRO, FO 371/98275 1123/17.
3. Ibid., FO 371/104206 XC13782.
4. Cited by Dan S. Chill, *The Arab Boycott of Israel* (New York: Praeger Publishers, 1976), p. 47.
5. Sarna, op. cit., p. 82, and American Jewish Congress, *Boycott Report*, May 1978, quoted in Teslik, op. cit., p. 54.
6. Arnold Forster, 'Fighting the Arab Boycott in the United States', in *Oxford Seminar on Oil Wealth, Discrimination and Freedom of Trade – Report* (Oxford, 1975), pp. 34–5.
7. Sarna, op. cit., p. 83.
8. Oded Remba, 'The Arab Boycott. A Study in Total Economic Warfare', *Midstream* (Summer 1960), p. 42 and Sarna, op. cit., p. 18.
9. Ibid.
10. Forster, op. cit., pp. 40–1.
11. Ibid., p. 54.
12. J. Hordes, talk given at the Seminar on Freedom of Trade with Israel, held in Brussels in June 1984, on 'The History of Anti-Boycott Legislation in the US', in Susan Hattis Rolef (ed.) *Freedom of Trade and the Arab Boycott* (Jerusalem: the Anti-Defamation League of B'nai B'rith, 1985), p. 64.
13. Remba, op. cit., p. 41.
14. Ibid., p. 54.
15. Ibid., p. 41 and Sarna, op. cit., pp. 83–4.
16. Susan Hattis Rolef, 'Israel's Anti-Boycott Policy', *Policy Studies* No. 28 (Jerusalem: The Leonard Davis Institute for International Relations at the Hebrew University of Jerusalem), p. 26.
17. Sarna, op. cit., p. 84.
18. See Chapter 6, pp. 132.
19. On the relation of the Sherman Antitrust Act to the battle against the Arab boycott, see Chapter 3, pp. 77–8.
20. Rolef, op. cit., p. 25.
21. Yosef Schechtman, *Haherem Ha'arvi Velikho* (The Arab Boycott and its Lessons), *Ha'umma*, 4, 13 (June 1965), p. 7.
22. Business International, 'Coping with the Arab Boycott', *Management Monographs*, No. 19 (New York: Business International, 1963).
23. Sol Stern, 'On and Off the Arabs' List', *The New Republic*, 27 March 1976, p. 7.
24. Ibid., pp. 10–11.
25. Terence Prittie and Walter Henry Nelson, *The Economic War against the Jews* (London: Secker & Warburg, 1978), p. 114.
26. Stern, op. cit.
27. See Chapter 6, pp. 132–3.
28. Rolef, op. cit., p. 29.

29. Sarna, op. cit., pp. 85–7 and Teslik, op. cit., p. 56.
30. Elizur, op. cit., p. 136.
31. Rolef, op. cit., pp. 29–30.
32. Sarna, op. cit., and Teslik, pp. 55–9.
33. Ibid. See also Chill, op. cit., pp. 49–51.
34. Teslik, op. cit., pp. 56–7.
35. Sarna, op. cit., pp. 86–8.
36. Meron Medzini (ed.) *Israel's Foreign Relations, Selected Documents 1947–1974* (Jerusalem: Ministry for Foreign Affairs, 1976), p. 281.
37. Report by the Department of Commerce, July 1975.
38. *The Arab Boycott and American Business*, Report by the Subcommittee on Oversight and Investigations of the Committee on Interstate and Foreign Commerce with Additional and Minority Views, House of Representatives, 94th Congress, 2nd Session, Washington DC, USGPO, 1976 (The Moss Report), pp. viii–ix; Teslik, op. cit., pp. 102–7, and *The Financial Times*, 8 September 1976, quoted in Prittie and Nelson, op. cit., p. 189.
39. J. Hordes, op. cit.
40. Teslik, op. cit., pp. 30–46.
41. Sarna, op. cit., p. 88, and Roy E. Licklider, *Political Power and the Arab Oil Weapon – the Experience of Five Industrial Nations* (Berkeley: University of California Press, 1988), pp. 189–271. It is interesting to note, however, that despite the vast growth in the wealth of the Arab oil-producing states, the percentage of exports to Israel of total US exports to the whole of the Middle East plus the Arab states in Africa was 21.2% in 1965, went down to 15.3% in 1975 and was up again to 19% in 1985 (calculations based on the IMF *Direction of Trade*, March 1966, April 1976 and April 1986).
42. Sarna, op. cit., pp. 88–9; Teslik, op. cit., pp. 68–72; Prittie and Nelson, op. cit., pp. 103–19.
43. J. Hordes, op. cit., p. 65 and Rolef, op. cit., p. 35.
44. M.S. Daoudi and M.S. Dajani, *Economic Sanctions: Ideals and Experience* (London: Routledge & Kegan Paul, 1983), p. 102.
45. Ibid., p. 103.
46. Ibid., p. 104.
47. Teslik, op. cit., p. 104 and Prittie and Nelson, op. cit., p. 186.
48. Roy M. Mersky, *Conference on Transnational Economic Boycotts and Coercion*, 19–20 February 1976, University of Texas Law School, papers presented at the Conference, Vol. 1 (New York: Oceana Publications, 1978), p. 193; Teslik, op. cit., pp. 102–3.
49. Stern, op. cit., p. 8.
50. Ibid., pp. 11–12.
51. For an analysis of the application to boycott-related activities of the Sherman Antitrust Act, Federal Civil Rights Laws and constitutional and statutory restrictions upon activities of federal agencies, see Antonin Scalia, 'Domestic Legal Issues Presented by the Arab Boycott', paper reproduced at the Conference on Transnational Economic Boycotts and Coercion, February 1976, University of Texas Law School, Vol. 1 (New York: Oceana Publications,

1978), p. 187.

52. Stern, op. cit., p. 11. In a consent judgment reached between Bechtel and the Department of Justice in 1977 and approved by the courts in 1979, Bechtel was enjoined and restrained for a period of 20 years from enforcing any contracts providing that it boycott or refuse to deal with any blacklisted American subcontractors or requiring other American firms to do the same (United States of America v. Bechtel Corporation et al., Civil No. 76-99, US District Court, Northern District of California, 16 January 1976). For a history of the Bechtel case see Holly L. Feder, 'US Companies and the Arab Boycott of Israel' (Texas Women's University, UMI 1988), pp. 24–38.

53. Sec. v. General Tyre and Rubber Co. Civil No. 76-0799, US District Court, District of Columbia, 10 May 1976. In this case the company consented to the entry of a permanent order of injunction against future violations of federal security laws.

54. Teslik, op. cit., pp. 76–114.

55. Ibid., pp. 82–3.

56. American Jewish Congress v. Richardson No. 75-1541.

57. Teslik, op. cit., pp. 96, 112.

58. Ibid., pp. 141–5, and Sarna, op. cit., pp. 98–9.

59. The language of the amendment was later changed to include any boycott not sanctioned by the US Administration, rather than just the Arab boycott – H.R. 10612. See Hordes, op. cit., p. 68.

60. Rolef, op. cit., pp. 38–9.

61. Teslik, op. cit., pp. 143, 152.

62. On the relationship between business and the boycott, see Nicolas Wolfson, 'The Need for Corporate Disclosure of Compliance with Arab Boycott Requests', reproduced at Conference on Transnational Economic Boycotts and Coercion, Vol. 1, op. cit., p. 347. See also Teslik, op. cit., pp. 131–5.

63. Ibid., pp. 153–60, 168–72.

64. See George Lenczowski, University of California, 'The Arab Boycott Issues – Comments and Reflections', and John Norton Moore, University of Virginia, 'United States Policy and the Middle East', papers presented at the April 1977 annual meeting of the American Society of International Law in San Francisco. See also *Wall Street Journal*, 13 September 1976; *Journal of Commerce*, 15 September 1976; *New York Times*, 16 September 1976; Congressional records – House, 21 September 1976 – testimony given by Edward Kock before the Federal Communications Commission, ADL press release, 12 January 1977, 'A national campaign against anti-boycott legislation.'

65. ADL press release, 12 January 1977.

66. Ibid, pp. 5–13.

67. In the second Carter–Ford debate on 10 June 1976, the two contestants had the following to say about the boycott:

> MR CARTER: I believe that the boycott of American businesses by the Arab countries because those businesses trade with Israel or because they have American Jews who are owners or directors in the company is an absolute dis-

grace. This is the first time that I remember in the history of our country when we've let a foreign country circumvent or change our Bill of Rights. I'll do everything I can as president to stop the boycott of American businesses by the Arab countries. It's not a matter of diplomacy or trade with me. It's a matter of morality. And I don't believe that Arab countries will pursue it when we have a strong president who will protect the integrity of our country, the commitment of our Constitution and Bill of Rights and protect people in this country who happen to be Jews. It may later be Catholics; it may later be Baptists who are threatened by some foreign country. But we ought to stand staunch. And I think it's a disgrace that so far Mr Ford's administration has blocked the passage of legislation that would've revealed by law every instance of the boycott and it would've prevented the boycott from continuing.

MR FORD: Again Governor Carter is inaccurate. The Arab boycott action was first taken in 1952. And in November of 1975 I was the first president to order the executive branch to take action, affirmative action, through the Department of Commerce and other cabinet departments, to make certain that no American businessman or business organization should discriminate against Jews because of an Arab boycott. And I might add that my administration – and I'm very proud or it – is the first administration that has taken an antitrust action against companies in this country that have allegedly cooperated with the Arab boycott. Just on Monday of this week I signed a tax bill that included an amendment that would prevent companies in the United States from taking a tax deduction if they have in any way whatsoever cooperated with the Arab boycott. And last week when we were trying to get the Export Administration Act through the Congress – necessary legislation – my administration went to Capital Hill and tried to convince the House and the Senate that we should have an amendment on that legislation which would take strong and effective action against those who participate or cooperate with the Arab boycott. One other point. Because the Congress failed to act, I am going to announce tomorrow that the Department of Commerce will disclose those companies that have participated in the Arab boycott. This is something that we can do; the Congress failed to do it, and we intend to do it.

68. Hordes, op. cit., p. 69.
69. Ibid., pp. 69–70; Teslik, op. cit., pp. 175–214; Nathan Perlmutter, 'ADL Fights Lies, Prejudice and Oppression', *National Jewish Monthly* (August 1980), p. 15. Speech by Robert Lipshutz, Counsel to President Carter, to the ADL, June 1977, and 'Knights of the Round Table', *Business Week*, 21 October 1988, p. 39; Sarna, op. cit., pp. 100–2.
70. Teslik, op. cit., p. 175 and Nancy Jo Nelson, *The Palestine Yearbook of International Law*, Vol. V (Nicosia: Al-Shaybani Society of International Law, 1989), pp. 129–83.
71. Sarna, op. cit., pp. 102–8.
72. Ibid., p. 117.
73. Teslik, op. cit., p. 231.

74. Cited in Barry E. Carter, *International Economic Sanctions: Improving the Haphazard US Legal Regime* (Cambridge: Cambridge University Press, 1988), p. 178.

75. W. Maslow, talk given at the Seminar on Freedom of Trade with Israel, held in Brussels in June 1984, on 'Enforcement of the US Anti-Boycott Laws', in Susan Hattis Rolef, op. cit., pp. 76–7.

76. 'Carter Signs Anti-Boycott Measure', Carter Library in Atlanta, Georgia.

77. Joint statement issued by the AJC, the AJCongress and the ADL on 3 May 1977.

78. Ibid, p. 84.

79. Sarna, op. cit., pp. 109–10. For review of the regulations see the Commerce Department's 116th Report on US Export Controls, Semiannual Report: April–September 1977, under the EAA.

80. Sarna, op. cit., pp. 110–11.

81. See memorandum from the General Counsel of the Department of Commerce to Domestic Affairs Adviser Stu Eizenstadt dated 31 August 1977, and Carter, op. cit., p. 179.

82. David Cain, 'International Business Communication and Free Speech: Briggs & Stratton Corp. v. Valdrige', *Boston College International and Comparative Law Review*, 9 (1985), pp. 137–9.

83. Speech given in Chicago, cited in 'The Impact of Anti-Boycott Laws on US Mideast Trade', paper prepared by the American Jewish Committee in May 1979.

84. OAC (1997), p. II–124

85. Sarna, op. cit. p. 118, and *An-Nahar Arab Report & Memo*, 28 December 1981.

86. 'The Operation and Effect of the International Boycott Provisions of the Internal Revenue Code: Fifth Annual Report', cited in the *Boycott Law Bulletin*, XV (February 1991), p. 4 and reaction by OAC Director William V. Skidmore in the *Boycott Law Bulletin*, XV (March and April 1991), pp. 14–18

87. *MEED*, 23 January 1988.

88. Sarna, op. cit., pp. 111–12; Feder, op. cit., pp. 67–8, and US Department of Commerce News BXA 880–8. For a year by year analysis of the enforcement of the EAA in the years 1979–88, see Feder op. cit., pp. 50–68. See also Export Administration Annual Reports, published by the US Department of Commerce.

89. *Boycott Law Bulletin*, July 1991, pp. 20–8

90. Sarna, op. cit., p. 112, and Cain, op. cit., p. 131.

91. See Dresser Industries Incorporated v. Baldridge 549 F. Supp. 198 (D.D.C. 1982) and Cain, op. cit., p. 140.

92. Howard N. Fenton III, 'United States Anti-Boycott Laws: An Assessment of their Impact Ten Years after Adoption', *Hastings International and Comparative Law Review*, 10, 2 (Winter 1987), p. 211.

93. 'The Future of Arab–US Trade', *MEED*, 31, 43 (17–23 October 1987), and Diraar Alghanin, 'US–Arab Business Opportunities', *American–Arab Affairs*, 4 (Spring 1983).

94. See *Boycott Report*, 13/6, June 1989.

95. Speech at the annual conference of the American Israel Public Affairs Committee (AIPAC) in Washington DC, 22 May 1989.
96. Paper prepared by Baxter, and distributed by the ADL together with a press release dated 25 March 1993.
97. Sue Shellenbarger, 'Did Hospital Supplier Dump its Israel Plant to Win Arabs' Favor?', *The Wall Street Journal*, 1 May 1990; Thomas M. Burton, 'Baxter Fails to Quell Questions on its Role in the Israeli Boycott', *The Wall Street Journal*, 25 April 1991; 'The Case against Baxter International', *Business Week*, 7 October 1991; Thomas M. Burton, 'How Baxter Got Off the Blacklist and How it Got Nailed', *The Wall Street Journal*, 26 March 1993; Burnaby J. Feder, 'Guilty Plea by Baxter on Boycott', *The New York Times*, 26 March 1993; Baxter press release: 'US Concludes Investigation of Baxter', Deerfield, Illinois, 25 March 1993.
98. For more details on this case see *Boycott Law Bulletin*, XV (March and April 1991), pp. 3–9, 23; *Boycott Law Bulletin*, XV (May and June 1991), pp. 3–6; *Business Week*, 7 October 1991.
99. *Boycott Report*, 12/5, May 1988; 12/8, October 1988, 14/9, November/December 1990, 15/3, March 1991.
100. Section 1403, Report on Compliance with foreign Boycott, amendment to the Foreign Aid Authorization bill. On GATT see also Chapter 3.
101. Department of Commerce, Bureau of Export Administration, 15 CFR Part 769, Restrictive Trade Practices or Boycotts, Interpretations, 26 September 1990 and *The Boycott Law Bulletin*, XIV, VIII (August 1990), p. 12.
102. *Boycott Report*, 15/4, April 1991.
103. Internal ADL and American Jewish Congress memoranda.
104. Ibid.
105. *The New York Times*, 23 March 1991.
106. Internal ADL and American Jewish Congress memoranda.
107. *Boycott Report*, 15/6, July 1991.
108. Internal ADL and American Jewish Congress memoranda.
109. *The Boycott Law Bulletin*, XV (May and June 1991), pp. 7–9, *Boycott Law Bulletin* update of 13 July; *Boycott Law Bulletin* (October and November 1991), p. 10 and *Boycott Report* 16/2, February 1992.
110. The full list of these bills and resolutions was published by the Washington DC office of the ADL on 11 June, 19 July and 19 December, 1991.
111. PR NEWSWIRE, 25 November 1991.
112. *Boycott Law Bulletin*, XV (October and November, 1991), p. 6.
113. Ibid.
114. 'Justification for certification and waiver by the Secretary of State under section 502 of the Departments of Commerce, Justice, and State, the Judiciary, and Related Agencies Appropriations Act relating to the prohibition against contracting with firms that comply with the Arab League boycott of the State of Israel or discriminate in the award of subcontracts on the basis of religion', attached to communication by Secretary of State James Baker dated 10 December 1991 to Senator Hollings, Chairman of the Subcommittee on Commerce, Justice, State and Judiciary, and Related Agencies, Committee on

Appropriations, United States of America.

115. *Boycott Report* 15/8, September/October 1991; 16/1, January 1992; 16/2, February 1992 and ADL memorandum 'Year End Status of Anti-Boycott Legislation – 102nd Congress, First Sessions', 19 December 1991.
116. *Middle East Executive Report*, June 1995, p. 20.
117. *Boycott Law Bulletin*, XV (July 1991), p. 3.
118. Editorial in *The Jerusalem Post*, 4 August 1991.
119. *Boycott Report* 16/7, August 1992.
120. *Boycott Report* 16/3, March 1992 and *Davar*, 2 February 1992.
121. Letter from Joe Kamalick, editor of *The Boycott Law Bulletin*, to the author, 4 February 1992.
122. *Boycott Report* Vol. 16/7, August–September, 1992.
123. According to the Egyptian weekly *Al-Muzwaar*, soon after becoming Foreign Minister Shimon Peres had stated in an interview that Israel would be willing to stop all the settlement activities in the territories, in return for the lifting of the boycott. It should be noted, however, that the new Israeli government was committed to stopping all settlement activities even without any *quid/pro quo* (*Davar*, 30 July 1992).
124. *Globes* (Hebrew), 24 July 1992, quoting radio Monte Carlo.
125. *Boycott Report*, 16/9, November/December 1992 and ADL memorandum.
126. Ibid.
127. *Boycott Report* 17/1, January 1993.
128. *Israel Business Today*, 12 March, 1993. Another 2,557 requests were from the United Arab Emirates (UAE) and 1,743 from Saudi Arabia. A total of 2,253 illegal requests came from other Arab or Muslim states including Algeria, India, Iran, Malaysia, Nigeria, Pakistan and Sudan.
129. *Wall Street Journal*, 23 February 1993.
130. Letter dated 29 March 1993. The State Department later used identical language in letters addressed to other American Jewish officials. see *The Jerusalem Post*, 30 April 1993.
131. *Agence France Press* (Damascus), 1 May 1993.
132. *The Jerusalem Post*, 14 May 1993.
133. *Arab News* (Dammam), 24 May 1993.
134. See for example letter sent by Representative Charles E. Schumer to fellow Congressmen on 28 April 1993 urging them to approach President Clinton on the issue.
135. Reuters (Tokyo), 8 July 1993.
136. Letter addressed to Secretary of State Warren Christopher in ADL press release, 17 August 1993.
137. Joel Glass, *Lloyd's List*, 19 August 1993.
138. Reuters (Damascus), 26 September 1993.
139. *New York Times*, 18 October 1993.
140. *Saudi Gazette*, 10 October 1993.
141. Julia Schîpflin, 'The Arab Boycott of Israel: Can it Withstand the Peace Process?', *Research Reports*, 4, March 1994, London, Institute of Jewish Affairs, p. 11.

142. The issue was hotly debated at two meetings of the International Steering Committee on Freedom of Trade with Israel, held on 14 October and 3 November 1993 in New York. See also *Washington Post* editorial on this topic, 2 November 1993.
143. Robert S. Greenberger in *The Wall Street Journal*, 7 February 1994.
144. *The Jerusalem Post*, 27 October 1993.
145. Jewish Telegraphic Agency (JTA) and *Ha'aretz*, 28 October 1993.
146. *Boycott Report*, 16/2, February 1992, and Allison Kaplan Sommer, in *The Jerusalem Post*, 15 April 1994.
147. Reuters (Washington), 21 November 1993.
148. Reuters News Service, 8 November 1993 and Lloyd's List, 14 December 1993.
149. Paper prepared by Baxter International and distributed by the ADL together with a press release dated 25 March 1993 *Yedi'ot 'Aharonot*, 26 March 1993, *Middle East Executive Reports*, June 1995, p. 20.
150. Ibid., pp. 20–1.
151. Jean Frydman, a Jewish businessman with dual French–Israeli citizenship, had claimed back in 1989 that the French cosmetics company L'Oréal had ousted him from a joint venture that he had signed with it the previous year, as part of the company's efforts to get itself removed from the Arab boycott blacklist (see Chapter 8, pp. 207–9). It should be noted that Frydman was one of the organizers of the peace rally in Tel Aviv at which Prime Minister Yitzhak Rabin was assassinated on 4 November 1995.
152. Corrze was not the only person connected with L'Oréal who, according to Frydman, had a Nazi past. Frydman also revealed that the deputy chairman of L'Oréal and husband of its controlling shareholder, Andre Bettencourt, had in the years 1940–42 written for *La Terre Française* – a weekly set up by Germany and aimed at rural populations in occupied France. Some of his articles were anti-Semitic in their content. Bettencourt did not deny his having written for the weekly, which he claimed had been a 'youthful error'. In December 1994 Bettencourt resigned his post in L'Oréal, apparently because of pressure by its board over this episode, though he denied that there had been any connection. (*Le Monde*, 11 February 1995, quoted by Reuters (Paris), 11 and 13 February 1995.)
153. Leah Nathans Spiro, Farah Nayei and Niel Sandler, 'The Shadow Across L'Oréal', *Business Week*, 21 March 1994.
154. L'Oréal denied that it had submitted to the boycott, arguing that while Helena Rubinstein products were no longer being manufactured in Israel, this was not due to the Arab boycott but to a policy of consolidation, which had involved the closing down of some 15 small plants world-wide. As part of this strategy, L'Oréal argued, Helena Rubinstein in Israel had turned into a distribution network called Interbeauty. (Nathans Spiro, Nayei and Sandler, op. cit.) It might be added that in May 1995, L'Oréal purchased a 30 per cent stake in Interbeauty, and the following month started producing at the Interbeauty Migdal Ha'emek plant.
155. PR Newswire (Washington), 29 August 1995.
156. Reuters (Washington), 5 July and 30 August 1995.

157. *MEED*, 11 February 1994.
158. Reuters (Amman), 17 January 1994.
159. Reuters (Riyadh), 16 January 1994. The Saudi Minister of Commerce, Suleiman al-Salim, had called for US support for GCC membership in GATT.
160. Ibid. See also *The Wall Street Journal*, 7 February 1994.
161. JTA, 5 April 1994. On 15 April the ADL issued a statement calling upon the Administration to speak out against the Arab League for 'violating commitments made to senior Administration officials'.
162. Meeting of the International Steering Committee on Freedom of Trade with Israel, held in New York on 5 January 1994.
163. Reuters (Washington), 24 August 1994.
164. *MEED*, 14 October 1994.
165. Reuters (Washington), 16 November 1994.
166. *Middle East Executive Reports*, June 1995, p. 21.
167. The Office of Antiboycott Compliance, 1997, pp. 11–116.
168. Press release by the Bureau of Export Administration in the US Department of Commerce, 26 February 1997 (Internet, http://www.bxa.doc.gov/Cacpress.htm) and *The New York Times*, 6 March 1997. As in many previous boycott cases in the US, so this issue was originally brought to the attention of the Department of Commerce and pursued, by the director of the ADL of B'nai B'rith, Dr Jess Hordes.
169. *Ha'aretz*, 1 December and 12 December 1996.

8

The Policy of the Major West European Countries

In 1977 it was estimated that as many as 2,000 west European firms were on the Arab blacklist.[1] At the same time there was widescale compliance with boycott requirements in all the member states of the EC, while generally speaking European companies have been more inclined than their American counterparts to give in to boycott demands. Thus for example in the sphere of computer components and software Israel managed, in the course of the 1980s, to penetrate the American market but not the European one. In 1980 IBM purchased $5 million worth of Israeli products, and in 1988 these purchases went up to $100 million. Already in 1949 IBM opened a small representation in Tel Aviv. For many years to come not a single European computer company chose to do business with Israel, with the boycott, rather than pure economic considerations, believed to be the main reason.

The states of western Europe were also much less prone than the US to participate in the battle against the Arab boycott. There were several reasons for this. The first was the fact that Jewish and pro-Israel lobbies are much weaker in Europe than across the Atlantic. The second was that traditionally Europe has followed a policy more partial to the Arabs in their conflict with Israel. The third was that Europe has been inclined to take a less ideological and more pragmatic attitude on issues such as the boycott. The fourth was that most European states were much more dependent on Arab oil and trade with the states of the Middle East than the US.

The initial reaction of the European Economic Community to the passage of anti-boycott legislation in the US was negative, and there were objections to the extraterritorial reach of the 1977 Export Administration Act.[2] Nevertheless, a study published by the Foreign

Affairs and National Defense Division of the (US) Congressional Research Service in 1979, which was carried out in West Germany, the Netherlands, France and Great Britain, found that some European businessmen, government officials, parliamentarians and interest groups were in sympathy with the American legislation. However, as a group, the study found, they disclosed a reluctance to adopt similar legislation because of fears of loss of trade and of jeopardizing good relations with the Arab world, and there was widespread willingness to comply with Arab boycott demands.[3]

Until the beginning of the 1990s the general consensus among European businessmen appeared to be that any action against the boycott should be taken by multilateral forums, so that no single European state would find itself at a disadvantage *vis-à-vis* the rest.[4] It was against this background that one should see the continuous efforts of Israel and its allies in the battle against the boycott to bring about a harmonization of anti-boycott legislation within the European community.[5]

Despite the negative atmosphere, as a result of the work of anti-boycott lobbies, towards the end of the 1970s both the British and Dutch parliaments established special committees to investigate the extent of compliance by their respective governments, business firms and financial institutions with Arab boycott requests. The French parliament enacted anti-boycott legislation in 1977, which the French Government chose at first not to implement on the grounds that it ran counter to the official French policy of expanding trade in the Middle East. However, after François Mitterrand became President of France the attitude started to change. The Benelux countries all passed some anti-boycott measures – not necessarily directed against the Arab boycott of Israel – in the course of the early 1980s, while Germany joined in 1992.

France

From British sources we learn that in November 1952, when the effects of the boycott started to be felt by other countries, and Britain invited the French Government to consider associating themselves in some concerted action against it, the impression that the French Government gave was that 'their interests were little affected and they were not concerned'.[6] Israel first approached France directly in a request to take measures against the Arab boycott in October 1955, at which time the French authorities expressed their willingness to join any initiative against the boycott, as long as the US and Britain were also involved.[7]

Several years later, in 1959, Renault, the state-owned car manufacturer, which had entered a contract with an Israeli firm to assemble 2,400 cars in Israel over an 18-month period, gave in to Arab boycott pressure, and broke its contract after only 800 cars had been assembled.[8] Renault announced that it had made repeated efforts to contend with the policy of 'certain states' to boycott firms having business dealings with Israel, and found itself forced 'to make a choice against its will'. Several weeks after the Renault affair, Air France broke off negotiations with El Al, the Israeli national airline, to establish an operational tie-up between the two airlines, for similar reasons.[9] Nevertheless, numerous major French companies, including the Marcel Dassault aircraft-manufacturing company, which was blacklisted for supplying Mirage jets to Israel in the early 1960s, refused to give in to Arab boycott demands.[10]

Towards the end of the 1970s there was a widespread application of a voluntary boycott against Israeli goods and companies, which was apparently affected by the large number of French firms that found themselves blacklisted, and by the generally cool relations prevailing between France and Israel in these years.[11] There was great resentment among French business circles against what they regarded as American pressure on France to adopt anti-boycott legislation and policies similar to those adopted in the US. French businessmen argued that the US was insensitive to Europe's economic problems, and resented the extraterritorial reach of the American legislation on American-owned or partially controlled subsidiaries based in France.[12]

Nevertheless, France was the first European state to pass an anti-boycott law on 7 June 1977.[13] The purpose of this legislation was to combat the secondary and tertiary boycotts in general, and in particular to stop the COFACE (*Compagnie Française d'Assurances pour le Commerce Extérieur*), the state-run and largest French foreign trade and credit insurance company, from providing financial guarantees on risks to companies that accept discriminatory conditions in their trade activities.[14] COFACE approved, as part of its export insurance guarantees for French exporters to Arab states, restrictive clauses requiring compliance with Arab boycott contractual conditions for clients enforcing the boycott. Furthermore it also indirectly enforced the Arab boycott by warning exporters that insurance for the risk of non-payment by Arab state clients or for confiscation of goods supplied, would not be effective if the exporter, having accepted the boycott condition as part of the contract, subsequently did not implement it for example, by refraining from supplying negative certificates of origin as required.[15]

Even before the passage of the 1977 legislation there were two provisions, related to the economic law, which were regarded as relevant to the battle against the boycott. Both originated from an ordinance dating back to 1945 and subsequently amended.[16] Article 37(1)a, enacted on 24 June 1958, made it an offence 'for any person engaged in the production of goods or services, commerce, industry or handicrafts, to refuse to satisfy requests of buyers for goods, or for the performance of services, within the limits of available resources and in conformity with commercial usage, if such requests were not abnormal, made in good faith, and on condition that the sale of such goods or the performance of such services was not forbidden by law or contrary to regulations issued by the competent authority'. It was subsequently argued that a refusal to sell in pursuance of a boycott policy was an offence under this article.[17]

Article 59b is of the same ordinance, as amended on 28 August 1967, defined as an offence 'actions taken in concert, express or implied agreements, understandings arrived at by associations in any form or for any purpose whatever, which have as their object or effect the prevention, restriction or distortion of competition'. This provision was regarded as the source of inspiration of article 85(1) of the Treaty of Rome.[18]

The legislation of June 1977 was effective for a period of only seven weeks. What happened was that on 24 July 1977 the French Government, headed by Raymond Barre, issued an *avis* (a nonbinding opinion) interpreting the law to the effect that in view of article 32(3) (the exception clause), COFACE would be exempted from the penalties contained in the legislation. The *avis* emphasized the necessity of reestablishing commercial equilibrium and increasing employment through the search for new markets, 'principally in oil-producing countries and developing industrial nations in the

Middle East, Southeast Asia, Latin America and certain African nations'.[19] Among the various groups in France which did their best to obstruct the implementation of anti-boycott legislation was the French section of the Parliamentary Association for Euro-Arab Cooperation, which consisted of over 350 members from all the members of the EEC. Of the 350 members about 50 were French.[20]

The legality of the *avis* regarding COFACE was challenged by several interest groups, including the *Mouvement pour la Liberté du Commerce* (MLC).[21] A complaint was made to the EEC Commission that COFACE was acting contrary to article 86 of the Treaty of Rome (abuse of a dominant position – see below) by virtue of its refusal to approve insurance contracts unless firms met Arab boycott requirements. The Commission responded that the policies of COFACE had no direct repercussions on any restrictions of competition that might derive from the boycott and therefore did not infringe article 86.[22] Towards the end of 1979 the Commission decided that COFACE was not in violation of any articles of the Treaty of Rome, and the MLC's case against it was dropped.

In addition to the EEC proceeding, in October 1977 the MLC filed a petition in the French Administrative Court (the *Conseil d'État*), to the effect that the *avis* was illegal. Despite the legal actions going on, the French business and financial community continued to rely on the *avis* as reflecting the Government's position and as justifying what they regarded as their primary aim of trade with the Third World and the OPEC (Organization of Petroleum Exporting Countries) countries. A paradoxical situation thereby ensued, whereby legally binding legislation was ignored by French governmental and business sectors, with the result that the issue of the boycott became one of extreme sensitivity in France.

After a court hearing on 21 March 1980 the French *Conseil d'État* decided that the Barre Government's decree had been issued in 'excess of authority', and that the law of 7 June 1977 should be implemented. On 9 May 1980, a new decree was promulgated by the French premier and the ministers for foreign trade and economic affairs. The new decree sought to limit the application of the anti-boycott law of 1977 by excluding discrimination on grounds of national origin. This meant that the French Government would recognize restrictive clauses as long as they were not specifically racist in character.[23]

In the same year two French associations, the League against Racism and Anti-Semitism (LICRA) and the Association for the Freedom of Trade (ALC), opened legal proceedings against *Aéroport de Paris*, on the grounds that it had agreed to boycott clauses in a consultancy contract for the airport in Tripoli (Libya) in 1977/78. A Paris court ruled in 1981 that *Aéroport de Paris* had not acted illegally because Barre's second directive was held to apply retroactively.[24]

In late June 1981 reports were published to the effect that the French Government under the premiership of the Socialist Pierre Mauroy had cancelled the previous decree of ex-premier Barre of 9 May 1980, thereby restoring the *Conseil d'État's* decision. The background to this decision was a promise made by the Socialist candidate for the presidency, François Mitterrand, several days before the second round of the presidential elections of May 1981, to the president of the Jewish community, Baron Alain de Rothschild, that he would support the implementation of the anti-boycott legislation.[25] An official statement to this effect was finally issued on 7 July 1981,[26] though the French Government reserved the right to exercise its discretion to deal with each case arising under the 1977 law on its individual merits.[27]

It was generally believed that the announcement by the CBO in Damascus on 17 December 1981, that Renault had been placed on the blacklist was prompted as a warning to the new French administration of the economic consequences of a move away from the pro-Arab policies of its predecessors in the course of the previous 15 years. The excuse for the blacklisting was a 46.6 per cent stake by Renault in American Motors, which had a Jeep production line in Israel at the time. However, Renault's involvement in American Motors was not new, nor the American firm's activities in Israel, which led observers to guess that the reason Renault had been chosen at this particular juncture was because it was state owned.[28]

Following the publication of the Mauroy statement, the question arose as to how the French anti-boycott regulations would be enforced within the French national jurisdiction. A technical committee was set up under the chairmanship of Prof. Jean-Louis Bismuth, and a political committee was established under the chairmanship of M. de Kemelaria. Following a visit to Saudi Arabia, Bahrain, the UAE, Iraq, Jordan, Kuwait, Oman, Qatar and North

Yemen, these countries agreed not to apply the Arab boycott to French enterprises or to enterprises trading from France, agreeing to accept 'positive' certificates of origin. It was agreed that these understandings would not be made public or the subject of political exploitation. The only countries which refused to eliminate the secondary and tertiary boycotts against French enterprises were Libya, Syria and South Yemen.[29]

Pursuant to these new arrangements, various organizations, including the Directorate of International Relations of the French Chamber of Commerce and Industry, COFACE, and the French Association of Banks, issued notices to their members in October 1983 explaining the new directives put out by the Government, and drawing attention to the establishment by the Directorate for External Economic Relations of 'the Centre for Information on Restrictive Clauses Affecting Foreign Trade', to which enquiries could be directed.[30] Under these new directives any restrictive practices affecting agreements with Arab importers had to be cleared with the official COFACE export insurance , which would no longer accept boycott-related conditions as valid for purposes of insurance coverage.[31]

These developments came about in parallel with an improvement in the relations between France and Israel, and French encouragement to businessmen and industrialists to normalize relations with Israel.[32] Nevertheless French companies continued to cooperate with the boycott, and as late as 1991 the French construction giant S.A.E. took another company – Yoro-Linia – to stand in for it in a massive bid for housing for new immigrants in Israel worth about $500 million, for fear of the boycott.[33]

Since 1991

Though France joined Britain in July 1992 in objecting to the G-7 issuing a statement calling on the Arabs to cancel the secondary boycott, at the end of November President Mitterrand issued a unilateral call for the end of the boycott, unlinked to any *quid pro quo* on Israel's part.[34] Again, before the G-7 meeting the following year, Mitterrand assured Israeli Prime Minister Yitzhak Rabin that the boycott issue would be addressed at the meeting in unequivocal terms.[35]

The L'Oréal Affair

However, the more significant development was that in 1991 for the first time the French anti-boycott law of 1977 was invoked in a legal case. The French cosmetics giant, L'Oréal, was served with an indictment, charging François Dalle, the company's President and General Manager in the years 1954–84, with fraud and racial discrimination under the French 1977 anti-boycott law.

L'Oréal's problems with the Arab boycott had begun in 1983, when it purchased Helena Rubinstein Inc., a US-based cosmetics manufacturer with manufacturing facilities in the development town of Mishmar Ha'ekem in Israel, for which it had been blacklisted. In 1985 the CBO in Damascus opened an investigation against L'Oréal, which soon found itself on the blacklist. Subsequently, L'Oréal opened a campaign to be removed from the list, *inter alia*, terminating the manufacturing of Helena Rubinstein products in Mishmar Ha'emek, though it never admitted that this move had been boycott related. In October 1986 L'Oréal made a formal declaration to the effect that it had no relations with Israel. On 5 July 1989 Patrick Salhov, a representative of L'Oréal, reported that the company had been removed from the blacklist.[36]

The French government was aware of L'Oréal's submission to the boycott. The French Foreign Ministry had, in 1986, stamped documents issued by L'Oréal, including a letter signed by Pascal Castres Saint Martin, who stood at the head of the financial and legal departments of the company, stating that the company 'had satisfied all the conditions of the boycott office', and declaring that 'L'Oréal did not and never had any connections with Israel or with Israeli companies abroad'. In addition, after the company was removed from the blacklist, L'Oréal sent a number of letters of appreciation to French official. One, sent to the Minister for Foreign Affairs, Jean-Marie Rausch, on 8 September 1989, stated:

> Since February 1988, our group of companies has been the target of a 'recommendation to be boycotted' issued by the conference of Offices of the Boycott of Israel. Recently this recommendation and the implementation of the measures resulting from it were suspended, which permits our companies to operate normally once again in the countries concerned. This result could not have been obtained without the efficient help and the unceasing support afforded us by the

services of the Ministry for Foreign Trade. We are particularly grateful for the concern that M. Olivier Louis [the commercial counsellor
in charge of the third sub-division] has shown.

However, the issue became complicated when in December 1990
one of Dalle's Jewish business partners, Jean Frydman (who held
dual French and Israeli nationality), made charges to the effect that
Dalle had forced him off L'Oréal's board of directors, as part of
L'Oréal's effort to curry favour with Arab boycott authorities. Dalle
was charged with forging minutes to show that Frydman had
resigned from the board. Frydman, who sued L'Oréal for money he
claimed was owing to him from a partnership in the film company
Paravision – a subsidiary of L'Oréal –, then filed his complaint with
the French courts, charging a violation of the French anti-boycott
law. An investigating magistrate, Jean-Pierre Getti, was appointed to
investigate the issue, and a compromise was reached towards the end
of December 1991.[37]

However, as a result of various pieces of information which started
to leak out in the course of this affair, and the intention of several
organizations to sue L'Oréal on the basis of the 1977 law, L'Oréal's
new President agreed that Professor Jean-Louis Bismuth, one of the
prime movers of the French anti-boycott legislation, should undertake an investigation of L'Oréal's alleged submission to the boycott.
Nineteen days before Bismuth's appointment, on 29 November 1991,
L'Oréal publicly acknowledged that it had indeed, in connection
with its purchase of Helena Rubinstein, negotiated with Arab inter-
mediaries to get itself off the blacklist, but denied that its actions
were in breach of the French law.[38]

Professor Bismuth passed away before completing his investigation, and his place was taken by Professor David Ruzie, who L'Oréal
refused to accept. Ruzie nevertheless published his decision on 2
November 1993. One of Ruzie's findings, on the basis of documents
which had come into his possession, was that L'Oréal, through some
of its subsidiaries, had given boycott assurances long before the
controversy linked to the conditions of its closure of Helena Rubinstein in Israel had emerged in 1988. Ruzie concluded that the
offences committed by L'Oréal included both material and moral
aspects, and were in breach of both the 1977 and 1980 laws.

L'Oréal rejected Ruzie's conclusion. However, by 1995 the whole picture had changed. In May 1995 L'Oréal purchased a 30 per cent stake in Interbeauty, Israel's largest cosmetics marketing organization and the principal distributor of L'Oréal's products. The following month it started producing at the Interbeauty Migdal Ha'emek plant. According to the company's chief executive officer, Lindsay Owen-Jones, the plan was not only increase sales in Israel by 30 per cent, but to start exporting from Israel to the other countries in the region. L'Oréal also initiated a venture with the Hadasah Medical Centre for cosmetics and dermatological studies that may lead to the marketing of new products, while a L'Oréal affiliate, Gladerma, entered into a joint venture with Teva laboratories, to develop a new treatment for psoriasis.[39]

Another court case in this period involved the chamber of commerce of the Loiret region, southwest of Paris. LICRA, one of France's main anti-racist organizations, brought charges against the chamber of commerce arguing that documents issued by the chamber of commerce to local firms working with Arab countries and testifying that the firms had no connections with Israel, or people residing there, were in violation to the French law banning economic discrimination on racial, ethnic or religious grounds. The court dismissed the charges on grounds that there were no identified victims in the case that it heard.[40]

Great Britain

In the first years of the boycott, when Palestine was still under the British Mandate, the Jewish Agency made efforts to get the British Government to take measures against it. In May 1946 for example, David Horowitz, Director of the Jewish Agency Economic Department, suggested to Sir Gerard Clauson, Assistant Under-Secretary of State in the Colonial Office, some concrete measures, which might be taken by Britain to combat the boycott. However, the British authorities were not in the least inclined to do anything about the boycott.[41]

In the early 1950s the Foreign Office seemed eager to coordinate its policy vis-à-vis the boycott with the US State Department and the French *Quai d'Orsay*, both of which were inclined to take a passive approach towards the issue.[42] In an undated memorandum prepared in 1953 by the Foreign Office, Britain's policy on the issue was explained in the following words:

> We do not condone the boycott or admit that it has any validity or justification. We do not, however, actively dispute the practice of the Arab states in controlling their trade with Israel except where this prejudices or threatens to prejudice British commerce. The Arab Governments are hardly amenable to reasoned argument concerning their boycott and we therefore avoid so far as possible becoming engaged in any dispute about its principles and confine our representations to particular cases in which British interests are attacked or threatened. In such cases we have, with certain exceptions, protested vigorously, making it clear that we cannot accept any discrimination against British concerns on account of the boycott. We have taken this action when executive measures have been immediately threatened or applied against British firms and have also made precautionary representations reserving our position where legislation has been passed which appears liable to lead to such measures. There have been exceptions to this policy in the cases of oil shipments from Kuwait to Haifa and of the denial of facilities to oil tankers. In these instances we have not taken a stand against interference with British activities by the boycott.[43]

The memorandum added that:

> [in] November 1952, when the boycott was becoming an increasing nuisance, we considered a proposal by the Board of Trade that we should combine with the other Western Powers and attempt to apply concerted pressure on the Arab Governments to drop those of their boycott measures which were harmful to our interests. After consulting Her Majesty's Missions concerned we decided that this would do more harm than good.[44]

The memorandum concluded that:

> It is hard to see how we can improve on our existing policy and practices, thankless though these have proved, of attempting to ward off by diplomatic methods particular threats to British interests when and where these arise ... The most difficult aspect arises when our representations are unsuccessful and we have to consider retaliation. It is hard to decide how far we should go with this in any particular case and [sic] is made more difficult by the fact that there are few measures of economic retaliation which we can apply to the Arab states without doing ourselves as much harm as them. We must not

allow boycott difficulties to damage our general relations with the Arab states ... and we have to remember that the possession of oil strengthens their position immensely, particularly if a situation should be allowed to develop where retaliation became likely.[45]

In October 1955 the Israeli Ministry for Foreign Affairs approached Britain, as well as the US and France, to take some concerted action against the boycott. This time the Foreign Office was a little more positive, responding that the boycott was unjustified, but that the companies concerned had to be left to decide for themselves how to react to it.[46]

In 1957/58 British Petroleum and Royal Dutch-Shell discontinued the marketing and distribution of oil products in Israel. This action terminated the last remaining link of major international oil companies with Israel. In the case of British Petroleum the British Government, as owner of BP, was certainly not free of responsibility for the decision.[47]

Britain was, however, one of the Western countries which was most cooperative in complying with the Arab boycott. The Norwich Union affair of 1963 involved direct Arab pressure to get a Jewish peer, Lord Manscroft, to resign from the board of directors of the Norwich Union Insurance Co. After the Norwich Union admitted publicly that Lord Mancroft had resigned as a result of Arab pressure, the Conservative British Government, then led by Prime Minister Sir Alec Douglas-Home, took swift action, and informed the Ambassadors of three Arab states that it opposed outside interference in British domestic affairs and in British companies's freedom to trade. The Ambassadors were further told that the British government strongly resented pressure on British firms to discriminate on any grounds among their British staff, and that it also strongly disapproved of action by the Arab embassies in London designed to bring pressure on British firms to comply with the boycott.[48]

On 20 June 1969 Mr G. O. Roberts, Minister of State for Foreign Affairs, wrote in a letter addressed to the Israeli Ambassador to London that 'The attitude of the British Government to the Arab boycott is well known, and has been reiterated many times in public statements. We neither accept nor condone the primary boycott of Israel, and are opposed to the secondary boycott. It is therefore part of our policy not to have any official dealings with the Central

Boycott Office in Damascus or with any of the Regional Offices, including the one in Beirut. This has always been our policy towards the boycott, and I can assure you that it remains unchanged today.'[49]

However, despite the fine words, cases of compliance with the boycott never elicited any reaction from the British Government. In 1970, for example, the Arabs decided that the modest investment which British Leyland, then the largest car-manufacturing conglomerate in Great Britain, had in Israel as a minority shareholder in an Israeli factory which assembled its Triumphs, was unbearably offensive. Though they continued to purchase Land Rovers from the company's Rover-Triumph subsidiary, they blacklisted the parent corporation to deny it potentially high truck and bus sales throughout the Arab world. Moves to get Leyland off the boycott blacklist began in 1972, and in December of that year the company was reported to have signed a £50 million deal to assemble 10,000 Land Rovers a year in Egypt (a plan which was later to be shelved). In Cairo the chairman of British Leyland was reported to have 'produced two documents affirming that the company was no longer collaborating with Israel' and that business in Israel had ended, which was not entirely true, though it did create the impression that it had surrendered to the boycotters. It was only in 1976 that Leyland was removed from the blacklist, even though some sales continued to Israel in a backhanded manner. At this stage the company considered rejoining the Anglo-Israel Chamber of Commerce which it had previously left, but as a result of Arab pressure it changed its position and joined the newly formed Arab–British Chamber of Commerce instead.[50] The British Government – which held 95 per cent of British Leyland shares at the time – did not openly intervene.

Again in 1975 the Israeli Ports Authority approached 18 British firms for tenders to construct tugboats worth more than $20 million, and this in a period in which the British shipyards were in dire economic straits. Only two of the firms approached replied, but both refused the contract, and the contract went to Norway.[51] In 1977, Metal Box, a blacklisted packaging firm, pulled out of a 25-year-old investment in Israel, after its food company customers were told to cease using Metal Box tin cans so long as the canning company maintained its long-standing links with the Israel Can Company.[52] Again, the British Government didn't intervene.

The British banking community adopted a similar attitude to that of industry, and the British Bankers Association presented testimony before the House of Lords Select Committee on the Byers Bill (see below), arguing that anti-boycott legislation would be ineffective while causing damage to Britain's business interests. Only Barclays Bank, which maintained links with Israel through the Barclays-Discount Bank, followed a different policy to the rest, and in October 1976 was blacklisted. While Barclays chairman stated in an address to the bank's stockholders on 13 March 1977 that 'In the last analysis ... we are convinced that an international bank cannot submit to pressure of this sort, and must work to support tolerance against intolerance', the British Government failed to take any action to defend a major British financial institution.[53]

While British companies were generally more cooperative than their counterparts in other European countries in complying with boycott demands, relatively more British companies were black-listed. In 1979, for example, about 1,150 British companies were to be found on the Saudi Arabian blacklist.[54]

While the British Government was not inclined to initiate anti-boycott legislation, in May 1977 the Anglo-Israeli Chamber of Commerce and Anti-Boycott Committee (ABC) and several Members of Parliament sent Labour Prime Minister James Callaghan a ten-point program, which called upon the Government to take action in the following spheres:

- to state unequivocally that it opposed all foreign boycotts directed against countries friendly to the United Kingdom, and to partici-pate in international action against boycott pressure;
- to require, or at least encourage, British companies to refuse to take action in support of foreign boycotts, while prohibiting the furnishing of boycott-related information;
- to prohibit the secondary boycott by making it illegal for a British company to refuse to do business with Israel in conformity with boycott requests;
- to outlaw the tertiary boycott by making it illegal for a company to refrain from dealing with a blacklisted non-Israeli firm;
- to prohibit the furnishing of information on business relationships with Israel or non-Israeli blacklisted firms, or concerning the religion or national origin of any British citizen;

- to take positive measures to prevent discrimination in employment or promotion arising from the boycott;
- to forbid the issuance of negative certificates of origin;
- to require companies to report boycott requests and/or the intention to comply with such requests and open these reports to public inspection;
- to prohibit banks and other financial institutions and shipping companies to require proof of boycott compliance in connection with the issuance of letters of credit or the processing and transport of export shipments;
- to deny public funds to firms practising discrimination in employment and make provision for firms suffering losses as a result of unfair business practices.[55]

Also in May an all-parliamentary committee was formed to draft anti-boycott legislation. The committee produced the Foreign Boycotts Bill of 1977, which was introduced in the House of Lords on 12 July 1977, by Lord Byers. The bill got as far as a second reading on 30 January 1978, and was subsequently referred to a House of Lords Select Committee. Throughout 1978 the Select Committee held hearings and called witnesses. The Committee took note of the existence of four types of boycotts, which were of particular concern to British citizens:

- the secondary boycott;
- the tertiary boycott;
- the demand that British firms supply information as to the religious affiliation of their owners and managers;
- the demand that British firms dispatch their products only on carriers which do not appear on Arab boycott lists, and that British banks and insurance companies agree to honour letters of credit or issue policies which contain explicit boycott clauses.[56]

The select committee published its report on 28 July 1978. It commented that the Government's policy of 'deploring the boycott and yet leaving all decisions to the commercial judgement of companies without any reference to the government's view is not wholly consistent'. It added 'that the government is vulnerable in its practice of authenticating negative certificates of origin' and recommended 'that Her Majesty's Government change its policy of authentication and that officials of the Foreign and Commonwealth Office should be directed not to authenticate the signatures on negative certificates of origin'. The committee also recommended that the Government reconsider the use of public funds for transactions involving submission to boycott requirements.

However, its main conclusion was that the provisions of the proposed bill clashed with Britain's relevant policy goals, which were to ensure a Middle East settlement, to maintain friendly relations with both the Arabs and Israel, to promote British exports, and to preserve the principle of non-discrimination in the United Kingdom among persons of different races, religions and ethnic origins. Therefore it recommended that further progress on the bill be stopped, adding that the most promising way of combating the secondary and tertiary Arab boycotts was through an initiative in the European Council. It added that 'Her Majesty's Government should undertake an initiative to put the subject on the agenda of the Council.'[57]

In February 1979 the committee's report was considered by the House of Lords. Many of its recommendations were rejected, though the Government did agree to review the Foreign Office practice of authenticating negative certificates of origin, to redraft the Department of Trade's guidelines to the business community, and to welcome the voluntary reporting of boycott requests by British companies.

At the same time Foreign Secretary Dr David Owen stated that 'Any change, whether legislative or administrative, which substantially changes the present situation would, in the Government's opinion, be bound to damage relations between the UK and the Arab states, who would regard it as a political act marking a shift in British policy in favour of Israel.' Dr Owen further remarked that he saw no reason for raising the matter with the European Community.[58]

The Government's position was officially presented in a note on the Arab boycott, issued by the Department of Trade in March 1979. The purpose of the note was, *inter alia*, 'to help remove misunderstandings and unnecessary anxieties among British businessmen' about the operation of the boycott as it affected British firms, and to set out Her Majesty's Government's (HMG) policy towards it. The note made it clear that its issue did not imply any recognition of the boycott by HMG, nor any willingness on its part to further its objectives by giving publicity to it. Nevertheless, the reluctance to take any firm stand or intervene in the business decisions of individual firms emerged clearly.

The Government's policy, as stated in the note, was as follows:

> H.M. Government is opposed to and deplores all trade boycotts that lack international support and authority. It does not recognize the boycott administration and has no formal communication with the boycott offices. The Government's policy is to maintain friendly relations with the Arab states and Israel, and it is therefore against the introduction, into commercial documents and transactions, of clauses and undertakings which are intended to restrict the commercial freedom of British firms to trade with all countries in the Middle East. Although the Government has no wish, and does not intend, to interfere with the ability of individual firms to decide in the light of their own commercial interests what their attitude should be towards the boycott and whether or not, or how far, they will complete and return questionnaires from boycott offices, it believes that companies will wish to bear in mind this statement of general policy and to avoid, as far as possible, giving undertakings which limit unnecessarily their commercial freedom.[59]

In 1981, the British Government gave the following three explanations to why it would not follow the American footsteps in passing anti-boycott legislation:

- the British economy was much more dependent on exports than the American one;
- if Britain passed anti-boycott legislation, the Arabs were likely to deliberately transfer export orders to Britain's foreign competitors;
- only concerted legislation by the European Community would be effective against the Arab boycott.[60]

By the mid-1980s the situation regarding the British government's attitude towards the Arab boycott was still considered unsatisfactory by those trying to get it to adopt a more active anti-boycott position. In June 1984, Terrence Prittie, one of the central figures within the ABC, enumerated three unsatisfactory features in this attitude:

> The first is the continuing readiness of the British Foreign Office to expedite boycott documents, in particular negative certificates of origin. The Arab Boycott offices have sought to implicate the Foreign Office, in order to lend strength and prestige to their campaign to undermine trade between Britain and Israel.

The second ... is governmental unreadiness to take any action to curb the boycott activities of the Arab–British Chamber of Commerce. This Chamber issues its own negative certificates and witnesses the signatures of public notaries expediting them. The British Government is well aware of this and has admitted it publicly. Indeed, government spokesmen have stated that many more boycott documents are dealt with by the Arab–British Chamber than by the British Foreign Office.

The third ... is contained in the Department of Trade's printed instructions to British firms who come under Arab boycott pressure. While 'deploring' the Arab boycott and pointing out that it has been rejected by the government, the Department advises firms to rely on their 'own commercial judgement'. Such a phrase implicitly suggests that the government will not intervene on behalf of such firms (nor does it do so).[61]

Following a visit to London by Israeli Prime Minister Shimon Peres in January 1986, the Foreign Office announced that it would stop cooperating with the Arab boycott in the form of authenticating negative certificates of origin.[62] Nevertheless, British companies, including government-owned ones such as British Aerospace, continued to fill negative certificates of origin. The sale of Tornadoes to Saudi Arabia towards the end of the 1980, provided an example of how British companies complied with the boycott. BAE purchased a component for the planes from Machine Components of Long Island in the US. In its contract with the American company of December 1988 there was a clause guaranteeing that none of the parts in these components was made in Israel or had been transported by any Israeli carrier.[63]

According to a document prepared by the Department of Trade and Industry in 1990, the boycott had deterred British Industry to the extent that it failed to tender for business in Israel potentially worth £325 million.[64]

Since 1991

Following the Gulf War, on several occasions the British government condemned the Arab boycott, but failed to take any practical steps in terms of legislation either domestically or on the European Community level.[65] In addition, during the meeting of the G-7 summit in Munich in July 1992, Britain, together with France, objected strongly to the issuing of a statement calling upon the Arab countries to end the secondary boycott, and this despite the fact that a new, Labor-led government was about to be formed in Israel, committed to freezing all Jewish settlement activities in the territories – the *quid pro quo* which the previous G-7 meeting had demanded for the ending of the boycott.

However, during a visit by Israeli Foreign Minister Shimon Peres to London in September, British Prime Minister John Major promised his guest that he would lead an EC effort to persuade the Arab states to end the boycott – without linkage to settlements or any other political issue.[66] On 9 December Yitzhak Rabin once again appealed to the British Government to take more positive steps to put an end to the Arab boycott.[67]

In the middle of April 1993 British Foreign Secretary Douglas Hurd called for the abolition of the secondary and tertiary Arab boycotts. 'Economically the boycott is wrong because it is an impediment to free flows of trade and investment both within the region and between the region and the rest of the world', he said in an address to the Arab Research Centre. 'I can accept that Arab states may choose not to trade directly with Israel', he said, 'but I cannot accept that they should boycott companies from third countries merely because of their links with Israel.'

Hurd then spoke of the *quid pro quo* – a freeze on Jewish settlement activities in the territories in return for the lifting of the secondary and tertiary boycotts. 'Last September', he added, after Israel had frozen the settlements, the European Community 'approached leading members of the Arab League and asked them to respond to the Israeli moves by taking steps to end the boycott'. 'But', he added, 'most of the states approached argued that the new Israeli government had not yet made sufficient moves to justify reciprocal action by the Arab League.'[68]

In 1993 a Private Member's Bill, designed to end boycott compliance and the completion of boycott declarations, was introduced in the House of Commons by Spencer Batiste, with the backing of members of the three main political parties. The Trades Boycotts Bill sought to prohibit UK companies from providing information for the purpose of a trade boycott, unless that boycott is approved by British law, the UN and the EC. However, Batiste's proposal fell.[69]

It was, however, in 1995 that a real change was finally discerned in the British attitude towards the Arab boycott and economic relations with Israel. On 13 March 1995, Prime Minister John Major came to Israel to participate in the opening session of a round table in which Israeli and British industrialists took part, after Britain had cancelled its long-standing arms embargo on Israel. Among other things Major stated in his speech that Britain was interested in investing in Israel and in having Israeli investments in Britain, while the round table itself dealt, *inter alia*, with technological cooperation.[70] Nine months later (and one month after the assassination of Israeli Prime Minister Yitzhak Rabin), a British–Israeli business council was inaugurated in London. It was no accident that on this occasion Israeli Prime Minister Shimon Peres sent a letter to Major with Israeli Minister of Industry and Trade, Micha Harish, who participated in the opening meeting of the Council, in which he wrote: 'After many years of the Arab boycott we are facing a new period of high hopes.' During his visit to Britain Harish met with the directors of several major British companies, who in the past would have nothing to do with Israel. These included the General Electric Company (GEC) and British Aerospace.[71]

Germany

In 1952, just before the Federal Republic of Germany (West Germany) signed the Restitution Agreement with Israel, the Arab League threatened to apply the Arab boycott directly against it. However, since in that period West Germany was in greater need of being accepted back into the family of nations than of Arab trade, the Arab threat failed completely.[72]

Following this event, and until 1979, neither the West German government nor the Bundestag (the West German parliament) took any action with regards to the Arab boycott. The official government position, as explained in an answer to a parliamentary question in 1975, was that: 'As a matter of principle ... the Federal government condemns any kind of boycott threat because of the adverse effect on international economic relations.' However, it was added that 'affected companies have to decide by themselves how best to react to threats of boycotts in their own particular case'.[73]

In practice, what this meant was that the Federal Republic was unwilling to enact anti-boycott legislation such as that which existed at the time in the US, France and the Netherlands. The main formal excuse given for the refusal to pass legislation on this subject was that such legislation would be contrary to the principles of the Basic Law of the Federal Republic, since it would constitute an interference with the freedom of business transactions. Another argument used was that there was no point in enacting such legislation because it could not effectively be enforced. However, the main reason for the refusal to introduce any effective measures against the boycott was that such measures were liable to endanger German economic relations with the Arab world, unless adopted simultaneously by all the Western industrialized states.

Nevertheless the German Ministry of Economics was willing, upon Israeli request, to inform German companies, which had given in to the boycott, that the government was opposed to it in principle.[74] The German government was also known to intervene on behalf of companies in danger of being blacklisted. Thus, for example, when the German car manufacturer Volkswagen (VW) received warning from the CBO in Damascus in connection with its licensing agreement with an Israeli firm for the production of its Wankel engine, the German Government intervened, and VW was able to continue operating simultaneously with both Israel and the Arab countries. In addition, unlike the practice in several other European states, after 1966 both the Federal Government and the German Chambers of Commerce refused to authenticate negative certificates of origin or boycott questionnaires.[75] Thus, in 1976 the Hamburg Chamber of Commerce described the Arab boycott of Israel as 'a particularly grotesque strain of discrimination against the freedom of trade', and noted that the Chamber's rejection of Arab boycott demands had not generated any disadvantages for German export businesses to the Arab world.[76]

In 1975 the West German banks were informed by the Arab League that if they continued to deal in the Eurobond market with Israel or pro-Israeli companies, they would be blacklisted. Most of the large German financial institutions refused to give in to these threats, and like many major German manufacturers (such as Mercedes-Benz) managed to maintain ties with both the Arab states and Israel without being blacklisted.

In 1977 a German–Arab Chamber of Commerce, called GHOURFA, was set up in Germany with independent financing, which made efforts to dictate the terms of German–Arab trade. This body was partially successful in its endeavors, but the Federal Government did not try to regulate its activities. Though German businessmen had stated to the researchers of the US Foreign Affairs and National Defense Division Congressional Research Service in the late 1970s, that on the whole the boycott did not confront them with any problems,[77] there is no question that many German manufacturers bent over backwards to try to avoid confrontation with the boycott authorities, and found various ways to circumvent their demands.

By the early 1980s many German companies had Israeli businessmen enter their offices only by the back door, and in large companies such as Höchst certain divisions refused to have any dealings with Israel, while others had direct or indirect contacts with it.[78] Furthermore, many German companies started trading with Israel, or alternatively with Arab trading partners, through third companies, subsidiaries or especially established straw companies, and engaging in such practices as changing labels on products, doctoring documents, or sending products through third countries.[79]

Other German companies trading with Arab countries did agree to sign clauses to the effect that they had no subsidiaries, representatives or any other sort of activities in Israel. Thus, for example, the German companies which exhibited products at the industrial fair in Baghdad in 1990 signed boycott declarations and filled questionnaires in which they denied any relations with Israel. In this particular case some businessmen were actually requested, before deals were signed with them, to confirm their Aryan origins.[80]

Though by 1990 Israeli trade with Germany amounted to about $1.1 billion, and Germany was Israel's third largest trading partner (after the US and Great Britain), German industry maintained few ties with Israeli industry beyond straightforward trade. There was very little German capital investment in Israel (mostly in the hotel business), no joint ventures or arrangements for the transfer of technology, and no purchases of Israeli goods by the German Government.[81]

Since 1991

In the aftermath of the Gulf War, after it had transpired that German companies had been involved in helping Iraq develop its non-conventional capability,[82] German Foreign Minister Hans Dietrich Genscher, during a visit to Israel at the end of January 1991, in order to observe the damage caused by the Iraqi Scud attacks, indicated to the Israeli Government that Germany would consider introducing anti-boycott legislation.[83] In May Genscher made a public commitment to the ADL leaders in New York that his country would soon enact anti-boycott legislation.[84]

This was in fact done the following year. On 23 July 1992 Germany passed an anti-boycott law forbidding German firms to honour Arab requests to isolate Israel economically by including clauses in commercial transactions for the sale or purchase of goods, which would have the effect of giving in to or complying with the Arab boycott.[85] A report by the German Embassy in Tel Aviv, submitted to the ADL Israel office, stated that 'the delivery of a declaration in foreign trade by which a legal entity would participate in a boycott against another state is forbidden'.[86]

Reporting on a private meeting which World Jewish Congress President Edgar Bronfman and the head of the Jewish community in Germany Ignatz Bubis held with Chancellor Helmut Kohl in Bonn in the third week of May 1993, a WJC spokesman issued a statement to the effect that Germany had finally instituted the anti-boycott regulations, and that the Jewish leaders were assured by the Chancellor that he would seek to introduce similar regulations within the European Community.[87]

In February 1994 Germany joined the US in conveying a request to the Arab League to relax the secondary and tertiary boycotts. The request was conveyed to the the Secretary General of the Arab League Esmet Abdel Meguid, during a visit to Bonn, by German Foreign Minister Klaus Kinkel. Abdel Meguid promised to lay it on the table of the League Ministerial Council which was to meet in Cairo on 29 March.[88]

In June 1995 Volkswagen became Germany's first major company to make a significant investment in Israel. Volkswagen agreed to invest $231 million in a magnesium plant at the Dead Sea. The decision, promoted by progress in the Middle East peace process, and Israel's generous grants for investments in the Negev, followed a visit by Chancellor Helmut Kohl to Israel early in June.[89] VW is interested in magnesium, which in future is to be used in the manufacture of its cars. Another major German company which previously avoided

contacts with Israel when it could, but is currently seeking technological contacts with Israeli high-tech companies, is Siemens.

The change in attitude in Germany has been exemplified by the
decision of the Deutsche Bank, which had previously kept a very low
profile with regards to its business dealings with Israel, to open up a
branch of its subsidiary, Roland Berger & Co., in Israel. Roland
Berger is an international consultancy firm, and it intends to offer its
services to foreign companies planning to participate in various
development projects in Israel, the Palestinian Authority, Jordan,
Egypt and other Middle Eastern states.[90]

The Netherlands

One of the first cases of a well known company giving in to the boycott involved the Dutch manufacturer of electrical goods Philips.
The company was placed on the blacklist after it opened a small
subsidiary in Israel for the manufacture of light bulbs in 1950. In
November 1952 Philips announced that it was closing its Israeli
plant down, allegedly for commercial reasons. Soon after closing
down its Israeli plant, Philips was taken off the blacklist, and in
January 1953 the CBO in Damascus announced that 'the representative of Philips in Damascus had declared that Philips had officially
promised the Arab states that its Israeli factory would not be
reopened, and its equipment would be transferred to an Arab state'.[91]
It was only at the beginning of 1998 that Philips officially announced
that it was no longer giving in to boycott demands.[92]

The subject of the boycott came up for serious discussion for the
first time in the Netherlands after Ronnie M. Naftaniel published, in
February 1978, a doctoral dissertation entitled 'The Arab Boycott
and the Netherlands', which revealed the extent of the compliance by
the Dutch government and business with the boycott. The work,
published by the *Centrum voor Informatie en Documentatie Israel*
(CIDI), found that in 1977 some 7,000 Dutch companies had filed
boycott-related documents with the Rotterdam Chamber of
Commerce.[93]

One year after the publication of this work, in February 1979, a
special committee, appointed by the second chamber of the Dutch
parliament, released a report on the effects of the Arab boycott on
Dutch business. The report found that Dutch companies were being

confronted with boycott demands in virtually all phases of their business transactions with Arab League states; many Dutch companies were being forced to sign negative certificates of origin; negative certificates of origin were being authenticated on a large scale by the Dutch Chamber of Commerce and Foreign Ministry; Dutch companies had issued declarations that employees to be sent to particular locations abroad were not Jewish; many Dutch businesses had discontinued trade or refused to trade with Israel in compliance with boycott demands; and both the Dutch government and the private sector seemed to comply with the Arab boycott to a greater extent than most other Western countries.[94]

Though the Netherlands was considered a country especially friendly to Israel, and an oil embargo was placed on it by the Arab oil-producing states owing to its alleged pro-Israeli position during the Yom Kippur War,[95] it should be noted that in 1979 over 40 per cent of the Dutch GNP derived from export earnings, of which approximately 10 per cent came from the Arab states. These figures reflected a doubling of Dutch exports to Arab countries since 1973, compared to the overall decline of 22 per cent in the exports of the OECD countries as a whole in the same period.

Nevertheless in October 1979, after difficult political debates, the Dutch government agreed to take the following measures:

- to stop the authentication of negative certificates of origin by the Ministry of Foreign Affairs;
- to forbid the Dutch export insurance company to insure contracts with discriminatory clauses, and to stop its practice of informing companies that with regard to contracts signed with Arab countries they must obey the Arab boycott regulations;
- to ask companies and chambers of commerce to use positive certificates of origin instead of negative ones;
- to inquire whether the application of the tertiary boycott could be stopped by means of the Dutch competition law;
- to forbid by law the use by companies of certificates of religious affiliation (non-Jew certificates) which stated that its management is non-Jewish and has no contacts with Israel;
- to initiate a bill which urges companies to inform the Ministry of Economic Affairs when approached with boycott requests for statements.[96]

In the beginning of 1981 an additional special parliamentary inquiry committee on the boycott was set up, in which all the Dutch political parties were represented.[97] As a result of this committee's report the Netherlands introduced, on 29 June 1981, a change in article 429 of the Dutch Penal Code, making it a criminal offence for anyone to discriminate in the course of practising a profession or trade against a person on grounds of race. This offence was made punishable by imprisonment of up to one month or a fine not exceeding 10,000 guilders. The provision was not to apply to cases of positive discrimination in favour of persons belonging to particular ethnic or cultural minorities. What it achieved was to do away with the non-Jew certificates.[98]

In May 1984 the legislation was extended, making it mandatory to register all foreign boycott-related requests within a specific period, their nature and the identity of those making such requests. Failure by companies to abide by these provisions was made punishable by a fine of up to 25,000 guilders or six months imprisonment. Further information could also be required by the authorities, and the measure established an independent commission to which injured parties domiciled in the Netherlands could turn.

Neither the 1981 legislation nor the 1984 legislation (which was originally intended to remain in force for three years only) prohibited the use of negative certificates of origin.[99] There was a lack of consensus in the Netherlands as to the need to address a problem specifically affecting Israel,[100] nor could either law be defined as 'anti-boycott legislation' in the strictest sense, as they were not directed against the boycott itself but against those consequences which are contrary to the legal order in the Netherlands. Moreover, both laws were intended to have a wider application. The 1981 law was intended to be applied in connection with problems arising from the increase of foreign residents in the Netherlands, whereas the 1984 measure was applicable to foreign boycotts in general.[101]

Nevertheless, the growing awareness regarding the Arab boycott and the two laws resulted in a 75 per cent drop in the number of requests for negative certificates of origin in the years 1979–83. In addition, in the years 1981–84 there was only one case of a company – the Swedish firm of Fläkt – being found guilty and fined for issuing a non-Jewish certificate.[102] This was probably due, however, to the fact that it was very difficult to prove that companies were committing an act of discrimination when they issued non-Jew declarations.[103]

In a report on the boycott, issued in October 1990 by the Dutch Economics Ministry, the effect of the legislation was evaluated. *Inter alia*, the report stated that while there had been some initial hesitation on the part of the industrial sector regarding the effects of the law, and despite the substantial administrative load which it had caused, the law had resulted in a large amount of information being collected and good cooperation between the government and industry.[104]

The report concluded with a statement of the government's policy on the boycott issue. These were summarized in three points:

- since the application of the law did not reveal mutual discrimination between persons or corporate bodies, legal measures need not be taken to prohibit the issue of certain boycott-related declarations;
- in view of boycott-related problems emerging in several European Community states in connection with the mixed Arab chambers of commerce, the Dutch government would raise the issue in the European Parliament and in talks between the Community and Gulf states;
- despite a certain 'reporting fatigue' among Dutch companies complying with the reporting duty in accordance with the law, in light of the absence of a satisfactory solution to the boycott problem on the European level, the government planned to retain the reporting duty for a further three years.

Luxembourg

On 9 August 1980 amendments were introduced to the Luxembourgian Penal Code, *inter alia* making it an offence to discriminate against any person on grounds of race, national or ethnic origin in the course of trading or offering to tender goods or services, to announce one's intention to refuse to provide goods or services, or to practice discrimination in the aforementioned circumstances. Article 454 of the Code made this offence punishable by imprisonment of up to six months and/or a fine of F100,000.

Article 455 of the Code made it an offence, punishable by the same penalties as apply to article 454, for anyone to carry out acts of incitement, in writing, by print or any other form of public communication, to commit the offences mentioned in article 454, or to commit acts of incitement to hatred or violence against any person, group or community, or against any of its members on any of the aforementioned grounds. It is also an offence to belong to any organization whose aims or activities are for the purpose of committing such acts.[105]

Belgium

A similar amendment to that enacted in Luxembourg was passed in Belgium on 30 July 1981. Article 1 of the Belgian law made punishable by a nominal fine and/or imprisonment for up to six months, certain acts of incitement specified under article 444 of the Penal Code – namely, incitement to discrimination, hatred or violence against a person, by reason of his race, colour, national or ethnic origin. The same offence is committed if directed against a group or community, or against certain members of such a group or community on the aforementioned grounds.

Article 3 of the law makes it an offence, punishable by a nominal fine and/or imprisonment for up to three months, for anyone committing a discriminatory act against any person on grounds of race, colour, national or ethnic origin, when tendering or offering to tender goods or services in a public place.

Notes

1. Daniel Lack, WJC memorandum, 'Arab Boycott: Submission of Test Case to EEC Commission', Geneva, 4 January 1977.
2. *Business International*, 30 December 1977, and Aaron Sarna, *Boycott and Blacklists – A History of Arab Economic Warfare against Israel* (Totowa, NJ: Rowman & Littlefield, 1986) p. 117
3. Charlotte A. Phillips, *The Arab Boycott of Israel – Possibilities for European Cooperation with US Anti-boycott Legislation* (Washington DC: Foreign Affairs and National Defense Division Congressional Research Service, May 1979).
4. Ibid., p. v.

5. See Chapter 9.
6. PRO, FO 371/104206 XC13782.
7. Susan Hattis Rolef, 'Israel's Anti-Boycott Policy', *Policy Studies*, 28 (Jerusalem: The Leonard Davis Institute for International Relations at the Hebrew University of Jerusalem, February 1989), p. 15.
8. Terence Prittie and Walter Henry Nelson, *The Economic War Against the Jews* (London: Secker & Warburg, 1978), p.139.
9. Oded Remba, 'The Arab Boycott. A Study in Total Economic Warfare', *Midstream* (Summer 1960), p. 47.
10. Ibid.
11. See 'France and the Boycott', *The Israel Economist*, 36 (January–February 1980), p. 21, and entry 'France and Israel' by Yohanan Manor, in Susan Hattis Rolef, *Political Dictionary of the State of Israel*, second edition (Jerusalem: The Jerusalem Publishing House, 1993) p. 118.
12. Phillips, op. cit., p. 45.
13. See Chapter 3, pp. 82–3.
14. Phillips, op. cit., p. 15.
15. WJC, 'Memorandum on the Status of Anti-Boycott Action and Anti-Terrorism Measures in France', 18 January 1984.
16. No. 45–1483 of 30 June 1945.
17. Daniel Lack, 'Memorandum on Recent Developments in Europe on Anti-Boycott Action', the WJC, Geneva, 8 June 1976.
18. Ibid. See also Chapter 9.
19. See French Embassy press and Information Division release of 8 August 1977, which took note of the concern expressed by the Israeli Government over this decree and the response of the French Ministry of Foreign Affairs that the government would continue actively to oppose discriminatory practices based on race, national or ethnic origin or religion, but that the law had been defined by the premier in view of its being capable of being interpreted as an impediment to foreign trade; see also Phillips, op. cit., p. 42.
20. Ibid., p. 52.
21. After its creation in 1976 the MLC became active in combatting the boycott in cooperation with the WJC.
22. Phillips, op. cit., p. 43.
23. Britain and Israel Information and Trade Centre, 'Memorandum for Lord Byers and Mr Kornberg France and the Arab Trade Boycott', 28 June 1981.
24. MEED, 12 March 1982, p. 14.
25. *Regards – Revue juive de Belgique*, 275, 20 June 1991, p. 12.
26. *Official Gazette*, 18 July 1981, p. 2003.
27. British–Israel Chamber of Commerce Information and Trade Centre, press release, 23 July 1981.
28. MEED, 12 March and 30 April 1982.
29. WJC memorandum, dated 18 January 1984.
30. Ibid.
31. 'The Arab Boycott', a WJC release, dated 9 January 1986, and WJC memorandum on Boycott legislation in Europe, dated May 1984.

32. Dr Shalom Shirman, at the Seminar on Freedom of Trade held in Brussels in March 1991 under the sponsorship of the BICC and CEJI.
33. ADL Memorandum, quoted in *Ha'aretz*, 21 June 1991.
34. Agence Europe (Brussels), 28 November 1992.
35. BBC Monitoring Service, 3 July 1993.
36. *Ha'aretz*, 11 June 1991.
37. Reuters, 20 and 21 December 1991, and *The Times*, 3 January 1992.
38. *Ha'aretz*, 1 December, 1991.
39. Reuters News Service, 'L'Oréal's Israeli Initiative', 5 July 1995. See also Leah Nathans Spiro, Farah Nayei and Niel Sandler, 'The Shadow Across L'Oréal', *Business Week*, 21 March 1994.
40. Reuter (Orléans), 7 December 1992.
41. Rolef, 'Israel's Anti-Boycott Policy', op. cit., p. 10.
42. PRO, FO 371/98275 1123/16 and 1123/17.
43. Ibid., FO 371/104206 XC13782.
44. Ibid.
45. Ibid.
46. Rolef, op. cit., p. 15.
47. Remba, op. cit., p. 47.
48. Prittie and Nelson, op. cit., pp. 59–63; see also Chapter 4.
49. Meron Medzini (ed.) *Israel's Foreign Relations. Selected Documents 1947–1974* (Jerusalem: Ministry for Foreign Affairs, 1976), p. 281.
50. Prittie and Nelson, op. cit., pp. 168–73.
51. *MEED*, 16 January 1976, p. 5.
52. Phillips, op. cit., p. 82.
53. See 'Memorandum: A Call for Effective Government Action Against the Arab Trade Boycott' issued by the Board of Deputies of British Jews, the Zionist Federation of Great Britain and Ireland and B'nai B'rith, dated 30 May 1977 and submitted to the House of Lords Select Committee.
54. Phillips, op. cit., p. 81, citing *The Economist*.
55. Ibid.
56. Statement by the President of the Board of Deputies of British Jews and the Chairman of the European branch of the WJC, Lord Fisher of Camden, made to the House of Lords Select Committee on 5 May 1978.
57. Phillips, op. cit., p. 30 and Terrence Prittie, 'Britain and the Arab Trade Boycott', in Susan Hattis Rolef (ed.) *Freedom of Trade and the Arab Boycott, Papers – Presentations and Discussions at the Seminar on Freedom of Trade with Israel, Brussels, June 1984* (Jerusalem: The Anti-Defamation League of B'nai Brith in cooperation with the Israel Institute of Coexistence, 1985), p. 126.
58. Phillips, op. cit., p. 79.
59. 'The Arab Boycott of Israel', note by the Department of Trade, March 1979.
60. 'The Arab Boycott', release by the Embassy of Israel in London, November 1981.
61. Terrence Prittie, op. cit., pp. 126–7.
62. *Financial Times*, 30 January 1986.

63. *Financial Times*, 27 July 1989.
64. Julia Schöpflin, 'The Arab Boycott of Israel: Can it Withstand the Peace Process?', London, Institute of Jewish Affairs, *Research Reports*, No. 4 (March 1994), p. 8.
65. See for example the answer by Foreign Secretary Douglas Hurd to an adjournment debate question in July 1991, where he declared that he regarded the boycott 'as a thoroughly undesirable policy'. Nevertheless, he did not believe legislation to be desirable because 'it would be unenforceable as to make the attempt undesirable' – see British–Israel Chamber of Commerce, 'Anti-Boycott Briefing Note', 8 July 1991.
66. *Boycott Report*, 16/9, November/December 1992, and 17/1, January 1993.
67. *Daily Telegraph*, 10 December, 1992.
68. BIPAC Newsbrief, 21 April 1993.
69. Martin Savitt, *Arab Trade Boycott of Israel Briefing Notes* (September 1993).
70. *Ma'ariv*, 14 March 1995, and *Haáretz*, 16 March 1995.
71. *Ma'ariv*, 12 December 1995.
72. Rolef, op. cit., p. 14.
73. Quoted in Susan Hattis Rolef, 'The Middle East Policy of the Federal Republic of Germany', *Jerusalem Papers on Peace Problems*, 39 (Jerusalem: The Magnes Press, the Hebrew University – The Leonard Davis Institute for International Relations, 1985), p. 41.
74. Ibid., pp. 41–2.
75. *Der Stern*, 'The Secret Boycott Against Israel ...' (German), 7 February 1991.
76. Jess Lukomski, 'West Germans Score Arab Boycott', *Journal of Commerce*, 3 March 1976, p. 27.
77. Phillip, op. cit., p. 57.
78. Transcript of interviews carried out by Susan Hattis Rolef in the early 1980s in Germany.
79. Phillips, op. cit., pp. 57–8. Rolef found that in this period major Israeli companies also engaged in similar manipulations to get around the boycott. Understandably, no German or Israeli company would openly admit to such practices.
80. *Der Stern*, op. cit.
81. Dr Ya'acov Cohen, 'Israel–FRG and the Arab Boycott', *Der Stern*, 7 February 1991.
82. See, for example *Ma'ariv*, 22 January and 25 January 1991, and *Yedi'ot 'Aharonot*, 28 January and 7 February 1991.
83. *Ha'aretz*, 31 January 1991.
84. ADL press release, May 10 1991, and *the Jerusalem Post*, 12 May 1991.
85. *Globes* (Hebrew), 23 July 1992.
86. German Embassy report of July 1992, and *Boycott Report*, 16/7, August/September 1992.
87. Reuters (New York), 21 May 1993.
88. Reuters (Cairo), 24 March 1994.
89. *Evening Standard*, 12 July 1995.
90. *Handelsblatt*, 15 September 1995.

91. *The Jerusalem Post*, 27 November 1952, 12 December 1952 and 23 January 1953.

92. *Het Financieele Dagblad*, 25 March 1998.

93. Ronnie M. Naftaniel, *Black List: The Arab Boycott and the Netherlands*, doctoral thesis, February 1978 (Dutch).

94. The report was the culmination of a year's hearings of the special committee, which was chaired by Mr Henry van den Bergh. That the Netherland's record of submission to the boycott was greater than that of other Western countries (quoted in Phillips, op. cit., p. 25), is not borne out by facts.

95. See entry 'oil in the Arab countries', in Ya'acov Shim'oni, *Political Dictionary of the Arab World* (New York: Macmillan Publishing Company, 1987), p. 361.

96. Ronni Naftaniel, 'The Arab Boycott in the Netherlands', in Susan Hattis Rolef (ed.) *Freedom of Trade and the Arab Boycott*, pp. 121–2.

97. WJC memorandum, 'Anti-Boycott Legislation in Europe', May 1984, p. 7.

98. Ibid, p. 8, *International Herald Tribune*, 23 June 1981; and WJC release dated 9 January 1986.

99. The difference between positive and negative certificates of origin is that while the former states where a product has been manufactured, a negative one states where is has not been manufactured – e.g. that it has *not* been manufactured in Israel.

100. See exchange of letters between CIDI and the British–Israel Chamber of Commerce in June–July 1981.

101. Letter from the Dutch Embassy (in London) to the British–Israel Chamber of Commerce, dated 20 July 1981.

102. Remarks by Mr Ronni Naftniel at the seminar on Freedom of Trade held in Brussels in March 1991.

103. Naftaniel, op. cit., p. 122.

104. *Ministerie van Economische Zaken, Eindrapportage Wet Amelding Buitenlandse Boycotmaatregelen, 1988*, October 1990, p. 5.

105. WJC memorandum, May 1984, op. cit., p. 9.

9

The Attitude of the European Community

THE BOYCOTT issue was first brought up with the European Community (EC) after the 1973 October War, when the application of the Arab boycott was intensified. In reply to a parliamentary question in February 1975, Israeli Minister of Foreign Affairs Yigal Allon, stated in the Knesset that in approaches to the west European countries Israel had drawn 'their attention to the fact that the intensification of the Arab boycott is totally at cross purposes with the aspiration to advance towards peace in the region, in addition to the fact that this boycott, by its very essence, does not correspond with all that the free states in the world stand for. We have called upon our interlocutors to act vigorously on this issue, and believe that we shall see decisive action by the Western states …'. Allon's optimism was based on the fact that a Free Trade Agreement was about to be signed between Israel and the EC. 'The fact that the European Economic Community has found it necessary to sign a comprehensive trade agreement with Israel, is an encouraging sign that the Nine are not ready to be pushed around. I hope none of them will bow to pressure or blackmail, either as individual nations or collectively', Allon stated in a press conference soon after the agreement had been signed on 11 May 1975.[1] The background to this statement were the overt efforts by the member states of the Arab League to stop the signing of the agreement.[2]

The issue of the Arab boycott against Israel came up on numerous occasions within different frameworks of the EC, almost invariably due to Israeli pressure or that of European pro-Israeli organizations. In June 1976 M. Claude Cheysson, who was Commissioner responsible for competition at the time, was first approached with a request that he act against discriminatory practices resulting from the Arab boycott. In these initial contacts with Cheysson, initiated by the World Jewish Congress (WJC), the whole barrage of arguments, based on the articles of the Treaty of Rome, was used.[3]

Demands for EC action to counteract the boycott traditionally fell under several headings: the alleged clash between certain articles of the Treaty of Rome, which had been signed on 25 March 1956, with compliance by European companies with boycott requirements; the fact that the boycott involved discrimination of a nature prohibited by the European Convention on Human Rights; the clash between the non-discrimination clauses in the agreements signed by the EC with the Maghreb countries (Algeria, Morocco and Tunisia) and the Mashreq countries (Egypt, Jordan, Lebanon and Syria) and boycott demands;[4] and the EC policy of harmonizing the legislation in member states to include anti-boycott laws.

It should be noted that after 1977 most of the anti-boycott activity at the Community level was initiated by organizations in several EC member states, such as the Anti-Boycott Committee (ABC) in London, *le Mouvement pour la Liberté du Commerce* (MLC) in Paris, and the *Centrum voor Informatie en Documentatie Israel* (CIDI) in the Hague. The work of these various organizations was closely co-ordinated by the European branch of the WJC.[5]

Boycott Requirements and the Treaty of Rome

There are two articles in the Treaty of Rome – articles 85 and 86 in the section of the Treaty dealing with the rules of competition – which have been cited as prohibiting the application of and compliance with the secondary and tertiary boycotts (see Chapter 3 pp. 66–7).

A note by the Commission's Legal Division regarding the boycott of 28 July 1976,[6] stated that the two articles apply to boycott measures in trade between undertakings, whether or not such undertakings are located within the Common Market, provided the Communities jurisdiction is established, and that it is a case of either *agreements* between undertakings, *decisions by associations* of undertakings, or *concerted practices* (article 85) or of *dominant positions* (article 86).

In addition there was regulation 17, promulgated in 1962, article 3(2) of which provides for a right of complaint by individuals, enterprises or interested parties in respect of breaches of the competition rules to the Commission, with a right of appeal to the European Court of Justice.[7] According to Daniel Lack of the WJC both the EC Commission and its Court had defined some of the essential characteristics of violations of the rules of competition, including boycott for general commercial motives, usually to enforce price maintenance, quotas or distributorship agreements. In order for such restrictive practices to qualify as violations they had to occur or the effects had to be felt within the EC area, with at least an affected subsidiary or affiliate in the Common Market area, and/or affect trade between member states.[8]

In one case – the Belgian Wallpaper Case of 1974[9] – the Commission recognized that a group or collective boycott is one of the most severe breaches of the competition rules in general and of articles 85(1) of the Treaty of Rome in particular, and that non-refusal to comply with boycott pressure is in itself in contravention of this article. The Luxembourg Court found against the Commission's decision on a separate point, but confirmed that collective boycotts, as a means of enforcing price maintenance by a group of manufacturers, is a violation of article 85(1) of the Treaty. In another case – CSC-Instituto v. Commission[10] – the Luxembourg Court dealt with a refusal to deal by an enterprise in a dominant market position. This refusal was held to be a violation of article 86 of the Treaty.

Similarly, in a number of decisions, the European Court of Justice confirmed the principle that concerted practices by enterprises *outside* the Community, aimed at restricting competition, but which had immediate, reasonable foreseeable and appreciably substantial effects *within* the EC, constitute a violation of article 85.[11]

The WJC had considered, in the late 1970s, bringing a test case before the Commission with regards to article 86, in connection with COFACE – the French state-run foreign trade and credit insurance company.[12] The WJC argued that COFACE was in breach of articles 86 and 90 (relating to public undertakings to which member states grant special or exclusive rights) when it required that exporters of goods to boycotting Arab countries meet the boycott-related conditions as a condition for approving insurance coverage for seizure, non-delivery or non-payment for such exports. The Inspectorate

Division of the European Commission was willing to consider the case, and prepared a voluminous and extensive internal report on the issue. However, the matter eventually lapsed as a result of the remedial action taken by the French government in the Mauroy circular.[13] According to the WJC, the equivalent organizations to the COFACE in other countries – the ECGD in Britain, the NCM (*Neder-landsche Credietverzekering Maatschappij*) in the Netherlands and the Office National Ducroire in Belgium – were guilty of similar transgressions.[14]

The European Convention on Human Rights

In 1975, an important decision was handed down by the European Court of Justice in Luxembourg, which those fighting the Arab boycott hoped could be used in their battle. This decision confirmed that the European Convention on Human Rights, passed in 1950, is part of Community law, binding on the members of the EC.[15] Article 14 of the Convention prohibits discrimination of any kind, although it might be argued that the non-discrimination provision applies only to the enjoyment of those specific rights and freedoms enumerated in the Convention itself.[16]

The human rights argument was not the one most frequently raised by those trying to combat the boycott at the EC level. However, at a meeting held by a delegation of the European branch of the WJC with the Dutch Foreign Minister, who was President of the EC Council in the first half of 1986, Mr Hans van den Broek conceded that effective anti-boycott action was desirable, but expressed the view that progress could best be assured by avoiding the political context of such action, while emphasizing the human rights aspect of preventing discrimination in trade and commerce on grounds of race, religion, ethnic or national origin. In this context Broek referred to a declaration which the Council, Commission and European Parliament were working on at the time (and subsequently adopted on 11 June 1986), which vigorously condemned all forms of intolerance, hostility and use of force against persons or groups of persons on the grounds of their racial, religious, cultural, social or national differences.[17]

The Boycott and the 1975 Free Trade Agreement between Israel and the EC

In March 1986 the European Court declared in an interim ruling that Britain's refusal to sell oil to Israel was not contrary to the 1975 Free Trade Agreement between Israel and the EC nor any of the EC's regulations. The case was brought to the Court by a Swiss registered company called Bulk Oil, which engaged in importing crude oil to Israel and exporting refined oil products from it. In April 1981 Bulk Oil signed an agreement with two companies called Sun Oil International and Sun Oil Trading – two companies registered in the US and Bermuda. The two companies undertook to sell Bulk Oil North Sea oil purchased by them from British Petroleum. When the latter found out that the oil was to be sold to Israel, it refused to supply the oil, arguing that the policy of the British Government prevented its fulfilling the terms of the contract. This policy, adopted by the British Government in January 1979, stated that North Sea oil would only be sold to the members of the Common Market, the member states of the OECD which are members of the International Energy Agency, as well as states which purchased oil from Britain in the past. The case was brought to an arbitrator, who decided in favour of Sun Oil. Bulk Oil appealed to the Supreme Court in Britain, which decided to pass the case on to the court in Luxembourg for its opinion.

In its interim ruling the court in Luxembourg stated that though article 3 of Israel's agreement with the EC prohibited any quantitative limitations on exports from the EC countries to Israel, article 4 added that these applied to limitations for purposes of customs exemptions, and not to limitations for other reasons. The court also rejected the argument that the British policy was contrary to article 85 of the Treaty of Rome.[18]

The Non-discrimination Clauses in the Agreements with the Maghreb and Mashreq States

In addition to complaints filed under the EEC competition rules, there were others filed under the relevant non-discrimination clauses in agreements signed by the Community with the Maghreb and

Mashreq states. The main distinction between complaints based on the free competition articles in the Treaty of Rome and the non-discrimination clauses in the agreements with the Arab states, was that the former had to do with trade between member states, while the latter was between an aggrieved European firm and a non-member state.[19]

The first set of such agreements was signed with the Maghreb states in December 1975, and a little over a year later similar agreements were signed with three of the four Mashreq states – in January 1976 (the agreement with Lebanon was signed in May).[20] The non-discrimination clauses which these agreements included stated that 'In the fields covered by the Agreement, the arrangements applied by [the name of the relevant Arab state] in respect of the Community shall not give rise to any discrimination between the Member States, their nationals or their companies or firms; the arrangements applied by the Community in respect of [the name of the relevant Arab state] shall not give rise to any discrimination between ... nationals, companies or firms.'[21]

Though the EC Committee on Development and Cooperation declared these clauses in the various agreements to be binding, notwithstanding the reservations made by the Mashreq states with regards to boycott related issues,[22] the fact is that these reservations were included in an exchange of letters which constituted an integral part of the agreements, and this contrary to the exchange of letters which accompanied the agreements with the Maghreb countries.[23] In the event of the unilateral reservations being cited by the Arab countries to justify the application of the secondary or tertiary boycott, the claim was to be submitted to the Joint Committee established between them and the EC, and the problem would be resolved on a political rather than a legal basis. Nevertheless, regulation 17 allowed the aggrieved party in the Community, with a complaint regarding breach of the EC competition rules, to apply to the Commission and the Luxembourg Court.[24]

In May 1975 M. Cheysson, the EC Commissioner for Development, stated that:

> The Commission considers that the measures of discriminatory boycotts are contrary to the spirit and principles of cooperation which the Community wishes to implement with the Arab countries; [and] that from a legal standpoint, the Commission will not accept any

formulation which could be interpreted as legalizing or recognizing the boycott, and that further the Commission will ensure that the principle of non-discrimination will be affirmed under conditions conforming to the practices of GATT, compatible with the sovereign rights of States and within the limits of the Community's agreements.

Resolutions in the same spirit were also adopted by the European Parliament. Thus, on 7 April 1976, the Parliament in Strasbourg adopted a resolution presented by the Committee on Political Affairs, on the so called 'Euro-Arab dialogue' which was going on at that time. The resolution, intended as a guide for the Community's forthcoming discussions with a delegation from the Arab League which were to be held in Luxembourg the following month, expressed the wish that particular attention be given in these talks to the principle of non-discrimination, adding that 'actual or threatened boycott measures will not be tolerated'.[25]

Two years later, when the report on the agreements with the Mashreq states came up for debate in the European Parliament, Cheysson reiterated the Commission's commitment that 'in accordance with instructions frequently received from this Parliament, [it] will be very strict in requiring compliance with the articles of the agreements dealing with non-discrimination. Non-discrimination is a fundamental principle in the life of the Community ...'.[26] Another EC Commissioner, Mr Burke, added that 'the Commission has come out, and without reservation, against any boycott of European firms which have links with Israel ... Any failure to keep this [non-discrimination] undertaking will be a violation of the agreement and the Commission will insist on strict respect of the undertaking.'[27]

The practical effect of such statements regarding the battle against the Arab boycott was, however, negligible. In its note to the Directorate General of Development on the issue, the Commission's Legal Division stated that the non-discrimination clause (article 24) in the EC's agreement with Israel, did not enable Israel to rely on the non-discrimination undertakings by the Arab League countries which had signed agreements with the Community *vis-à-vis* its relations with the European states. The Legal Division added that the above article did not prevent discrimination on the part of the Community as between Israeli nationals or firms on the one hand, and nationals or firms of other third countries on the other. Its sole aim was to prevent any discrimination as between Israeli nationals. Furthermore, it noted that, with regard to the agreements with the Mashreq and Maghreb countries, the Community was not prevented from discriminating between Arab countries and Israel. Similarly, these provisions did not prevent undertakings in the Arab countries from discriminating against undertakings and nations within the EC.[28]

In the case of the Euro-Arab dialogue, the final communiqué of the meeting, which took place in May 1976, spoke of general directives regarding the terms for foreign investments and their protection, and concerning the terms of contracts, especially with regard to questions of guarantees and arbitrations. Neither the boycott itself, nor the principle of non-discrimination were mentioned.[29]

The following year the Committee on External Economic Relations of the European Parliament held a meeting on the Additional Protocol to the Agreement between the Community and Israel, and recommended that the Parliament unequivocally oppose any boycott from whatever quarter against firms having business contacts with Israel, noting that investments by European firms in Israel are impeded by the Arab boycott. In an annex to the report the President of the Parliament noted the Community's commitment 'to pursuing a policy of non-discrimination, based on principles of parallelism with all the Mediterranean countries'. In May 1977 the Parliament adopted a resolution in this vein.[30]

The debate as to whether the non-discrimination clauses in the EC's agreements with the Maghreb and Mashreq states excluded application of the secondary and tertiary boycotts in EC member states, remained largely on the theoretical and argumentative level. A decade after these agreements were signed, Claude Cheysson, now as Commissioner for Mediterranean Policy and North–South Relations, replying to a written question by Dutch member of the European Parliament M. Gijsbert de Vries in April 1985, expressed the view that indeed the secondary and tertiary boycotts did not tally with the non-discrimination clauses in the agreements signed by the EC with various groups of Arab states. He added that '[the] secondary and tertiary boycotts, including non-Israeli declarations, are entirely contrary to the spirit and letter of the agreements concluded by the Community with the Maghreb and Mashreq countries. The clause contained in all these agreements, which prohibits discrimination between nationals or undertakings of the Member States, constitutes a clear ban on boycotts.'[31]

Harmonization of Legislation

With regards to the harmonization of legislation or 'approximation of laws', the two relevant articles in the Treaty of Rome are articles 100 and 101, which deal with the measures which the Council and Commission may take in cases where 'a difference between the provisions laid down by law, regulation or administrative action in Member States is distorting the conditions of competition in the Common Market' (article 101).[32] Since in the late 1970s it was only France which had any sort of anti-boycott legislation,[33] it was primarily the adoption of the French legislation by other states which one was speaking of, though eventually the Benelux countries also passed some legislative measures,[34] and much later Germany joined as well.[35]

The approach which favoured harmonization, or an approximation of laws, was based on the grounds that if a community-wide measure against the boycott were not introduced, there would be discrimination on the grounds of nationality, in violation of article 7 of the Treaty of Rome, since EC members with no anti-boycott laws would benefit from preferential trade relations with boycotting countries, and those with anti-boycott laws would be discriminated against.[36] This approach was supported by the EC Commission's Legal Division, which stated in a document already mentioned, that while the regulatory procedures available to the Community for dealing with certain trade aspects of the secondary boycott offered means of action of which appropriate use could be made, only *ad hoc* legislation would be likely to encompass all of the commercial implications of the secondary boycott.[37]

However, both the Council and Commission of the EC were reluctant to deal with the issue of harmonization of laws, in view of the lack of consensus among member states in support of legislation, and the inability to agree on the nature and extent of legislation among the few who did advocate such measures being taken.[38] In a written question posed to the Commission towards the end of 1976, M. Giraud asked to know whether the Commission was willing to force European firms 'to participate in boycott activities inside as well as outside the Community, and to inform the Commission of pressure or threats to which they are being submitted'. The Commission answered that 'where the relevant conditions are fulfilled, articles 85 and 86 of the Treaty [of Rome] also apply to agreements which oblige firms to discriminate in the choice of the parties with whom they have industrial and/or trade dealings ... [and that] the provisions of the EEC Treaty and the non-discrimination clauses forming part of the cooperation agreements do not presently justify drawing up a specific law in the context of a code of conduct'.[39] At this time the Commission took the view that it would be most appropriate for a solution to be sought, not in the form of harmonization of European laws, but within the wider framework of the OECD, in which the US was also a member.[40]

The official attitude of the EC towards harmonization over the years was greatly influenced by the state holding the presidency of the Council at any given time. Thus in the first half of 1982, during the presidency of the Belgian Foreign Minister Leo Tindemans, the idea of harmonization found support.[41] However, in part owing to the opposition of Greece, which regarded the boycott as a political issue to be resolved within the framework of an overall solution of the Middle East problem,[42] nothing practical resulted from this support.

In the course of the subsequent Danish presidency in the second half of 1982 it was proposed that the Council, meeting informally at the level of Ministers of Justice within the framework of 'the political cooperation', should request that the Commission draft a directive in favour of harmonization. During the presidency of the Federal Republic, which followed in the first half of 1983, the idea was dropped,[43] to be raised again early in 1984 during the French presidency. M. Claude Cheysson, as President of the European Council, expressed support for the discrimination argument, but Saudi Arabian opposition prevented any practical measures being taken towards harmonization, while stopping France from extending the bilateral non-discrimination undertakings it had obtained from the EEC countries to its EEC partners, in contradiction to the Mauroy circular of 1981.[44]

In the second half of 1985, the International Steering Committee to Combat the Arab Boycott – a body founded in March 1985 to coordinate the activities of the WJC and B'nai B'rith International *vis-à-vis* the UN, the EC and other international organizations and bodies[45] – managed to meet with the Luxembourgian president of the Council, Foreign Minister Jacques F. Poos. This meeting led to an understanding that proposals for a harmonization directive of an anti-boycott measure, based on the existing legislation in four members of the EC, would be pursued under the Dutch presidency which was due to begin on 1 January 1986.[46]

Despite this understanding M. Poos expressed two objections to harmonizing legislation on the basis of article 100 of the Treaty of Rome. The first was that while the Jewish organizations might see racist overtones in the Arab boycott, the Arab point of view – that the boycott was a political weapon that they were exercising within the context of a right of belligerency – had to be considered. Poos's second objection was that article 100 required unanimity for the adoption of a harmonization directive when acting on a proposal from the Commission.

The International Steering Committee countered Poos's objections by pointing out that while the primary boycott could be justified on grounds of the right of belligerency, the principle of non-discrimination was being violated by the secondary and tertiary boycotts, and that in the years 1976–79 the Commission had on several occasions acknowledged that secondary and tertiary boycott practices, including negative certificates of origin which referred specifically to Israel, were in violation of both the letter and spirit of the non-discrimination clauses in the EC's agreements with the Maghreb and Mashreq countries.[47]

As to article 100, the Committee argued that it could not be denied that application of the secondary and tertiary boycotts resulted in unacceptable discrimination against the nationals of those states which had passed anti-boycott legislation compared to those of states which had not, and that this was expressly prohibited by article 7 of the Treaty of Rome. In addition, it was pointed out that, following the Milan EC Summit of June 1985, the Council was seeking to change the requirement for unanimity and replace it by decision based on qualified majorities.[48] This was in fact achieved, and on the basis of the new articles 8A and 100A of the Treaty of Rome harmonization was one of the issues on which decisions could be taken by a qualified majority.[49]

The Boycott within the Context of the Arab–Israeli Conflict

There is no question that one of the causes for the inclination of the Community not to take any practical measures with regards to the Arab boycott, at least until the early 1990s, was that most of the member states viewed the issue as an inseparable part of the Arab–Israeli conflict, which would be resolved within the framework of progress in the peace process. Towards the end of 1990 the link between the boycott and the Arab–Israeli conflict, and between the Community's relations with Israel and the Middle East peace process, was emphasized in a statement by Italian Foreign Minister Gianni de Michelis, as acting President of the Council.[50] However, it was only in the aftermath of the Gulf War in January/February 1991 that this position was finally put to the test.

Since 1991

On 14 May Israeli Foreign Minister David Levy met EC leaders in Brussels, asking them to help end the secondary boycott by harmonizing the anti-boycott legislation of the member states, and noting that the post-war Middle East 'must bring to an end the economic war waged against Israel'.[51] The Foreign Minister of Luxembourg, Jacques Poos, who held the rotating EC presidency at that time, responded to Levy that 'the EC is aware of your concern over a problem that has complex political, economic and legal implications'.[52] Ten days later, at a meeting of the EC–Israel Cooperation Council, European officials hinted that the Community might be prepared to act against the boycott, and ensure that its member states would vote for the repeal of the infamous 'Zionist-equals-Racism' resolution which the United Nations General Assembly had passed in November 1975 (resolution 3379), if Israel would accept an active EC role in the planned Middle East peace conference.[53]

At around the same time the 12 foreign ministers of the EC member states met with representatives of the six Gulf Cooperation Council (GCC) member states, and for the first time issued a coordinated European request for Arab relaxation of the boycott.[54] An attempt by the Euro-Arab Parliamentary Conference, that met in Lisbon at the end of October 1991 to issue a joint communiqué stating that Israel's colonization of the occupied territories should end in return for the lifting of the Arab boycott of Israel, failed due to the efforts of the Libyan representatives, who rejected any sort of *quid pro quo* with Israel.[55]

After a lengthy delay the European Parliament's Committee on External Economic Relations (REX) agreed in February 1992 to study and act on a resolution, introduced to the European Parliament in July 1991 by MP Derek Prag (UK), calling upon the EC 'to propose measures outlawing and effectively combating all the unacceptable aspects of the [Arab] boycott [of Israel]'. The action was the result of a successful lobbying effort begun in March 1991 by the *Centre Européen Juif d'Information* (CEJI) based in Brussels.[56]

The REX Committee's rapporteur, Jan Sonneveld, issued his report on the boycott in July 1992, urging 'rigorous observance of the non-discrimination clauses contained in EC association agreements with the Arab countries', and recommending that 'non-discrimination should be expressed as a binding principle' in free-trade agreements with Gulf states that were under negotiation. But Sonneveld asserted that the primary *and secondary* boycotts were 'admissible under international law ... insofar as the intention [of the secondary boycott] exists to circumvent the primary boycott by shifting trade flows'. Against the tertiary boycott, and the Arab boycott of individuals and firms that have 'Zionist tendencies', the EC should 'speak out decisively against them', Sonneveld concluded. Debate on his controversial report was delayed in the REX Committee until November, keeping the issue on a diplomatic back-burner.[57]

The REX Committee report was then referred to the European Parliament's Foreign Affairs and Security Committee for 'further study'. One of the obstacles on the way to getting the European Parliament in this period to pass resolutions in favour of anti-boycott measures was, curiously enough, the peace process. 'There is an expectation that anti-boycott legislation will be part of an overall peace plan, so the process of passing legislation is being dragged out'.[58]

On 16 November 1992 the London firm of solicitors S.J. Berwin & Co. submitted a memorandum on the infringement of the competition rules of the EC to the EC Commissioner responsible for competition, on behalf of the EEC–Israel Chamber of Commerce and the

CEJI. Following a detailed and well documented analysis of the secondary and tertiary Arab boycott, its means of application and, because of its distinct nature, the difficulty of quantifying its disruptive and distortional effect on world trade in general and that within the EC in particular, the memorandum concluded that 'losses and damage inflicted upon EC manufacturing and trade is very substantial'. The memorandum then went on to cite 12 illustrative cases, six of the secondary boycott and six of the tertiary boycott, demonstrating that these were in breach of articles 85 and 86 of the Treaty of Rome. All this was done in order to provide the Commission with evidence and documentation required by it in order to launch an investigation into the operation of the boycott in the EC, in accordance with Council Regulation 17/62.[59]

When the memorandum was submitted, those who stood behind it apparently did not expect a positive response from the Commission. Three reasons were given for this. The first was that the mandate of the Commissioner who was responsible for competition at the time was about to end. The second was that there was a clear inclination on the part of the Commission, in accordance with the draft Anti-Trust Enforcement (National Courts) Guidelines issued in 1991, to encourage resort to courts in the member states for the application of the EC competition rules, rather than at the EC level. The third was that in a boycott case, unrelated to the Arab boycott of Israel, which had come before Court of First Instance of the EC on 10 July 1990, the Commission's position was that there was not sufficient interest in the issue to justify pursuing the case.[60]

In June 1993, following a half-year delay, the REX Committee issued a six-page working document on the boycott. Later, in November, the European Parliament approved two resolutions related to the boycott. The Foreign Affairs Committee resolution (A3-322/93 Piecyk) stated that a decision by the Arab League to list the primary boycott would represent an important confidence building measure for the Middle East peace process and that the lifting of the secondary boycott affecting European companies should be negotiated directly with the Arab countries within the framework of the Cooperation Council. The External Economic Relations Committee resolution (A3-239/93 – Sonneveld) also called for an end to the boycotts.[61]

The parliament then proceeded to adopt a 12-point 'explanatory statement' regarding the Arab boycott, based on the two resolutions. While stating that the direct boycott is not contrary to international law, it called on the Arab states to put an end to all forms of the indirect boycott, within the framework of the peace process. The EP went on to call upon the member states to adopt legislation and regulations prohibiting companies from complying with boycott demands, except in those cases where the European Union (EU) did not object. It went on to urge the Commission to propose preventive legal arrangements which would enable the EU, on the basis of political criteria drawn up by the Council, to protect Community companies from any boycott measures imposed on them by third countries. Finally, the Parliament welcomed the fact that the EU intended to play an active role in supporting and monitoring the Middle East peace process, while encouraging close cooperation between states in the region.[62] The following week the President of the Israeli Manufacturers' Association, Dan Propper, met with senior officials of the EU to discuss means of bringing about the cancellation of the Arab boycott. Propper sought to get the Union to place more pressure on the Arab countries to cancel the boycott and to issue a directive against it.[63]

Notes

1. Susan Hattis Rolef, 'Israel's Anti-Boycott Policy', *Policy Studies*, 28 (Jerusalem: The Leonard Davis Institute for International Relations at the Hebrew University, February 1989), p. 33.
2. Muhammad ʿAbd al-'Aziz Ahmad wa-Muhammad al-Jabali, *Al-Difaʾ al-Iqtisadi Didda al-Atmaʾ al-Istighlaliyaa al-Isra*'iliyya (Arabic) (The Economic Protection from Israel's Ambitions to Exploit the Region), pp. 89–91.
3. Rolef, op. cit., p. 44.
4. Charlotte A. Phillips, *The Arab Boycott of Israel – Possibilities for European Cooperation with US Antiboycott Legislation* (Washington, DC: Foreign Affairs and National Defense Division Congressional Research Service, May 1979), pp. 38–9. See also note by the EC Commission's Legal Division to the Directorate-General for Development re: 'Secondary boycott measures of Arab League Countries against undertakings having relations with Israel', Note VIII/1/9129, dated 28 July 1976.
5. WJC memorandum, 'Anti-Boycott Legislation in Europe', May 1984.
6. Note VIII/1/9129, op. cit.
7. See Daniel Lack, note of December 1975.
8. Ibid.

9. Case IV/426, OJL 237 of August 1974, overruled in No. 73/74, 1975 Recueil p. 1491.
10. Cases No. 6 and 73, 1974 Recueil p. 223. In the case of United Brands, decided on 17 December 1975, the Court once again considered the abuse of a dominant position by an enterprise using the boycott as a weapon.
11. See, for example, the Beguelin case, 1971 Recueil 249, and the Dyestuffs case, 1972, Recueil p. 692.
12. See Chapter 8, pp. 202–4.
13. Ibid., p. 205.
14. See WJC memorandum, 'Arab Boycott – Submission of Test Case to the Commission of the EEC – the COFACE Case', 21 November 1977 and Lecture by Daniel Lack on 'Enforcement of Anti-Boycott Measures in Europe', delivered in Geneva, December 1992.
15. Rutili case of 28 October 1975, Ref. 36/75.
16. Daniel Lack, WJC Memorandum 'Steps Taken at the Council of Europe to Initiate Measures against the Arab Boycott', 9 February 1976.
17. Daniel Lack, 'Memorandum to the President of the Council of Ministers of the European Community, concerning certain discriminatory practices in the Common Market area', January 1987.
18. Yuval Elizur, *'Aflayat Yisrael Biydey Britania – Hukit'* (Hebrew) (Discrimination by Britain against Israel is Legal), *Ma'ariv-Asskim*, 1 April 1986.
19. See Daniel Lack, 'Developments in the Field of Anti-boycott Measures at Regional and National Levels', 15 June 1978.
20. Ibid.
21. See WJC memorandum 'The Non-Discrimination Clauses in the Interim Agreements between the EEC and the Mashreq Countries', Geneva, 7 February 1977; WJC memorandum, 10 June 1977.
22. Ibid., and note by the EC Commission Legal Division of 28 July 1976, op. cit., pp. 7–9.
23. See agreements signed by the EC with Egypt, Jordan, Syria and Lebanon, *Keesings Contemporary Archives*, 1977, p. 28657.
24. WJC memorandum of 7 February 1977, op. cit., p. 4.
25. Daniel Lack, WJC memorandum, 8 June 1976.
26. Daniel Lack, memorandum of 15 June 1978, op. cit., p. 6.
27. WJC memorandum, 10 June 1977, op. cit., p. 8.
28. Note of the EC Commission Legal Division of 28 July 1976, op. cit.
29. Ibid.
30. Report 67/77 dated 14 May 1977. See also WJC paper of 10 June 1977, op. cit., p. 4.
31. Written question C435/84. See also Official Journal of the European Communities 135/17, 3 June 1985.
32. *Treaties Establishing the European Communities, Treaties Amending these Treaties, Documents Concerning the Accession* (Luxembourg: European Communities, 1973), p. 255.
33. See Chapter 8, pp. 202–5.
34. Ibid., pp. 223–7.

35. Ibid., pp. 222–3.
36. WJC memorandum of 18 January 1984, op. cit., p. 4 and Daniel Lack, paper of 15 June 1978, op. cit., p. 9.
37. Note by the EC Commission Legal Division of 28 July 1976, op. cit.
38. Phillips, op. cit., p. 39.
39. Question No. 308/76 to the EC Commission on Freedom of Trade, Official Journal of the European Communities, No. C 305/3 of 27 December 1976.
40. Daniel Lack, memorandum of 15 June 1978, op. cit., pp. 10, 25–6.
41. WJC Report 'WJC European Branch: EEC Committee meeting with Mr Leo Tindemans, Foreign Minister of Belgium and President-in-office of the Council of the European Community', Brussels, 12 March 1982, p. 2.
42. WJC Memorandum, 'EEC and Arab Boycott', in respect of meetings held with M. Jean Gol, Belgian Minister of Justice on 29 November 1982.
43. WJC Memorandum of May 1984, p. 9.
44. WJC report of 29 March 1985 on meeting of the International Steering Committee to Combat the Arab Boycott, p. 2. Regarding the Mauroy circular see Chapter 8, p. 205.
45. Daniel Lack of the WJC assumed the role of legal advisor to the International Steering Committee.
46. Daniel Lack, 'Memorandum – Visit to President of the EEC Council, Luxembourg, 20 and 21 November 1985', 28 November 1985.
47. Ibid.
48. Ibid, and B'nai B'rith-WJC paper, 'The European Community and the Arab Boycott', 6 November 1989, p. 3.
49. Ibid.
50. The Journal of Commerce, 2 October 1990.
51. The Financial Times, 14 May 1991.
52. Associated Press, reported in The Jerusalem Post, 15 May 1991.
53. Mideast Markets, 1 April 1991.
54. Boycott Report, 15/6, July 1991.
55. Agence Europe, press releases of 29 and 30 October 1991.
56. CEJI communiqué.
57. Ibid. See also Boycott Reports, 16/5, May 1992, and 17/3, March 1993.
58. Statement by Martin Savitt, chairman of the Britain–Israel Chamber of Commerce Anti-Boycott Committee, WJC Intelligence Report, 14 September 1992.
59. Lecture by Daniel Lack on 'Enforcement of Anti-Boycott Measures in Europe', delivered in December 1992 in Geneva.
60. Ibid.
61. European Union press release, 16 November 1993.
62. Agence Europe, Brussels, 18 November 1993.
63. Davar, 26 November 1993.

10

The Policies of Japan, South Korea, Australia and Canada

Japan

The effect of the Arab boycott on Japanese–Israeli economic ties was always extremely strong, even before the 1973 oil crisis. While in most instances nothing seemed to stop Japanese sales and investment abroad, in the case of Israel Japanese businessmen not only willingly gave in to Arab boycott demands, but operated a voluntary boycott which went far beyond anything ever demanded by the Arab boycott authorities. Unlike their European counterparts, who gave in to Arab boycott demands, most Japanese were not ashamed to admit that the source of their unwillingness to have any dealings with Israeli businessmen was the boycott, and for many years Israeli businessmen experienced having their phone calls to Japanese companies disconnected as soon as they identified themselves as Israelis.[1]

In 1968 the three largest Japanese automobile manufacturers, Toyota, Honda and Nissan were explicitly warned by boycott officials not to sell their products in Israel.[2] Among the Japanese companies, which refused to have anything to do with Israel were Bridgestone, C. Itoh, Fuji-Telecommunication, Hitachi, Kawasaki, Mitsui, Nippon Steel, Sumitomo, Toshiba, as well as all the Japanese companies offering financial and transportation services. Insofar as the products of Japanese manufacturers that boycotted Israel were sold in Israel, this was usually done through third countries, and none of those engaged in their marketing in Israel was a direct agent of the producers.[3]

The major exceptions to the refusal to have any contacts with Israel were to be found in the diamond and chemical sectors.[4] In addition Sony maintained normal economic ties with Israel (it is said that this was due to reasons which had nothing to do with business), for which it was blacklisted in 1974, and from 1969 until the late 1980s, the relatively unknown Subaru, manufactured by Fuji Industries, was the only Japanese car sold in Israel. Subaru was originally developed more or less exclusively for the Israeli market.

In the field of transportation, in the late 1960s, there were incidents of Japanese companies refusing to enable the Israeli shipping companies Zim and El-Yam to carry goods to Japan, even when these ships were not carrying Israeli goods, and until quite recently Japan Air Lines (JAL) boycotted Israel, and El-Al was not allowed to land in Japan.[5] In 1981 the Japanese car manufacturer Toyota, gave in to the tertiary boycott, when it cancelled a joint venture with the blacklisted Ford, after being warned by the Saudi Arabian Minister of Commerce that if the deal with Ford went through, Toyota itself would be blacklisted.[6]

Until the late 1980s, and to a lesser extent until after the Gulf War at the beginning of 1991, the Japanese government displayed unwillingness to criticize the boycott or discourage Japanese companies from complying with it, though it consistently denied that anti-Israel or anti-Semitic sentiments had anything to do with its approach.[7] The three most common grounds cited for this attitude of the Japanese government were Japan's dependence on Middle East oil,[8] the infinitely greater importance of the Arab markets to Japan than that to Israel (to which Japanese products were nevertheless sold indirectly),[9] and the traditional non-interference by the government with business decisions.[10]

By the mid-1980s Japan had begun to show greater interest in Israel. This led to the invitation of the Israeli Foreign Minister, Yitzhak Shamir, to visit Japan in 1985.[11] In November 1987, the first Japanese economic mission of the Japanese Federation of Economic Organizations – Keidanren – paid an official visit to Israel, and six months later Foreign Minister Sosuke Uno became the first Japanese government minister to visit Israel. Though the boycott issue was not publicly raised with Sosuke Uno during his visit, various projects for economic cooperation were presented to him. The Japanese response was that such cooperation could take place once progress was made in the Middle East peace process.[12] In 1988 there was a visible increase in trade between the two countries.[13] Two additional Japanese car manufacturers – Daihatsu and Suzuki –

started quietly selling cars in the mid-1980s, and towards the end of 1988 Mitsubishi joined as well. In June 1988 the first visit to Israel by a Japanese Foreign Minister took place.

American pressure undoubtedly played a role in the change in the Japanese position,[14] though the decline of the Arab oil economies in the 1980s, and growing appreciation in Japan for Israel's scientific achievements in certain fields, such as biochemistry, also played a role.[15] In December 1988 the US Congress had included a statutory note in the US Trade Act regarding its dissatisfaction with Japanese boycott compliance. 'It is the sense of Congress that the US should encourage the Government of Japan in its efforts to expand trade relations with Israel and to end compliance by Japanese commercial enterprises with the economic boycott of Israel.'[16] In the winter of 1989/90 100 Representatives wrote to the Japanese and South Korean Prime Ministers protesting the flagrant participation of their countries in the Arab boycott. In November 1990 the Japanese government decided, for the first time, to send a commercial attaché to the Japanese embassy in Tel Aviv.[17] The first joint Japanese–Israeli venture of any kind was in the diamond retail trade, as was the second, with the establishment of the Tasaki Riger diamond factory in Beit Sh'an. In 1991 a gemalogical laboratory was opened at the Ramat Gan diamond exchange, as a joint venture between the Gemalogical Association of All Japan-Zenhokyo (GAAL) and two Israeli institutions, GIL and GIPS.[18]

Despite all these developments, the Japanese government continued to assure Arab representatives in Tokyo that its pro-Arab orientation, which had been introduced in the early 1970s, would continue,[19] and refused to open a branch of the Japanese Trade Relations Organization (JETRO), which had branches in 65 states, in Israel.[20] Furthermore, Japanese companies continued to reject letters of credit drawn by Israeli buyers, on the grounds that Japanese banks refused to accept them, and demanded advance payments for goods and raw materials.[21]

Since 1991

Following the Gulf War of January/February 1991 the Japanese policy *vis-à-vis* Israel underwent an additional change. This development resulted both from the new hopes for a Middle East settlement and Israel's potential as a regional centre of commerce and economic and scientific technology,[22] and from increased American pressure.[23] In April 1991 nine leading Senators, led by Senator Jay Rockefeller (D – W.VA), sent a letter to Japanese Prime Minister Toshiki Kaifu, urging him to end boycott compliance by Japanese firms. Later that month Kaifu visited California where he met with President Bush, and was picketed by protesters carrying banners reading 'Stop Japan's Boycott'.

During a visit to Israel at the end of May 1991 the Japanese Foreign Minister, Taro Nakayama, indicated, for the first time, that his country's Export-Import Bank would 'consider' requests for financing exports to Israel, and referred to the boycott as 'undesirable'. A Japanese spokesman, accompanying the Foreign Minister, made it clear, however, that the Japanese Government would not make a public statement on the boycott, nor move to outlaw it.[24]

The same month the Japanese car manufacturers Toyota and Nissan announced that they would begin direct sales in Israel, and were followed by Mazda.[25] Soon thereafter Honda joined in as well, though it circumvented Arab pressure by selling Israel cars manufactured in its Ohio plant in the US.[26] The American Jewish Committee and American Jewish Congress had launched a wide-ranging effort to focus pressure on Japanese and South Korean companies suspected of boycotting Israel. These included Hitachi, Hyundi Electronics, Lucky Goldstar, Samsung and Toshiba. That winter both Hitachi and Toshiba informed the Jewish organizations that they were soon to begin marketing their cars directly in Israel.[27] Though the change in the attitude of the Japanese car manufacturers towards Israel was undoubtedly connected with progress in the Arab–Israeli peace process following the Madrid Conference of October/November 1991, there were apparently also purely economic reasons for this development.[28]

While compliance with the boycott started to decline, it did not come to a complete halt. Thus for example in the summer of 1991 Tadiran, a major communications company in Israel, reached an agreement with the British company Fulcrum by which the two companies were to have made a joint offer in a tender opened by British Telecom. However, the plan fell through when the Japanese company owning 75 per cent of Fulcrum – Fujitsu – objected to the cooperation on grounds of 'political sensitivity'.[29]

In this period Japanese investments in Israel reached a mere $19 million dollars,[30] and while in 1992 Japan had turned into Israel's third largest export market,[31] Israel was still relatively insignificant on the list of Japan's export markets. Nevertheless, as 1992 progressed, change was in sight. In February Mitsubishi, which had started selling cars to Israel the previous year, sent a representative to Israel at the invitation of the Israel Export Institute and the Foreign Trade Administration at the Ministry of Industry and Trade, to investigate additional export and import possibilities, including purchases of Israeli tyres, quality textiles, medical equipment and flowers.[32]

In June 1992 the Japanese Ambassador to Israel, Mr Kazuhisa Oshida, stated that Japanese businessmen still saw economic ties with Israel as involving high business risks, and he therefore did not foresee a major increase in investments in the foreseeable future, adding that Arab markets were infinitely larger and more attractive.[33] Israeli companies also still came across manifestations of the Arab boycott in their contacts with Japanese firms. Thus at the end of 1992 the Israel Aircraft Industries (IAI) Ltd filed a $20 million lawsuit in the northern district of Illinois against Sanwa Business Credit Corporation and Sanwa Bank of Japan, on grounds that Sanwa had refused to extend credit to a venture involving the IAI and another company – Quadrant Management Inc. – because it is an Israeli company.[34]

In November the Deputy Minister at the Japanese Foreign Trade Ministry (MITI), Naburu Hatakiyama, arrived in Israel for a visit, the goal of which was to work towards closer economic relations between the two countries.[35] Two and a half weeks later the Japanese Foreign Minister, Michio Watanabe, told a visiting AJC delegation on a visit to Japan, that: 'The Japanese government has advised leading Japanese firms to stop complying with the Arab boycott of Israel. The Japanese government has asked its ambassadors to various Arab League states to urge their host governments to end the blacklisting of companies trading with Israel.' He added that Japanese chambers of commerce had agreed to stop issuing negative certificates of origin, and that Japan planned to expand its financial contacts with Israel.[36] At the same time the Japanese addressed a request to the Secretary General of the Arab League, Ahmed Esmet Abdel Meguid, asking that the Arab states stop requiring Japanese companies doing business with them to pledge that they had no commercial ties with Israel. According to Japanese Foreign Ministry sources the background to Japan's request was the policy of the government of Yitzhak Rabin to suspend new settlement in the occupied territories.[37]

The Israeli press was, however, sceptical, pointing out that JETRO had still not opened a branch in Israel. Nor had Japanese banks begun to grant long-term credit for trade with Israel, making it difficult for Israeli firms to purchase Japanese equipment. Also none of the large Japanese trading companies, which control the bulk of Japanese exports, had opened an office in Israel.[38]

The Japanese followed up on their December 1992 declaration with a visit in April 1993 to Israel by representatives of the Keidanren, the powerful manufacturers association. The 15 members of the delegation, headed by Keidanren President Masaya Miyoshi, included representatives of the largest Japanese commercial and banking firms. Speaking to reporters, Miyoshi attributed the change in Japan's trade policy towards Israel to the 1991 G-7 anti-boycott declaration. He added that if Middle East peace was achieved, he would seriously consider moving the Keidanren Middle East headquarters from Cairo to Tel Aviv.

Despite all of this, by the end of 1994 many Japanese companies were still wary of entering the Israeli market. During a visit to Japan in the middle of December Israeli Prime Minister Yitzhak Rabin called on Japanese companies to start viewing Israel as a business partner. 'European and Japanese companies should no longer fear the Arab boycott', he said at a luncheon in Tokyo with businessmen.[39] In the course of this visit the Japanese government agreed to enable Japanese companies seeking to invest in Israel to receive guarantees for their investments. The Japanese Brokers Association also decided to permit Japanese companies to invest in the Tel Aviv Stock Exchange, and an R&D deal was signed between the two governments.[40]

On 17 September 1995, Japanese Prime Minister Tomiichi Murayama announced that Japan was finally considering opening a JETRO in Israel, 'probably in 1997'.[41] Also in September, Fuji Bank agreed to take the lead in arranging a $100 million loan for Israel, something totally unthinkable in the past.[42] Nevertheless, Japanese businessmen were wary about becoming involved in Middle East regional projects in general and investments in Israel in particular, and it was reported that Japanese participation in the Casablanca Economic Conference in October/November 1994, the Amman Economic Conference in November 1995 and the Cairo Conference in November 1996 resulted from pressure by the Japanese government, which in turn acted under American pressure.[43]

The Likud victory in the elections of May 1996 in Israel, caused somewhat of a reversal in the situation.[44] Nevertheless, in August 1996 Japan's Nissho Iwai joined the Tomen Corporation in Israel in opening a Tel Aviv office, and in the beginning of 1997 announced its intention to become the first major Japanese trading house to establish comprehensive business ties with Israel. The company is presently in negotiations with over a dozen Israeli companies, including Clal (Israel) Ltd, one of the largest Israeli business groups.[45]

South Korea

After Israel closed down its embassy in Seoul in 1978 for budgetary reasons, South Korea refused to allow Israel to reopen it. Subsequently Korea managed to obtain numerous major construction contracts in Saudi Arabia and other Gulf States, and its large consumer conglomerates made no bones about refusing to do business with Israel. As late as January 1990 Samsung published an advertisement in the *Korean Times*, in which it declared that the firm 'will never violate the Arab regulations'.[46]

However, after South Korea was admitted to the United Nations 1991, a change started to take place in its policy. On 15 December 1991 it voted in the General Assembly in favour of the repeal of the 'Zionism equals Racism' resolution of 1975. In a meeting with US Jewish leaders in October 1991 South Korea's Foreign Minister, Choi Ho Joong, declared that his country was taking steps to allow Israel to reopen its embassy, and that a South Korean embassy would be opened for the first time in Tel Aviv. This was done in November 1992. After that Korean companies started showing interest in establishing economic contacts in Israel, though at this stage there was no sign of the major Korean conglomerates Lucky Goldstar, Samsung or Daewoo entering the Israeli market.[47]

A further change occurred in the summer of 1993. Hyundai Heavy Industries contracted to build a $60 million plant at Israel's Dead Sea Works; the South Korean Dacom entered into a venture with Israel's Bezek Telephone Corporation; and Samsung and Lucky Goldstar started selling computers in Israel.[48] By the end of 1994, shortly before a visit by Prime Minister Yitzhak Rabin to South Korea,[49] Israeli officials in the Israeli Ministry of Industry and Trade reported that Korean companies were flocking into Israel, and were demonstrating great boldness in their penetration of the Israeli market.[50] One example was a $17 million contract signed between Daewoo and Ta'as – Israel's military industries – to set up a factory in Israel to produce automobile airbags, with Daewoo undertaking to purchase all of the output.[51] In March 1995, following Rabin's visit, Samsung announced that it would open an office in Israel in order to scout out opportunities for industrial and technological joint ventures in Israel,[52] and the following year signed a joint production agreement with the Israeli high-tech firm.

Australia

Like companies in other parts of the world Australian companies were subjected to pressure by the Central Boycott Office in Damascus, and Jewish businessmen and companies dealing with Jews were discriminated against. Despite all this, anti-boycott legislation was never enacted, nor even considered.[53] In one blatant example of the operation of the boycott, Quantas Airline decided, for a brief period in 1978, to prohibit Jews from enjoying transit rights on international flights stopping in Damascus. The decision was rescinded within a week, and Quantas eventually even opened an office in Tel Aviv.[54]

Also, like most other countries, Australia was reluctant to act against the boycott. This reluctance resulted from fear of Arab retaliation and loss of trade.[55] Australia's dependence on Arab trade was traditionally heavy. In 1988 for example more than 40 per cent of the Arab countries' coal imports came from Australia, and the Arab states were the largest outlet for Australian mutton. Until 1987 Australia was also the largest supplier of grain to the Arab world.[56] However, following the Gulf War, a change occurred in the

Australian position vis-à-vis the Arab boycott, as in that of other countries. In May 1992 Australia's largest business association, the New South Wales Chamber of Commerce, offered categorical assurances that it would no longer issue negative certificates of origin. This move followed criticism by Bob Carr, leader of the Labour Party opposition, of a document issued by the Chamber which not only contained the compliance stamp of the CBO, but also listed 'Palestine' as one of the destinations for which the stamp was required.[57]

Canada

Like Australia, Canada has not enacted any specific anti-boycott legislation, though the government did issue various policy statements which condemned economic boycotts as instruments of foreign policy in general, and the Arab boycott in particular. In addition, existing human rights legislation was extended to apply to proscribe discrimination in a manner which could apply to certain boycott situations.

The wariness of the Canadian government from doing anything on the legislative level, resulted from the fact that in the aftermath of the 1973/74 oil crisis there had been heavy Arab investments in Canada, while trade with the Arab states and Arab oil imports greatly increased. The boycott issue was first raised publicly in Canada in 1975 in connection with the alleged practice of the Export Development Corporation (EDC) – a federal crown agency – of providing financing and insurance coverage for export transactions with Arab states which included boycott provisions.[58] It was in this connection that Prime Minister Pierre Elliott Trudeau issued a statement in the House of Commons on 8 May 1975 to the effect that 'the boycott is alien to everything the government stands for, and indeed to what Canadian ethics stand for'. In more concrete terms Minister of Industry, Trade and Commerce Alastair Gillespie announced on 2 June 1975 that the government would no longer permit the EDC to insure discriminatory boycott clauses.[59] But words apart and deeds apart, on 14 January 1976 a Canadian–Saudi Arabian trade agreement was signed in which it was agreed that each government should promote trade 'according to its respective laws and regulations'.[60]

On 21 October 1976, External Affairs Minister Donald C. Jamieson issued a strongly worded statement in which he affirmed the Canadian government's opposition to discrimination and boycotts based on race, national or ethnic origin or religion, and announced that the government would take measures to deny its support of facilities to various kinds of trade transactions in order to combat any discriminatory effects which such boycotts might have on Canadian firms and individuals. Mr Jamieson stated that Canadian firms would be required to report all instances of compliance with the boycott, and that such information would be made public. However, the statement did not include proposals for new legislation, and did not list any sanctions which would be imposed on firms that failed to report the receipt of and compliance with boycott provisions. Mr Jamieson stated that for the implementation of this policy the government would rely primarily on the honesty and cooperation of the Canadian companies.[61]

Following a visit to Israel in January 1977 William Davis, the Conservative premier of Ontario, made a bold anti-boycott statement in which he declared that his government was 'opposed to compliance and complicity with the boycott in both the public and private sector'. He added that since 'the policy of the Federal Government has not had any noticeable effect so far ... I intend to take certain steps to lessen the effect of the boycott as far as firms over which Ontario has control are concerned.'[62] On 9 November 1978, Davis finally managed to get a bill through in Ontario, prohibiting discrimination in business practices, which addressed itself to the secondary and tertiary boycotts.[63]

The law prohibiting discrimination in business relationships was designed to prevent discrimination in the business community on the basis of race, creed, colour, nationality, ancestry, place of origin or geographical location. It provided for orders of compliance, assurances of voluntary compliance, and enforcement of orders and assurances. Provision was also made for sanctions and compensation in the event of breach of the provisions of the law, although it was non-penal by nature.[64]

Though Davis's initiative did not result in similar legislation being passed on the federal level, new policy guidelines were introduced by the Department of Industry, Trade and Commerce, after the Commission on Economic Coercion and Discrimination – a citizens' commission headed by international law professor Irwin Cotler – published a report in January 1977 on the manifestations of the Arab boycott in Canada and recommended anti-boycott action.[65] The report brought many examples of the operation of the boycott in Canada, listing the types of declarations commonly required by the Arab boycott authorities and noting that the major chartered banks (including the Bank of Montreal, the Royal Bank of Canada, the Toronto Dominion Bank and the Bank of Nova Scotia) regularly processed letters of credit containing boycott clauses. The report instanced examples of religious discrimination, including the practice of the Canadian High Commission in London of authenticating 'non-Jewish' certificates. It was also found that a majority of the Canadian export transactions with Arab League countries involved boycott compliance, while major Canadian corporations, including consulting firms, insurance companies, engineering and construction firms had been complying with the boycott. Most serious, however, was the fact that evidence was adduced to the effect that the EDC had insured a number of contracts containing boycott clauses and that the boards of trade in major Canadian cities were authenticating documents containing boycott clauses. In addition, the Canadian government itself was not only circulating information on trade opportunities with Arab partners, which involved boycott related conditions, but was also providing information about compliance with the boycott.[66]

The report received a good deal of attention both from the press and from academic and legal circles which criticized the government. 'The report', wrote the *Montreal Star*, 'is on almost every page, a moral affront to this country and a classic example of a process which should be unacceptable to any decent society.'[67] Much of the media attention was directed at calling upon the government to enact anti-boycott legislation and using Quebec legislation on human rights adopted in 1975 to try and counteract the effects of the boycott. The new policy guidelines hardly fulfilled these demands, but constituted a certain improvement.

During a visit to Israel the Canadian Secretary for Trade stated, on 27 May, that 'Canada firmly disagrees with economic boycotts as instruments of foreign policy ... Nor do we allow foreign countries to restrict the right of Canadians to do free commerce with whom they wish. That is the position we have taken with respect to the

Arab Boycott of Israel.'[68] Then in July 1977 the federal parliament extended the Canadian Human Rights Act to proscribe discrimination on the basis of race, national or ethnic origin, colour, religion, age, sex or marital status. Tertiary boycotts involving refusal to sell to blacklisted Jewish firms would, arguably, violate this provision.[69]

In its semi-annual report, covering the period 1 August 1977 to 31 January 1978, which *inter alia* dealt with international economic boycotts, the Department of Industry, Trade and Commerce made it clear that only the following types of boycotts were forbidden under Canadian law:

- discrimination based on the race, national or ethnic origin or religion of any Canadian firm or individual;
- refusal to purchase from or sell to any other Canadian firm or individual;
- refusal to sell Canadian goods to any other country;
- refrainment from purchases from any country;
- restricting commercial investment or other economic activity in any country.[70]

This report was strongly criticized for failing to deal with the real problems created by the boycott, like the banning of negative or exclusionary certificates of origin; allowing unilateral 'statements of facts' with information, such as that the company does not have an office or branch in Israel, being issued; or specific exemptions in respect of letters of credit requiring blacklist certifications.[71]

Although Joe Clark, leader of the Progressive Conservative Party, promised after a visit to Israel in January 1979 that if his party won the forthcoming federal elections he would move the Canadian Embassy from Tel Aviv to Jerusalem and introduce anti-boycott legislation, the first pledge caused such a furore that during his brief premiership from April to December of 1979, the Embassy was not moved, nor was any anti-boycott legislation proposed.[72]

In the absence of federal legislation, all that exists in Canada in the way of anti-boycott legislation is the Ontario law and US anti-boycott laws as they apply to some business activities of American-owned companies in Canada.

Notes

1. This information was gathered by Dr Susan Hattis Rolef in 1982 from Israeli businessmen who experienced such behaviour on the part of the Japanese.
2. Aaron Sarna, *Boycott and Blacklist* (Totowa, NJ: Rowman & Littlefield Publishers, 1986), p. 172.
3. Ibid. p. 165; 'Japan's Israel Problem', *The New Republic*, 9 March 1987, p. 11; 'Japan's Free Trade Charade', *The New York Times*, 13 October 1987; ADL Special Report 'Blacklisting Israel: A Current Perspective on the Arab Boycott', (Spring 1989), p. 30.
4. ADL Report, op. cit., p. 30.
5. Dan S. Chill, *The Arab Boycott of Israel* (New York: Praeger Publishers, 1976), pp. 28–9. In 1997 JAL (Japanese Air-Lines), which had a representative in Tel Aviv, still was not flying to Israel.
6. Ford Motor Company was blacklisted in 1966 for licensing an Israeli firm to assemble Ford trucks and tractors. Ford continued doing business with Israel and was banned from selling its cars in all Arab countries. In 1980 Toyota sold 256,000 cars in the Middle East, approximately 50 per cent of them in Saudi Arabia (Sarna, op. cit., p. 170).
7. *Jerusalem Post*, 23 December 1991.
8. Even in the late 1980s, 70 per cent of all Japanese oil imports still came from the Middle East – down from 90 per cent in the late 1970s, Alan Richard and John Waterbury, *A Political Economy of the Middle East* (Boulder, CO: Westview Press, 1990), p. 63.
9. For example, in 1980, out of $14,152 million worth of Japanese exports to the Middle East, only $110 million were to Israel, and of $44,612 million worth of Japanese imports from the Middle East $228 million were from Israel, mainly diamonds. By 1986 the situation had somewhat improved: of $9,535 million worth of exports $227 million were to Israel, and of $18,585 million worth of imports $325 million were from Israel. By 1994, both exports to and imports from Israel had grown to $872 and $979 million respectively (*Direction of Trade Statistics, Yearbook 1987*, Washington DC: International Monetary Fund, 1987, and *Direction of Trade*, September 1995).
10. 'Japan's Free Traders Boycott Israel', *Tokyo Business Today*, November 1987; 'Unwilling Japan Bows to Boycott Pressure', *The Jewish Week*, 18 March 1988; Institute of Jewish Affairs (IJA) Research Report No. 2, 1991.
11. *Near East Report*, 'Japanese Boycott Weakening', 2 October 1989.
12. Rolef, op. cit.
13. Until 1991 Israel was the only Western country with a balance of trade surplus with Japan, mostly resulting from Israeli diamond sales to Japan. For example in 1980 Israel had a $109.5 million surplus with Japan. In 1986 this surplus was down to $15.9 million. By 1994 the surplus was once again over 100 million dollars (*Direction of Trade Statistics, Yearbook 1987*, Washington DC: International Monetary Fund, 1987 and *Direction of Trade*, September 1995).
14. 'Japan and the Arab Boycott' in ADL Special Report, op. cit.; Harry Wall and David M. Weinberg, 'Japan should Show it Means Business', *The Jerusalem Post*,

7 June 1991; 'Japanese Compliance with the Arab Boycott of Israel', *Institute of Jewish Affairs, Research Report* No. 2, London, 1991.
15. Susan Hattis Rolef, 'Israel's Anti-Boycott Policy' *Policy Studies*, 28 (Jerusalem: The Leonard Davis Institute for International Relations at the Hebrew University of Jerusalem, February 1989), p. 52.
16. US Trade Act of December 1988, Section 2209.
17. Voice of Israel in English, 15 November 1990.
18. *Link*, op. cit., p. 30, and memorandum prepared by Harriet Mandel of the JCRC dated 15 August, 1990.
19. ADL Special Report, op. cit., pp. 32–3.
20. IJA Research Report, op. cit.
21. *Yedi'ot Aharonot*, 27 February 1991.
22. *Israel Business Today*, 'Japan–Israel Trade – Seductive but Slow', 5 December 1991; *Globes* (Hebrew), 3 March 1992.
23. Reuters (USA), 22 March 1991.
24. Reuters (Israel), 30 and 31 May 1991.
25. *The Washington Post*, 12 April 1991; *The New York Times*, 11 April 1991; *Yedi'ot Aharonot*, 26 April 1991 and 13 May 1991; *Jewish Telegraphic Agency* (JTA), 3 May 1991.
26. *The Link*, March–April 1992, p. 34
27. PR Newswire, 22 August 1991.
28. Seminar paper presented to Dr Gil Feiler by Sharon Berger in the Spring of 1995.
29. Letter from the marketing manager of Tadiran to the director general of the Industrial Cooperation Authority, 17 November 1991.
30. *Globes* (Hebrew), 16 November 1992.
31. Diamonds remained Israel's largest item of exports to Japan. Outside diamonds, Scitex – an Israeli company which manufactures computerized colour graphics workstations for the printing and publishing industry, and had developed a joint venture with the Tokyo Ink Corporation called Nihon-Scitex – was Israel's largest exporter to Japan in 1992, *Link*, op. cit.
32. *Ta'asiyot*, 134, 16 February 1992.
33. 'Taxation Interferes with Japanese Investment', *Globes* (Hebrew), 6 October 1992.
34. ADL memorandum dated 5 January 1993 and *Chicago Tribune*, 1 March 1993.
35. *Globes* (Hebrew), 12 and 16 November 1992.
36. *Jerusalem Post* and *Ma'ariv*, 4 December 1992.
37. Jiji Press (Tokyo), 3 December 1992.
38. 'Economic Analysis: Israel Doesn't Get Fair Economic Treatment from Japan', *Ha'aretz*, 17 June 1992.
39. Reuters (Israel), 11 December 1994; Reuters (Tokyo), 14 December 1994.
40. *Israel Business Today*, 23 December 1994.
41. Mike Tobin, Associated Press, 17 September 1995.
42. *The Guardian*, 26 October 1995.
43. *MEED*, 13 December 1996.
44. Ibid.
45. *Nikkei Weekly*, 17 February 1997.

46. *Korean Times*, 17 January 1990.
47. *Israel Business Today*, 5 June 1992.
48. *Boycott Report*, 17/5, May 1993.
49. Rabin had first visited South Korea in the beginning of 1967, when he was Chief of Staff (*Korea Economic Daily*, 15 December 1994).
50. Reuters (Israel), 11 December 1994.
51. *Israel Business Today*, op. cit.
52. Reuters (Israel), 19 March 1995.
53. See 'Arab Boycott now Spreads Down Under', *Jerusalem Post*, 12 December, 1991, and 'Arab Boycott Surfaces Down Under', *Israel Business Today*, 6, 274, 24 April 1992, p. 9.
54. See 'Blacklisting Report: A Current Perspective on the Arab Boycott', ADL Special Report, Spring 1989.
55. Ibid., citing Dr Colin Rubenstein, who noted that the Australian government's fear of offending Arab trading partners led it to become increasingly critical of Israel, while at the same time turning a blind eye on 'Arab economic blackmail at home'.
56. ADL Special Report, op. cit.
57. 'Australian Business Council Won't Comply with Arab Boycott', *Daily News Bulletin*, 20 May 1992; *Boycott Report*, 16/6 June/July 1992.
58. Rolef, op. cit., pp. 42–3.
59. Ibid.
60. See 'Views on the Arab Boycott and its Implications for Canada', presentation of the Hon. Herb Grey to the Canada–Israel Committee in April 1976, and WJC report, op. cit.
61. 'The Arab Boycott in Canada', Report of the Commission on Economic Coercion and Discrimination in association with the Center for Law and Public Policy, Montreal, 11 January 1977, pp. 9–11.
62. *Jerusalem Post*, 23 January 1977.
63. Howard Stanislawski, 'The Impact of the Arab Boycott of Israel on the United States and Canada', in David Leyton-Brown (ed.) *The Utility of Economic Sanctions* (London: Croom Helm, 1987), pp. 246–8 and *The Toronto Star*, 22 January 1977.
64. Daniel Lack, 'Developments in the field of anti-boycott measures at regional and national levels', 15 June 1978, p. 22.
65. 'Directive on International Economic Boycotts', Department of Industry, Trade and Commerce, 21 January 1977; 'Canada and the Arab Boycott: Developments and Proposals', Canada–Israel Committee, Montreal, April 1977; Rolef, op. cit.
66. Canada–Israel Committee report above, and Report of the Commission on Economic Coercion and Discrimination, op. cit.
67. *Montreal Star*, 15 January 1977.
68. Embassy of Israel in Ottawa release dated 30 May 1977.
69. ADL Special Report, op. cit. p. 25.
70. 'Canada's Ineffective Anti-Boycott Policy', *Petroeconomic File* 19, August 1978.
71. Ibid.
72. Stanislawski, op. cit. pp. 243–4.

11

The Boycott's Effectiveness and Cost

The Problem of Measuring the Boycott's Effectiveness

Trying to evaluate the extent of the boycott's effectiveness, and its cost to the Israeli economy, is not an easy task, for reasons which will be explained below. The main problem in trying to evaluate its effectiveness is that there are no absolute criteria for doing so. Insofar as the original goal of the boycott, in the eyes of the Arabs, was to prevent the establishment of a Jewish state in the Middle East, and later to help bring about its collapse and demise, the boycott was clearly a complete failure, and nothing more need be said on the subject. However, as explained in Chapter 4, over the years the Arab states modified their goals, first to causing the Israeli economy as much hardship as possible, and later as a means of attaining concrete returns within the framework of the Middle East peace process.

With regards to the peace process, so far the main use made of the boycott by the Arab states engaged in this process (except for Egypt and Jordan, that have already signed separate peace treaties with Israel involving the formal cancellation of the boycott), has been to refuse to lift the primary boycott, and in some cases the secondary and tertiary boycotts as well, until Israel terminates its occupation of Arab lands and recognizes the rights of the Palestinians to a state of their own. However, even though the Arabs will probably explain Israel's withdrawal from the remaining territories, which it occupied during the Six Day War, as proof of the boycott's effectiveness (i.e. that it was so effective, that Israel was willing to pay a very high price to get it cancelled), if and when such a withdrawal occurs, it will be in return for a comprehensive peace treaty, in which the cancellation of the boycott will constitute only a small part.

What we are left with is the question of how much damage and dislocation the boycott caused the Israeli economy over the years. Since the official imposition of the boycott preceded the establishment of the State of Israel by two and a half years, the Israeli economy developed from the very start within a reality of no formal economic contacts with its neighbours (the primary boycott), and various constraints in establishing normal economic contacts with third states (the secondary and tertiary boycotts). It is thus impossible to compare the 'before' and 'after' situation, as one can do in the case of other examples of economic sanctions.

Though one may examine trade patterns between pre-1948 Palestine (or the pre-1948 Jewish community in Palestine) and its neighbouring states, the long-term conclusions one can draw from such an examination are extremely limited, because pre-1948 Mandatory Palestine was a very different sort of entity from post-1948 independent Israel in part of Palestine, with a very different population make-up, different policies and different priorities.

That the boycott was unsuccessful in preventing the development of Israel into a strong, vital and modern state, with a sophisticated economy, high rates of economic and industrial growth and an impressive record of exports, is an undeniable fact (see Table 1).

Table 1: Statistics Indicating the Growth of the Israeli Economy 1950–97

Year	Total use of resources		GDP		GDP of business sector		Exports[a]	
1950	17,418	—	12,806	—	7,062	—	562	—
1951	21,172	(21.6)	16,663	(30.1)	9,275	(32.1)	783	(39.3)
1952	21,256	(0.4)	17,397	(4.4)	9,672	(4.3)	1,025	(30.9)
1953	21,169	(−0.4)	17,145	(−1.4)	9,349	(−3.3)	1,260	(22.9)
1954	24,679	(16.6)	20,471	(19.4)	11,268	(20.5)	1,793	(42.3)
1955	27,619	(11.9)	23,265	(13.6)	12,676	(12.5)	1,843	(2.8)
1956	30,655	(11.0)	25,340	(8.9)	13,915	(9.8)	2,099	(13.9)
1957	32,508	(6.0)	27,580	(8.8)	15,273	(9.8)	2,512	(19.7)
1958	35,320	(8.7)	29,600	(7.3)	16,494	(8.0)	2,797	(11.3)
1959	39,271	(11.2)	33,374	(12.8)	18,858	(14.3)	3,686	(31.8)
1960	42,720	(8.8)	35,578	(6.6)	20,203	(7.1)	4,654	(26.3)
1961	48,831	(14.3)	39,455	(10.9)	22,637	(12.0)	5,399	(16/0)
1962	54,420	(11.4)	43,395	(10.0)	25,149	(11.1)	6,342	(17.5)
1963	59,555	(9.4)	47,968	(10.5)	27,977	(11.4)	7,286	(14.9)
1964	66,148	(11.1)	52,728	(9.9)	30,987	(10.8)	7,728	(6.1)

Table 1 (*contd.*)

Year	Total uses of resources		GDP		GDP of business sector		Exports[a]	
1964[b]	64,959	—	52,059	—	30,792	—	7,563	—
1965	69,635	(7.2)	56,957	(9.4)	33,657	(9.3)	8,200	(8.4)
1966	70,020	(0.6)	57,527	(1.0)	33,470	(−0.5)	9,065	(10.5)
1967	73,053	(4.3)	58,853	(2.3)	33,569	(0.3)	9,818	(8.3)
1968	87,390	(19.6)	67,900	(15.4)	39,879	(18.8)	12,540	(27.7)
1969	99,166	(13.5)	76,536	(12.7)	45,756	(14.7)	13,409	(6.9)
1970	109,939	(10.9)	82,403	(7.7)	49,167	(7.5)	14,712	(9.7)
1971	122,099	(11.1)	91,687	(11.3)	55,513	(12.9)	18,187	(23.6)
1972	132,537	(8.5)	102,907	(12.2)	63,332	(14.1)	20,649	(13.5)
1973	151,523	(14.3)	107,916	(4.9)	64,338	(1.6)	21,779	(5.5)
1974	157,181	(3.7)	113,870	(5.5)	67,880	(5.5)	22,995	(5.6)
1975	163,412	(4.0)	118,231	(3.8)	70,067	(3.2)	23,400	(1.8)
1976	163,251	(−0.1)	120,098	(1.6)	70,045	(0)	26,840	(14.7)
1977	163,472	(0.1)	122,529	(2.0)	70,874	(1.2)	29,983	(11.7)
1978	174,037	(6.5)	127,562	(4.1)	73,633	(3.9)	31,361	(4.6)
1979	180,971	(4.0)	133,588	(4.7)	77,288	(5.0)	32,304	(3.0)
1980	180,852	(−0.1)	138,343	(3.6)	80,592	(4.3)	34,819	(7.8)
1981	193,068	(6.7)	144,844	(4.7)	85,467	(6.0)	36,645	(5.2)
1982	197,405	(2.2)	146,889	(1.4)	85,968	(0.6)	35,370	(−3.5)
1983	205,722	(4.2)	150,644	(2.6)	88,565	(3.0)	35,957	(1.7)
1984	207,549	(0.9)	153,940	(2.2)	90,709	(2.4)	40,839	(13.6)
1985	212,390	(2.3)	160,781	(4.4)	96,288	(6.2)	44,929	(10.0)
1986	224,522	(5.7)	166,503	(3.6)	101,346	(5.3)	47,425	(5.6)
1987	248,337	(10.6)	176,881	(6.2)	109,787	(8.3)	52,274	(10.2)
1988	251,116	(1.1)	183,065	(3.5)	113,739	(3.6)	51,510	(−1.5)
1989	248,944	(−0.9)	185,547	(1.4)	115,115	(1.2)	53,566	(4.0)
1990	266,440	(7.0)	196,622	(6.0)	123,764	(7.5)	54,624	(2.0)
1991	289,334	(8.6)	207,341	(5.4)	131,566	(6.3)	53,214	(−2.6)
1992	310,563	(7.3)	220,979	(6.6)	142,568	(8.4)	60,501	(13.7)
1993	332,414	(7.0)	228,511	(3.4)	147,428	(3.4)	66,835	(10.5)
1994	359,870	(8.3)	243,962	(6.8)	159,057	(7.9)	75,278	(12.6)
1995	387,247	(7.6)	261,172	(7.1)	173,029	(8.8)	82,918	(10.1)
1996	408,534	(5.5)	272,816	(4.5)	182,089	(5.2)	87,079	(5.0)
1997	417,334	(2.2)	278,099	(1.9)	—		92,394	(6.1)

Notes: Figures are in constant 1995 prices in millions of NIS (New Israeli Shekels), and those in brackets indicate percentage changes over previous years (thus there are no percentage figures for 1950 as there are no figures for 1949).

[a]   Goods and services
[b]   New series

Source: The Central Bureau of Statistics. *Statistical Yearbook of Israel,* Vol. 48 (1997), pp. 174–5; *Monthly Bulletin of Statistics,* Vol. 49, No. 3 (March 1998), p. 19.

Nevertheless the boycott most certainly had an effect on the direction of this development, and in its absence (and of the Arab–Israeli conflict in general) such inherent problems as relatively high rates of inflation and a chronic balance of trade deficit, might at least have been less severe.

On the most general level, the costs of the boycott to Israel can be divided into three categories:

1. *Direct costs*, which include immediate real costs resulting directly from the imposition of the boycott
2. *Indirect costs*, resulting from production disruption, originating from the disruption of normal trade relations. The importation of intermediary products and raw materials is an important component in this sphere of costs;
3. Costs resulting from potential opportunities which cannot be realized.[1]

Among the specific economic difficulties caused to Israel by the boycott have been the following:

(a) the inability to develop normal economic relations with its closest neighbours;
(b) difficulties in selling Israeli products to third states;
(c) difficulties in purchasing certain products from third states;
(d) the refusal of many foreign companies to invest in Israel, and the decision of certain foreign companies which had invested in Israel to leave;[2]
(e) difficulties of the Israeli government in contracting commercial loans from banks abroad;[3]
(f) the refusal of many commercial airlines and shipping companies to stop over in Israel, or carry Israeli cargoes.

One might add, on the basis of general economic truisms, that:

(a) the larger the number of boycotting states, so the damage caused to the boycotted state grows, since the alternatives open to it diminish;
(b) the greater the ratio of exports and imports to national product, so the effects which can be caused by the boycott are more negative;
(c) the less flexible the demand for imports of the boycotted state the more vulnerable it is.[4]

However, as we shall see below, it is extremely difficult, if not impossible, to determine what the exact cost of each of these problems actually was to the Israeli economy.

One reason has to do with the fact that neither foreign nor Israeli companies are eager to divulge information about the boycott. Foreign companies have usually been reluctant to admit that their economic relations with Israel, or refusal to have such relations, are in any way affected by the boycott.[5]

Israeli companies on the other hand have been extremely wary of speaking of how they are affected by the boycott or what they do to circumvent it.[6] Among the reasons for this wariness have been: the fear of damaging existing trade relations; the fact that as of mid-1975 the ministry officially in charge of dealing with the boycott was the Ministry of Finance, which is *inter alia* also responsible for tax collection and thus a body to which most businesses would rather divulge as little information as possible; and the fact that not all the means used to circumvent the boycott have been legal.[7]

With regards to investment there are additional difficulties in coming up with an accurate picture of what Israel lost because of the boycott. In the first place, especially with regard to the early years of the state's existence, no one ever calculated what its capacity for absorbing foreign investment really was. Furthermore, while one may assume that the boycott was an important factor in keeping many foreign investors out of Israel in the past, it would be wrong to blame the boycott alone for this. In addition to the boycott, the overall security situation, more attractive targets for investment and labour unrest in certain periods and sectors have been among the reasons why foreign investors have shied away from Israel. In the mid-1970s an Israeli commentator described the problem in the following terms: 'In most cases ... it is quite impossible to disentangle the effect of the Arab boycott from other objective factors at play in the difficulties encountered by the young Israeli economy. Also it is impossible to know whether a foreign firm simply does not operate in Israel or has refused to extend its operation there because of the boycott.'[8] More recently it has been pointed out that many American companies are wary of opening operations Israel because of cultural reasons, including the aggressiveness, rudeness and disrespect of their Israeli counterparts, and the Israeli bureaucracy.[9] Under the circumstances we can compute known cases of foreign investors who withdrew from Israel, or from plans to invest in Israel, because of Arab pressure, but have no way of knowing how much foreign investment would have poured into Israel in its absence.[10]

What we do have are lists of thousands of companies the world round that refused to give in to the boycott. The boycott authorities and various Arab states published, over the years, blacklists of companies accused by them of maintaining 'prohibited' economic contacts with Israel. Thousands of names of companies appeared on these lists, and the longer the lists the greater the proof that no matter how successful the Arab boycott was in curtailing Israel's ability to act on the international market as a free and equal agent, it was unable to keep it out of this market.

From a study of the 1968 lists, prepared under the auspices of the Institute for Palestine Studies in Beirut in 1970, we learn that the boycotted companies were from all industrial branches, and based in most of the Western industrial countries.[11] The study tells us for example that in 1968 44 American companies in the Chemicals and Pharmaceuticals branch were on the Arab boycott list, another ten from the UK, four from Turkey, six from France, four from West Germany, two from Cyprus, four from Italy, four from Switzerland and three from Japan.[12] In other words, according to the boycott lists at least 81 foreign companies in the chemical and pharmaceutical industries maintained economic contacts with Israel, and this at a time when in Israel itself impressive chemical and pharmaceutical industries were being established (see below, pp. 276–8).

On the other hand an Israeli study published five years later demonstrated that 'a close examination of the British blacklists of 1968 ... revealed that 10 per cent of the names on the list referred to Israeli firms in Britain, 35 per cent of these firms were subsidiaries of branch companies of other firms whose names were listed, and 25 per cent of the firms did not exist or were not engaged in international business.'[13] In other words, the CBO in Damascus apparently believes that the longer the list the better the deterrent, and regarded it as an effective propaganda device.

Another problem which emerges when one tries to calculate the economic effect of the boycott relates to the fact that even though the boycott undoubtedly raised economic difficulties for Israel certain spheres, this was counter-balanced by Israel's having been forced to be self-sufficient in certain sectors, and that many sophisticated industries might never have been developed in Israel if it had not been for the boycott and the Arab–Israeli conflict.[14] This being the case, when one tries to evaluate the cost of the boycott to Israel, one must also take the benefits into account, which makes the calculation even more difficult and illusive.

Finally one cannot overlook the fact that over the years direct trade between Israel and various Arab states has taken place by various means, but that no official figures exist as to the exact scope of this trade.[15]

A General Evaluation of the Boycott's Effect over the Years

In the years since 1946 there were periods in which the boycott was more effective in causing difficulties for the Israeli economy, and others in which it was less so. As already pointed out, in the early years of Israel's existence the boycott, and the unresolved state of war between Israel and its neighbours, forced the Israeli economy to develop in certain directions which it might not otherwise have followed. But other factors, having nothing whatsoever to do with the boycott and the conflict – such as the mass immigration of Jews to Israel, the mobilization of the Jewish world to assist the new state, the 1952 reparations agreement with Germany, and economic aid from various international sources – also affected this development.[16]

In the early 1960s the Israeli economy was in a state of rapid economic growth, accompanied by a relatively high rate of inflation and a massive balance of trade deficit. While the balance of trade deficit was temporarily reduced by means of a major devaluation of the currency, inflationary pressures and a full employment policy soon eroded the effect of the devaluation. The government then tried an economic slowdown policy, that greatly curtailed new investment and finally resulted in a major economic slump from which Israel managed to recover only during the post-Six Day War boom.[17] What effect did the boycott have on all this? Israeli economists were inclined to ignore the boycott,[18] while Arab economists analyzing the Israeli economy were inclined to attribute to the boycott a major role in Israel's economic problems.[19] All one can say with any certainty is that in the absence of the boycott, Israel's balance of trade problems would probably not have been so severe.

After 1973 the economic power amassed by the Arab oil-producing states by means of their petro-dollars, and the subsequent desire of both the industrialized and developing countries to remain on good terms with the Arab states, greatly increased the boycott's effectiveness insofar as many third states started to implement a voluntary boycott against Israel, i.e. they refused to do business with Israel even if not approached by the Arabs.[20] At the same time the fact that the boycott apparatus in the Arab world did not become more efficient,[21] the introduction of relatively effective anti-boycott legislation in the US, which affected the implementation of the secondary and tertiary boycotts,[22] and the opening of both overt and covert trade routes between Israel and the Arab world after 1975,[23] acted in the opposite direction.

In the early 1980s the boycott started losing some of its potency for a variety of reasons. On the one hand the effects of the oil-crisis started to melt away, and at the same time the consumption boom in Israel convinced many foreign companies that the Israeli market was, after all, something to be reckoned with.[24] As the 1980s progressed another development made the implementation of the boycott regulations more difficult, which was the growing fragmentation of the production process to sub-contractors, who in turn frequently made use of additional sub-contractors. It thus became increasingly difficult to follow where all the various components of a particular product were manufactured, and to verify the accuracy of negative certificates of origin which stated that none of these components were manufactured in Israel.[25] Nevertheless, the fragmentation in production also acted in the opposite direction, insofar as a single company in a business pyramid, which still felt obliged to apply a voluntary boycott or 'shadow boycott' for fear of losing business in the Arab world, could prevent contacts of any sort with Israel.[26] Furthermore, many Israeli manufacturers of electronic and computer components complained in these years that due to the practice of many Arab states of demanding 'negative certificates of origin', which *inter alia* required European manufacturers, who were interested in selling sophisticated products to them, to state that none of the components in these products had been manufactured in Israel, they lost many business opportunities.[27]

By the early 1990s the Middle East peace process made the effective implementation of the boycott increasingly difficult, though several Arab states (such as Syria) continued to apply it rigorously, while others (such as the Gulf States) started applying it less rigorously.[28]

The Cost of the Boycott to Israel

Efforts to calculate the cost of the boycott to Israel have taken place at least at three levels:

- at the first level, on the basis of the trade statistics relating to trade between Palestine and its neighbours in the years preceding the establishment of the State of Israel, which were examined in Chapter 2, an attempt is made to evaluate the effect of this cessation of trade on Israel's trade patterns;
- at the second level an attempt is made to quantify, or at least describe the effect of the boycott on specific sectors of the Israeli economy;
- at the third level a look is taken at various attempts which were made over the years to calculate the cost to the Israeli economy of the boycott by playing around with Israel's aggregate economic statistics, in other words, to calculate what these aggregates might have been in the boycott's absence.

The Effect of the Arab Boycott on Economic Relations between the Jewish Community in Palestine and its Arab Neighbours before 1948 and in the Immediate Post-1948 Years

As indicated in Chapter 2 economic boycotts were declared by the Arabs against the Jewish community in Palestine – the Yishuv – since the 1920s. However, it was only upon the outbreak of the Arab revolt in 1936 that such a boycott was implemented in earnest. The reaction of the Yishuv was to strengthen the Jewish economy (including the construction of a port in Tel Aviv), and this in a period when there was a major inflow of consumer and capital goods from Germany, within the framework of the 'transfer' arrangement, which until 1938 enabled many German Jews to save at least some of their capital.[29] At least some of these German goods found their way to Arab markets. It is thus extremely difficult to measure the effect of the boycott on the Jewish economy.

However, by 1938 the boycott was effectively imposed only on land sales to Jews, while all other trading transactions between the Jewish and Arab sectors – including purchases of Arab agricultural produce by the Jews and the purchase by the Arabs of manufactured goods from the Jewish economy – took place without serious interference, though theoretically the boycott was still on. A good deal of trade took place by means of brokers, in cash or by means of mutual trust arrangements, in order to conceal any traces of direct dealings. Though such procedures caused some price rises, on the whole prices were relatively stable in this period. It should be noted, however, that the countries of the Middle East (including Turkey), were not Palestine's most important trading partners in this period. Thus in the years 1936–39 these countries furnished only 20 per cent of Palestine's imports and purchased only 12 per cent of its exports.[30]

The effect of the boycott on the Jewish economy further declined during the years of the Second World War when, after 1941, the economy of the Yishuv entered a period of prosperity due to major orders from the allied forces in the Middle East, and increased orders from Arab markets due to the difficulties in obtaining goods from European sources. In addition, because of the disruption of trade routes between Europe and Palestine, the share of imports into Palestine from other Middle Eastern countries increased from about 20 per cent of the total in the years 1936–39 to 52.7 per cent in 1944.[31]

Following the establishment of the Arab League in 1945, the Arab boycott entered a new phase upon the proclamation of a more institutionalized and controlled Arab boycott. Nevertheless, in 1947 trade between Palestine – in whose economy the Yishuv was predominant – and the Arab states was still substantial,

Until the beginning of 1948 Palestine continued to serve as an important outlet for the agricultural surpluses of its Arab neighbours, and its balance of trade with them in the last years of the Mandate was negative (over 3 to 1 in favour of the Arab countries).[32] Since this imbalance had existed before the boycott was formally instituted in 1946 one may assume that it had little if anything to do with the boycott. All this suggests that when all trade between Israel and the Arab world came to a complete halt in the middle of 1948, the Arab economies were more seriously affected than that of Israel.

The complete cessation of all trade relations between Israel and the Arab world in 1948 caused an immediate trade-diversion reaction. Thus, for example, Israel was forced to start purchasing frozen beef and preserved meat from Argentina and other countries, since it could no longer buy beef-on-the-hoof from the Sudan and Egypt. This both raised the price of meat in Israel (because of the higher cost of the meat and the higher transportation costs), and resulted in a loss to Israel of the by-products from locally slaughtered beef. While rationing of meat (and other foodstuffs) in Israel in the immediate post-independence years was not due to the boycott but to the large influx of immigrants and the shortage of foreign currency, there is no doubt that the boycott aggravated the situation.

With regards to eggs, prior to 1948 most of the eggs consumed by the Yishuv came from Egypt, Syria and Lebanon. Now Israel was forced to start developing its own poultry industry, while temporarily making up for shortages with imported powdered eggs. However, unlike the situation with regards to meat, soon Israel became self-sufficient in egg production.

Similar developments took place in other areas of food production in Israel, including the growing of fruit and vegetables, and fishing. An initial need to import from more expensive sources abroad, was followed by rapid development of local production. It should be pointed out, however, that at first the increased production did not have a major effect on imports, both because of the large increase in the Israeli population resulting from the mass immigration, and because of improved diet.[33]

Nevertheless, there were certain agricultural products in which Israel could not possibly become self-sufficient. In addition to beef and mutton this involved rice and barley, as well as certain types of wheat. Overall, however, in the sphere of agricultural products, the shift from Arab to alternative sources of supply and self-production was smooth and resulted in developments which were more beneficial than harmful to the Israeli economy.

The effect of the Arab boycott on oil imports was more serious. Until 1948 Palestine received all its oil by means of the 12.45-inch oil pipe-line from Kirkuk in Iraq to Haifa, which had an annual capacity of 2 million tons of unrefined fuel. When the 1948 Arab–Israeli War broke out plans to construct a second, 16-inch pipe-line were abandoned, while the old pipe-line fell into desuetude.[34] Even though Israel continued to dream of finding oil in commercial quantities under its soil, replacing imports by local production was not an immediate option, and it was only in the period between the Six Day War and the return of the Abu-Rudeis oil fields to Egypt in 1975 that Israel produced substantial quantities of oil.

Thus for many years after 1948 Israel was forced to purchase most of its oil from afar. The result was that Israel had to pay a much higher price for its oil than if regional sources had been open to it, primarily as a result of transportation and brokerage costs added to the cost of the oil itself.[35] In 1971 *Time* magazine wrote that Israeli oil purchases from Venezuela had added $15 million to its annual oil bill,[36] which was, at the time, close to $90 million).[37] The only problem with this figure is that Israel purchased only very small quantities of oil from Venezuela on an occasional basis,[38] and the official figure for imports from Venezuela in 1971 was less than a million dollars.[39]

Despite the boycott, until 1979 Israel was, however, able to import large quantities of oil from Iran, which arrived by tanker to Eilat and was then transported by pipe to Ashkelon, which had been officially opened in 1970.[40] After the return of the Abu-Rudeis oil fields to Egypt in 1975 and the signing of the peace treaty between the two countries in 1979 Israel started importing Egyptian oil by the same route.

The Effect of the Arab Boycott on Particular Sectors

There has been no systematic study of how the various sectors in the Israeli economy have been affected by the boycott, though articles and studies about particular industries have been written, some taking a descriptive approach, others a statistical one.

Shipping

In the case of both Israeli imports and exports restrictions imposed by the Arab boycott on transportation to and from Israel resulted in the extension of supply and export lines, accompanied by a steep rise in transport costs and protracted delivery timetables.

The closure of the Suez Canal to Israeli shipping from 1956 (when the canal was nationalized by Egypt) until the signing of the Interim Agreement between Egypt and Israel in 1975[41] forced ships coming from the East and heading for Israel either to sail around Africa, or in the case of smaller vessels – after the opening of the Gulf of Aqaba to Israeli bound shipping in the aftermath of the 1956 Sinai Campaign – to use the port of Eilat on the Red Sea. In 1967 the Egyptian decision to close the Straits of Tiran for shipping bound for Israel was one of the causes for the outbreak of the Six Day War. The effect of all of this was to increase most transportation costs between Israel and the East significantly.

But it was not only a problem of the extension of supply and export lines which caused Israel economic damage, but the black-listing of ships which frequented Israeli ports. Between 1954 and 1968, 772 vessels were placed on the Arab blacklist. Of these 260 were finally removed after their owners agreed to comply with the boycott, but the net result was that most shipping lines (and for many years many airlines) boycotted Israel.[42] This once again increased transportation costs for Israel, since Israel was not free to choose the cheapest available means of transportation. Though the boycott resulted in the development of a significant merchant fleet sailing under the Israeli flag, Israeli ships were not cheap. According to figures supplied by the ADL in the early 1990s, there were some 600 vessels on the blacklist.

Another reason for the increased costs to Israel of ocean and air transport, not caused directly by the Arab boycott but rather by the geopolitical and security situation, has been the high insurance rates fixed by Lloyds Underwriters regarding cargoes imported to or exported from Israel. In addition to the usual insurance premiums, Israeli importers and exporters are charged an addition 2.25 thousandths of the value of the goods in respect of air transport, and 2.75 thousandths in respect of ocean transport.[43] Having said all this, it should be added that no one has ever calculated the actual cost to Israel of the boycott in the sphere of shipping.

The Chemical Industry

The chemical industry in Israel, which is considered a success story, was the subject of an article on the effects of the boycott, which appeared in *Israel Business Today* in July 1994. In 1993, the article stated, sales by the industry rose by 10.5 per cent, amounting to $4.67 billion of which $1.89 billion were exports. Nevertheless the industry had suffered from the fact that 'in the past a few multi-national corporations set up subsidiaries in Israel, but they all left', the article quoted Ya'acov Makov, director of the Israeli chemical company Pazchim, as having said that 'after that, we were denied full access to the knowledge acquired by the big corporations'.[44] Another expert, Ya'acov Lustig, a former Director of the Chemicals Division at the Israel Export Institute added that 'there is no doubt that the multi-nationals all caved in. When we need to buy a license for know-how, we have to promise to change the name of a product, hide any connection to the licensor, and then claim we developed the technology on our own. Household chemicals are more expensive in Israel, partly because of the costs of hiding their sources.' Insiders in the industry were reluctant to reveal which technologies had been acquired in this way, but the article claimed that PVC, polypropylene processes and a catalytic cracker had been acquired from companies which preferred to remain anonymous. 'Products such as oven cleaners and industrial detergents', the article continued, 'may be sold under a local brandname, but the technology came from somewhere else. The extra cost incurred is passed on to the Israeli consumer.'

When necessary know-how has been restricted, the government has taken steps to make it more available. The government permits local companies to exploit existing patents and pay royalties to foreign companies who will not release their rights. This happens whether or not the foreign companies are willing to accept payment from Israeli companies. Using this aggressive method, local companies have been able to manufacture Ampicillin from Beecham in England, and Captropil from Squibb in the US.

Israel is a country with very few natural resources, and the only natural resources found in abundance in it are the phosphate, potash and bromine extracted from the Dead Sea. *Inter alia* these resources are used in the chemical industry for the manufacture of of pesticides, herbicides, fire retardants, etc. Two of the largest manufacturers of these products in Israel are Machteshim and Agan. 'Both began business by exploiting process patents that were not registered in Israel, or by circumventing patents with a different chemical synthesis', the article explains. 'If it hadn't been for the Arab boycott', it continues 'the same patents would have surely been registered in Israel and loophole techniques would have been replaced with direct access to the original technology. As it stands the two companies are doing hundreds of million dollars of business without doing much original research.'

But the problem of the high cost and difficulties in acquiring technology, has not been the only problem of the chemical industry in Israel resulting from the boycott. 'Our biggest loss is not being able to sell to the Arab market. It's rich, big and close and we can't get to it directly', Makov said. One way of getting around this problem was for Israeli companies to open subsidiaries abroad, though circumventing the boycott was not the only reason for doing so.[45] In 1995 Teva Pharmaceuticals acquired Prosintex, an Italian bulk pharmaceutical chemical company (BPC), after having purchased a bankrupt Dutch chemical company in 1977.[46] In 1994 Bromine Compounds spent $30 million expanding its own Dutch operation. The foreign subsidiaries of Israeli chemical companies were frequently engaged in repackaging Israeli-manufactured products, hiding all traces of their origin, then transferring them to third companies which sold them to Arab states or others that had been intimidated by the boycott out of trading with Israel directly. However, in the course of the 1990s, as the application of the boycott started to weaken, such activities became less necessary.[47]

Car Imports

In 1995, about five years after the major Japanese car manufacturers started marketing their cars in Israel, an attempt was made to calculate how much the boycott had cost Israel in terms of its car imports.[48] Until the mid-1980s the only Japanese make to be sold in Israel was Subaru, when it was joined by Daihatsu and Suzuki. All the other major Japanese car manufacturers, including Mitsubishi, Mitusi, Nissan, Toyota and Mazda, refused to sell in Israel until the early 1990s. The fact that soon after these companies lifted their boycott of Israel, Japanese (and Korean) cars replaced European vehicles in most categories as the most popular among Israeli consumers, was proof to the extent of the trade diversion caused by the boycott in previous years.

Using sophisticated statistical methods, Fershtman and Gandal concluded that had the boycott continued, the new car market in Israel would have been approximately 12 per cent smaller in 1994 (20 per cent smaller if Subaru, Daihatsu and Suzuki had also stayed out of the Israeli market), the percentage of small, less expensive cars being sold would have been somewhat larger, while that of compact cars would have been smaller, but that the prices of cars would have been only slightly higher than they turned out to be because of the relatively high level of competition in the Israeli market.[49] In terms of the welfare gain from the end of the boycott, they calculated that in 1994 this amounted to $870 per purchase (it would have been $1,280 if Subaru, Daihatsu and Suzuki had not been in the market).[50]

Attempts to Calculate the Aggregate Cost of the Boycott to the Israeli Economy

Over the years all sorts of aggregate figures have been quoted as representing the cost of the boycott to the Israeli economy. These figures have never been the product of a comprehensive study, but rather the result of calculations of how a 5, 10 or 20 per cent increase in such economic parameters as investments, exports or job opportunities, would have affected the Israeli economy, assuming that the lifting of the boycott would have resulted in such increases. The fact that an increase in exports, for example, would have automatically led to an increase in the imports of inputs, was never taken into account in these calculations. Some widely quoted figures in the past were no more than the product of a some quick scribbling of figures by a government official or businessman trying to make a point. In most cases those who produced estimated figures did not explain how these were arrived at.

In 1953 Gardner Patterson estimated that the annual cost of the boycott to Israel was $25–30 million.[51] In 1957 Harry Ellis estimated the annual cost to Israel at $40 million.[52] Another source gave a higher estimate. Writing in 1960 Oded Remba stated that in the early 1950s it had been estimated that the cost to the Israeli economy of the absence of normal economic relations with the Arab countries was approximately $60–70 million annually. This calculation included such factors as the additional expenditures incurred for fuel and other imports (including higher ocean freight charges), the denial to Israel of foreign exchange earnings from operating the Haifa refineries at full capacity, etc. It also included the loss of export opportunities to Arab countries and of prospective investments by foreign companies. By the late 1950s, according to Remba, the loss had fallen to $30–40 million annually.[53]

In 1975 Shalom Schirman of the Israeli Ministry for Foreign Affairs stated that, according to calculations based on a static model that compared the foreign trade structure of Israel and its neighbours during the late 1960s, if it hadn't been for the primary boycott, Israel could have diverted 20 per cent of its actual exports (in value) to the neighbouring Arab countries and that some 'immediate gain' would have resulted for the Israeli economy from the diversion to closer markets. However, Schirman did not present the calculations themselves.[54]

In 1984 economists in the Israeli Ministry of Finance calculated that, if in the period 1972–83 exports had increased by one per cent every year, in the absence of the boycott, in 1983 exports would have amounted to $11.5 billion, rather than $10.3 billion. The increase in exports (assuming that they would not be accompanied by an increase in imports) would have caused a decrease in Israel's balance of payments deficit of $700 million a year. For the entire period an additional $6 billion worth of exports would have been generated, and the foreign debt would have decreased by $3.5 billion.[55]

Apparently relating to these figures, Hamza argued that they appeared to be on the high side. His explanation was that Israel was using them for propaganda purposes.[56]

In 1985 Gary Clyde Hufbauer and Jeffrey J. Schott offered the following calculation:[57]

Reductions in Israeli exports	*Annual cost to target country*
Reduction in Israeli exports resulting from Arab boycott; welfare loss valued at 15 per cent of estimated lost sales.[a]	
1951–60 $25 million	
1961–72 $69 million	
1973–80 $667 million	
Annual average, 1951–80	$214 million

Reductions in Israeli imports	Annual cost to target country
Reduction in Israeli imports caused by Arab boycott; welfare loss valued at 15 per cent of estimated lost trade[a]	

1951–60	$16 million
1961–72	$12 million
1973–80	$127 million

Annual average, 1951–80	$44 million
Total annual average 1951–80	$258 million

Note: [a] Assumes potential Israeli trade with Arab League would be same share of total trade as Lebanon once enjoyed. In 1957–62, Lebanon sold about 60 per cent of exports, and took 22 per cent of imports from other Middle East in countries; in 1968–72, the figures were 44 per cent and 6 per cent respectively.

In the summer of 1992, the Federation of Israeli Chambers of Commerce (FICC) came out with the figure of $45 billion, as the loss incurred to the Israeli economy as a result of the boycott in the previous 40 years.[58] How was this sum arrived at? The first element in this sum concerned foreign investments in Israel. Comparing Israel to Ireland and New Zealand, the FICC pointed out that while in a good year total foreign investment in Israel reached no more than $200 million, in 1990 alone American companies had invested around $1 billion in Ireland and $2 billion in New Zealand. Furthermore, out of the 500 largest companies in the world, most of which are multinationals, only five had overt investments in Israel. If investments in Israel had been 10 per cent larger in the years 1950–90, investments in Israel would have been $16 billion larger than they actually were. Had they been 15 per cent larger, the sum would have been $24 billion (in 1986 prices).

In terms of exports, the FICC calculation continued, assuming that in the absence of the boycott Israeli exports would have been 10 per cent higher in each of the years from 1950–90, Israeli exports would have been $20 billion higher. This figure was compared with Israel's foreign debt, which in 1992 amounted to $24 billion. The rest of the economic cost to Israel was, according to the FICC, made up of the effect of the boycott on the structure of Israel's industry, resulting from the fact that while many foreign companies are happy to purchase Israeli knowhow they are unwilling to set up manufacturing facilities in Israel to take advantage of this knowhow; the efforts that must frequently be made to conceal the true origin of products manufactured in Israel; the fact that Israel cannot always purchase goods from the cheapest source; and supply lines that are frequently longer than they would have been if it were not for the boycott.

In 1994, after the Saudi Foreign Minister announced that the six Gulf States would lift the secondary and tertiary boycotts, Dan Propper, President of the Manufacturers' Association, announced that Israel's loss in foreign investments of approximately $300–600 million per annum would now be reduced.[59]

According to Shafiq Ahmad Ali, author of a recently published book on the Arab boycott, the CBO in Damascus calculated that the cost of the boycott to Israel was over $100 billion. The figure was based on the fact that, according to the CBO, since 1948 the US had granted Israel $107 billion in assistance and grants, and that in fact the US paid the cost of the Arab boycott to Israel.[60]

Thus, we see that the estimates regarding the cost to Israel of the boycott over the years have varied, with the Israelis being inclined to minimize the boycott's effect and the Arabs being inclined to exaggerate it. All one can really say with certainty is that there is no doubt that the boycott harmed the Israeli economy in some respects and encouraged its development in others, and that if one wants to come up with any meaningful figures, a much more serious and sophisticated model will have to be developed than the ones that have been used to the present.[61]

Notes

1. This division is given by Menahem Ronen, '*Haherem Hakalkali al Yisrael – Skira Tamtzitit*' (The Economic Boycott of Israel – a Concise Survey), *Kalkala Va'avoda* (Economics and Labour), 8, (November 1992), p. 110.
2. In 1990, of the 500 largest companies in the world, only five admitted to having investments in Israel, *Ha'aretz*, 10 March 1993.
3. It was only in 1988 that the Israeli government was first able to contract a $50 million loan from a group of 14 banks in the US, Europe and Australia.
4. Ronen, op. cit., p. 111.
5. In the L'Oréal case (see Chapter 7, pp. 186–7 and Chapter 8, pp. 207–9) the French company refused to admit that certain actions it had taken were in any way connected to the Arab boycott rather than pure commercial reasons. It persisted in its refusal to admit this even after agreeing to pay a large fine for violating the US anti-boycott legislation.

6. The means used have included working through straw companies or third parties, the falsification of certificates of origin and misleading packaging.

7. See Chapter 6, pp. 136 and 138.

8. Shalom Schirman, 'The History of the Arab Boycott, 1921–1975, *Middle East Review* (Winter 1975/76), p. 41.

9. See Haim Handworker, *Helem Tarbuti* (Cultural Shock) (Hebrew), *Ha'aretz*, 26 March 1997.

10. As early as May 1965 the *Near East Report* pointed out that it was impossible to evaluate how many companies had refrained from investing in Israel because of the boycott. See Yosef Schechtman, *Haherem Ha'arvi Velikho* (The Arab Boycott and its Lessons), *Ha'umma*, 4, 13 (June 1965), p. 11.

11. Amer A. Sharif, 'A Statistical Study on the Arab Boycott of Israel', *Monograph Series*, 26, Beirut, the Institute for Palestine Studies, 1970.

12. Ibid., Table 4.

13. Schirman, op. cit.

14. See for example comments by MK Dan Tichon during Knesset debate on a motion for the agenda on the Arab boycott on 5 October 1994.

15. See Chapter 5.

16. See, for example, Yoram Ben-Porath, 'The Entwined Growth of Population and Product, 1922–1982', in Yoram Ben-Porath (ed.) *The Israeli Economy – Maturing through Crises* (Cambridge, MA: Harvard University Press, 1986), pp. 27–41.

17. See for example entry by Prof. Haim Barkai 'economic policy', in Susan Hattis Rolef (ed.) *Political Dictionary of the State of Israel*, second edition (Jerusalem: The Jerusalem Publishing House, 1993), p. 79.

18. See for example Jacob Metzer, 'The Slowdown of Economic Growth: A Passing Phase or the End of the Big Spurt?', in Yoram Ben-Porath, op. cit., pp. 75–100.

19. Ja'far Tah Hamza, *Al-Muqata'a al-'Arabiyya li-Isra'il* (Arabic) (The Arab Boycott of Israel), 1973, pp. 141–5.

20. Schirman, op. cit., p. 42.

21. Ibid.

22. See Chapter 7.

23. See Chapter 5.

24. Gad Gilber, '*Lo Bodkim Bataviyot*' (Hebrew) (One Doesn't Check the Labels), *Ha'aretz*, 26 April 1991

25. Ibid.

26. Yuval Elizur, '*Herem Hatzlalim Zover Nekudot*' (Hebrew) (The Shadow Boycott Gains Points), *Ha'aretz*, 2 May 1991.

27. Transcript of interviews carried out by Susan Hattis Rolef in the early 1980s.

28. See Chapters 5 and 11.

29. For a serious discussion on the 'transfer' see Werner Feilchenfeld, Dolf Michaelis and Ludwig Pinner, *Ha'avara – Transfer nach Palästina und Ein-wanderung deutscher Juden 1933–1939*, Introduction (Tübingen: Siegfried Moses, 1972).

30. Robert R. Nathan, Oscar Gass and Daniel Creamer, *Palestine: Problem and Promise – an Economic Study* (Washington DC: Public Affairs Press, American

Council of Public Affairs, 1946), p. 325.
31. Ibid., p. 333.
32. Oded Remba, 'The Arab Boycott: A Study in Total Economic Warfare', *Midstream* (Summer 1960), p. 40.
33. Gardner Patterson 'Israel's Economic Problems', *Foreign Affairs*, 32 (January 1954), p. 317.
34. Gershon Maron, '*Haharem Ha'aravi Verishumo Hakalkali*' (Hebrew) (The Arab Boycott and its Economic Impact), '*Riv'on Lekalkala*', January 1954.
35. See for example Dan Chill, *The Arab Boycott of Israel* (New York: Praeger Publishers, 1976), p. 16.
36. *Time* magazine, 19 July 1971.
37. The Central Bureau of Statistics, *The Statistical Yearbook of Israel*, 1972.
38. Talk with Zevi Dienstein on 21 February 1997.
39. The Central Bureau of Statistics, op. cit.
40. A pipeline of much smaller capacity had been opened between Eilat and the refineries in Haifa in 1958 in the aftermath of the Sinai Campaign.
41. On 28 September the Egyptians actually detained an Israeli ship – the *Bat Galim* – which attempted to sail through the Suez Canal, confiscating its cargo and imprisoning its crew. Egypt was, in fact, compensated by the Arab League for income lost to it due to the closure of the canal to ships bound for or leaving Israeli ports.
42. Amar Shariff, op. cit. p. 4.
43. Information supplied by customs brokers EPI Ltd.
44. Barry Chamish, 'Boycott Still Holds Back Israel's Chemical Industry', *Israel Business Today*, 1 July 1994.
45. For example, in the case of phosphates, in the late 1970s Israel Chemicals purchased a failing German company in order to get around the cartel established by the European Community in this sphere. This case was alluded to (but not mentioned specifically for obvious reasons) in an article on 'Israeli Production in Europe' by the editor of *Hashuk Hameshutaf* (The Common Market), Susan Hattis Rolef, published in Tel Aviv by the Association of Kibbutz Industries, the Manufacturers Association in Israel, Hevrat Ha'ovdim and the Ministry of Industry, Trade and Tourism, January 1979.
46. *Ha'aretz*, 2 March 1997.
47. Chamish, op. cit.
48. Chaim Fershtman and Neil Gandal, 'The Effect of the Arab Boycott on Israel: the Automobile Market', *Discussion Paper No. 3–95*, The Pinhas Sapir Centre for Development (Tel Aviv: Tel Aviv University, November 1995).
49. Ibid., p. 17.
50. Ibid., p. 19.
51. Patterson, op. cit., p. 321.
52. Harry B. Ellis, *Heritage of the Desert – the Arabs and the Middle East* (New York: Ronald Press Co., 1956) p. 162.
53. Remba, op. cit., p. 51.
54. Schirman, op. cit.
55. Ministry of Finance Report 1985, p. 62.

56. Hamza, op. cit., pp. 175–85.
57. Gary Clyde Hufbauer and Jeffrey J. Schott, *Economic Sanctions Reconsidered* (Washington DC: Institute for International Economics, 1985), pp. 183–4.
58. FICC press release, 5 August 1992.
59. *Globes*, 2–3 October 1994.
60. Shafiq Ahmad Ali, 11th article on the Arab boycott in *Al-Wattan*, 11 January 1997.
61. The author is, in fact, currently engaged in working out such a model.

12

From Boycott to Economic
Cooperation

THE ARAB–ISRAELI peacemaking process, as it developed in the
aftermath of the Madrid Conference in October/November 1991, and
especially after the signing of the Declaration of Principles between
Israel and the PLO on 13 September 1993, offered the leaders of
those Arab states willing to come to terms with Israel the political
excuse to start dismantling the Arab boycott of Israel and moving
towards a new reality of economic cooperation.[1]

The difficulties have been the result of several factors, of which the
main ones are the very different, frequently diametrically opposed,
expectations of the Arab side and the Israeli side regarding the
essence of 'economic cooperation', the imbalance between the Israeli
economy and the economies of its neighbours,[2] and the frequent
crises, which have emerged in the course of the peacemaking process
itself, especially since Binyamin Netanyahu formed his Likud-led
government in June 1996.

Removal of the Secondary and Tertiary Boycotts

The first manifestation of the change in the Arab attitude has been
on the level of the secondary and tertiary boycotts, even though
these are still being widely applied, albeit, in an increasingly haphazard and inconsistent manner.

The positive change has manifested itself in various ways. Most
immediately many major foreign companies, which were on the blacklist for many years, have been removed from it. These include Cad-
bury, Coca-Cola, Colgate-Palmolive, Ford, Fuji, Jaguar, Schweppes

and Xerox to mention a few. Furthermore, on 30 September 1994, the member states of the Gulf Cooperation Council (GCC) decided, partially as a result of American pressure, to lift the secondary and tertiary boycotts,[3] though the decision has since been inconsistently applied.

The main effect of the removal of the secondary and tertiary boycotts has been to make life much simpler for foreign companies wishing to operate simultaneously in both Israel and the Arab countries. Some companies, such as the McDonald's fast food chain, entered Israel first, and then expanded into the Arab countries. More frequently, companies, such as 3M, entered the Arab countries first and only later came to Israel. For other companies, with long established business connections in Israel, such as the Rover Group, Jaguar, JCB and Unilever, the new situation opens opportunities for expansion to other countries in the region. Marks & Spencer, for example, opened its first franchise in the Gulf in 1997. Until recently, Marks & Spencer's close ties with Israel had made it virtually impossible for it to establish contacts with Arab companies,[4] even though Arabs visiting Britain did not refrain from shopping in the chain's stores there.

The effect of the removal of the secondary and tertiary boycotts has been especially noticeable in the case of companies in countries such as Japan and South Korea, and other Far Eastern and South-East Asian countries, which for many years avoided contacts with Israel. Now they are openly pursuing Israeli contacts in the fields of technology, telecommunications, and construction products.[5] Though Europe never submitted to the boycott as the Asian countries did, many European companies that refused to have anything to do with Israel are now seeking economic and technological cooperation with it.[6]

The end of the secondary and tertiary boycott has not only brought foreign companies to Israel in search of economic and technological cooperation, but has also enabled them to start addressing the region as a single market, rather than separate, mutually exclusive ones. In dollar terms this has meant that between 1991 and 1995 total direct foreign investment in Israel increased six-fold from $686 million to about $3.6 billion, while foreign investment in financial assets grew 15-fold from $133 million to $2.054 billion.[7]

On another level, there is no doubt that the impressive rise in

Israeli exports has been due to the melting away of the boycott, and the opening up of many new markets previously closed to Israel – such as those of the Far East (including China) and Central Asia (including India), and a broadening of the possibilities in markets that were previously open (for example, in west European countries). Thus between 1990 and 1997 Israeli exports to India grew from $69.6 million to $364.8 million dollars, to Japan from $546.5 million to $1,029.4 million, and total exports to Asia grew from $1,047.8 million to $4,094.2 million.[8]

The increase in foreign investments and Israeli exports (added to the effects of the arrival to Israel since 1989 of over 600,000 immigrants from the former Soviet Union) has resulted in an impressive average annual growth in GDP of 6 per cent in the years 1991 to 1995, a fall in the rate of inflation to plus/minus 10 per cent (from a three-digit figure ten years earlier) and to relatively low levels of unemployment, with per capita income reaching approximately $16,000 – a figure higher than that in Spain, Greece, Portugal and Ireland.[9] Thus the benefits to Israel from the elimination of the secondary and tertiary boycotts have been tangible and clear. To the Arab states the benfits and payoffs seem much less obvious.

Removal of the Primary Boycott

Though Egypt and Jordan have formally cancelled all the various forms of the boycott, in conformity with the peace treaties they signed with Israel in 1979 and 1994 respectively,[10] and *de facto* direct trade and economic relations have been established between Israel several other Arab states in North Africa and the Gulf, formally the primary boycott still exists. Its continued existence was reconfirmed in a resolution passed by the Arab foreign ministers meeting in Cairo at the end of March 1997, which called for 'the continued preservation of the primary Arab boycott against Israel, until a comprehensive and just peace is attained in the region'.[11]

There are, incidentally, differences of opinion among economists as to how much direct trade will actually be generated between Israel and the Arab states once the primary boycott is eliminated, since there is no assurance that the Arab states will necessarily opt for Israeli goods competing with those of other industrialized countries, and Israel is already purchasing much of its oil requirements from Egypt. Furthermore the Arab states as a whole present a market smaller than Italy's, and only 6 per cent of Arab trade is within the region. The Arab countries as a group, with a population of 270 million people, import less than $140 billion per annum,[12] less than either South Korea or Japan.

There are also no reliable figures as to how much direct trade is taking place between Israel and the Arab world today. Some estimates put Israeli annual exports to the Arab world at several hundred million dollars or even as much as $1 billion.[13] The problem is that much of the direct trade that is taking place is still going via third countries and false brand names are still current.

Economic Cooperation

It is not surprising that the earliest plans for Middle East economic cooperation started to crystallize in Israel. Already in the course of the late 1980s and early 1990s many Israeli economists started working on models of cooperation involving bilateral cooperation on particular projects between Israel and its immediate neighbours, major regional infrastructure projects, etc.[14] While the Oslo talks were still being held in secret, Israeli Minister for Foreign Affairs, Shimon Peres, put pen to paper and wrote his book *The New Middle East* – in which he spread out a blueprint for regional cooperation.[15] It has also been suggested that there is a large potential for cooperation by means of joint Arab–Israeli ventures, to be located in industrial parks along Israel's borders with its neighbours, which will utilize Israeli technology and low cost Arab labour. Most of the output of these joint ventures would not be consumed within the region but would be exported outside the Middle East. It is, of course, very difficult to estimate exactly what the potential is. Israel has not made it a secret that its ultimate goal in this sphere 'is the creation of a regional community of nations, with a common market and elected centralized bodies, modelled on the European Community.'[16]

The Arab attitude towards such cooperation has been much more hesitant and ambivalent than that on the Israeli side. Many observers in the Arab world view the word 'cooperation', when coming from Israeli mouths, to imply 'Israeli economic imperialism', and one of the messages coming out of the Cairo Conference in November 1996 was that the Arab world is wary (see below, pp. 295–7). Egyptian columnist Mahmoud Abdel-Fadil wrote, in the course of the Conference that a Middle East free-trade area was synonymous with Israeli regional hegemony, and that while the Western media was excessively optimistic regarding the potential economic gains from the peace process, not all Arabs expressed such optimism. Abdel-Fadil also noted that it would be primarily Israel that stood to gain from the fusion of its sophisticated technology with inexpensive high-quality Arab labour, and that one of the problems was that Israel did not recognize the existence of an Arab economy, preferring to establish a Middle Eastern economy with Israel as its heart.[17]

Dr Abdul Qader Tash, an Egyptian intellectual and strong critic of the peace process with Israel, has argued that Israel was advocating the establishment of a Middle East common market, not only to break down the wall of isolation between Israel and its Arab neighbours, but to turn Israel into the dominant player in the region, first in the economic sphere, and later in the political and cultural ones. 'Zionists have failed to achieve their ambition of a Greater Israel with weapons and military superiority', he wrote. 'Hence economic overlordship is the new weapon they want to use to convert their idea of a Greater Israel into a concrete reality. That will be hegemony gained without war or bloody confrontation.'[18]

These fears of Israel, smacking of the forged nineteenth-century *Protocols of the Elders of Zion* which suggested that there was a Jewish plot to gain control over the world, might well be sincere, but totally unrealistic. 'The fear expressed by some Arab countries of Israel's economic dominance', the German Axel Halbach has written, 'is based on a considerable overestimation of the relatively small Israeli economy, in international comparison.'[19]

Economic Cooperation before or after the Establishment of Peace

One of the questions which has been raised in connection with Arab–Israeli economic cooperation has been whether it should be one of the means used to facilitate the establishment of peace in the Middle East, or whether economic cooperation will be one of the outcomes of a peace, following the resolution of the various political issues in dispute. Seen from the Arab perspective the question may be posed in a different manner: should the economic boycott of Israel be formally cancelled as an indication that the Arab world is willing to enter a new era in its relations with Israel, or should the boycott be used as a lever to force Israel to change objectionable policies?

Shimon Peres has continuously argued that cancellation of the boycott and economic cooperation should precede an actual settlement, since the potential economic payoffs from this will encourage the peace makers in their work. Many experts have tended to support this position, arguing that economic cooperation and integration ought to be addressed early on in the peace negotiations, both as a catalyst and guarantor of peace, and possibly even as a card in negotiations.[20] This support has, however, been accompanied by a warning that 'the potential symbolic and political effects of cooperation ... can be exaggerated as much as the economic benefits can be. It cannot be a panacea for the problems of the region.'[21] However, Nimrod Novik, in the past one of Peres's senior aides and currently a vice-president of an Israeli company involved with Egyptian and other partners in the construction of an oil refinery in Alexandria and other projects, stated in April 1997 that 'we thought business interests would act as a safety net, but these expectations were exaggerated, to say the least'.[22]

Experience teaches us that economic cooperation does not necessarily resolve political differences, though as the example of the scientific cooperation between Israel and Egypt has shown, they might persist despite the differences.[23] Even when improved political relations have followed the establishment of economic or scientific cooperation, it is very difficult to prove that the one led to the other rather than that it was easier to start with the latter.[24] It has been argued, however that in the case of Israel's relations with the Gulf Cooperation Council 'economic ties ... are likely to continue to proceed rather faster than diplomatic ties, a pattern which is not new to Israel. Indeed it often has sought exactly this process in the past in order to create conditions which make it difficult for a process of rapprochement – however slow – to be reversed.'[25]

On the other hand Arab countries, especially those that have not yet established formal economic relations with Israel, argue that the only way to get Israel to change its policies, especially regarding the

Palestinians and Jerusalem, is by denying it the economic cooperation that it seeks.[26]

In actual fact both approaches have manifested themselves simultaneously. On the one hand the beginning of cooperation may be discerned and is slowly contributing to the establishment of a modified
Middle East, even if not yet a totally new one.[27] Furthermore, even
in Israel, it has been appreciated that in the first stages it is not the
mega-projects which will be realized in the foreseeable future, but
more limited ones in areas which will be of obvious mutual benefit
to the countries concerned, in the spheres of education, agriculture,
health, water resources, energy and environmental issues.[28]

On the other hand, the Arab states, including those that have
established various levels of relations with Israel – such as Morocco,
Oman, Qatar and Tunisia – keep conditioning further normalization
in the development of these relations and on a change in the Israeli
policy and attitude, and have even threatened to reverse the process
– as was done at the meeting of the Arab foreign ministers in Cairo
at the end of March 1997.

There are also those, such as Egyptian President Hosni Mubarak,
who believe that cooperation with Israel should be preceded by
greater economic integration among the Arab states,[29] which is tantamount to putting off economic cooperation with Israel to the distant
future without conditioning it on progress in the peace process.
There are currently more than 60 official pan-Arab and inter-Arab
organizations in existence, many of them designed to deal with
economic issues. However progress towards Arab integration has
been slow. 'Most [of the Arab] economies ... remain highly protected', Halbach explains. 'The reasons are clear: protected sectors
wield political power; governments rely heavily on tariffs as a source
of revenue; and there is fear of massive layoffs and social unrest
associated with liberalizing formerly protected, uncompetitive
industries. ... [In addition] regional economic cooperation between
states, that are non-democratic in nature, spells failure. Political
reform and the prevalence of democracy is considered by many as a
precondition to successful Arab regional cooperation.'[30]

A Reality of Cooperation

Despite the over optimism on the one hand and exaggerated fears on the other, the peacemaking process, as it has evolved since the Madrid Conference, has the concept of economic cooperation built into it. Thus one of the five forums for multilateral talks which started to convene after Madrid, with the participation of Israel, a large number of Arab states and countries from outside the region, has dealt specifically with economic cooperation. Since the signing of the Declaration of Principles (DoP) between Israel and the Palestinians on 13 September 1993, four economic conferences – officially referred to as Middle East and North African (MENA) economic conferences – with the participation of businessmen from the Arab world, Israel and third countries, have been convened. The first conference was held in Casablanca in October/November 1994; the second was held in Amman in November 1995; the third in Cairo in November 1996; and the fourth in Doha in November 1997.

The Casablanca Conference

The Casablanca Conference, hosted by King Hassan II of Morocco, convened on 30 October with the participation of 61 states and 1,114 businessmen, under the sponsorship of the US Council on Foreign Relations and the Geneva-based World Economic Forum.[31] The Conference was in fact convened at the insistence of the US, and in conformity with Israel's desire to push forward normalization in the economic relations between itself and the Arab states, even before a comprehensive and permanent peace was attained. Israel also hoped that the Conference would constitute a formal end to the Arab boycott, in conformity with the assurances which Peres had received from the Moroccan Prime Minister, Abdel Latif Filal.[32]

Israel, understandably enthusiastic about the event, was represented by a delegation, which in addition to Prime Minister Yitzhak Rabin and Foreign Minister Shimon Peres, included eight ministers and approximately 130 businessmen. To Arab observers this enthusiasm seemed like proof of Israel's economic hegemonial designs on the Arab world, and the Israelis were criticized for their arrogant behaviour. The Arabs were also disappointed because the Conference did not lead to massive European and American investments in the less prosperous Arab states, as expected. Few concrete deals were actually concluded at Casablanca, and those that were were harshly criticized in many Arab capitals, where they were termed premature. Nevertheless, the fact that Israeli and Arab politicians and businessmen openly and publicly mingled in Casablanca was seen as a clear signal to foreign companies that a new era had, in fact, begun.[33]

The Amman Conference

Prior to the convention of the Amman Conference in October 1995, several Arab states suggested that they were having second thoughts about the holding of additional economic conferences with Israel's participation, and that the Arab boycott should continue to be applied until a comprehensive and permanent peace was reached with Israel.[34] Israel and the US on the other hand reasserted their belief that Arab–Israeli economic relations should expand as early as possible without conditioning them on the attainment of such a peace first.

The Amman Conference opened on 29 October – one day after the opening of an international business conference in Jerusalem, and continued until 3 November – one day before the assassination of Yitzhak Rabin in Tel Aviv. Seventy states participated in the Conference, including Egypt, the Gulf states, Jordan, Morocco, Saudi Arabia and Tunisia. Israel turned up with a thick project book, proposing 218 different joint projects worth $24.7 billion.[35] Though most of the projects were destined to remain on paper, a business partnership was signed between Jordan and Israel for the construction of a joint bromide plant along the Jordanian shore of the Dead Sea. The agreement was signed by the new owner of Israel Chemicals, Shaul N. Eisenberg, and the Jordanian Government Potash Company, and the cost of the project was estimated at $50 million.[36] Israeli Minister of Energy, Gonen Segev, and the American Gas company Euron also signed a memorandum of understanding regarding the supply to Israel of natural gas from Qatar.

But the main achievement of the conference was the 'Amman Declaration', which spoke of the establishment of regional institutions, including a bank for economic cooperation and development to be based in Cairo with capital of $5 billion; a regional tourism board; a summit secretariat to be based in Rabat; a regional economic development monitoring committee to be located in Amman; and a regional business council, with the participation of Egypt, Israel, Jordan and the Palestinians.[37]

One of the corner-stones of Peres's dream of a new Middle East had been the establishment of a Middle East Regional Development Bank. Concrete plans for the establishment of such a bank had already been made in the early 1990s, with the cooperation of certain personalities in Egypt, who insisted however that for the time being the plans remain secret.[38] In Casablanca in 1994 no progress was made because of differences of opinion between the US and the European Union. At Amman an agreement was reached despite the fact that 12 of the 15 countries of the European Union, including France, Germany and Great Britain, still had reservations. Once the bank is established it will finance investment projects initiated both by the governments of the region and the private sector.[39]

The Cairo Conference

Whereas at the 1996 Amman Conference the Egyptians were very eager that the next conference be held in their capital, as the date of the Cairo Conference drew near, doubts were raised as to whether the Conference would take place, and this against the background of deadlock in the negotiations between Israel and the Palestinian Authority over the Hebron Agreement and the policies of the Netanyahu Government in Israel. As a result of massive pressure on the part of the US and the World Economic Forum, the Conference was finally convened on 13 November 1996 – though instead of being called a 'business summit' with the participation of prime ministers and heads of states, it was called 'The Middle East and North Africa Business Conference.'[40]

The Cairo Conference, as it finally evolved, was much less political than the previous conferences, and while Israeli politicians were not made to feel welcome,[41] despite claims in the Arab press that Israeli businessmen, seeking to normalize relations with their Arab colleagues, were nothing but 'pipe-dreamers',[42] they were, in fact, made to feel very comfortable.

The Doha Conference

The Doha Conference opened on 16 November 1997 against the background of stalemate in the Middle East peace process, increased tension between Iraq and the United Nations, following the halting of the inspections by UNSCOM – the UN body formed to carry out weapons inspections in Iraq – by Iraqi President Saddam Hussein, and threats by various Arab and Muslim states against the Government of Qatar. The conference was held without the participation of official delegations from Bahrain, Egypt, Morocco, the Palestinian Authority, Saudi Arabia and the United Arab Emirates, in addition to those Arab states which had refused to participate in previous conferences. Nevertheless, representatives from all these countries were among the 800 businessmen who officially participated in the Conference, which was much less political in its content than previous ones, even though US Secretary of State Madeleine Albright – the only foreign minister to participate in the event – took advantage of the conference to chastize the Israeli Prime Minister Binyamin Netanyahu for his rigid policy on the Middle East peace process.[43]

It should be noted that not all the Arab states were willing to participate in the MENA conferences. Syria was one of those that refused to join. Two weeks after the Amman Conference in 1995 Syrian Deputy President Abd el Halim-Hadim severely criticized the Arab states that had attended the Casablanca and the Amman conferences, arguing that bilateral agreements between Israel and various Arab states merely strengthened Israel while weakening the Arabs. 'How can a partnership develop between the occupier and the occupied?' he added, alluding to the refusal of the Israeli government to talk about an Israeli withdrawal from the Golan Heights.[44] Lebanon also officially stayed away from all the conferences, even though Lebanese businessmen attended as individuals.

It is too early to evaluate the contribution of the MENA conferences to the economies of the states involved, and in May 1998 it was not even clear that a fifth one would take place.[45] It has been noted, however, that most of the major projects presented at these conferences have been 'mega-projects' in the domain of the public sector, and for the time being it is not clear how these are to be financed. This has not prevented Arab opponents of the conferences to argue that their only beneficiary has been Israel. This is how

Hassan Tahsin, a senior columnist of the *Saudi Gazette*, summed up the first three conferences:

> The Jewish state has done its best to establish economic relations with Arab countries in order to become an economic power in the region. Looking closely at the three economic conferences held in Morocco, Jordan and Egypt, we may conclude the following:
> - At the Rabat [sic] Conference, Israel partially freed itself from the Arab economic embargo. This helped to increase Israel's GNP.
> - At the Amman Conference, the United States exerted tremendous pressure on the Arabs to end their boycott of Israel. For the first time, Peres called on the Arabs to divorce politics from economics: in other words, economic cooperation is possible regardless of the political situation. Yet again, we see Israel's plan of establishing economic relations with the Arabs before making peace with them.
> - In the recent Cairo Conference, the participants agreed upon the final status of the Mid-East and Mediterranean Tourism Organization in Tunisia. Further, they endorsed a proposal for the establishment of a Mid-East and North Africa Bank in addition to another agreement for setting up an oil refinery in Egypt to be financed by both Egypt and Israel. Israel must be made to understand that any economic gains it has made cannot last. Economic gains are rooted in real progress toward peace. The roots of these gains, however, are in sandy rather than solid ground. Israel can, it believes, change earlier agreements it has made without regard to the consequences. This cannot be allowed to happen.[46]

Joint Ventures

It should be noted that there are already numerous functioning joint-ventures between Israeli companies or their subsidiaries, in Jordan, Egypt, Morocco and Oman. For example, Israel's Delta Galil textile company, has been involved in a $5 million factory with Egypt since the early 1990s, and towards the end of 1997 joined forces with Jordan's Century to set up a clothing factory in Irbid.[47] There is a potential to develop such activities, for example in the construction industry.[48] Other spheres with vast potential include the production of minerals, chemicals[49] and pharmaceuticals,[50] in which Israel comes with relevant experience and a record of success. Whether or not substantial cooperation in the form of joint ventures materializes, will be a function of the availability of funds and the ability to form an atmosphere of partnership rather than Israeli predominance and an Arab sense of exploitation by Israel. It is no secret that the Egyptians, Jordanians and Palestinians have reservations about Israeli economic domination.[51] It is a fact that most of the joint ventures already operating involve Israeli firms utilizing low-skill, low-cost Arab labour, for the production of semi-finished goods, which are then sent to Israel for finishing and export.

Nevertheless, there is no doubt that both sides benefit from the joint ventures, even in their present form. For the Arab partners they offer jobs in markets where jobs are badly needed. For Israel it is no secret that they help Israeli manufacturers bypass what remains of the Arab boycott, since in MENA and world markets the products of these joint ventures are perceived as Arab. In addition, 'Israel perceives joint ventures as an advanced stage of normalization and acceptance in the region, which Israelis have been denied during many decades of hostility and total boycott.'[52]

Regional Infrastructure Projects

One of the pillars of Peres's 'New Middle East',[53] is the prospect for the construction of major regional infrastructure projects in the spheres of transportation, telecommunication, water,[54] sewage, energy systems, fuel transportation and tourism.[55] However, without the cancellation of the primary boycott by all of Israel's immediate and more distant neighbours, such projects have little chance of being implemented. Some projects proposed at early stages of the peace process, such as Egyptian–Israeli and a Qatar–Aqaba–Eilat gas pipeline, have since come to a standstill due to the slowdown in the peace process. Nevertheless, multinationals hoping to become involved in future regional projects are setting foot in the region through participation in small nation-based projects by means of which they are hoping to establish useful contacts for future use. For the foreseeable future the construction of industrial parks along Israel's border with Jordan and the Palestinian Authority, are more realistic, but also not free of problems. Such parks are also possible along Israel's borders with Egypt, Lebanon, and Syria.

Finance

Something missing from all three MENA conferences so far has been adequate funding proposals for the ambitious public sector projects presented. True, progress in the peace process, especially the signing of the DoP, brought with it a flood of commitments from states outside the region to finance development projects. However, while such commitments have served as encouragement to the region's leaders and to some prospective investors, they have been relatively small compared to the potential presented by private financing. In 1995, for example, worldwide donor aid, referred to as 'Organizational Development Assistance' (ODA), reached $62 billion. During the same period foreign direct investment (FDI) reached $315 billion (a 40 per cent increase over the previous year) of which over $100 billion was directed at developing economies.[56]

In the long run the real hope is not donor assistance, which in any case is assumed to be temporary, but direct private investment. Accepting this reality, Israel's economic leaders have done everything in their power to encourage private investment. 'Private participation does not have to wait for the consummation of the peace process', wrote Israeli Minister of Finance Avraham Beiga Shohat in 1995. 'Economic relations can precede diplomatic relations and flexible contract-based arrangements can be made in a manner which allows political issues to be addressed at the project level.'[57] However, for private investment to materialize there is need, in addition to progress in the peace process, for sound development strategies, as well as cooperation by Middle Eastern and foreign public and private banking systems. It is to this end that the idea of a regional development bank was raised (see above).

Among the developments in the banking sphere worth mentioning has been cooperation between the International Gulf Bank of Bahrain and three Saudi banks, in order to finance the $500 million Ghuzlan power station project in Saudi Arabia.[58] Other project finance methods, such as build–operate–transfer (BOT), build–own–operate (BOO) and build–own–operate–transfer (BOOT), get around the problem of shortage of capital for investment, and are becoming increasingly popular throughout the Middle East. Oman became the first Gulf Arab state to issue a BOOT project when the Manah power station came on stream in April 1996. Oman also plans to use BOOT in the Muscat and Salalah waste water projects.[59] Though none of these projects is connected to the peace process, the manner in which they have been financed points to the desired direction of development in this sphere.

It should be pointed out that at the end of 1995 the combined assets of Arab banks increased by around 11.9 per cent to $911 billion while credits grew by 8.1 per cent to $262.7 billion.[60] Furthermore, it is hoped that increased security in the region will result in at least some of the $900 billion of Arab capital investments abroad being rechannelled to the the MENA countries.

Conclusion

While the 52-year-old formal Arab boycott of Israel is undoubtedly close to disappearing, despite the setbacks, the reality of cooperation has not yet been fully realized. As this book goes to print it is not yet clear whether the peace process will continue to advance and the Arab boycott will continue to disintegrate, or whether the process might be reversed – as several Middle Eastern states, headed by Syria, would like to see happen. Despite everything, it is my belief that the gradual movement towards a different, even if not completely new Middle East, will overcome all the political obstacles. No matter how worrisome the setbacks, it is hard to imagine McDonald's pulling out of Israel or Saudi Arabia kicking IBM out of Riyadh. There is a growing number of vested interests, in the Arab world as in Israel, that do not want to see a reversal in the process. It is, however, impossible to predict what the future has in stock. The Middle East and the states that inhabit it always were, and remain, unpredictable.

Notes

1. Gil Feiler and Yaacov Yisraeli, *Business Laws and Economics Prospects in the Middle East and North Africa* (Federation of Israeli Chambers of Commerce, 1996). See also Simcha Bahiri and Samir Huleileh, *Peace Pays: Palestinians, Israelis and the Regional Economy* (Israel/Palestine Center for Research and Information, 1993); Rodney Wilson, *The Palestinian Economy and International Trade*, CMEIS Occasional Papers, Centre for Middle Eastern and Islamic Studies at the University of Durham, 45 (November 1994).

2. The former British Secretary for Trade and Industry, Lord Young, commented in February 1997 that 'You look at the map and Israel looks small, but it has a gross domestic product of $90 billion. Egypt, Jordan, Syria, Lebanon and the Palestinians combined have just over $60 billion' (*Birmingham Post*, 8 February 1997, p. 19).
3. See Chapter 2, pp. 54–5.
4. *Globe and Mail*, Toronto, 7 February 1997.
5. See Chapter 10, sections on Japan and South Korea.
6. See Chapter 8.
7. The Israeli Bureau for Statistics, *The Annual Statistical Abstract of the State of Israel, for 1995* (Jerusalem, 1996).
8. Ibid., p. 272, and *the Monthly Bulletin of Statistics*, March 1998, p. 40.
9. *The Annual Statistical Abstract of the State of Israel, for 1995*, op. cit.
10. Nevertheless Israeli exports to Egypt amounted in 1996 to only $57 million and those to Jordan to $8 million (*The Economist*, 5 April 1997).
11. *Ha'aretz*, 1 April 1997.
12. Herb Keinon, 'Biteless Boycott', *Jerusalem Post*, 4 April 1997.
13. Feiler, *Scientific and Technological Cooperation Between Israel and Egypt: Possibilities and Achievements*, Tel Aviv University, The Armand Hammer Fund for Economic Cooperation in the Middle East, January 1991.
14. See, for example, Susan Hattis Rolef, 'Economic Prospects for Peace', *Spectrum* (June 1990), pp. 26–7.
15. Shimon Peres, *The New Middle East* (New York: Henry Hold & Company, 1993).
16. Ministries of Foreign Affairs and Finance, Government of Israel, *Development Options for Cooperation: The Middle East/East Mediterranean Region*, Version IV, August 1995, pp. 1–2. This document was officially presented at the Amman Economic Conference.
17. Mahmoud Abdel-Fadil, *Al Ahram*, 14 November 1996.
18. Abdul Qader Tash, *Arab News*, 12 November 1996.
19. Axel J. Halbach, 'New Potential for Cooperation and Trade in the Middle East', *IFO Research Report*, 85 (Department for Development and Transformation Studies, Weltforum Verlag, 1995).
20. See 'Economic Cooperation in the Middle East and North Africa', The World Bank, September 1993; Stanley Fischer in 'Securing Peace in the Middle East: Project on Economic Transition', The Institute for Social and Economic Policy in the Middle East at the John F. Kennedy School of Government, Harvard University, June 1993, p. 129; and Meir Merhav (ed.), 'The Research Project for Economic Cooperation in the Middle East: An Overview' (The Armand Hammer Fund for Economic Cooperation in the Middle East, Tel Aviv University, December 1986), pp. 2–8.
21. 'Regional Cooperation in the Middle East', Agency for International Development, US Department of State, 1 February 1979.
22. *The Economist*, 5 April 1997.
23. Feiler, op. cit.
24. For example it has been pointed out that the exchange program for scientists

organized by the Weizmann Institute in Israel and the Max-Planck Society in Germany at the end of the 1950s preceded the institution of diplomatic relations between the two countries by more than five years (S. Freier, 'Science for Development in a Region at Peace', paper presented at the Middle East Development Conference, Geneva, 23–6 March 1989), but it cannot be proven that the former paved the way for the latter, rather than merely being a more convenient means of maintaining contact at the time.

25. Emma C. Murphy, 'The Arab–Israeli Peace Process: Responding to the Economics of Globalization', *Critique*, 9 (Fall 1996), pp. 69–71.
26. See for example the Bahraini position as expressed towards the meeting of the Cairo Conference, *Al-Ra'i al-Am* (Kuwait), 13 November 1996.
27. *Globes*, op. cit.
28. Gil Feiler, 'From Boycott to Limited Scientific and Technological Cooperation', in Efraim Inbar (ed.) *Regional Security Regimes* (Albany, NY: State University of New York Press, 1995), pp. 253–269.
29. *Tishrin*, op. cit.
30. Halbach, op. cit. On the subject of Arab cooperation see Pierre van den Boogaerde, *Financial Assistance from Arab Countries and Arab Regional Institutions*, Occasional Paper 87, International Monetary Fund, Washington DC, September 1991.
31. Ami Ayalon and Bruce Maddy-Weitzman (eds) *Middle East Contemporary Survey*, The Moshe Dayan Centre for Middle Eastern and African Studies, Tel Aviv University, published by Westview, 1996, p. 61.
32. BBC Monitoring Service Middle East, 4 October 1994.
33. *Ma'ariv*, 24 October 1995.
34. Hassan Tahsin, *Saudi Gazette*, 7 November 1995.
35. *Ha'aretz*, 29 October 1995.
36. *Yedi'ot 'Aharonot*, 30 October 1995.
37. Ibid., and Jordan TV in English, 31 October 1995.
38. Notes taken by Susan Hattis Rolef during the visit to Israel in November 1991 by former Egyptian Prime Minister Mustafa Halil, as guest of the Israel Labor Party Fifth Conference.
39. *Davar*, 3 November 1995.
40. *Globes* (Hebrew), 12 November 1996.
41. For example the head of the Israeli delegation, Minister for Foreign Affairs David Levy, was not even allowed to speak at the opening session, which prompted him to boycott later sessions.
42. *The Star* (Jordan), 28 November 1996.
43. *Ma'ariv*, 21 November 1997.
44. *Tishrin* (Syria), 14 November 1995.
45. *Al-Thawra* (Damascus), 28 April 1998.
46. 'Will the Middle Eastern Volcano Erupt?' Arab View – The Internet Home of Independent Arab Opinions, 26 November 1996.
47. IPR database.
48. Gil Feiler, 'Housing Policy in Egypt', *Middle Eastern Studies* (28), 2 April 1992, pp. 295–312.

49. *Chemical Market Reporter*, Schnell Publishing Company, 251, 8 (24 February 1997).
50. *Industry Express*, Market Letter Publications Ltd, UK, 17 March 1997.
51. Murphy op. cit., pp. 69–71.
52. Halbach, op. cit.
53. Peres, op. cit., especially Chapters 9–11, pp. 123–47.
54. Back in 1953 the US tried to initiate regional cooperation for the utilization of the waters of the Jordan River. The Johnston Plan was presented to the states of the riparian states – Lebanon, Syria, Jordan and Israel – in 1955 but the Arab states refused, at the time, to concur in any scheme to which Israel would be an active partner.
55. The potential for increasing the number of tourists visiting the Middle East is enormous, but awaits progress in the peace process, and reduction of xenophobic violence by Muslim extremists. There is believed to be a high potential for shared tourist projects along the Red Sea and Dead Sea.
56. 'Foreign Direct Investment', *Business Middle East*, The Economist Intelligence Unit, 16–30 November 1996.
57. Avraham Beiga Shohat, 'The Role of the Private Sector in the Middle East Peace Process' (Jerusalem: Ministry of Finance, Government of Israel, 1995).
58. 'Arab Banking: Less is More', *Middle East Briefing*, Info-Prod Research (Middle East) Ltd, 2 January 1997.
59. 'BOT: Growing Private Finance Methods in the Region', *Middle East Briefing*, Info-Prod Research (Middle East) Ltd, 13 March 1997.
60. Ibid.

Bibliography

Archives and Other Documentary Sources

Archives

Carter Presidential Library in Atlanta, Georgia, USA
Central Zionist Archives in Jerusalem, Israel
Public Record Office in London, Great Britain

Other Sources of Documents

American Jewish Congress, New York
Anti-Defamation League of B'nai Brith in Washington DC, New York and
    Jerusalem
Buy-Back Authority in Tel Aviv
Central Boycott Office in Damascus, Syria
Centre Européen Juif D'Information, Brussels
Economic Warfare Authority in the Ministry of Finance in Jerusalem
Office of Antiboycott Compliance (OAC) of the US Department of Com-
    merce in Washington DC
World Jewish Congress, Geneva

Books and Articles

Abbott, Kenneth W., 'Coercion and Communications: Frameworks for
    Evaluation of Economic Sanctions', *New York University Journal of
    International Law and Politics*, 19 (1987).
——, 'Economic Sanctions and International Terrorism', *Venderbilt Journal
    of Transnational Law*, 29 (1987).
Agency for International Development, *Regional Cooperation in the Middle
    East* (US Department of State, 1 February 1979).

Ahmad, Muhammad 'Abd al-'Aziz wa-al-Jabali, Muhammad, *Al-Difa' al-Iqtisadi Didda al-Atma' al-Istighlaliyaa al-Isra'iliyya* (The Economic Protection from Israel's Ambitions to Exploit the Region) (Arabic).

Alghanin, Diraar, 'US–Arab Business Opportunities', *American–Arab Affairs*, 4 (Spring 1983).

Ali, Shafiq Ahmad, series of 16 articles on the Arab Boycott in *Al-Wattan* (Qatar), (January 1997), (Arabic).

Ali-Raddam, A., 'The US and the Arab Boycott', *Majalat Markaz al-Dirasat al-Filastiniyah* 30 (September–October 1979), pp. 5–22 (Arabic).

'Analysis and Application of the Anti-Boycott Provisions of the Export Administration Amendments of 1977', *Law and Policy in International Business*, 9 (1977), pp. 915–57.

'Anti-Boycott Legislation – the Export Administration Amendments of 1977, Pub. 1, 95–72 stat. 235', *Harvard International Law Journal*, 19 (Winter 1978), pp. 343–72.

Anti-Defamation League, B'nai B'rith, *Japan's Foreign Trade and the Arab Boycott of Israel* (New York: Anti-Defamation League, 1968).

'Antitrust as an Antidote to the Arab Boycott', *Law and Policy in International Business*, 8 (1976), pp. 799–828.

'The Antitrust Implications of the Arab Boycott', *Michigan Law Review*, 74, 4 (March 1976), pp. 795–819.

Aplatoni, Arye, *'Milliard Dollar'* (A Billion Dollars), *Ma'ariv – Assakim* (29 October, 1991).

'The Arab Boycott: An Instrument of Peaceful Self-Defense', *Arab Report* (15 January 1976).

'The [Arab] Boycott – a Two-Edged, Flexible and Powerful Weapon', *Middle East Economic Digest (MEED)* (16 January 1976).

'Arab Boycott and the Bechtel Case', *Journal of World Trade Law*, 11 (1977).

'Arab Boycott and the International Response', *Georgia Journal of International and Comparative Law*, 8 (Spring 1978).

'The Arab Boycott in Canada', Report of the Commission on Economic Coercion and Discrimination in association with the Center for Law and Public Policy, Montreal (11 January 1977).

'Arab Boycott's Effects on Britain', *Middle East Review* (Winter 1975–76).

'The Arab Boycott Within the European Community', memorandum by the EEC Israel Chamber of Commerce and the Centre Européen Juif D'Information to the Commission of the European Communities, Brussels, n.d.

Areeda, Phillip, 'Remarks on the Arab Boycott', *Texas Law Review*, 54 (1976), pp. 1432–7.

'Awf, 'Ali Abd Al-Rahman, *Isra'il wal-Hisar al-'Arabi* (Israel and the Arab Blockade), (Cairo, 1965) (Arabic).

Ayalon, Ami, and Maddy-Weitzman, Bruce (eds), *Middle East Contemporary*

Survey, XVIII, 1994 (The Moshe Dayan Centre for Middle Eastern and African Studies, Tel Aviv University, published by Westview, 1996).

Bahiri, Simcha and Huleileh, Samir, *Peace Pays: Palestinians, Israelis and the Regional Economy* (Israel/Palestine Centre for Research and Information, 1993).

Bahti, James H., *The Arab Economic Boycott of Israel* (Washington DC: The Brookings Institute, 1967).

Balabkins, Nicholas, *West German Reparations to Israel* (New Brunswick, NJ: Rutgers University Press, 1971).

Bar-Siman-Tov, Yaàcov, 'The Limits of Economic Sanctions: The American–Israeli Case of 1953', *Journal of Contemporary History*, 23 (1988).

Barber, James, 'Economic Sanctions as a Policy Instrument', *International Affairs*, 55, 3 (1979).

Basisu, Fu'ad Hamdi, '*Al-Watan al-Muhatall Bayna Mutatallabat Da'am al-Sumud wa-Iltizamat al-Muqata'a al-'Arabiyya li-Isar'il*' (The Occupied Homeland between the Demands of the 'Sumud' and the Commitment to the Arab Boycott of Israel), *Shu'un 'Arabiyya*, 42 (June 1985) (Arabic).

Becker, Charles M., 'The Impact of Sanctions on South Africa and its Periphery', *African Studies Review*, 31, 2 (1988).

Beilin, Yossi, *Hataàsiya Halvrit – Shorashim* (Roots of Israeli Industry), (Jerusalem: Keter, 1987) (Hebrew).

Ben-Aharon, Yossi, *Eretz Yisrael 1951* (1989).

Ben-Porath, Yoram, 'The Entwined Growth of Population and Product, 1922–1982', in Yoram Ben-Porath (ed.) *The Israeli Economy – Maturing through Crises* (Cambridge, MA: Harvard University Press, 1986).

Besok, Motti, '*Yemei Haherem Haàharonim*' (Last Days of the Boycott), *Davar* (1 February 1994) (Hebrew).

Bismuth, Jean-Louis, *Le boycottage dans les echanges économiques internationaux au regard du droit* (Paris: Economica, 1980).

'Blacklisting Report: A Current Perspective on the Arab Boycott', ADL Special Report (Spring 1989).

Blum, Yehuda Z., 'Economic Boycotts in International Law', *Texas International Law Journal*, 12 (1977), pp. 5–15.

B'nai B'rith and the World Jewish Congress, 'The European Community and the Arab Boycott' (6 November 1989).

The Board of Deputies of British Jews, the Zionist Federation of Great Britain and Ireland and B'nai B'rith, 'Memorandum: A Call for Effective Government action Against the Arab Trade Boycott' submitted to the House of Lords Select Committee on the Foreign Boycotts Bill (30 May 1977).

Van den Boogaerde, Pierre, 'Financial Assistance from Arab Countries and Arab Regional Institutions', *Occasional Paper* 87, International Monetary

Fund, Washington DC (September 1991).

Boudin, Leonard B., 'Economic Sanctions and Individual Rights', *International Law and Politics*, 19 (1987).

Boutros-Ghali, Boutros, 'The Arab League: Ten Years of Struggle', *International Conciliation* (May 1954).

Bowett, Derek William, 'Economic Coercion and Reprisal by States', *Virginia Journal of International Law*, 13 (1972).

British–Israel Chamber of Commerce, 'Anti-Boycott Briefing Note' (8 July 1991).

Burton, Thomas M., 'Baxter Fails to Quell Questions on its Role in the Israeli Boycott', *The Wall Street Journal* (25 April 1991).

——, 'How Baxter Got Off the Blacklist and How it Got Nailed', *The Wall Street Journal* (26 March 1993).

Business International, 'Coping with the Arab Boycott of Israel', *Management Monograph*, 19 (New York: Business International, 1963).

Cain, David, 'International Business Communication and Free Speech: Briggs & Stratton Corp. v. Valdrige', *Boston College International and Comparative Law Review*, 9 (1985), pp. 137–9.

'Canada and the Arab Boycott: Developments and Proposals' (Canada–Israel Committee, Montreal, April 1977).

'Canada's Ineffective Anti-Boycott Policy', *Petroeconomic File*, 19 (August 1978).

Carswell, Robert, 'Economic Sanctions and the Iran Experience', *Foreign Affairs*, 60, 2 (Winter 1981/82).

Carter, Barry E., *International Economic Sanctions: Improving the Haphazard US Legal Regime* (Cambridge: Cambridge University Press, 1988).

Chamish, Barry, 'Boycott Still Holds Back Israel's Chemical Industry', *Israel Business Today*, 1 July 1994.

Chaudhri, Welu and Zaucha, 'Sanctions against Iraq and Occupied Kuwait', *Middle East Executive Report*, 13 (1990).

Chill, Dan S., *The Arab Boycott of Israel – Economic Aggression and World Reaction* (New York: Praeger Publishers, 1976).

Clute, N. Vander (chairman), *Legal Aspects of the Arab Boycott* (New York: Practising Law Institute, 1977).

Cohen, Ya'acov, 'Israel–FRG and the Arab Boycott', *Der Stern* (7 February 1991) (German).

Coleman, Clarence L., Jr., 'Boycott Not Religious, Arabs Tell State Department', *Issue* (Spring 1962), pp. 79–80.

Dagan, A., 'The Arab Boycott', in *The Israel Year Book 1966* (Jerusalem: Israel Yearbook Publications, 1966), pp. 252–4.

Daoudi, M.S. and Dajani, M.S., *Economic Sanctions: Ideals and Experience* (London: Routledge & Kegan Paul, 1983).

Al-Dajani, Mundir Sulayman, 'Al-Muqat'a al-'Arabiyyha li-Isra'il: Ahdafuha wa-Fa'aliyyatuha' (The Arab Boycott of Israel: Its Goals and Activities), Al-Nadwa (February 1990) (Arabic).

Deutschkron, Inge, 'Ham'a'avak Neged Haherem Ha'aravi Be'artzot Habrit' (The Struggle Against the Arab Boycott in the United States), Ma'ariv-Assakim (18 February 1986).

Dodell, Sue Allen, 'United States Banks and the Arab Boycott of Israel', Columbia Journal of Transnational Law, 17 (1978), pp. 119–43.

Doxey, Margaret P., Economic Sanctions and International Enforcement (Oxford University Press for the Royal Institute of International Affairs, 1971).

——, 'Economic Sanctions: Benefits and Costs', The World Today, 36, 12 (December 1980).

——, International Sanctions in Contemporary Perspective (London: Macmillan Press; New York: St Martin's Press: second edition, 1996).

——, 'International Sanctions: The Lessons of Experience', Harvard International Review, 10, 5 (1988).

Dworkin, Susan, 'The Japanese and the Arab Boycott', Near East Report, Supplement (October 1968), pp. 374–9.

Eban, Abba, 'The Answer to the Arab Boycott', in The Israel Yearbook 1966 (Jerusalem: Israel Yearbook Publications, 1966), pp. 19–21.

——, Voice of Israel (New York: Horizon Press, 1957).

'Economic Analysis: Israel Doesn't Get fair Economic Treatment from Japan', Ha'aretz (17 June 1992).

'Economic Cooperation in the Middle East and North Africa,' (The World Bank, September 1993).

Egyptian Society of International Law, Egypt and the United Nations, (New York: Manhattan Publishing 1957).

Elali, Amer al-Roubaie and Wajeeh, 'The Financial Implications of Economic Sanctions against Iraq', Arab Studies Quarterly, 17, 3 (Summer 1993).

Elizur, Yuval, 'Aflayat Yisrael Biydey Britania – Hukit' (Discrimination by Britain against Israel is Legal), Ma'ariv-Asskim (1 April 1986) (Hebrew).

——, 'Herem Hatzlalim Zover Nekudot' (The Shadow Boycott Gains Points), Ha'aretz, 2 May 1991 (Hebrew).

——, Lohama Kalkalit – Me'a Shnot Imut Kalkali Bein Yehudim Le'Aravim (The Hundred-year Economic Confrontation between Jews and Arabs) (Kinereth Publishers, 1997) (Hebrew).

Ellings, Richard J., 'Embargoes and World Power: Lessons from American Foreign Policy', in Westview Special Studies in International Relations (Boulder, CO: Westview Press, 1985).

Ellis, Harry B., Heritage of the Desert – the Arabs and the Middle East (New York: Ronald Press 1956).

ESCO Foundation for Palestine, *Palestine: a Study of Jewish, Arab and British Policies* (New Haven, CT: Yale University Press, 1947).

European Jewish Information Centre, 'The Arab Boycott and its Impact on the European Community' (3 June 1992).

'Export Policy, Antitrust and the Arab Boycott', *New York University Law Review* (1976), pp. 94–132.

Feder, Burnaby J., 'Guilty Plea by Baxter on Boycott', *The New York Times* (26 March 1993).

Feder, Holly L., 'US Companies and the Arab Boycott of Israel' (Texas Women's University, UMI 1988).

Feilchenfeld, Werner, Michaelis, Dolf and Pinner, Ludwig *Ha'avara – Transfer nach Palästina und Einwanderung deutscher Juden 1933–1939*, (Tübingen, Introduction: Siegfried Moses, 1972).

Feiler, Gil, 'The Arab Boycott – A Political Weapon', *Israel British Trade* (January 1992), pp. 32–3.

——, 'Arab Boycott Getting Worse', *Israel Business Today*, 6, 255 (13 December 1991).

——, 'From Boycott to Limited Scientific and Technological Cooperation', in Efraim Inbar (ed.) *Regional Security Regimes* (Albany: State University of New York Press, 1995), pp 253–69.

——, *Hameshek Hasuri Ve'efsharuyot Leshituf Pe'ula 'Im Yisra'l* (The Syrian Economy and the Potential for Cooperation with Israel) (Tel Aviv: Armand Hammer Fund for Economic Cooperation in the Middle East, Tel Aviv University, November 1992).

——, 'Ha'omnam Nehlash Haherem?' (Has Indeed the Boycott Weakened?), *Ha'aretz* (30 July 1991).

——, 'Israel, Jordan and the Palestinian Authority: The Competition for Investments', *Justice* (11 December 1996), pp. 25–8.

——, *Shituf Pe'ulah Mada'i Vetechnologi Bein Yisra'el Umitsrayim – Kivunim, Efsharuyot Vehsegim* (Scientific and Technological Cooperation Between Israel and Egypt: Possibilities and Achievements) (Tel Aviv: Armand Hammer Fund for Economic Cooperation in the Middle East, Tel Aviv University, January 1991).

——, *Shituf Pe'ulah Ta'asukati Bein Yisra'el Umitsrayim – Kivunim Ve'efsharuyot* (Israel–Egypt Cooperation in the Field of Employment – Directions and Possibilities) (Tel Aviv: David Horowitz Institute, sponsored by Armand Hammer Fund for Economic Cooperation in the Middle East Tel Avin University, 1990).

——, *Rethinking Business Strategy for the Middle East and North Africa* (London: The Economist Intelligence Unit, 1997).

——, 'The End of the Arab Boycott of Israel?', *Israel–British Trade* (Winter 1998).

Feiler, Gil, and Yisraeli, Yaacov, *Business Laws and Economics Prospects in the Middle East and North Africa* (Federation of Israeli Chambers of Commerce, 1996).

Feinerman, 'Arab Boycott and State Law: the New York Anti-Boycott Statute', *Harvard International Law Journal*, 18 (Spring 1977), pp. 343–63.

Feldman, Lily Gardner, *The Special Relationship Between West Germany and Israel* (London: George Allen & Unwin, 1984).

Fenton, Howard N., 'United States Anti-Boycott Laws: An Assessment of their Impact, Ten Years after Adoption', *Hastings International and Comparative Law Review*, 10, 2 (Winter 1987).

Fernandez, Jose I., 'Dismantling Apartheid: Counterproductive Effects of Conitnuing Economic Sanctions', *Law and Policy in International Business*, 22 (1991).

Fershtman, Chaim, and Gandal, Neil, 'The Effect of the Arab Boycott on Israel: the Automobile Market', *Discussion Paper 3–95*, The Pinhas Sapir Centre for Development (Tel Aviv: Tel Aviv University, November 1995).

Flander, 'Foreign Sovereign Compulsion and the Arab Boycott: A State Action Analogy', *Georgetown Law Journal*, 65 (April 1977), pp. 1001–23.

Forster, Arnold, 'Fighting the Arab Boycott in the United States', in *Oxford Seminar on Oil Wealth, Discrimination and Freedom of Trade – Report* (Oxford 1975).

Freier, S., 'Science for Development in a Region at Peace', paper presented at the Middle East Development Conference, Geneva 23–6 (March 1989).

Friedman, H.M., 'Confronting the Arab Boycott: A Lawyer's Baedeker', *Harvard International Law Journal*, 19 (Summer 1978), pp. 443–533.

Galtung, Johan, 'On the Effects of International Economic Sanctions – With Examples from the Case of Rhodesia', *World Politics*, 19 (1967).

General Principles for Boycott of Israel, League of Arab Countries General Secretariat, Head Office for the Boycott of Israel, Damascus (June 1972).

General Union of Arab Chambers of Commerce, Industry and Agriculture, *Arab Boycott of Israel: Its Grounds and Its Regulations* (Beirut: General Union of Arab Chambers of Commerce, 1959).

George, Alexander L., Hall, David K. and Simons, William R., *The Limits of Coercive Diplomacy: Laos–Cuba–Vietnam* (Boston: Little, Brown, 1971).

Gilber, Gad, *'Lo Bodkim Bataviyot'* (Labels Aren't Checked), *Ha'aretz* (26 April 1991) (Hebrew).

Green, Mark and Solow, Steven, 'The Arab Boycott of Israel: How the US and Business Cooperated', *The Nation* (17 October 1981).

Greene, P. L., 'Arab Economic Boycott of Israel: The International Law Perspective', *Vanderbilt Journal of Transnational Law*, 11 (Winter 1978), pp. 77–94.

Greilsammer, Ilan, 'European Sanctions Revisited', *Policy Studies*, 31 (Jerusalem: The Leonard Davis Institute for International Relations at the Hebrew University of Jerusalem, February 1989).

Haberman, Clyde, 'Though still in Effect, Arabs' Economic Boycott of Israel Weakens', *New York Times* (11 May 1993).

Halbach, Axel J., *New Potential for Cooperation and Trade in the Middle East*, IFO Research Report, 85 (Department for Development and Transformation Studies, Weltforum Verlag, 1995).

Hamadah, Mustafa, 'A Look at the Arab Boycott of Israel', *Shu'un Arabiya* (Arab Affairs), 2 (Beirut, May 1981), pp. 107–20 (Arabic).

Hamza, Jafar Tah, *Al-Muqata'a al-'Arabiyya li-Isra'il* (The Arab Boycott of Israel) (1973) (Arabic).

Handworker, Haim, *Helem Tarbuti* (Cultural Shock), *Ha'aretz* (26 March 1997) (Hebrew).

Al-Hassan, Omar, *Economic Sanctions and the Middle East in 1996* (London: Gulf Centre for Strategic Studies, 1996).

Hedges, Chris, 'Despite US Urging, Arab Lands Hold Firm to their Israel Boycott', *New York Times* (6 October 1993).

Al-Hindi, Hani, coordinator and editor of a symposium on the Arab Boycott, *Shu'un Falestiniyya*, 46 (June 1975).

Horowitz, David, *Hayim Bamoked* (In the Heart of Events) (Tel Aviv: Masada, 1975) (Hebrew).

Hotaling, E., *The Arab Blacklist Unveiled* (Beverly Hills, CA: Landia, 1977).

House of Lords Select Committee on the Foreign Boycotts Bill, Vols I and II (Report and Minutes of Proceedings) (London: HMSO, July 1978).

Hufbauer, Gary C. and Elliot, Kimberly, 'Qualified Success: Financial Sanctions and Foreign Policy', *Harvard International Review*, 10, 5 (1988).

Hufbauer, Gary C. and Schott, Jeffrey J., *Economic Sanctions Reconsidered: History and Current Policy* (Washington, DC: Institute for International Economics, 1985, second edition 1990).

Iskandar, Marwan, 'Arab Boycott of Israel', *Middle East Forum* (October 1960), pp. 27–30.

——, *The Arab Boycott of Israel* (Beirut: PLO Research Center, 1966).

'Japan–Israel Trade – Seductive but Slow', *Israel Business Today* (5 December 1991).

'Japan's Free Traders Boycott Israel', *Tokyo Business Today* (November 1987).

Jonah, James O. C., 'Sanctions and the United Nations', *Harvard International Review*, 10 (1988).

Joyner, Nelson T., *Arab Boycott/Anti-Boycott – The Effects on US Business* (MacLean, VI: Rockville Consulting Group, December 1976).

Kaempfer, William H. and Lowenberg, Anton D., 'The Theory of International Economic Sanctions: A Public Choice Approach', *American Economic Review*, 78 (September 1988).

——, 'Sanctioning South Africa: the Politics Behind the Policies', *Cato Journal*, 8 (Winter 1989).

Kaikati, J., 'The Arab Boycott: Middle East Business Dilemma', *California Management Review*, 20, 3 (1978), pp. 32–46.

Keimach, Burt, 'The Arab Boycott of Israel – an Exercise in Failed Economic Warfare', *Focus*, published by BIPAC (May 1991).

Keinon, Herb, 'Biteless Boycott', *Jerusalem Post* (4 April 1997).

Kellner, Peter, 'The Boycott – a Two-Edged, Flexible and Powerful Weapon', *Middle East Economic Digest* (16 January 1976).

Kestenbaum, Lionel, 'The Antitrust Challenge to the Arab Boycott: Per Se Theory, Middle East Politics and United States v. Bechtel Corporations', *Texas Law Review*, 54 (1976), pp. 1411–31.

Kestin , Hesh, 'Israel's Best-Kept Secret', *Forbes*, 134 (22 October 1984).

Khan, Haider Ali, 'The Impact of Trade Sanctions on South Africa: A Social Accounting Matrix Approach', *Contemporary Policy Issues*, 6 (October 1988).

Kimche, Jon, 'The Arab Boycott of Israel: New Aspects', *Midstream* (September 1964).

Lack, Daniel, 'Arab Boycott: Submission of Test Case to EEC Commission', a WJC memorandum (4 January 1977).

——, 'Developments in the Field of Anti-boycott Measures at Regional and National Levels', 15 June, 1978, a WJC memorandum.

——, 'Memorandum to the President of the Council of Ministers of the European Community, concerning certain discriminatory practices in the Common Market area', January 1987.

——, 'Note on Identifying Potentially Actionable Cases of Boycott under EEC Competititon Rules', a WJC memorandum (December 1975).

——, 'Recent Developments in Europe on Anti-Boycott Action', a WJC memorandum (8 June 1976).

——, 'Steps Taken at the Council of Europe to Initiate Measures against the Arab Boycott', a WJC memorandum (9 February 1976).

——, 'Visit to President of the EEC Council, Luxembourg, 20 and 21 November, 1985', a WJC memorandum (28 November 1985).

Lande, Robert H., 'Arab Boycott and Title VII', *Harvard Civil Rights–Civil Liberties Law Review*, 12 (Winter 1977), pp. 181–205.

Lansing , Paul and Kuruvilla, Sarosh, 'Business Divestment in South Africa: In Whose Best Interest?', *Journal of Business Ethics* (7 August 1988).

Leyton-Brown, David (ed.), *The Utility of Economic Sanctions* (London: Croom Helm, 1987).

Licklider, Roy E, *Political Power and the Arab Oil Weapon – the Experience of*

Five Industrial Nations (Berkeley: University of California Press, 1988).

Lombard, Joseph C., 'The Survival of Noriega: Lessons from the US Sanctions Against Panama', *Stanford Journal of International Law*, 26 (1989).

Losman, Donald L., *International Economic Sanctions: The Cases of Cuba, Israel and Rhodesia* (Albuquerque: University of New Mexico Press, 1979).

Lukomski, Jess, 'West Germans Scorn Arab Boycott', *Journal of Commerce* (3 March 1976).

MacDonald, Robert W., *The League of Arab States – A Study in the Dynamics of Regional Organization* (Princeton, NJ: Princeton University Press, 1965).

Maddox, William S., 'The Comprehensive Anti-Apartheid Act: A Case Study in the Legality of Economic Sanctions', *Washington and Lee Law Review*, 44 (1987).

Mansfield, Edward D., 'International Institutions and Economic Sanctions', *World Politics*, 47 (July 1995), pp. 575–605.

Marcuss, S. and Thomas, R., Chairman, *The Proposed Anti-Boycott Regulations under the Export Administration Act of 1977: Compliance and Understanding* (New York: Law Journal Press, 1977).

Marcuss, Stanley J. and Richard, Eric L., 'Extraterritorial Jurisdiction in United States Trade Law, The Need for a Consistent Theory', *Columbia Journal of Transnational Law*, 20, 3 (1981), pp. 439–83.

Maron, Gershon, 'Haherem Ha'aravi Verishomo Hakalkali' (The Arab Boycott and its Economic Ramifications), *Riv'on Lekalkala* (January 1954).

Medzini, Meron (ed.), *Israel's Foreign Relations: Seclected Documents 1947–1974* (Jerusalem: Ministry for Foreign Affairs, 1976).

Van Meerhaeghe, M.A.G., *International Economic Institutions* (London: Longman, second edition, 1971).

Meo, Leila (ed.), *The Arab Boycott of Israel* (Detroit: Association of Arab-American University Graduates, 1976).

Merhav, Meir (ed.), 'The Research Project for Economic Cooperation in the Middle East – An Overview' (Tel Aviv: Armand Hammer Fund for Economic Cooperation in the Middle East, Tel Aviv University, December 1986).

Mersky, Roy M. (ed.), *Conference on Transnational Economic Boycotts and Coercion*, paper presented at the Conference on Transnational Economic Boycott and Coercion, 19–20 February (New York: University of Texas Law School, Oceana Publications, 1978), Vol. 1.

Miller, Judith, 'When Sanctions Worked', *Foreign Policy*, 39 (1980).

Moberly, Sir Patrick, 'Assessing Their Effectiveness: South African Sanctions', *Harvard International Review*, 10, 5 (1989).

Moore, John Norton, 'United States Policy and the Arab Boycott', *Proceedings of the American Society of International Law* (1977).

Mourad, Rashad, 'The Arab Boycott – Its Application', *American–Arab Trade Newsletter* (Spring/Summer 1966), pp. 5–6.

Mughayzal, Juzif, *Al-Muqata'a al-'Arabiyya wal-Qanun al-Dawli* (The Arab Boycott and International Law) (Beirut: M.T.F., Markaz al-Abhath, 1968) (Arabic).

Muir, Dupray, 'The Boycott in International Law', *The Journal of International Law and Economics*, 9 (2 August 1974), pp. 187–204.

Murphy, Emma C., 'The Arab–Israeli Peace Process: Responding to the Economics of Globalization', *Critique*, 9 (Fall 1996).

Naftaniel, Ronnie M., *Black List: The Arab Boycott and the Netherlands*, doctoral thesis (February 1978).

Nagan, Winston P., 'Economic Sanctions, US Foreign Policy, International Law and the Anti-Apartheid Act of 1986', *Florida International Law Journal*, 4 (1988).

Al-Najar, Sa\`id, *Likrat Estrategyat Shalom Aravi* (Towards an Arab Peace Strategy) (Tel-Aviv: The The Tami Steinmitz Centre for Peace Research, *Translation Series*, 1, 1994) (Hebrew).

Nanda, V. and Lake, R. (eds), 'International Boycotts', in *The Law of Transnational Business Transactions* (Clark, Boardman, Callaghan, a division of Thomson Legal Publishing, 1995).

Nathan, Robert R., Gass, Oscar and Creamer, Daniel, *Palestine: Problem and Promise – an Economic Study* (Washington, DC: Public Affairs Press, American Council of Public Affairs, 1946).

Neff, Stephen C., 'Boycott and the Law of Nations: Economic Warfare and Modern International Law in Historical Perspective', *The British Yearbook of International Law* (1988).

———, 'Economic Warfare in Contemporary Interantional Law: Three Schools of Thought, Evaluated According to an Historical Method', *Stanford Journal of International Law*, 26 (1989).

Nelson, Nancy Jo, 'The United States Legal Response to the Arab Boycott – a Quagmire for the Innocent', in *The Palestine Yearbook of International Law* (Nicosia: Al-Shaybani Society of International Law, 1989).

Nincic, Miroslav and Wallenstein Peter (eds), *Dilemmas of Economic Coercion* (New York: Praeger Publishers, 1983).

Nur-Allah, N. A., 'Counter-Legislation to the Arab Boycott of Israel', *Shulun Arabiya* (October 1981), pp. 7–20 (Arabic).

Palestine Royal Commission Report (The Peel Commission Report) (London: HMSO, 1937).

Patterson, Gardner, 'Israel's Economic Problems', *Foreign Affairs*, 32 (January 1954).

Paust, Jordan J. and Blaustein, Albert P., 'The Arab Oil Market – a Threat to International Peace', *American Journal of International Law*, 68 (1974).

Peres, Shimon, *The New Middle East* (New York: Henry Hold & Company, 1993).

Phillips, Charlotte A., *The Arab Boycott of Israel – Possibilities for European Cooperation with US Anti-boycott Legislation* (Washington DC: Congressional Research Service, Library of Congress, May 1979).

Porath, Yehoshua, *From Riots to Rebellion – the Palestinian–Arab National Movement 1929–1939* (London: Frank Cass, 1977).

Post, H.H.G. (ed.), *International Economic Law and Armed Conflict* (Alphen aan den Rijn: Martinus Nijhoff, 1994).

Prittie, Terence Prittie and Nelson, Walter Henry, *The Economic War Against the Jews* (London: Secker & Warburg, 1978).

Prittie, T., 'The Secondary Arab Boycott and Britain', *Middle East Review* (Winter, 1975/76), pp. 46–7.

Remba, Oded, 'The Arab Boycott. A Study in Total Economic Warfare', *Midstream*, 6, 3 (Summer 1960), pp. 40–55.

Richard, Alan and Waterbury, John, *A Political Economy of the Middle East* (Boulder, CO: Westview Press, 1990).

Rolef, Susan Hattis, '*Yitzur Yisraeli Be'europa*' (Israeli Production in Europe), *Hashuk Hameshutaf* (The Common Market) (January 1979).

—— (ed.), *Freedom of Trade and the Arab Boycott* (Jerusalem: The Anti-Defamation League of B'hai Brith, 1985).

——, 'The Middle East Policy of the Federal Republic of Germany', *Jerusalem Papers on Peace Problems*, 39 (Jerusalem: The Magnes Press, the Hebrew University – The Leonard Davis Institute for International Relations, 1985).

——, 'Israel's Anti-Boycott Policy', *Policy Studies*, 28 (Jerusalem: The Leonard Davis Institute for International Relations at the Hebrew University of Jerusalem, February 1989).

——, 'Economic Prospects for Peace', *Spectrum* (June 1990), pp. 26–7.

——, *Political Dictionary of the State of Israel* (Jerusalem: The Jerusalem Publishing House, second edition, 1993).

Ronen, Menahem, '*Haherem Hakalkali al Yisrael – Skira Tamtzitit*' (The Economic Boycott of Israel – a Concise Survey), *Kalkala Va'avoda* (Economics and Labour) (Hebrew) (8 November 1992).

Roth, A., 'Arab Boycott and the Federal Securities Laws', *Securities Regulations Law Journal*, 5 (Winter 1978), pp. 318–47.

al-Roubaie, Amer and Elali, Wajeeh, 'The Financial Implications of Economic Sanctions Against Iraq', *Arab Studies Quarterly*, 17, 3 (Summer 1993), pp. 53–68.

Roudot, Pierre, 'Arab Boycott as Myth', *New Outlook*, 6 (5 June 1963), pp. 17–24.

Salpeter, Eliahu, 'Hifkiru et Haherem' (The Boycott Has Been Neglected), Ha'aretz (14 June 1990) (Hebrew).

Sarna, Aaron, Boycott and Blacklists – a History of Arab Economic Warfare Against Israel (Totowa, NJ: Rowman & Littlefield, 1986).

Savitt, Martin, Arab Trade Boycott of Israel Briefing Notes (September 1993).

Scalia, Antonin, 'Domestic Legal Issues Presented by the Arab Boycott', paper presented at the Conference on Transnational Economic Boycotts and Coercion, February 1976, Vol. 1 (New York: University of Texas Law School, Oceana Publications, 1978).

Schechtman, Yosef, Herem Ha'arvi Velikho (The Arab Boycott and its Lessons), Ha'umma, 4 (13 June 1965).

Schirman, Shalom, 'The History of the Arab Boycott, 1921–1975', Middle East Review (Winter 1975/76), pp. 40–2.

Schöpflin, Julia, 'The Arab Boycott of Israel: Can it Withstand the Peace Process?', London, Institute of Jewish Affairs, Research Reports (4 March 1994).

Schreiber, Anna, 'Economic Coercion as an Instrument of Foreign Policy', World Politics, 25 (3 April 1973).

Schrijver, Nico, 'The Use of Economic Sanctions by the UN Security Council: An International Law Perspective', in H.H.G. Post (ed.), International Economic Law and Armed Conflict (Alphen aan den Rijn: Martinus Nijhoff, 1994), pp. 123–61.

Seaga, Edward, 'Impact of Economic Sanctions on the South African Economy', Round Table, 306 (1988).

'Securing Peace in the Middle East: Project on Economic Transition', The Institute for Social and Economic Policy in the Middle East at the John F. Kennedy School of Government, Harvard University (June 1993).

Select Committee on the Foreign Boycotts Bill, House of Lords, Report and Minutes of (London: HMSO, July 1978).

Sharif, Amer A., 'A Statistical Study on the Arab Boycott of Israel', Monograph Series 26 (Beirut: The Institute for Palestine Studies, 1970).

Shellenbarger, Sue, 'Did Hospital Supplier Dump its Israel Plant to Win Arabs' Favor?', The Wall Street Journal (1 May 1990).

Shihata, Ibrahim F.I., 'Destination Embargo of Arab Oil: its Legality under International Law', The American Journal of International Law, 68 (1974).

Shimoni, Ya'acov, Political Dictionary of the Arab World (New York: Macmillan 1987).

Shohat, Avraham, 'The Role of the Private Sector in the Middle East Peace Process' (Jerusalem: Ministry of Finance, Government of Israel, 1995).

Shorer, Oded, Ma'ariv Assakim (16 April 1991) (Hebrew).

Snyder, Louis L. (ed.), Fifty Major Documents of the Twentieth Century

(Princeton, NJ: D. Van Nostrand, 1985), p. 169.

Sokol, Albert, 'State Reaction to the Arab Boycott of Israel, Legislative and Constitutional Preemption', *Boston University Law Review*, 57 (March 1977), pp. 335–67.

Spiro, Leah Nathans, Nayei, Farah and Sandler, Niel, 'The Shadow Across L'Oréal', *Business Week* (21 March 1994).

Sporn, Chalres M., 'Complicity with the Arab Blacklist, Business Expedience versus Abridgement of Constitutional Rights', *Brooklyn Journal of International Law*, 2, 2 (Spring 1976), pp. 228–49.

Stanislawski, Howard, 'The Impact of the Arab Boycott of Israel on the United States and Canada', in David Leyton-Brown (ed.) *The Utility of Economic Sanctions* (London: Croom Helm, 1987), pp. 246–8.

Steiner, Henry J., 'International Boycotts and Domestic Order, American Involvement in the Arab–Israeli Conflict', *Texas Law Review*, 54 (1976), pp. 1355–410.

Stern, Sol, 'On and Off the Arabs' List', *The New Republic* (27 March 1976).

Strack, Harry R., 'The Effectiveness of Rhodesian Sanctions: Symbolism and Influence', *Harvard International Review*, X, 5 (1988).

——, *Sanctions: the Case of Rhodesia* (Syracuse: Syracuse University Press, 1978).

Der Stern, 'The Secret Boycott Against Israel ...' (7 February 1991) (German).

Teslik, Kennan Lee, *Congress, the Executive Branch, and Special Interests: the American Response to the Arab Boycott of Israel* (Westport, CT: Greenwood Press, 1982).

Thomas, John, 'Arab Boycott: a Legislative Solution to Multidimensional Problem', *University of Pittsburgh Law Review*, 39 (Fall 1977), pp. 63–86.

Treaties Establishing the European Communities, Treaties amending these Treaties, Documents Concerning the Accession (Luxembourg: European Communities, 1973).

Turck, Nancy, 'The Arab Boycott of Israel', *Foreign Affairs*, 55 (April 1977), pp. 472–93.

Wall, Harry and Weinberg, David M., 'Japan should Show it Means Business', *Jerusalem Post* (7 June 1991).

Wallenstein, Peter, 'Characteristics of Economic Sanctions', *Journal of Peace Research*, 5 (1968).

UN Resolutions, General Assembly, Series I, compiled and edited by Dusan J. Djonovich (New York: Oceana Publications/Dobbs Ferry, VIII 1960–62, 1974; IX 1962–63, 1974; XIII 1970–71, 1976; XIV 1972–74, 1978).

UN Resolutions, Security Council, Series II, compiled and edited by Dusan J. Djonovich (New York: Oceana Publications/Dobbs Ferry, VI 1966–67, 1989; VII 1968–70, 1990; X 1976–77, 1992).

'Unwilling Japan Bows to Boycott Pressure', *The Jewish Week* (18 March 1988).

US Congress, House of Representatives, Committee on Foreign Affairs, *Discriminatory Arab Pressure on US Business*, Hearings, Subcommittee on International Trade and Commerce, Committee on International Relations, 94th Congress, 1st Session, 6 March–11 December 1975 (Washington DC, 1976).

US Congress, *The Arab Boycott*, Hearings on S. 69 and S. 92 before the Subcommittee on International Finance of the Senate Committee on Banking, Housing and Urban Affairs, 95th Congress, 1st Session (1977).

US Congress, *The Arab Boycott and American Business*, Report by the Subcommittee on Oversight and Investigations of the Committee on Interstate and Foreign Commerce with Additional and Minority Views, House of Representatives, 94th Congress, 2nd Session (The Moss Report) (1976).

US Congress, *Discriminatory Arab Pressure on U.S. Business*, Hearings Before the Subcommittee on International Trade and Commerce of the House Committee on International Relations, 94th Congress, 1st Session (1975).

'US Legislation of Foreign Investments and the Arab Boycott' and 'Boycott of Banking and Underwriting Firms', and 'US Anti-Boycott Legislation and Action, 1975', *Middle East Review*, 7 (Winter 1975/76), pp. 22–6.

Weigard, Robert, 'The Arab League Boycott of Israel', *Michigan State University Business Topics* (Spring 1968), pp. 74–80.

Weinberg, David M., 'Japan Should Show it Means Business', *Jerusalem Post* (7 June 1991).

Weintraub, Sydney (ed.), 'Economic Coercion and US Foreign Policy: Implications of Case Studies from the Johnson Administration', in *Westview Special Studies in International Relations* (Boulder, CO: Westview Press, 1982).

Weisburg, Henry, 'Unilateral Economic Sanctions and the Risks of Extraterritorial Application: the Libyan Example', *International Law and Politics*, 19 (1987).

Williams, J. L., 'US Regulation of Arab Boycott Practices', *Law and Politics of International Business*, 10 (1978), pp. 815–86.

Wilson, Rodney, *The Palestinian Economy and International Trade*, CMEIS Occasional Papers, Centre for Middle Eastern and Islamic Studies at the University of Durham, 45 (November 1994).

Woolbert, R. G., 'Pan-Arabism and the Palestine Problem', *Foreign Affairs* (January 1938).

World Jewish Congress, 'Consequences of Arab Measures of Economic Coercion, with Particular Reference to Boycott Practices, from the Standpoint of International Law, International Trade Law, and the Law of Certain European Institutions' (October 1975).

——, 'The Non-Discrimination Clauses in the Interim Agreements between the EEC and the Mashreq Countries' Geneva (7 February 1977).

——, 'Recent Anti-Boycott Developments in France and the EEC' Geneva (10 June 1977).

——, 'Arab Boycott – Submission of Test Case to the Commission of the EEC – the COFACE Case' Geneva (21 November 1977).

——, 'WJC European Branch: EEC Committee meeting with Mr Leo Tindemans, Foreign Minister of Belgium and President-in-Office of the Council of the European Community' Brussels (12 March 1982).

——, 'EEC and Arab Boycott' (in respect of meetings held with M. Jean Gol, Belgian Minister of Justice) (29 November 1982).

——, 'Memorandum on the Status of Anti-Boycott Action and Anti-Terrorism Measures in France' (18 January 1984).

——, 'Anti-Boycott Legislation in Europe' (May 1984).

——, 'The Arab Boycott' (9 January 1986).

Yosef, Lieutenant Colonel, *'Halohama Hakalkalit Ha'aravit Neged Yisrael'* (Arab Economic Warfare against Israel), *Ma'archot*, 275 (August 1980), (Hebrew).

Index

328 *From Boycott to Economic Cooperation*

International Gulf Bank of Bahrain, 299
International Medical Technology Ltd,
  186
International Steering Committee to
  Combat the Arab Boycott, 138–9,
  241, 242
International Trade Commission (ITC),
  185–6
International Trade Organization, 74
Intra Investment Company, 158
Iran, 13–14, 28, 34, 39, 40, 119
Iran–Iraq War, 14
Iraq, 10–11, 22, 24, 26, 32, 38, 41, 43,
  66, 140, 205, 221–2, 274, 296
Irbid, 297
Ireland, 281, 288
Iron & Gate, 41
IRS *see* Inland Revenue Service
Islamic Amal movement, 45–6
Islamic Conference Organization, 39
Islamic Office for the Boycott of Israel,
  39
Israel Aircraft Industries Ltd, 253
Israel Can Company, 212
Israel Chemicals, 294
Israel Business Today, 276–7
Israel Export Institute, 253, 277
Israel Institute of Coexistence (IIC),
  134
Israel Year Book (1966), 133
Israeli Economic Mission, 133, 155
Israeli Manufacturers' Association, 134,
  139, 144, 246
Israeli Ministry of Commerce and
  Industry, 132, 133; Investment
  Centre, 132
Israeli Ministry of Defence, 132
Israeli Ministry of Finance, 133, 134,
  139, 145, 268, 280; Investment
  Authority, 132; *see also* Economic
  Warfare Authority
Israeli Ministry of Foreign Affairs, 130,
  131, 134, 137, 138, 139, 143, 145,
  211, 280; Economic Department,
  130, 134; Energy Department, 134;
  Matmach, 131, 132, 133, 134;
  Research Department, 130
Israeli Ministry of Industry and Trade,
  134, 138, 139, 256; Foreign Trade
  Administration, 253

Israeli Ports Authority, 212
Italy, 9, 289
ITC *see* International Trade
  Commission
Iwai, Nissho, 255
Izmir Fair, 30
Izzat, Ibrahim, 94

al-Jabali, Muhammad, 100
Jaffa, 22, 23
Jaguar, 286, 287
Jamieson, Donald C., 258
Japan, 5, 48, 71, 73, 101, 138–9, 140,
  171, 145, 171–2, 249–55, 278, 287,
  288, 289; Foreign Ministry, 254;
  Foreign Trade Ministry (MITI), 253
Japan Air Lines (JAL), 250
Japanese Brokers Association, 254
Japanese Federation of Economic
  Organizations *see* Keidanren
Japanese Trade Relations Organization
  (JETRO), 251, 254
Javits, Jacob, 156
JCB, 287
Jecho-Metal, 47
Jedda, 39
Jeep, 40
Jerusalem, 21, 22, 23, 49, 51, 57, 109,
  111, 112, 130, 139, 145, 183, 260,
  292, 294
JETRO *see* Japanese Trade Relations
  Organization
Jewish Agency, 25, 72, 128, 129, 131,
  209; External Relations Department,
  130, 131; Political Department, 72,
  128, 129
Jewish Manufacturers' Association of
  Palestine, 128
Jewish National Home policy, 22
Jeyes, 40
Joint Arab–British Chamber of
  Commerce, 100
Joint Statement of Principles (1977),
  163–4
Jordan, 38, 39, 49, 51, 52, 53, 54, 55,
  57, 103, 107, 112, 118, 119, 120,
  144, 184, 188, 205, 223, 233, 264,
  288, 294, 295, 297, 298
Jordanian Government Potash
  Company, 294

For Product Safety Concerns and Information please contact our EU representative GPSR@taylorandfrancis.com Taylor & Francis Verlag GmbH, Kaufingerstraße 24, 80331 München, Germany

T - #0058 - 230425 - C0 - 229/152/19 - PB - 9780714644233 - Gloss Lamination